RUSSIA

GOLD MINING AND MINING INDUSTRY DIRECTORY

VOLUME 1

STRATEGIC, PRACTICAL INFORMATION, CONTACTS

International Business Publications, USA
Washington DC, USA - Russia

RUSSIA

GOLD MINING AND MINING INDUSTRY DIRECTORY

VOLUME 1 STRATEGIC, PRACTICAL INFORMATION, CONTACTS

UPDATED ANNUALLY

Cover Design: **International Business Publications, USA**

We express our sincere appreciation to all government agencies and international organizations which provided information and other materials for this directory

2017 Edition Updated Reprint International Business Publications, USA
ISBN 1-4330-4161-8

This directory provides basic information for starting or/and conducting business in the country. The extraordinary volume of materials covering the topic, prevents us from placing all these materials in this directory. For more detailed information on issues related to any specific investment and business activity in the country, please contact Global Investment Center, USA

Please acquire the list of our business intelligence and marketing reports and other business publications. We constantly update and expand our business intelligence and marketing materials. Please contact the center for the updated list of reports on over 200 countries.

For additional analytical, business and investment opportunities information,
please contact Global Investment & Business Center, USA
at (703) 370-8082. Fax: (703) 370-8083. E-mail: ibpusa3@gmail.com
Global Business and Investment Info Databank - www.ibpus.com

Printed in the USA

RUSSIA

GOLD MINING AND MINING INDUSTRY DIRECTORY

VOLUME 1

STRATEGIC, PRACTICAL INFORMATION, CONTACTS

TABLE OF CONTENTS

STRATEGIC AND DEVELOPMENT PROFILES

IMPORTANT FACTS

Capital (and largest city)	Moscow 55°45′N 37°37′E55.75°N 37.617°E
Official language(s)	Russian official throughout the country; 27 others co-official in various regions
Ethnic groups	81% Russians 3.7% Tatars 1.4% Ukrainians 1.1% Bashkirs 1% Chuvashes 11.8% others and unspecified
Demonym	Russian
Government	Federal semi-presidential constitutional republic
- President	Vladimir Putin
- Prime Minister	Dmitry Medvedev
Legislature	Federal Assembly
- Upper house	Federation Council
- Lower house	State Duma
	Formation
- Rurik Dynasty	862
- Kievan Rus'	882
- Vladimir-Suzdal Rus'	1169
- Grand Duchy of Moscow	1283
- Tsardom of Russia	16 January 1547
- Russian Empire	22 October 1721
- Russian Soviet Federative Socialist Republic	7 November 1917
- Union of Soviet Socialist Republics	10 December 1922
- Russian Federation	25 December 1991
	Area
- Total	17,075,400 km^2 (1st) 6,592,800 sq mi
- Water (%)	13 (including swamps)
	Population
- 2012 estimate	143,100,000 (9th)
- Density	8.3/km^2 (217th) 21.5/sq mi
GDP (PPP)	2011 estimate
- Total	$2.383 trillion
- Per capita	$16,736
GDP (nominal)	2011 estimate
- Total	$1.850 trillion
- Per capita	$12,993
Gini (2008)	42.3 (83rd)
HDI (2011)	▲0.755 (high) (66th)

Currency	Ruble (RUB)
Time zone	(UTC+3 to +12 (exc. +5))
Date formats	dd.mm.yyyy
Drives on the	right
ISO 3166 code	RU
Internet TLD	.ru, .su, .рф
Calling code	+7

Russia also officially known as the **Russian Federation** (Russian: is a country in northern Eurasia. It is a federal semi-presidential republic, comprising 83 federal subjects.

From northwest to southeast, Russia shares borders with Norway, Finland, Estonia, Latvia, Lithuania and Poland (both via Kaliningrad Oblast), Belarus, Ukraine, Georgia, Azerbaijan, Kazakhstan, China, Mongolia, and North Korea. It also has maritime borders with Japan by the Sea of Okhotsk, and the US state of Alaska by the Bering Strait. At 17,075,400 square kilometres (6,592,800 sq mi), Russia is the largest country in the world, covering more than one eighth of the Earth's inhabited land area. Russia is also the ninth most populous nation with 143 million people as of 2012.

Extending across the whole of northern Asia and most of eastern Europe, Russia spans nine time zones and incorporates a wide range of environments and landforms. Russia has the world's largest reserves of mineral and energy resources and is the largest producer of oil and natural gas globally. Russia has the world's largest forest reserves and its lakes contain approximately one-quarter of the world's fresh water.

The nation's history began with that of the East Slavs, who emerged as a recognizable group in Europe between the 3rd and 8th centuries AD. Founded and ruled by a Varangian warrior elite and their descendants, the medieval state of Rus arose in the 9th century. In 988 it adopted Orthodox Christianity from the Byzantine Empire, beginning the synthesis of Byzantine and Slavic cultures that defined Russian culture for the next millennium. Rus' ultimately disintegrated into a number of smaller states; most of the Rus' lands were overrun by the Mongol invasion and became tributaries of the nomadic Golden Horde.

The Grand Duchy of Moscow gradually reunified the surrounding Russian principalities, achieved independence from the Golden Horde, and came to dominate the cultural and political legacy of Kievan Rus'. By the 18th century, the nation had greatly expanded through conquest, annexation, and exploration to become the Russian Empire, which was the third largest empire in history, stretching from Poland in Europe to Alaska in North America.

Following the Russian Revolution, Russia became the largest and leading constituent of the Soviet Union, the world's first constitutionally socialist state and a recognized superpower, which played a decisive role in the Allied victory in World War II. The Soviet era saw some of the most significant technological achievements of the 20th century, including the world's first human spaceflight. The Russian Federation was founded following the dissolution of the Soviet Union in 1991, but is recognized as the continuing legal personality of the Soviet state.

The Russian economy is the world's ninth largest by nominal GDP and sixth largest by purchasing power parity, with the 3rd largest nominal military budget. Russia is one of the world's fastest growing major economies. It is one of the five recognized nuclear weapons states and possesses the largest stockpile of weapons of mass destruction.

Russia is a great power and a permanent member of the United Nations Security Council, a member of the G8, G20, the Council of Europe, the Asia-Pacific Economic Cooperation, the Shanghai Cooperation Organisation, the Eurasian Economic Community, the Organisation for Security and Cooperation in Europe (OSCE), the World Trade Organisation (WTO), and is the leading member of the Commonwealth of Independent States.

Background:	Founded in the 12th century, the Principality of Muscovy, was able to emerge from over 200 years of Mongol domination (13th-15th centuries) and to gradually conquer and absorb surrounding principalities. In the early 17th century, a new Romanov Dynasty continued this policy of expansion across Siberia to the Pacific. Under PETER I (ruled 1682-1725), hegemony was extended to the Baltic Sea and the country was renamed the Russian Empire. During the 19th century, more territorial acquisitions were made in Europe and Asia. Repeated devastating defeats of the Russian army in World War I led to widespread rioting in the major cities of the Russian Empire and to the overthrow in 1917 of the imperial household. The Communists under Vladimir LENIN seized power soon after and formed the USSR. The brutal rule of Josef STALIN (1928-53) strengthened Russian dominance of the Soviet Union at a cost of tens of millions of lives. The Soviet economy and society stagnated in the following decades until General Secretary Mikhail GORBACHEV (1985-91) introduced glasnost (openness) and perestroika (restructuring) in an attempt to modernize Communism, but his initiatives inadvertently released forces that by December 1991 splintered the USSR into 15 independent republics. Since then, Russia has struggled in its efforts to build a democratic political system and market economy to replace the strict social, political, and economic controls of the Communist period. While some progress has been made on the economic front, recent years have seen a recentralization of power under Vladimir PUTIN and an erosion in nascent democratic institutions. A determined guerrilla conflict still plagues Russia in Chechnya.

GEOGRAPHY

Location:	Northern Asia (that part west of the Urals is included with Europe), bordering the Arctic Ocean, between Europe and the North Pacific Ocean
Geographic coordinates:	60 00 N, 100 00 E
Map references:	Asia
Area:	total: 17,075,200 sq km land: 16,995,800 sq km water: 79,400 sq km
Area - comparative:	approximately 1.8 times the size of the US
Land boundaries:	total: 20,017 km border countries: Azerbaijan 284 km, Belarus 959 km, China (southeast) 3,605 km, China (south) 40 km, Estonia 294 km, Finland 1,340 km, Georgia 723 km, Kazakhstan 6,846 km, North Korea 19 km, Latvia 217 km, Lithuania (Kaliningrad Oblast) 227 km, Mongolia 3,485 km, Norway 196 km, Poland (Kaliningrad Oblast) 206 km, Ukraine 1,576 km
Coastline:	37,653 km
Maritime claims:	territorial sea: 12 nm exclusive economic zone: 200 nm continental shelf: 200-m depth or to the depth of exploitation

Climate:	ranges from steppes in the south through humid continental in much of European Russia; subarctic in Siberia to tundra climate in the polar north; winters vary from cool along Black Sea coast to frigid in Siberia; summers vary from warm in the steppes to cool along Arctic coast
Terrain:	broad plain with low hills west of Urals; vast coniferous forest and tundra in Siberia; uplands and mountains along southern border regions

Elevation extremes:	lowest point: Caspian Sea -28 m highest point: Gora El'brus 5,633 m
Natural resources:	wide natural resource base including major deposits of oil, natural gas, coal, and many strategic minerals, timber note: formidable obstacles of climate, terrain, and distance hinder exploitation of natural resources

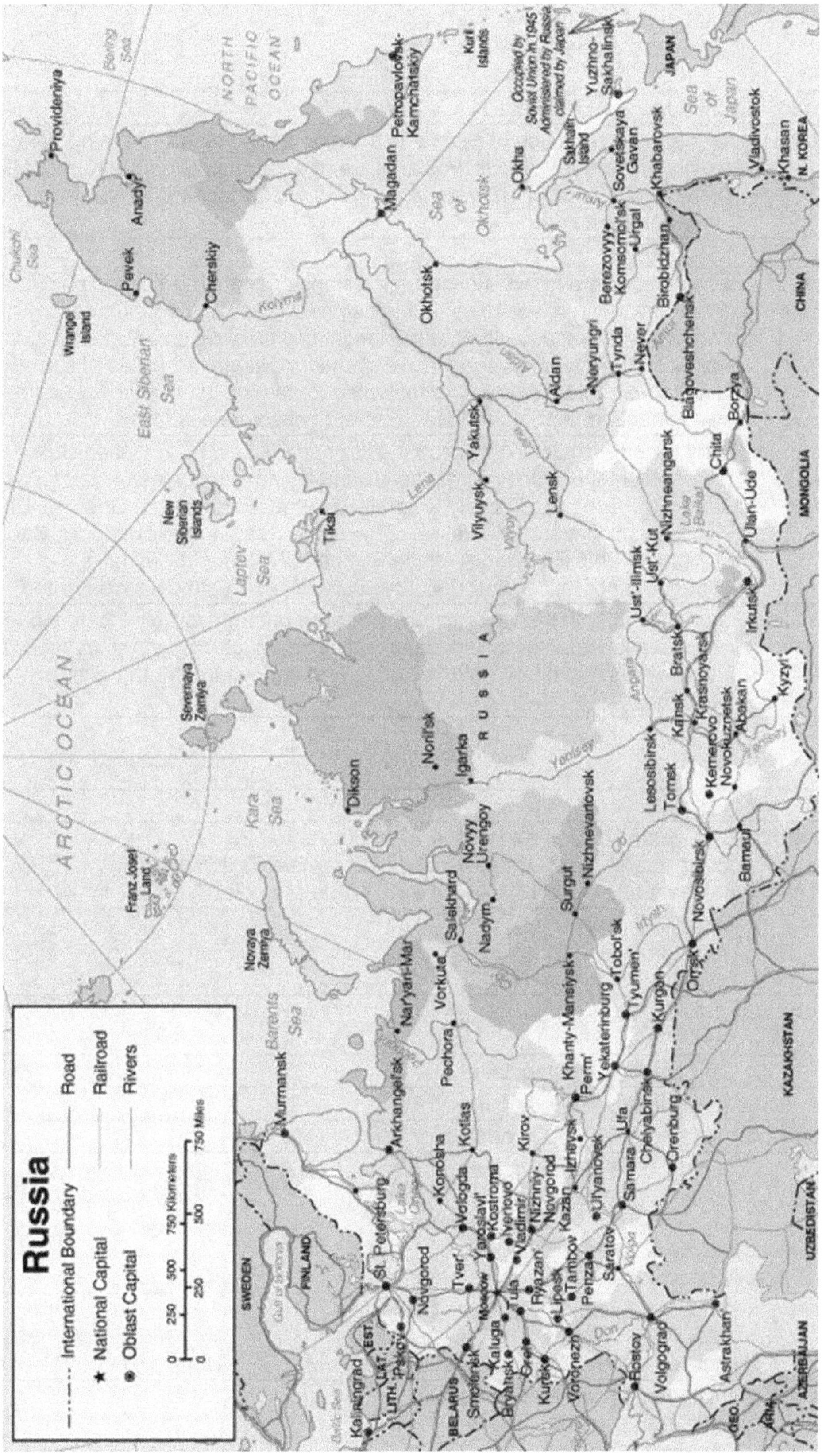
Russia
International Boundary
National Capital
Oblast Capital
Road
Railroad
Rivers
0 250 500 750 Kilometers
0 250 500 750 Miles
ARCTIC OCEAN
NORTH PACIFIC OCEAN
Barents Sea
Kara Sea
Laptev Sea
East Siberian Sea
Chukchi Sea
Bering Sea
Sea of Okhotsk
Sea of Japan
RUSSIA
Novaya Zemlya
Franz Josef Land
Severnaya Zemlya
New Siberian Islands
Wrangel Island
Kuril Islands
Sakhalin Island
JAPAN
CHINA
MONGOLIA
KAZAKHSTAN
UZBEKISTAN
AZERBAIJAN
N. KOREA
FINLAND
SWEDEN
BELARUS
Moscow
St. Petersburg
Murmansk
Arkhangel'sk
Nar'yan-Mar
Vorkuta
Salekhard
Dikson
Noril'sk
Igarka
Tiksi
Yakutsk
Magadan
Petropavlovsk-Kamchatskiy
Provideniya
Anadyr'
Pevek
Cherskiy
Okhotsk
Khabarovsk
Vladivostok
Yuzhno-Sakhalinsk
Irkutsk
Ulan-Ude
Chita
Krasnoyarsk
Novosibirsk
Omsk
Tomsk
Surgut
Yekaterinburg
Perm'
Chelyabinsk
Samara
Volgograd
Rostov
Astrakhan'
Kaliningrad

Land use:	arable land: 7.33% permanent crops: 0.11% other: 92.56%
Irrigated land:	46,630 sq km (1998 est.)
Natural hazards:	permafrost over much of Siberia is a major impediment to development; volcanic activity in the Kuril Islands; volcanoes and earthquakes on the Kamchatka Peninsula; spring floods and summer/autumn forest fires throughout Siberia and parts of European Russia

Environment - current issues:	air pollution from heavy industry, emissions of coal-fired electric plants, and transportation in major cities; industrial, municipal, and agricultural pollution of inland waterways and seacoasts; deforestation; soil erosion; soil contamination from improper application of agricultural chemicals; scattered areas of sometimes intense radioactive contamination; groundwater contamination from toxic waste; urban solid waste management; abandoned stocks of obsolete pesticides
Environment - international agreements:	party to: Air Pollution, Air Pollution-Nitrogen Oxides, Air Pollution-Sulfur 85, Antarctic-Environmental Protocol, Antarctic-Marine Living Resources, Antarctic Seals, Antarctic Treaty, Biodiversity, Climate Change, Endangered Species, Environmental Modification, Hazardous Wastes, Law of the Sea, Marine Dumping, Ozone Layer Protection, Ship Pollution, Tropical Timber 83, Wetlands, Whaling signed, but not ratified: Air Pollution-Sulfur 94, Climate Change-Kyoto Protocol
Geography - note:	largest country in the world in terms of area but unfavorably located in relation to major sea lanes of the world; despite its size, much of the country lacks proper soils and climates (either too cold or too dry) for agriculture; Mount El'brus is Europe's tallest peak

PEOPLE

Population:	143,782,338
Age structure:	0-14 years: 15% (male 11,064,109; female 10,518,595) 15-64 years: 71.3% (male 49,534,076; female 52,958,107) 65 years and over: 13.7% (male 6,177,580; female 13,529,871)
Median age:	total: 37.9 years male: 34.7 years female: 40.7 years
Population growth rate:	-0.45%
Birth rate:	9.63 births/1,000 population
Death rate:	15.17 deaths/1,000 population
Net migration rate:	1.02 migrant(s)/1,000 population
Sex ratio:	at birth: 1.06 male(s)/female under 15 years: 1.05 male(s)/female 15-64 years: 0.94 male(s)/female 65 years and over: 0.46 male(s)/female total population: 0.87 male(s)/female
Infant mortality rate:	total: 16.96 deaths/1,000 live births male: 19.58 deaths/1,000 live births female: 14.18 deaths/1,000 live births
Life expectancy at birth:	total population: 66.39 years male: 59.91 years female: 73.27 years

Total fertility rate:	1.26 children born/woman
HIV/AIDS - adult prevalence rate:	0.9%
HIV/AIDS - people living with HIV/AIDS:	700,000
HIV/AIDS - deaths:	9,000
Nationality:	noun: Russian(s) adjective: Russian
Ethnic groups:	Russian 81.5%, Tatar 3.8%, Ukrainian 3%, Chuvash 1.2%, Bashkir 0.9%, Belarusian 0.8%, Moldavian 0.7%, other 8.1% (1989)
Religions:	Russian Orthodox, Muslim, other
Languages:	Russian, other
Literacy:	definition: age 15 and over can read and write total population: 99.6% male: 99.7% female: 99.5%

GOVERNMENT

Country name:	conventional long form: Russian Federation conventional short form: Russia local long form: Rossiyskaya Federatsiya local short form: Rossiya former: Russian Empire, Russian Soviet Federative Socialist Republic
Government type:	federation
Capital:	Moscow
Administrative divisions:	49 oblasts (oblastey, singular - oblast), 21 republics (respublik, singular - respublika), 10 autonomous okrugs (avtonomnykh okrugov, singular - avtonomnyy okrug), 6 krays (krayev, singular - kray), 2 federal cities (singular - gorod), and 1 autonomous oblast (avtonomnaya oblast') : oblasts: Amur (Blagoveshchensk), Arkhangel'sk, Astrakhan', Belgorod, Bryansk, Chelyabinsk, Chita, Irkutsk, Ivanovo, Kaliningrad, Kaluga, Kamchatka (Petropavlovsk-Kamchatskiy), Kemerovo, Kirov, Kostroma, Kurgan, Kursk, Leningrad, Lipetsk, Magadan, Moscow, Murmansk, Nizhniy Novgorod, Novgorod, Novosibirsk, Omsk, Orenburg, Orel, Penza, Perm', Pskov, Rostov, Ryazan', Sakhalin (Yuzhno-Sakhalinsk), Samara, Saratov, Smolensk, Sverdlovsk (Yekaterinburg), Tambov, Tomsk, Tula, Tver', Tyumen', Ul'yanovsk, Vladimir, Volgograd, Vologda, Voronezh, Yaroslavl' : republics: Adygeya (Maykop), Altay (Gorno-Altaysk), Bashkortostan (Ufa), Buryatiya (Ulan-Ude), Chechnya (Groznyy), Chuvashiya (Cheboksary), Dagestan (Makhachkala), Ingushetiya (Magas), Kabardino-Balkariya (Nal'chik), Kalmykiya (Elista), Karachayevo-Cherkesiya (Cherkessk), Kareliya (Petrozavodsk), Khakasiya (Abakan), Komi (Syktyvkar), Mariy-El (Yoshkar-Ola), Mordoviya (Saransk), Sakha [Yakutiya] (Yakutsk), North Ossetia (Vladikavkaz), Tatarstan (Kazan'), Tyva (Kyzyl), Udmurtiya (Izhevsk) : autonomous okrugs: Aga Buryat (Aginskoye), Chukotka (Anadyr'), Evenk (Tura), Khanty-Mansi, Komi-Permyak (Kudymkar), Koryak (Palana), Nenets (Nar'yan-Mar), Taymyr [Dolgano-Nenets] (Dudinka), Ust'-Orda Buryat (Ust'-Ordynskiy), Yamalo-Nenets (Salekhard) : krays: Altay (Barnaul), Khabarovsk, Krasnodar, Krasnoyarsk, Primorskiy (Vladivostok), Stavropol'

	: federal cities: Moscow (Moskva), St. Petersburg (Sankt-Peterburg) : autonomous oblast: Yevrey [Jewish] (Birobidzhan) note: administrative divisions have the same names as their administrative centers (exceptions have the administrative center name following in parentheses)
Independence:	24 August 1991 (from Soviet Union)
National holiday:	Russia Day, 12 June (1990)
Constitution:	adopted 12 December 1993
Legal system:	based on civil law system; judicial review of legislative acts
Suffrage:	18 years of age; universal
Executive branch:	chief of state: President Vladimir Vladimirovich PUTIN (since 7 May 2012) head of government: Dmitriy Anatolyevich MEDVEDEV (since 8 May 2012); First Deputy Premier Igor Ivanovich SHUVALOV (since 12 May 2008); Deputy Premiers Arkadiy Vladimirovich DVORKOVICH (since 21 May 2012), Olga Yuryevna GOLODETS (since 21 May 2012), Aleksandr Gennadiyevich KHLOPONIN (since 19 January 2010), Dmitriy Nikolayevich KOZAK (since 14 October 2008), Dmitriy Olegovich ROGOZIN (since 23 December 2011), Vladislav Yuryevich SURKOV (since 27 December 2011) cabinet: the "Government" is composed of the premier, his deputies, and ministers; all are appointed by the president, and the premier is also confirmed by the Duma note:there is also a Presidential Administration (PA) that provides staff and policy support to the president, drafts presidential decrees, and coordinates policy among government agencies; a Security Council also reports directly to the president elections: president elected by popular vote for a six-year term (eligible for a second term); election last held 4 March 2012 (next to be held in March 2018); note - the term length was extended from four to six years in late 2008 and went into effect after the 2012 election; there is no vice president; if the president dies in office, cannot exercise his powers because of ill health, is impeached, or resigns, the premier serves as acting president until a new presidential election is held, which must be within three months; premier appointed by the president with the approval of the Duma election results: Vladimir PUTIN elected president; percent of vote - Vladimir PUTIN 63.6%, Gennadiy ZYUGANOV 17.2%, Mikhail PROKHOROV 8%, Vladimir ZHIRINOVSKIY 6.2%, Sergey MIRONOV 3.9%, other 1.1%; Dmitriy MEDVEDEV approved by Duma 299 to 144
Legislative branch:	**description:** bicameral Federal Assembly or Federalnoye Sobraniye consists of the Federation Council or Sovet Federatsii (166 seats; 2 members in each of the 83 federal administrative units (see note below) - oblasts, krays, republics, autonomous okrugs and oblasts, and the federal cities of Moscow and Saint Petersburg - appointed by the top executive and legislative officials; members serve 4-year terms) and the State Duma or Gosudarstvennaya Duma (450 seats; as of February 2014, the electoral system reverted to a mixed electoral system for the 2016 election, in which one-half of the members are directly elected by simple majority vote and one-half directly elected by proportional representation vote; members serve 5-year terms) **elections:** State Duma - last held on 18 September 2016 (next to be held in fall 2021) **election results:** State Duma - United Russia 54.2%, CPRF 13.3%, LDPR 13.1%, A Just Russia 6.2%, Rodina 1.5%, CP 0.2%; seats by party - United Russia 343, CPRF 42, LDPR 39, A Just Russia 23, Rodina 1, CP 1,

	independent 1 **note:** the State Duma now includes 3 representatives and the Federation Council 2 each from the Republic of Crimea and the Federal City of Sevastopol, two regions that Russia occupied and attempted to annex from Ukraine and that the US does not recognize as part of Russia
Judicial branch:	Constitutional Court; Supreme Court; Superior Court of Arbitration; judges for all courts are appointed for life by the Federation Council on the recommendation of the president
Political parties and leaders:	A Just Russia [Sergey MIRONOV] Civic Platform or CP [Rifat SHAYKHUTDINOV] Communist Party of the Russian Federation or CPRF [Gennadiy ZYUGANOV] Liberal Democratic Party of Russia or LDPR [Vladimir ZHIRINOVSKIY] Rodina [Aleksei ZHURAVLYOV] United Russia [Dmitriy MEDVEDEV] **note:** 72 political parties are registered with Russia's Ministry of Justice (as of August 2017), but only six parties maintain representation in Russia's national legislature, and two of these only have one deputy apiece
Political pressure groups and leaders:	NA
International organization participation:	APEC, ARF, ASEAN (dialogue partner), BIS, BSEC, CBSS, CE, CERN (observer), CIS, EAPC, EBRD, G- 8, IAEA, IBRD, ICAO, ICC, ICCt (signatory), ICFTU, ICRM, IDA, IFC, IFRCS, IHO, ILO, IMF, IMO, Interpol, IOC, IOM (observer), ISO, ITU, LAIA (observer), MIGA, MINURSO, MONUC, NAM (guest), NSG, OAS (observer), ONUB, OPCW, OSCE, Paris Club, PCA, PFP, SCO, UN, UN Security Council, UNAMSIL, UNCTAD, UNHCR, UNIDO, UNITAR, UNMEE, UNMIK, UNMIL, UNMISET, UNMOVIC, UNOCI, UNOMIG, UNTSO, UPU, WCO, WFTU, WHO, WIPO, WMO, WToO, WTrO (observer), ZC
Diplomatic representation in the US:	chief of mission: Ambassador Anatoliy Antonov chancery: 2650 Wisconsin Avenue NW, Washington, DC 20047 telephone: (202) 298-5700, 5701, 5704, 5708 FAX: (202) 298-5735 consulate(s) general: New York, San Francisco, and Seattle
Diplomatic representation from the US:	chief of mission: Ambassador Jon Huntsman embassy: Bolshoy Devyatinskiy Pereulok No. 8, 121099 Moscow mailing address: PSC-77, APO AE 09721 telephone: (095) 728-5000 FAX: (095) 728-5090 consulate(s) general: Saint Petersburg, Vladivostok, Yekaterinburg
Flag description:	three equal horizontal bands of white (top), blue, and red

ECONOMY

Russia has undergone significant changes since the collapse of the Soviet Union, moving from a centrally planned economy towards a more market-based system. Both economic growth and reform have stalled in recent years, however, and Russia remains a predominantly statist economy with a high concentration of wealth in officials' hands. Economic reforms in the 1990s privatized most industry, with notable exceptions in the energy, transportation, banking, and defense-related sectors. The protection of property rights is still weak, and the state continues to interfere in the free operation of the private sector.

Russia is one of the world's leading producers of oil and natural gas, and is also a top exporter of metals such as steel and primary aluminum. Russia's reliance on commodity exports makes it vulnerable to boom and bust cycles that follow the volatile swings in global prices.

The economy, which had averaged 7% growth during 1998-2008 as oil prices rose rapidly, has seen diminishing growth rates since then due to the exhaustion of Russia's commodity-based growth model.
A combination of falling oil prices, international sanctions, and structural limitations pushed Russia into a deep recession in 2015, with the GDP falling by close to 4%. Most economists expect this downturn will continue through 2016. Government support for import substitution has increased recently in an effort to diversify the economy away from extractive industries. Although the Russian Ministry of Economic Development is forecasting a modest growth of 0.7% for 2016 as a whole, the Central Bank of Russia (CBR) is more pessimistic and expects the recovery to begin later in the year and a decline of 0.5% to 1.0% for the full year. Russia is heavily dependent on the movement of world commodity prices and the CBR estimates that if oil prices remain below $40 per barrel beyond 2016, the resulting shock would cause GDP to fall by up to 5%.

GDP (purchasing power parity):
$3.718 trillion (2015 est.)
$3.862 trillion (2014 est.)
$3.834 trillion (2013 est.)
note: data are in 2015 US dollars
country comparison to the world: 7

GDP (official exchange rate):
$1.325 trillion (2015 est.)

GDP - real growth rate:
-3.7% (2015 est.)
0.7% (2014 est.)
1.3% (2013 est.)
country comparison to the world: 210

GDP - per capita (PPP):
$25,400 (2015 est.)
$26,400 (2014 est.)
$26,700 (2013 est.)
note: data are in 2015 US dollars
country comparison to the world: 73

Gross national saving:
23.4% of GDP (2015 est.)
24% of GDP (2014 est.)
22.3% of GDP (2013 est.)
country comparison to the world: 62

GDP - composition, by end use:
household consumption: 53.2%
government consumption: 20.2%
investment in fixed capital: 19.1%
investment in inventories: -3.3%
exports of goods and services: 32.2%
imports of goods and services: -21.4% (2015 est.)

GDP - composition, by sector of origin:
agriculture: 4.4%
industry: 35.8%
services: 59.7% (2015 est.)

Agriculture - products:
grain, sugar beets, sunflower seeds, vegetables, fruits; beef, milk
Industries:
complete range of mining and extractive industries producing coal, oil, gas, chemicals, and metals; all forms of machine building from rolling mills to high-performance aircraft and space vehicles; defense industries (including radar, missile production, advanced electronic components), shipbuilding; road and rail transportation equipment; communications equipment; agricultural machinery, tractors, and construction equipment; electric power generating and transmitting equipment; medical and scientific instruments; consumer durables, textiles, foodstuffs, handicrafts

Industrial production growth rate:
-3.5% (2015 est.)
country comparison to the world: 185

Labor force:
74.89 million (2015 est.)
country comparison to the world: 8

Labor force - by occupation:
agriculture: 9.4%
industry: 27.6%
services: 63% (2014)

Unemployment rate:
5.4% (2015 est.)
5.2% (2014 est.)
country comparison to the world: 59

Population below poverty line:
11.2% (2014 est.)

Household income or consumption by percentage share:
lowest 10%: 5.7%
highest 10%: 42.4% (2011 est.)

Distribution of family income - Gini index:
42 (2014)
41.7 (2011)
country comparison to the world: 54

Budget:
revenues: $216.3 billion
expenditures: $251.6 billion (2015 est.)

Taxes and other revenues:
17.5% of GDP (2015 est.)
country comparison to the world: 175

Budget surplus (+) or deficit (-):
-2.9% of GDP (2015 est.)
country comparison to the world: 107

Public debt:
13.5% of GDP (2015 est.)
10.4% of GDP (2014 est.)
note: data cover general government debt, and include debt instruments issued (or owned) by government entities other than the treasury; the data include treasury debt held by foreign entities; the data include debt issued by subnational entities, as well as intra-governmental debt; intra-governmental debt consists of treasury borrowings from surpluses in the social funds, such as for retirement, medical care, and unemployment, debt instruments for the social funds are not sold at public auctions
country comparison to the world: 163

Fiscal year:
calendar year

Inflation rate (consumer prices):
15.5% (2015 est.)
7.8% (2014 est.)
country comparison to the world: 217

Central bank discount rate:
11% (31 December 2015 est.)
17% (31 December 2014)
note: this is the so-called refinancing rate, but in Russia banks do not get refinancing at this rate; this is a reference rate used primarily for fiscal purposes
country comparison to the world: 20

Commercial bank prime lending rate:
15.9% (31 December 2015 est.)
11.14% (31 December 2014 est.)
country comparison to the world: 33

Stock of narrow money:
$171.5 billion (31 December 2015 est.)
$201.4 billion (31 December 2014 est.)
country comparison to the world: 24

Stock of broad money:
$926.8 billion (31 October 2014 est.)
$1.087 trillion (31 December 2013 est.)
country comparison to the world: 19

Stock of domestic credit:
$676.5 billion (31 December 2015 est.)
$664.8 billion (31 December 2014 est.)
country comparison to the world: 20

Market value of publicly traded shares:
$874.7 billion (31 December 2012 est.)
$796.4 billion (31 December 2011)

$1.005 trillion (31 December 2010 est.)
country comparison to the world: 17

Current account balance:
$65.8 billion (2015 est.)
$59.46 billion (2014 est.)
country comparison to the world: 9

Exports:
$337.8 billion (2015 est.)
$497.8 billion (2014 est.)
country comparison to the world: 15

Exports - commodities:
petroleum and petroleum products, natural gas, metals, wood and wood products, chemicals, and a wide variety of civilian and military manufactures

Exports - partners:
Netherlands 11.9%, China 8.3%, Germany 7.4%, Italy 6.5%, Turkey 5.6%, Belarus 4.4%, Japan 4.2% (2015)

Imports:
$197.3 billion (2015 est.)
$308 billion (2014 est.)
country comparison to the world: 23

Imports - commodities:
machinery, vehicles, pharmaceutical products, plastic, semi-finished metal products, meat, fruits and nuts, optical and medical instruments, iron, steel
Imports - partners:
China 19.2%, Germany 11.2%, US 6.4%, Belarus 4.8%, Italy 4.6% (2015)

Reserves of foreign exchange and gold:
$377.8 billion (31 December 2015 est.)
$385.5 billion (31 December 2014 est.)
country comparison to the world: 7

Debt - external:
$599 billion (31 December 2014 est.)
$728.9 billion (31 December 2013 est.)
country comparison to the world: 23

Stock of direct foreign investment - at home:
$360.9 billion (31 December 2015 est.)
$353.4 billion (31 December 2014 est.)
country comparison to the world: 20

Stock of direct foreign investment - abroad:
$404.4 billion (31 December 2015 est.)
$388.4 billion (31 December 2014 est.)
country comparison to the world: 19

Exchange rates:
Russian rubles (RUB) per US dollar -

61.27 (2015 est.)
38.378 (2014 est.)
38.378 (2013 est.)
30.84 (2012 est.)
29.382 (2011 est.)

ENERGY

Electricity - production:
1.064 trillion kWh (2014 est.)
country comparison to the world: 4

Electricity - consumption:
1.065 trillion kWh (2014 est.)
country comparison to the world: 4

Electricity - exports:
8.12 billion kWh (2014 est.)
country comparison to the world: 25

Electricity - imports:
8.87 billion kWh (2014 est.)
country comparison to the world: 24

Electricity - installed generating capacity:
242.2 million kW (2013 est.)
country comparison to the world: 6

Electricity - from fossil fuels:
68.8% of total installed capacity (2012 est.)
country comparison to the world: 110

Electricity - from nuclear fuels:
10.1% of total installed capacity (2012 est.)
country comparison to the world: 18

Electricity - from hydroelectric plants:
20.2% of total installed capacity (2012 est.)
country comparison to the world: 92

Electricity - from other renewable sources:
0.4% of total installed capacity (2012 est.)
country comparison to the world: 104

Crude oil - production:
10.84 million bbl/day (2014 est.)
country comparison to the world: 1

Crude oil - exports:
4.594 million bbl/day (2014 est.)
country comparison to the world: 2

Crude oil - imports:
29,650 bbl/day (2014 est.)
country comparison to the world: 62

Crude oil - proved reserves:
103.2 billion bbl (1 January 2015 est.)
country comparison to the world: 7

Refined petroleum products - production:
6.053 million bbl/day (2014 est.)
country comparison to the world: 4
Refined petroleum products - consumption:
2.8 million bbl/day (2014 est.)
country comparison to the world: 8

Refined petroleum products - exports:
3.3 million bbl/day (2014 est.)
country comparison to the world: 1

Refined petroleum products - imports:
44,600 bbl/day (2014 est.)
country comparison to the world: 83

Natural gas - production:
578.7 billion cu m (2014 est.)
country comparison to the world: 2

Natural gas - consumption:
409.2 billion cu m (2014 est.)
country comparison to the world: 2

Natural gas - exports:
201.9 billion cu m (2014 est.)
country comparison to the world: 1

Natural gas - imports:
24.2 billion cu m (2014 est.)
country comparison to the world: 14

Natural gas - proved reserves:
32.6 trillion cu m (1 January 2015 est.)
country comparison to the world: 2

Carbon dioxide emissions from consumption of energy:
1.782 billion Mt (2012 est.)
country comparison to the world: 5

COMMUNICATIONS

Telephones - fixed lines:
total subscriptions: 36,524,978
subscriptions per 100 inhabitants: 26 (July 2015 est.)
country comparison to the world: 7

Telephones - mobile cellular:
total: 227.288 million
subscriptions per 100 inhabitants: 160 (July 2015 est.)
country comparison to the world: 7

Telephone system:
general assessment: the telephone system is experiencing significant changes; more than 1,000 companies licensed to offer communication services; access to digital lines has improved, particularly in urban centers; progress made toward building the telecommunications infrastructure necessary for a market economy; the estimated number of mobile subscribers jumped from fewer than 1 million in 1998 to more than 235 million in 2011; fixed-line service has improved but a large demand remains
domestic: cross-country digital trunk lines run from Saint Petersburg to Khabarovsk, and from Moscow to Novorossiysk; the telephone systems in 60 regional capitals have modern digital infrastructures; cellular services, both analog and digital, are available in many areas; in rural areas, telephone services are still outdated, inadequate, and low-density
international: country code - 7; connected internationally by undersea fiber -optic cables; satellite earth stations provide access to Intelsat, Intersputnik, Eutelsat, Inmarsat, and Orbita systems

Broadcast media:
13 national TV stations with the federal government owning 1 and holding a controlling interest in a second; state-owned Gazprom maintains a controlling interest in 2 of the national channels; government-affiliated Bank Rossiya owns controlling interest in a fourth and fifth, while a sixth national channel is owned by the Moscow city administration; the Russian Orthodox Church and the Russian military, respectively, own 2 additional national channels; roughly 3,300 national, regional, and local TV stations with over two-thirds completely or partially controlled by the federal or local governments; satellite TV services are available; 2 state-run national radio networks with a third majority-owned by Gazprom; roughly 2,400 public and commercial radio stations (2016)

Radio broadcast stations:
AM 323, FM about 1,500, shortwave 62

Television broadcast stations:
7,306

Internet country code:
.ru; note - Russia also has responsibility for a legacy domain ".su" that was allocated to the Soviet Union and is being phased out

Internet hosts:
14.865 million
country comparison to the world: 10

Internet users:
total: 104.553 million
percent of population: 73.4% (July 2015 est.)
country comparison to the world: 7

TRANSPORTATION

Airports:
1,218 (2013)
country comparison to the world: 5

Airports - with paved runways:
total: 594
over 3,047 m: 54
2,438 to 3,047 m: 197

1,524 to 2,437 m: 123
914 to 1,523 m: 95
under 914 m: 125

Airports - with unpaved runways:
total: 624
over 3,047 m: 4
2,438 to 3,047 m: 13
1,524 to 2,437 m: 69
914 to 1,523 m: 81
under 914 m: 457

Heliports:
49

Pipelines:
condensate 122 km; gas 163,872 km; liquid petroleum gas 1,378 km; oil 80,820 km; oil/gas/water 40 km; refined products 13,658 km; water 23 km

Railways:
total: 87,157 km
broad gauge: 86,200 km 1.520-m gauge (40,300 km electrified)
narrow gauge: 957 km 1.067-m gauge (on Sakhalin Island)
note: an additional 30,000 km of non-common carrier lines serve industries (2014)
country comparison to the world: 3

Roadways:
total: 1,283,387 km
paved: 927,721 km (includes 39,143 km of expressways)
unpaved: 355,666 km
country comparison to the world: 5

Waterways:
102,000 km (including 48,000 km with guaranteed depth; the 72,000-km system in European Russia links Baltic Sea, White Sea, Caspian Sea, Sea of Azov, and Black Sea)
country comparison to the world: 2

Merchant marine:
total: 1,143
by type: bulk carrier 20, cargo 642, carrier 3, chemical tanker 57, combination ore/oil 42, container 13, passenger 15, passenger/cargo 7, petroleum tanker 244, refrigerated cargo 84, roll on/roll off 13, specialized tanker 3
foreign-owned: 155 (Belgium 4, Cyprus 13, Estonia 1, Ireland 1, Italy 14, Latvia 2, Netherlands 2, Romania 1, South Korea 1, Switzerland 3, Turkey 101, Ukraine 12)
registered in other countries: 439 (Antigua and Barbuda 3, Belgium 1, Belize 30, Bulgaria 2, Cambodia 50, Comoros 12, Cook Islands 1, Cyprus 46, Dominica 3, Georgia 6, Hong Kong 1, Kiribati 1, Liberia 109, Malaysia 2, Malta 45, Marshall Islands 5, Moldova 5, Mongolia 2, Panama 49, Romania 1, Saint Kitts and Nevis 13, Saint Vincent and the Grenadines 11, Sierra Leone 7, Singapore 2, Spain 6, Vanuatu 7, unknown 19) (2010)
country comparison to the world: 11

Ports and terminals:
major seaport(s): Kaliningrad, Nakhodka, Novorossiysk, Primorsk, Vostochnyy
river port(s): Saint Petersburg (Neva River)

oil terminal(s): Kavkaz oil terminal
container port(s) (TEUs): Saint Petersburg (2,365,174)
LNG terminal(s) (export): Sakhalin Island

MILITARY

Military branches:
Ground Troops (Sukhoputnyye Voyskia, SV), Navy (Voyenno-Morskoy Flot, VMF), Air Forces (Voyenno-Vozdushniye Sily, VVS); Airborne Troops (Vozdushno-Desantnyye Voyska, VDV), Missile Troops of Strategic Purpose (Raketnyye Voyska Strategicheskogo Naznacheniya, RVSN) referred to commonly as Strategic Rocket Forces, and Aerospace Defense Troops (Voyska Vozdushno-Kosmicheskoy Oborony or Voyska VKO) are independent "combat arms," not subordinate to any of the three branches; Russian Ground Troops include the following combat arms: motorized-rifle troops, tank troops, missile and artillery troops, air defense of the Ground Troops (2014)

Military service age and obligation:
18-27 years of age for compulsory or voluntary military service; males are registered for the draft at 17 years of age; 1-year service obligation (conscripts can only be sent to combat zones after 6 months of training); reserve obligation for non-officers to age 50; enrollment in military schools from the age of 16, cadets classified as members of the armed forces

note: the chief of the General Staff Mobilization Directorate announced in March 2015 that for health reasons, only 76% of draftees called up during the spring 2015 draft campaign were fit for military service (2015)

Military expenditures:
3.49% of GDP (2014)
3.18% of GDP (2013)
2.92% of GDP (2012)
2.71% of GDP (2011)
country comparison to the world: 16

TRANSNATIONAL ISSUES

Disputes - international:
Russia remains concerned about the smuggling of poppy derivatives from Afghanistan through Central Asian countries; China and Russia have demarcated the once disputed islands at the Amur and Ussuri confluence and in the Argun River in accordance with the 2004 Agreement, ending their centuries-long border disputes; the sovereignty dispute over the islands of Etorofu, Kunashiri, Shikotan, and the Habomai group, known in Japan as the "Northern Territories" and in Russia as the "Southern Kurils," occupied by the Soviet Union in 1945, now administered by Russia, and claimed by Japan, remains the primary sticking point to signing a peace treaty formally ending World War II hostilities; Russia's military support and subsequent recognition of Abkhazia and South Ossetia independence in 2008 continue to sour relations with Georgia; Azerbaijan, Kazakhstan, and Russia ratified Caspian seabed delimitation treaties based on equidistance, while Iran continues to insist on a one-fifth slice of the sea; Norway and Russia signed a comprehensive maritime boundary agreement in 2010; various groups in Finland advocate restoration of Karelia (Kareliya) and other areas ceded to the Soviet Union following World War II but the Finnish Government asserts no territorial demands; Russia and Estonia signed a technical border agreement in May 2005, but Russia recalled its signature in June 2005 after the Estonian parliament added to its domestic ratification act a historical preamble referencing the Soviet occupation and Estonia's pre-war borders under the 1920 Treaty of Tartu; Russia contends that the preamble allows Estonia to make territorial claims on Russia in the

future, while Estonian officials deny that the preamble has any legal impact on the treaty text; Russia demands better treatment of the Russian-speaking population in Estonia and Latvia

Lithuania and Russia committed to demarcating their boundary in 2006 in accordance with the land and maritime treaty ratified by Russia in May 2003 and by Lithuania in 1999; Lithuania operates a simplified transit regime for Russian nationals traveling from the Kaliningrad coastal exclave into Russia, while still conforming, as an EU member state with an EU external border, where strict Schengen border rules apply; preparations for the demarcation delimitation of land boundary with Ukraine have commenced; the dispute over the boundary between Russia and Ukraine through the Kerch Strait and Sea of Azov is suspended due to the occupation of Crimea by Russia; Kazakhstan and Russia boundary delimitation was ratified on November 2005 and field demarcation should commence in 2007; Russian Duma has not yet ratified 1990 Bering Sea Maritime Boundary Agreement with the US; Denmark (Greenland) and Norway have made submissions to the Commission on the Limits of the Continental Shelf (CLCS) and Russia is collecting additional data to augment its 2001 CLCS submission

Refugees and internally displaced persons:
refugees (country of origin): 311,407 (Ukraine) (2015)
IDPs: 27,000 (armed conflict, human rights violations, generalized violence in North Caucasus, particularly Chechnya and North Ossetia) (2015)
stateless persons: 101,813 (2015); note - Russia's stateless population consists of Roma, Meskhetian Turks, and ex-Soviet citizens from the former republics; between 2003 and 2010 more than 600,000 stateless people were naturalized; most Meskhetian Turks, followers of Islam with origins in Georgia, fled or were evacuated from Uzbekistan after a 1989 pogrom and have lived in Russia for more than the required five-year residency period; they continue to be denied registration for citizenship and basic rights by local Krasnodar Krai authorities on the grounds that they are temporary illegal migrants

Trafficking in persons:
current situation: Russia is a source, transit, and destination country for men, women, and children who are subjected to forced labor and sex trafficking; with millions of foreign workers, forced labor is Russia's predominant human trafficking problem and sometimes involves organized crime syndicates; workers from Russia, other European countries, Central Asia, and East and Southeast Asia, including North Korea and Vietnam, are subjected to forced labor in the construction, manufacturing, agricultural, textile, grocery store, maritime, and domestic service industries, as well as in forced begging, waste sorting, and street sweeping; women and children from Europe, Southeast Asia, Africa, and Central Asia are subject to sex trafficking in Russia; Russian women and children are victims of sex trafficking domestically and in Northeast Asia, Europe, Central Asia, Africa, the US, and the Middle East

tier rating: Tier 3 - Russia does not fully comply with the minimum standards for the elimination of trafficking and is not making a significant effort to do so; prosecutions of trafficking offenders remained low in comparison to the scope of Russia's trafficking problem; the government did not develop or employ a formal system for identifying trafficking victims or referring them to protective services, although authorities reportedly assisted a limited number of victims on an ad hoc basis; foreign victims, the largest group in Russia, were not entitled to state-provided rehabilitative services and were routinely detained and deported; the government has not reported investigating reports of slave-like conditions among North Korean workers in Russia; authorities have made no effort to reduce the demand for forced labor or to develop public awareness of forced labor or sex trafficking (2015)

Illicit drugs:
limited cultivation of illicit cannabis and opium poppy and producer of methamphetamine, mostly for domestic consumption; government has active illicit crop eradication program; used as

transshipment point for Asian opiates, cannabis, and Latin American cocaine bound for growing domestic markets, to a lesser extent Western and Central Europe, and occasionally to the US; major source of heroin precursor chemicals; corruption and organized crime are key concerns; major consumer of opiates

IMPORTANT INFORMATION FOR UNDERSTANDING RUSSIA

PROFILE

Geography
Area: 17 million sq. km. (6.5 million sq. mi.); about 1.8 times the size of the United States.
Cities: *Capital*--Moscow (pop. 10.4 million). *Other cities*--St. Petersburg (4.6 million), Novosibirsk (1.4 million), Nizhniy Novgorod (1.3 million).
Terrain: Broad plain with low hills west of Urals; vast coniferous forest and tundra in Siberia; uplands and mountains (Caucasus range) along southern borders.
Climate: Northern continental.

People
Nationality: *Noun and adjective*--Russian(s).
Population (August 2011): 142.9 million.
Annual population growth rate (2011 est.): -0.07%.
Ethnic groups (2002 census): Russian 79.8%, Tatar 3.8%, Ukrainian 2%, Bashkir 1.2%, Chuvash 1.1%, other 12.1%.
Religion: Russian Orthodox, Islam, Judaism, Roman Catholicism, Protestant, Buddhist, other.
Language: Russian (official); more than 140 other languages and dialects.
Education (total pop.): *Literacy*--99.4%.
Health: *Life expectancy* (2011 est.)--63.03 years men, 74.87 years women.
Work force (75.49 million, 2010 est.): *Services*--58.1%, *industry*--31.9%, *agriculture*--10%.

Government
Type: Federation.
Independence: August 24, 1991.
Constitution: December 12, 1993.
Branches: *Executive*--president, prime minister (chairman of the government). *Legislative*--Federal Assembly (Federation Council, State Duma). *Judicial*--Constitutional Court, Supreme Court, Supreme Court of Arbitration, Office of Procurator General.
Political parties: There are seven registered political parties in Russia: United Russia, the Communist Party (KPRF), the Liberal Democratic Party (LDPR), Just Russia, Yabloko, Patriots of Russia, and Right Cause. Yabloko, Patriots of Russia, and Right Cause did not win enough votes in the December 2011 election to be represented in the Duma. The next Duma election will be held in December 2016.
Subdivisions: 83 federal subjects (members of the Federation), including 21 republics, 9 krays, 46 oblasts, 2 federal cities, 1 autonomous oblast, and 4 autonomous okrugs.
Suffrage: Universal at 18 years.

Economy
Natural resources: Petroleum, natural gas, timber, furs, precious and nonferrous metals.
Agriculture: *Products*--Grain, sugar beets, sunflower seeds, meat, dairy products.
Industry: *Types*--Complete range of manufactures: automobiles, trucks, trains, agricultural equipment, advanced aircraft, aerospace, machine and equipment products; mining and extractive industry; medical and scientific instruments; construction equipment.
Trade (2010): *Exports*--$376.7 billion: petroleum and petroleum products, natural gas, woods and wood products, metals, chemicals. *Major markets*--EU, CIS, China, Japan. *Imports*--$191.8 billion: machinery and equipment, chemicals, consumer goods, medicines, meat, sugar, semi-finished metal products. *Major*

partners--EU, CIS, Japan, China, U.S. *U.S. exports*--$6.0 billion. *Principal U.S. exports to Russia* (2010)--oil/gas equipment, meat, motor vehicles and parts, aircraft, electrical machinery, automatic data processing machines and parts, medical equipment, plastics, cosmetics, and chemicals. *U.S. imports*--$25.7 billion. *Principal U.S. imports from Russia* (2010)--oil, chemicals (including fertilizer), radioactive materials, iron/steel, precious stones, nickel, aluminum, fish and crustaceans, alcoholic beverages, and base metals.

PEOPLE

Russia's 142.9 million citizens descend from more than 100 ethnic groups. Russian is the official language of Russia and is one of the six official languages of the United Nations. Russian is also the language of such giants of world literature as Pushkin, Tolstoy, Dostoevsky, Chekhov, Pasternak, and Solzhenitsyn.

Russia's educational system has produced nearly 100% literacy. About 8.1 million students attended Russia's 1,108 institutions of higher education in 2008, but continued reform is critical to producing students with skills to adapt to a market economy. Because great emphasis is placed on science and technology in education, Russian mathematical, scientific, and space and aviation research is still generally of a high order. The number of doctors in relation to the population is high by American standards, although medical care in Russia, even in major cities, is generally far below Western standards. The unraveling of the Soviet state in its last decades and the physical and psychological traumas of transition during the 1990s resulted in a steady decline in the health of the Russian people. Currently Russia faces a demographic crisis as births lag far behind deaths. While its population is aging, the high number of deaths of working-age males due to cardiovascular disease is a major cause of Russia's demographic woes. A rapid increase in HIV/AIDS infections and tuberculosis, added to rising deaths from cancer, compounds the problem. In 2011, life expectancy at birth was estimated at 63.03 years for men and 74.87 years for women. The large annual excess of deaths over births, if unabated, could cut Russia's population by 30% over the next 50 years, though inward migration could change this picture. At the end of 2010, there were 60 million Internet users in Russia, with the number growing by 15% a year. Industry watchers forecast that Russia will be Europe's largest Internet market within the next 2 years.

The Russian labor force, amounting to nearly 76 million workers in 2010, is undergoing tremendous changes. Although well educated and skilled, it is largely mismatched to the rapidly changing needs of the Russian economy. Official unemployment dropped to its lowest rate of 5.4% in May 2008, and labor shortages appeared in some high-skilled job markets. The economic crisis that began in late 2008, however, quickly reversed this trend and the ranks of unemployed swelled to an International Labor Organization (ILO)-estimated 8.2% in 2009; 1.8 million Russians lost their jobs in the first quarter of 2009 alone. By the end of 2010, the Russian economy showed signs of recovery, with the unemployment rate falling to 7.4% by the end of the second quarter, according to the Russian Government statistics agency, Rosstat. Following the 1991 collapse of the Soviet Union and the economic dislocation it engendered, the standard of living fell dramatically. Real disposable incomes then doubled between 1999 and 2009, and experts estimate that the middle class constitutes approximately one-fourth of the population. The economic crisis, however, interrupted this trend, as real disposable incomes grew by only 1.9% in 2009 and wages fell by 2.8% during the same period. The stock of wage arrears, which peaked during the crisis at almost 9 billion rubles, had fallen by almost half by February 2010. Government anti-crisis measures to bolster wages, pensions, and other benefits helped reduce the poverty rate in 2009 to an estimated 14%, bringing the number of people living below the subsistence minimum (equivalent to about $169 per month) to below 20 million. The official poverty rate was estimated as 13.1% by the World Bank at the end of 2010. According to Russian statistics, the poverty level increased to 14.9% of the population in the first half of 2011 because of an increase in the official poverty threshold and because average real income fell slightly in 2011.

Moscow is Russia's capital and largest city. Moscow is also increasingly important as an economic and business center; it has become Russia's principal magnet for foreign investment and business presence. Its cultural tradition is rich, and there are many museums devoted to art, literature, music, dance, history, and science, as well as hundreds of churches and dozens of notable cathedrals.

The second-largest city in Russia is St. Petersburg, which was established by Peter the Great in 1703 to be the capital of the Russian Empire as part of his Western-looking reforms. The city was called Petrograd during World War I and Leningrad after 1924. In 1991, as the result of a city referendum, it was renamed St. Petersburg. Under the tsars, the city was Russia's cultural, intellectual, commercial, financial, and industrial center. After Lenin moved the capital back to Moscow in 1918, the city's political significance declined, but it remained a cultural, scientific, and military-industrial center. The Hermitage, formerly the Winter Palace of the tsars, is one of the world's great fine arts museums.

Russia has an area of about 17 million square kilometers (6.5 million sq. mi.); in geographic terms, this makes Russia the largest country in the world by more than 2.5 million square miles. But with a population density of about 22 persons per square mile (9 per sq. km.), it is sparsely populated, and most of its residents live in urban areas.

HISTORY

Although human experience on the territory of present-day Russia dates back to Paleolithic times, the first lineal predecessor of the modern Russian state was founded in 862. The political entity known as Kievan Rus was established in Kiev in 962 and lasted until the 12th century. In the 10th century, Christianity became the state religion under Vladimir, who adopted Greek Orthodox rites. Consequently, Byzantine culture predominated, as is evident in much of Russia's architectural, musical, and artistic heritage. Over the next centuries, various invaders assaulted the Kievan state and, finally, Mongols under Batu Khan destroyed the main population centers except for Novgorod and Pskov in the 13th century and prevailed over the region until 1480. Some historians believe that the Mongol period had a lasting impact on Russian political culture.

In the post-Mongol period, Muscovy gradually became the dominant principality and was able, through diplomacy and conquest, to establish suzerainty over European Russia. Ivan III (1462-1505) referred to his empire as "the Third Rome" and considered it heir to the Byzantine tradition. Ivan IV (the Terrible) (1530-1584) was the first Russian ruler to call himself tsar, a word derived from the Old Russian term for Caesar. He pushed Russia eastward with his conquests but his later reign was marked by the cruelty that earned him his familiar epithet. He was succeeded by Boris Godunov, whose reign commenced the so-called Time of Troubles. Relative stability was achieved when Mikhail Romanov established the dynasty that bore his name in 1613.

During the reign of Peter the Great (1689-1725), modernization and European influences spread in Russia. Peter created Western-style military forces, subordinated the Russian Orthodox Church hierarchy to the tsar, reformed the entire governmental structure, and established the beginnings of a Western-style education system. He moved the capital westward from Moscow to St. Petersburg, his newly-established city on the Baltic. His introduction of European customs generated nationalistic resentments in society and spawned the philosophical rivalry between "Westernizers" and "Slavophiles" that remains a key dynamic of current Russian social and political thought.

Catherine the Great continued Peter's expansionist policies and established Russia as a European power. During her reign (1762-96), power was centralized in the monarchy, and administrative reforms concentrated great wealth and privilege in the hands of the Russian nobility. Catherine was also known as an enthusiastic patron of art, literature and education and for her correspondence with Voltaire and other Enlightenment figures. Catherine segregated the large Jewish population Russia inherited during the partitions of Poland (1772-95) into an area known as "The Pale of Settlement," where great numbers of Jews were concentrated and later subject to vicious attacks known as pogroms.

Alexander I (1801-1825) began his reign as a reformer, but after defeating Napoleon's 1812 attempt to conquer Russia, he became much more conservative and rolled back many of his early reforms. During this era, Russia gained control of Georgia and much of the Caucasus. Throughout the 19th century, the Russian Government sought to suppress repeated attempts at reform and attempts at liberation by various national movements, particularly under the reign of Nicholas I (1825-1855). Its economy failed to compete with those of Western countries. Russian cities were growing without an industrial base to generate employment, although emancipation of the serfs in 1861 foreshadowed urbanization and rapid industrialization late in the century. At the same time, Russia expanded into the rest of the Caucasus, Central Asia and across Siberia. The port of Vladivostok was opened on the Pacific coast in 1860. The Trans-Siberian Railroad opened vast frontiers to development late in the century. In the 19th century, Russian culture flourished as Russian artists made significant contributions to world literature, visual arts, dance, and music. The names of Dostoyevsky, Tolstoy, Gogol, Repin, and Tchaikovsky became known to the world.

Alexander II (1855-1881), a relatively liberal tsar, emancipated the serfs, reformed the judiciary, and established elected local councils (zemstvos). His 1881 assassination, however, prompted the reactionary rule of Alexander III (1881-1894). At the turn of the century, imperial decline became evident. Russia was defeated in the unpopular Russo-Japanese war in 1905. The Russian Revolution of 1905 forced Tsar Nicholas II (1894-1917) to grant a constitution and introduce limited democratic reforms. The government suppressed opposition and abetted anti-Semitic pogroms. Attempts at economic change, such as land reform, were incomplete.

1917 Revolution and the U.S.S.R.

The ruinous effects of World War I, combined with internal pressures, sparked the March 1917 uprising that led Tsar Nicholas II to abdicate the throne. A provisional government came to power, headed by Aleksandr Kerenskiy. On November 7, 1917, the Bolshevik Party, led by Vladimir Lenin, seized control and established the Russian Soviet Federated Socialist Republic. Civil war broke out in 1918 between Lenin's "Red" army and various "White" forces and lasted until 1920, when, despite foreign interventions and a war with Poland, the Bolsheviks triumphed. After the Red army conquered Ukraine, Belarus, Azerbaijan, Georgia, and Armenia, a new nation, the Union of Soviet Socialist Republics (U.S.S.R.), was formed in 1922.

First among its political figures was Lenin, leader of the Bolshevik Party and head of the first Soviet Government, who died in 1924. In the late 1920s, General Secretary of the Communist Party of the Soviet Union (CPSU) Josef Stalin emerged as the dominant figure in the aftermath of intra-party rivalries; he maintained complete control over Soviet domestic and international policy until his death in 1953. In the 1930s, Stalin oversaw the forced collectivization of tens of millions of its citizens in state agricultural and industrial enterprises. Millions died in the process from state-created famines. Millions more were executed or died in the vast penal and labor system known as the Gulag. Initially allied to Nazi Germany, which resulted in significant territorial additions on its western border, the U.S.S.R. was attacked by the Axis on June 22, 1941. More than twenty million Soviet citizens died during World War II in the successful effort to defeat the Axis, in addition to over two million Soviet Jews who perished in the Holocaust. After the war, the U.S.S.R. became one of the Permanent Members of the UN Security Council. In 1949, the U.S.S.R. developed its own nuclear arsenal.

Stalin's successor, Nikita Khrushchev, served as Communist Party leader until he was ousted in 1964, and presided over an era of cautious liberalization known as the Thaw. Aleksey Kosygin became Chairman of the Council of Ministers, and Leonid Brezhnev was made First Secretary of the CPSU Central Committee in 1964. In 1971, Brezhnev rose to become "first among equals" in a collective leadership. During this period, the Soviet economy entered a period of stagnation from which it never recovered. Brezhnev died in 1982 and was succeeded by Yuriy Andropov (1982-84) and Konstantin Chernenko (1984-85). In 1985, Mikhail Gorbachev became the next (and last) General Secretary of the CPSU. Gorbachev introduced policies of *perestroika* (restructuring) and *glasnost* (openness). But his efforts to reform the creaky Communist system from within failed. The people of the Soviet Union were not content with half-freedoms granted by Moscow; they demanded more and the system collapsed. Boris Yeltsin was elected the first president of the Russian Federation in 1991. Russia, Ukraine, and Belarus formed the Commonwealth of Independent States in December 1991. Gorbachev resigned as Soviet President on December 25, 1991.

The Russian Federation

After the December 1991 dissolution of the Soviet Union, the Russian Federation became its successor state, inheriting its permanent seat on the UN Security Council, most of its military assets, as well as the bulk of its foreign assets and debt. By the fall of 1993, politics in Russia reached a stalemate between President Yeltsin and the parliament elected in the waning days of the Soviet Union. The parliament had succeeded in blocking, overturning, or ignoring the President's initiatives on drafting a new constitution, conducting new elections, and making further progress on democratic and economic reforms.

In a dramatic speech in September 1993, President Yeltsin dissolved the Russian parliament in contravention of the existing constitution, and called for new national elections and a new constitution. In response, the parliament sought to depose Yeltsin and instigate an armed insurrection. Yeltsin ordered the army to respond with force to capture the parliament building and crush the insurrection. In December 1993, voters elected a new parliament and approved a new constitution that had been drafted by the Yeltsin government. Yeltsin remained the dominant political figure, although a broad array of parties, including ultra-nationalists, liberals, agrarians, and communists, had substantial representation in the parliament and competed actively in elections at all levels of government.

In late 1994, the Russian security forces launched a brutal operation in the Republic of Chechnya against rebels who were intent on separation from Russia. The protracted conflict, which received close scrutiny in the Russian media, raised serious human rights and humanitarian concerns abroad as well as within Russia, with violations committed on both sides of the fighting. After numerous unsuccessful attempts to institute a cease-fire, in August 1996 the Russian and Chechen authorities negotiated a settlement that resulted in a complete withdrawal of Russian troops and the holding of elections in January 1997. A peace treaty was concluded in May 1997. Following a number of terrorist incidents blamed on Chechen separatists, the Russian Government launched a new military campaign into Chechnya in 1999. By spring 2000, federal forces claimed control over Chechen territory, but fighting continued as rebel fighters regularly ambushed Russian forces in the region. Throughout 2002 and 2003, the ability of Chechen separatists to battle the Russian forces waned but they claimed responsibility for numerous terrorist acts. In 2005 and 2006, key separatist leaders were killed by Russian forces. Large-scale violence was quelled after Ramzan Kadyrov was confirmed as Chechen President in 2007, though many human rights groups accused him of committing serious human rights violations. In April 2009, the Russian Government announced the end of counterterrorism operations in Chechnya; however, the specter of potential conflict in the North Caucasus was raised again by the March 2010 bombing of the Moscow Metro, the January 2011 explosion in Moscow's Domodedovo airport, and the continuing violence in the republic of Dagestan.

On December 31, 1999 Boris Yeltsin resigned, and Vladimir Putin was named Acting President. In March 2000, he won election in his own right as Russia's second president with 53% of the vote. Putin moved quickly to reassert Moscow's control over the regions, whose governors had confidently ignored edicts from Boris Yeltsin. He ended direct elections for regional leaders and sent his own "plenipotentiary representatives" (commonly called 'polpred' in Russian) to ensure that Moscow's policies were followed in recalcitrant regions and republics. He won enactment of liberal economic reforms that rescued a faltering economy and stopped a spiral of hyperinflation. Putin achieved wide popularity by stabilizing the government, especially in marked contrast to what many Russians saw as the chaos of the latter Yeltsin years. The economy grew both because of rising oil prices and, in part, because Putin was able to achieve reforms in banking, labor, and private property. During this time, Russia also moved closer to the U.S., especially after the terrorist attacks of September 11, 2001. In 2002, the NATO-Russia Council was established, giving Russia a voice in NATO discussions.

U.S.-Russian relations cooled over the ensuing years given concerns over domestic developments in Russia, including political freedoms and human rights, as well as over foreign policy differences. Dmitriy Medvedev was elected President in March 2008 and inaugurated in May. Relations during the first few months of his presidency were affected by the August 2008 Russia-Georgia war and subsequent decision by Russia to recognize the territories of South Ossetia and Abkhazia. As a result, U.S.-Russian contact decreased significantly and the NATO-Russia Council was suspended temporarily.

With the change of U.S. administration in January 2009, U.S.-Russian relations have markedly improved as both sides sought to change the tone of the relationship and to cooperate in areas of mutual interest. At a July 2009 summit in Moscow, Presidents Barack Obama and Medvedev created the U.S.-Russia Bilateral Presidential Commission to pursue joint projects and improve cooperation between the two countries. Recent years have also seen increased cooperation with U.S. and NATO, leading to a new strategic concept proposed at the November 2010 Lisbon Summit that strives to develop a "true strategic partnership between NATO and Russia." In February 2011, the New START Treaty, which significantly reduced each country's deployable nuclear weapons, came into effect. The new 123 Agreement between the U.S. and Russia establishes a legal framework for advancing joint work on peaceful uses of nuclear energy. The U.S., NATO, and Russia have also worked closely together to bring stability to Afghanistan. To address Iran's failure to abide by its international commitments regarding its nuclear program, the U.S. and Russia coordinated multilateral approaches to demonstrate to Iran the consequences of its intransigence.

GOVERNMENT AND POLITICAL CONDITIONS

In the political system established by the 1993 constitution, the president wields considerable executive power. There is no vice president, and the legislative branch is far weaker than the executive. The bicameral legislature consists of the lower house (State Duma) and the upper house (the Federation Council). The president nominates the highest state officials, including the prime minister, who must be approved by the Duma. The president can pass decrees without consent from the Duma. He also is head of the armed forces and of the Security Council.

Elections to the Duma, the 450-seat lower house of parliament, were held most recently on December 4, 2011, and presidential elections on March 4, 2012. The pro-government party, United Russia, polled 49 percent of the Duma vote, which translated to 53 percent of seats under Russia's proportional representation system. This was a much weaker result than in 2007, when the party won more than two thirds of seats, enabling it to change the Constitution at will. The three minority parties elected to the Duma in 2007- the Communists, Just Russia and the Liberal Democratic Party – all increased their representation in the 2011 election. Three other parties – Yabloko, Right Cause, and Patriots of Russia – contested the elections but did not meet the 7 percent threshold for representation.

The Party of People's Freedom, a liberal opposition party, had its party registration invalidated and could not participate in the elections. In contrast to 2007, the Organization for Security and Cooperation in Europe's (OSCE) Office of Democratic Institutions and Human Rights (ODIHR) sent a mission to observe the Duma elections. The ODIHR mission's post-election statement identified discrepancies in voting, counting, and tabulation procedures, and noted that the elections took place in an atmosphere which seriously limited political competition. Frequent abuses of administrative resources and media coverage strongly in favor of United Russia combined to hinder political pluralism. The next Duma election must occur before December 2016, as a December 2008 law extended the mandate of the Duma, beginning with the 2011 elections, to five years from four.

On September 24, 2011 Prime Minister Vladimir Putin announced his intention to seek a new term as Russia's president. Putin was elected to a third term – he served the constitutional maximum two consecutive terms from 2000-2008 – as Russia's president on March 4, 2012. He officially garnered 63.4 percent of the vote against four rivals, including leaders of the minority parties in the Duma and a self-nominated candidate, Mikhail Prokhorov. The OSCE/ODIHR observed the election and noted similar shortcomings to those noted in the Duma elections, including the lack of genuine competition and biased media coverage affecting the fairness of the election. The December 2008 law that extended the Duma's mandate also lengthened the term of Russia's president, beginning with the 2012 election, to six years, so the next presidential election is scheduled for 2018.

Russia is a federation, but the precise distribution of powers between the central government and the regional and local authorities is still evolving. The Russian Federation consists of 83 administrative units, including two federal cities, Moscow and St. Petersburg. The constitution explicitly defines the federal government's exclusive powers, but it also describes most key regional issues as the joint responsibility of the federal government and the regional administrative units. In 2000, President Putin grouped the regions into seven federal districts, with presidential appointees established in Moscow and six provincial capitals. In March 2004, the constitution was amended to permit the merger of some regional administrative units. A law enacted in December 2004 eliminated the direct election of the country's regional leaders. Governors are now nominated by the president and subject to confirmation by regional legislatures.

Judicial System
The Russian judicial system consists of the Constitutional Court, courts of general jurisdiction, military courts, and arbitrage courts (which hear commercial disputes). The Constitutional Court of the Russian Federation is a court of limited subject matter jurisdiction. The 1993 constitution empowers the Constitutional Court to arbitrate disputes between the executive and legislative branches and between Moscow and the regional and local governments. The court also is authorized to rule on violations of constitutional rights, to examine appeals from various bodies, and to participate in impeachment proceedings against the president. The July 1994 Law on the Constitutional Court prohibits the court from examining cases on its own initiative and limits the scope of issues the court can hear. The system of general jurisdiction courts includes the Supreme Court of the Russian Federation, regional level courts, district level courts and justices of the peace.

The Duma passed a Criminal Procedure Code and other judicial reforms during its 2001 session. These reforms help make the Russian judicial system more compatible with its Western counterparts. The reforms reintroduced jury trials in certain criminal cases and created a more adversarial system of criminal trials that protect the rights of defendants more adequately. Another significant advance in the Code is the transfer, from the Procuracy to the courts, of authority to issue search and arrest warrants. There are concerns, however, that prosecutors have selectively targeted individuals for political reasons, as in the prosecution of Yukos Oil CEO Mikhail Khodorkovskiy.

In spite of some efforts to increase judicial independence (for example, through a considerable salary increase for judges several years ago), many judges still see their role not as impartial and independent arbiters, but as government officials protecting state interests. See below for more information on the commercial court/business law.

Human Rights
Russia's human rights record remains uneven and poor in some areas. Despite significant improvements in conditions following the end of the Soviet Union, problem areas remain. In particular, the Russian Government's policy in the North Caucasus has been a cause for international concern. Although the government has recognized the legitimacy of international human rights standards, the institutionalization of procedures to safeguard these rights has lagged. There are, however, some indications that the law is becoming an increasingly important tool for those seeking to protect human rights.

The judiciary is not independent, is often subject to manipulation by political authorities, and is plagued by large case backlogs and trial delays. Lengthy pretrial detention remains a serious problem. Russia has one of the highest prison population rates in the world, at 613 per 100,000. There are credible reports of beating and torture of inmates and detainees by law enforcement and correctional officials, and brutality perpetrated by the prisoners themselves, some of whom are informally granted authority to enforce order within the prisons. Prison conditions fall well below international standards and extreme overcrowding is common. In 2001, President Putin ordered a moratorium on the death penalty. There are reports that the

Russian Government might still be violating promises it made upon entering the European Council, especially in terms of prison control and conditions. A 2008 law established an independent association of prison monitors, which began work in 2009. The association has had mixed results in its work, with some prison officials cooperating, and others obstructing its work. Highly publicized cases, such as the November 2009 death of lawyer Sergey Magnitsky, who died in pre-trial detention due to lack of access to medical care, have increased pressure on the authorities to ensure effective prison monitoring.

In the North Caucasus, there have been credible allegations of violations of international human rights and humanitarian law committed by both government and non-government forces. Despite an official end to the counterterrorism campaign in Chechnya in April 2009, there was an upsurge in violence in the North Caucasus starting in 2009 and continuing to the present, especially in the republic of Dagestan. Russian authorities have introduced some improvements, such as requiring the presence of civilian investigators during all large-scale military operations and targeted search and seizure operations. Human rights groups and non-governmental organization (NGO) leaders in the region claim that most abuses remain uninvestigated and unpunished and have spread more broadly in the North Caucasus. Chechen leader Ramzan Kadyrov, in power since 2007, was unanimously approved by the Chechen parliament for a new 5-year term beginning in April 2011. Kadyrov has reportedly begun imposing strict Islamic rules on women in the Russian republic, including mandatory headscarves and other restrictive dress code and workplace policies. In 2010, there were paintball attacks in the Chechen capital of Grozny on women who did not have their heads covered, but were otherwise modestly dressed.

The Russian constitution provides for freedom of religion, the equality of all religions before the law, and the separation of church and state. More than 70% of Russians identify themselves as Russian Orthodox. While Muslims, Jews, and other religious minorities continue to encounter prejudice and societal discrimination, they have not been inhibited by the government in the free practice of their religion. High-ranking federal officials have condemned anti-Semitic hate crimes, but law enforcement bodies have not always effectively prosecuted those responsible. The Federal Registration Service and some local officials continue to prevent some religious minority groups from registering locally or from acquiring property. Jehovah's Witnesses, readers of Said Nursi, and Scientologists have all reported problems with registration and harassment. All have also had religious literature declared extremist by regional courts.

The constitution provides for freedom of speech and of the press; however, in practice government pressure on the media persists, resulting in numerous infringements of these rights. The government uses direct ownership or ownership by large private companies with links to the government to control or influence the major media outlets, especially television, through direct control and through self-censorship by editors and journalists. This results in restricted access to information about issues deemed sensitive, including coverage of opposition political parties and movements. Unsolved murders of journalists, including the murder of respected investigative reporter Anna Politkovskaya in October 2006, have caused significant international concern and increased the reluctance of journalists to cover controversial subjects. In another unsolved case, environmentalist journalist Mikhail Beketov was beaten nearly to death in November 2008 after he published articles attacking local authorities' development plans for the Khimki forest. The November 2010 beating of Kommersant reporter Oleg Kashin led President Medvedev to pledge to capture those who committed the crime and prompted over 200 journalists to sign a petition to the President asking for protection.

The 2006 law on NGOs created a burdensome registration process for all NGOs, with stricter requirements for foreign-funded NGOs and more relaxed requirements for religious organizations. Authorities also have used a separate law against extremism as a pretext for closing opposition NGOs and media entities, doing so for the first time in January 2007. In 2010, the State Duma passed a law easing registration requirements for NGOs, but critics alleged that this law was largely symbolic, as it did nothing to reinstate the tax-exempt status of foreign grants.

The constitution guarantees citizens the right to choose their place of residence and to travel abroad. Some big-city governments, however, have restricted this right through residential registration rules that closely resemble Soviet-era restrictions. These restrictions, though, are widely circumvented, as evidenced by the large number of undocumented foreign workers in these cities. The freedom to travel abroad and emigrate is respected although restrictions may apply to those who have had access to state secrets, or who have court orders against them for default on debts. Since 1994, the U.S. President has found Russia to be in full compliance with the provisions of the Jackson-Vanik Amendment.

Principal Government Officials

Pres., **Vladimir Vladimirovich PUTIN**
Premier, **Dmitriy Anatolyevich MEDVEDEV**
First Dep. Premier, **Igor Ivanovich SHUVALOV**
Dep. Premier, **Arkadiy Vladimirovich DVORKOVICH**
Dep. Premier, **Olga Yuryevna GOLODETS**
Dep. Premier, **Aleksandr Gennadiyevich KHLOPONIN**
Dep. Premier, **Dmitriy Nikolayevich KOZAK**
Dep. Premier, **Dmitriy Olegovich ROGOZIN**
Dep. Premier, **Vladislav Yuryevich SURKOV**
Min. of Agriculture, **Nikolay Vasilyevich FEDOROV**
Min. of Civil Defense, Emergencies, & Natural Disasters, **Vladimir Andreyevich PUCHKOV**
Min. of Communications & Mass Media, **Nikolay Anatolyevich NIKIFOROV**
Min. of Culture, **Vladimir Rostislavovich MEDINSKIY**
Min. of Defense, **Anatoliy Eduardovich SERDYUKOV**
Min. of Economic Development, **Andrey Removich BELOUSOV**
Min. of Education & Science, **Dmitriy Viktorovich LIVANOV**
Min. of Energy, **Aleksandr Valentinovich NOVAK**
Min. of Far East Development, **Viktor Ivanovich ISHAYEV**
Min. of Finance, **Anton Germanovich SILUANOV**
Min. of Foreign Affairs, **Sergey Viktorovich LAVROV**
Min. of Health, **Veronika Igoryevna SKVORTSOVA**
Min. of Industry & Trade, **Denis Valentinovich MANTUROV**
Min. of Internal Affairs, **Vladimir Aleksandrovich KOLOKOLTSEV**
Min. of Justice, **Aleksandr Vladimirovich KONOVALOV**
Min. of Labor & Social Protection, **Maksim Anatolyevich TOPILIN**
Min. of Natural Resources & Ecology, **Sergey Yefimovich DONSKOY**
Min. of Regional Development, **Oleg Markovich GOVORUN**
Min. of Sport, **Vitaliy Leontyevich MUTKO**
Min. of Transportation, **Maksim Yuryevich SOKOLOV**
Min. for Liaison With Open Govt., **Mikhail Anatolyevich ABYZOV**
Dir., Foreign Intelligence Service (SVR) (Acting), **Mikhail Yefimovich FRADKOV**
Dir., Federal Security Service (FSB) (Acting), **Aleksandr Vasilyevich BORTNIKOV**
Head, Govt. Apparatus, **Vladislav Yuryevich SURKOV**
Sec., Security Council, **Nikolay Platonovich PATRUSHEV**
Procurator Gen., **Yuriy Yakovlevich CHAYKA**
Chmn., Central Bank of Russia, **Sergey Mikhaylovich IGNATYEV**
Ambassador to the US, **Sergey Ivanovich KISLYAK**
Permanent Representative to the UN, New York, **Vitaliy Ivanovich CHURKIN**

The Russian Federation maintains an **embassy** at 2650 Wisconsin Ave., NW, Washington, DC 20007 (tel. 202-298-5700) and a consular section at 2641 Tunlaw Road, Washington, DC (tel. 202-939-8907/8913/8918). Russian consulates also are located in Houston, New York, San Francisco, and Seattle.

ECONOMY

Rank	8th (nominal) / 6th (PPP) (2013)
Currency	Russian ruble (RUB)

Fiscal year	calendar year
Trade organizations	WTO, CIS, APEC, EURASEC, G-20 and others
	Statistics
GDP	$2.118 trillion (nominal) $3.461 trillion (PPP) (WB)
GDP growth	0.7%
GDP per capita	$14,818 (2013) (nominal) $23,589 (2012-2014) (PPP) (WB)
GDP by sector	agriculture: 4.4% industry: 37.6% services: 58%
Inflation (CPI)	7.8%
Population below poverty line	11.2%
Labour force	75.5 million
Labour force by occupation	Agriculture: 4.4%, Industry: 37.6%, Services: 58%
Unemployment	4.9%
Average gross salary	32,715 rubles
Main industries	
Ease-of-doing-business rank	92nd
	External
Exports	$542.5 billion
Export goods	petroleum and petroleum products, natural gas, metals, wood and wood products, chemicals, and a wide variety of civilian and military manufactures
Main export partners	Netherlands 14.6% People's Republic of China 6.8% Germany 6.8% Italy 6.2% Turkey 5.2% Ukraine 5.2% Belarus 4.7%
Imports	$358.1 billion
Import goods	consumer goods, machinery, vehicles, pharmaceutical products, plastic, semi-finished metal products, meat, fruits and nuts, optical and medical instruments, iron, steel
Main import partners	People's Republic of China 16.6% Germany 12.2% Ukraine 5.7% Japan 5% United States 4.9% France 4.4% Italy 4.3%
FDI stock	$552.8 billion
Current account	$34.1 billion
Gross external debt	$720.9 billion
	Public finances
Public debt	7.9% of GDP
Revenues	$469 billion
Expenses	$414 billion
Credit rating	andard & Poor's: BBB (Domestic) BBB- (Foreign) BBB- (T&C Assessment)

	Outlook: Negative
	ɔody's:
	Baa1
	Outlook: Negative
	tch:
	BBB
	Outlook: Negative
Foreign reserves	$467.2 billion

Economy of Russia is a mixed economy with state ownership in strategic areas of the economy. Market reforms of the 1990s privatized much of Russian industry and agriculture, with notable exceptions in the energy and defense-related sectors.

Russia is unusual among the major economies in the way it relies on energy revenues to drive growth. The country has an abundance of natural resources, including oil, natural gas and precious metals, which make up a major share of Russia's exports. As of 2012 oil and gas sector accounted for 16% of the GDP, 52% of federal budget revenues and over 70% of total exports

Russia has a large and sophisticated arms industry, capable of designing and manufacturing high-tech military equipment, including a fifth-generation fighter jet. The value of Russian arms exports totalled $15.7 billion in 2013—second only to the US. Top military exports from Russia include combat aircraft, air defence systems, ships, submarines.

Russian economy is the sixth largest in the world by PPP. Between 2000 and 2012, Russia's energy exports fuelled a rapid growth in living standards, with real disposable income rising by 160%.In dollar-denominated terms this amounted to more than sevenfold increase in disposable incomes since 2000. However, these gains have been distributed unevenly as 110 wealthiest individuals were found to own 35% of all financial assets held by Russian households. Since 2008 Moscow has been repeatedly named the "billionaire capital of the world" by Forbes.

According to the IMF, the Russian economy was already in recession from early 2014 mainly as a result of the 2014 Crimean crisis and the subsequent capital flight. But this turned out to be false and the IMF revised it's rhetoric to *close to being in recession* and a forecast of 0.2% growth in 2014 and 1.0% through 2015

The Russian economy underwent tremendous stress in the 1990s as it moved from a centrally planned economy to a free market system. Difficulties in implementing fiscal reforms aimed at raising government revenues and a dependence on short-term borrowing to finance budget deficits led to a serious financial crisis in 1998. Lower prices for Russia's major export earners (oil and minerals) and a loss of investor confidence due to the Asian financial crisis exacerbated financial problems. The result was a rapid and steep decline (60%) in the value of the ruble, flight of foreign investment, delayed payments on sovereign and private debts, a breakdown of commercial transactions through the banking system, and the threat of runaway inflation.

The Russian economy bounced back quickly from the 1998 crisis and enjoyed over 9 years of sustained growth averaging about 7% due to a devalued ruble, implementation of key economic reforms (tax, banking, labor and land codes), tight fiscal policy, and favorable commodities prices. Household consumption and fixed capital investments both grew by about 10% per year during this period and replaced net exports as the main drivers of demand. Inflation and exchange rates stabilized due to a prudent fiscal policy (Russia ran a budget surplus from 2001-2008). Foreign exchange reserves grew to almost $600 billion by mid-2008, the third-largest in the world, of which more than $200 billion were classified as stabilization funds designed to shelter the budget from commodity price shocks. The balance of payments experienced twin surpluses until mid-2008 in the current and capital accounts, which accounted for the phenomenal growth of reserves. As of July 1, 2006, the ruble became convertible for both current and capital transactions. Russia repaid its entire Soviet-era Paris Club debt of $22 billion in late 2006, but by October 2008 foreign external debt totaled $540 billion, of which $500 billion was owed by banks and corporations, including state-owned enterprises.

The global economic crisis hit Russia hard, starting with heavy capital flight in September 2008, which caused a crisis in its stock market. Several high-profile business disputes earlier in 2008, such as TNK-BP and Mechel, as well as the Georgian war helped drive capital out of Russia. By mid-September, Russia's stock market had collapsed, as businesses sold shares to raise collateral for margin calls required by international lending institutions. As the global financial crisis gathered steam in the fall of 2008, the accompanying steep fall in global demand, commodity prices, and tightening of credit served to almost bring Russia's economic growth to a halt in the fourth quarter of 2008, to 1.1% down from 9.5% during the same period in 2007. The Central Bank of Russia responded by pumping liquidity into Russian banks, which helped avert a banking crisis. At the same time, the government attempted a managed devaluation, which successfully avoided a run on the ruble and bank deposits but at the cost of a steep decline in foreign exchange reserves to $387 billion by mid-February 2009. This in turn prompted the S&P and Fitch rating agencies to downgrade Russia's sovereign debt to the lowest investment grade. By 2010, however, the Russian economy had begun a modest recovery, bolstered by government anti-crisis policies, the global rebound, and a rise in oil prices. Russia's leaders put renewed emphasis on promoting innovation as key to economic modernization as well as on the need to diversify the economy away from oil and gas.

Government Spending/Taxation

The Russian federal budget ran growing surpluses from 2001-2007, as the government taxed and saved much of the rapidly increasing oil revenues. The government overhauled its tax system for both corporations and individuals in 2000-2001, introducing a 13% flat tax for individuals and a unified tax for corporations, which improved overall collection. Responding to demands from the oil sector, the government reduced the tax burden on oil production and exports, but only marginally. Tax enforcement of disputes continues to be uneven and unpredictable. In 2007 the federal budget surplus was 5.5% of GDP, and in 2008 the government ended the year with a surplus of 4.1% of GDP. Although the government revised its budget projections during 2009 to reflect lower oil prices and the effects of the economic crisis, it ended the year with a budget deficit amounting to 7.9% of GDP, which it financed from the Reserve Fund, one of the government's two stabilization funds. The government's anti-crisis package in 2008 and 2009 amounted to about 6.7% of GDP, according to World Bank estimates. The package provided support to the financial sector and enterprises--through liquidity injections to banks and tax cuts/fiscal support to enterprises--as well as modest support for households and small and medium enterprises (SMEs) and increased unemployment benefits. By the end of 2010, due to improving economic conditions, Russia had lowered its budget deficit to 3.9% of GDP. Due to relatively high oil prices through the first half of the year, many officials believed there would not be a budget deficit for 2011.

Population

Russia's population was 142.9 million as of August 2011. Life expectancy remains low compared to developed countries, averaging 63.03 years for men and 74.87 years for women in 2011. The UN predicts that Russia may lose one-third of its population by 2050. Cardiovascular diseases, cancer, traffic accidents, and violence continue to be major causes of death among working age men. Many premature deaths are attributed to excessive alcohol consumption and smoking. A truly healthy Russia will require serious improvements in the health sector and some major changes in current cultural norms. To combat the looming demographic crisis, in October 2007 then-President Putin approved the concept of demographic policy for the years 2008-2025. The program aims to increase life expectancy, reduce mortality, increase the birth rate, improve the population's health, and develop a sound migration policy. The government instituted the National Priority Health Project and "mother's capital" in order to slow the population decline. These programs had short-term success; Russia's natural population decline, the absolute difference between births and deaths, diminished from more than 800,000 in 2005 to roughly 200.000 in 2010, as the birthrate grew from 10.2 to 12.5 per 1,000 in the same period. In April 2008, the government signed the World Health Organization's Framework Convention on Tobacco Control, then approved a tobacco control policy in September 2010 designed to reduce extremely high smoking rates. Results of the 2010 Global Adult Tobacco Survey showed tobacco is the third-leading cause of premature death in Russia, amounting to 17% of all deaths. Nearly 40% of Russia's adult population, or nearly 44 million people, are smokers, more than any other country surveyed on a per capita basis.

HIV/AIDS
Rhere were 592,110 HIV cases officially registered in Russia, though some experts believe the actual number may be over 1 million HIV cases. Statistics show 58,663 new HIV cases documented in Russia in 2010, which is not a significant change from 58,448 new cases recorded in 2009. However, the prevalence of HIV cases was 369 per 100,000 people in 2010, higher than the 2009 indicator of 323 per 100,000. The chief form of transmission continues to be intravenous drug use, which accounted for over 59.2% of new HIV cases in 2010, slightly down from 61.3% in 2009, suggesting an increase in transmission from at-risk groups into the general population via sexual contact. More than 40% of new HIV cases are identified in females, and transmission through heterosexual sex has grown rapidly.

The Government of Russia implements HIV treatment and prevention programs through its National Priority Health Project and Federal Targeted Program. The government currently spends over $250 million per year on HIV/AIDS treatment programs and allocated over $42 million for the period of 2007-2010 to support HIV/AIDS vaccine research. Approximately 74,000 patients are receiving antiretroviral therapy, and the government projects that number will exceed 100,000 patients by 2012. Russia's government-procured antiretroviral therapy (ART) supplies have been affected by a series of shortages and inconsistent delivery to ART recipients.

Commercial Law

Russia has a body of conflicting, overlapping and rapidly changing laws, decrees and regulations, which has resulted in an ad hoc and unpredictable approach to doing business. In this environment, negotiations and contracts from commercial transactions are complex and protracted. Uneven implementation of laws creates further complications. Regional and local courts are often subject to political pressure, and corruption is widespread.

Natural Resources

The mineral-rich Ural Mountains and the vast oil, gas, coal, and timber reserves of Siberia and the Russian Far East make Russia rich in natural resources. However, most resources are located in remote and climatically unfavorable areas that are difficult to develop and far from Russian ports. Nevertheless, Russia is a leading producer and exporter of minerals, gold, and all major fuels. Natural resources, especially energy, dominate Russian exports. Over two-thirds of Russian exports to the United States are fuels, mineral oil, or metals.

Industry
Russia is one of the most industrialized of the former Soviet republics. However, years of very low investment have left much of Russian industry antiquated and highly inefficient. Besides its resource-based industries, it has developed large manufacturing capacities, notably in metals, food products, and transport equipment. Russia is now the world's third-largest exporter of steel and primary aluminum. Russia inherited most of the defense industrial base of the Soviet Union, so armaments remain an important export category for Russia. Efforts have been made with varying success over the past few years to convert defense industries to civilian use, and the Russian Government is engaged in an ongoing process to privatize many of the state-owned enterprises.

Agriculture
Although Russia has 9% of the world's arable land and abundant fresh water, the relative lack of investment and modernization has made agriculture one of Russia's lagging economic sectors. But significant change has occurred in recent years. Grain production for export is concentrated in the south

Deputy Chief of Mission--Sheila Gwaltney
Counselor for Political Affairs--Michael Klecheski
Counselor for Economic Affairs--Stuart Dwyer
Counselor for Commercial Affairs--John McCaslin
Counselor for Consular Affairs--Doron D. Bard
Counselor for Management Affairs--Michael Hoza
Counselor for Public Affairs--Michael J. Hurley
Counselor for Environment, Science, Technology, and Health--Lynette Poulton
Director, U.S. Agency for International Development--Charles North
Legal Attache--David Rubincan
Law Enforcement Section--Tom Firestone and Luke Dembosky
DHS/Citizenship and Immigration Services (CIS)--Susan Aikman
Department of Energy--Christine Buzzard
National Aeronautics and Space Administration (NASA)--Patrick Buzzard
Senior Defense Official and Defense Attache--Rear Admiral Douglas Venlet

TRAVEL

TRAVEL ALERTS, TRAVEL WARNINGS, TRIP REGISTRATION

The U.S. Department of State's Consular Information Program advises Americans traveling and residing abroad through Country Specific Information, Travel Alerts, and Travel Warnings. **Country Specific Information** exists for all countries and includes information on entry and exit requirements, currency regulations, health conditions, safety and security, crime, political disturbances, and the addresses of the U.S. embassies and consulates abroad. **Travel Alerts** are issued to disseminate information quickly about terrorist threats and other relatively short-term conditions overseas that pose significant risks to the security of American travelers. **Travel Warnings** are issued when the State Department recommends that Americans avoid travel to a certain country because the situation is dangerous or unstable.

For the latest security information, Americans living and traveling abroad should regularly monitor the Department's Bureau of Consular Affairs Internet web site at http://travel.state.gov, where current Worldwide Caution, Travel Alerts, and Travel Warnings can be found. The travel.state.gov website also includes information about passports, tips for planning a safe trip abroad and more. More travel-related information also is available at http://www.usa.gov/Citizen/Topics/Travel/International.shtml.

The Department's Smart Traveler app for U.S. travelers going abroad provides easy access to the frequently updated official country information, travel alerts, travel warnings, maps, U.S. embassy locations, and more that appear on the travel.state.gov site. Travelers can also set up e-tineraries to keep track of arrival and departure dates and make notes about upcoming trips. The app is compatible with iPhone, iPod touch, and iPad (requires iOS 4.0 or later).

The Department of State encourages all U.S. citizens traveling or residing abroad to enroll in the State Department's Smart Traveler Enrollment Program (STEP). A link to the registration page is also available through the Department's Smart Traveler app. U.S. citizens without internet access can enroll directly at the nearest U.S. embassy or consulate. By enrolling, you make your presence and whereabouts known in case it is necessary to contact you in an emergency and so you can receive up-to-date information on security conditions.

Emergency information concerning Americans traveling abroad may be obtained by calling 1-888-407-4747 toll free in the U.S. and Canada or the regular toll line 1-202-501-4444 for callers outside the U.S. and Canada.

PASSPORTS

The National Passport Information Center (NPIC) is the U.S. Department of State's single, centralized public contact center for U.S. passport information. Telephone: 1-877-4-USA-PPT (1-877-487-2778);

TDD/TTY: 1-888-874-7793. Passport information is available 24 hours, 7 days a week. You may speak with a representative Monday-Friday, 8 a.m. to 10 p.m., Eastern Time, excluding federal holidays.

SELECTED U.S. AND RUSSIAN CONTACTS

RUSSIAN GOVERNMENT AGENCIES:

*Ministry of Trade and Industry:
Yuri Dmitrievich Maslyukov, Minister-Designate
18/1, Ovchinnikovskaya Nab., Moscow
Tel: (095) 220-1064; Fax: (095) 220-1684, 231-9220
*Note: The Russian Government announced that in August 1998, the
Ministry for Foreign Economic Relations and Trade would be abolished,
and that some of its functions would be assumed by a new Ministry of
Trade and Industry. Mr. Maslyukov was appointed by President Yeltsin
in July 1998.

Ministry of Finance:
Mikhail Mikhailovich Zadornov, Minister of Finance
Ulitsa Ilyinka 9, Entrance 1, Moscow
Tel: (095) 298-9130; Fax: (095) 925-0889

Ministry of Fuel and Energy:
Sergei Vladimirovich Generalov, Minister of Fuels and Energy
7, Kitaigorodskiy Proyezd, Moscow 103074
Tel: (095) 220-4659; Fax: (095) 975-2045
(International Dept.)

Ministry of Agriculture and Food:
Viktor A. Semyonov, Minister of Agriculture and Food
Orlikov Pereulok, 1/11, Moscow
Tel: (095) 207-4243; Fax: (095) 207-8362

State Customs Committee:
Vitaly G. Draganov, Chairman, State Customs Committee
1a, Komsomolskaya Ploshchad, Moscow 107842
Phone: (095) 975-1918; Fax: (095) 975-4823

State Committee for Standardization, Metrology and Certification
(GOSSTANDART
Gennady Petrovich Voronin, Chairman
9, Leninskiy Prospekt, Moscow 117049
Phone: (095) 236-6208, -4044; Fax: (095) 236-6231, 237-6032

Russian Copyright Agency:
Georgiy Artashessovich Ter-Gazariyants, Chairman of the Board;
Vadim Serafimovich Dunin, Head of Foreign Relations Department
6a, Bolshaya Bronnaya Ul., Moscow 103670
Phone: (095) 203-2996, -4599; Fax: (095) 200-1263

Committee for Patents and Trademarks (Rospatent
Alexander Dmitrievich Korchagin, General Director
2/6 Cherkasskiy Pereulok, Moscow
Tel: (095) 206-6203; Fax: (095) 923-4093

State Investment Corporation:
Yuriy Vladimirovich Petrov, Chairman
35, Myasnitskaya Ul., Moscow 103685
Phone: (095) 925-6796; Fax: (095) 207-6936
Regional Governments:

Moscow City Administration:
Iosif N. Ordzhonikidze,
Deputy Mayor and Minister for External Relations
13 Tverskaya Ulitsa, 103032, Moscow
Tel: 095-229-6360; Fax: (095) 883-6208

Moscow Registration Chamber:
Vladimir Ivanovich Sobolyev, Chairman
Mokhovaya Ul., 11, Bld. 8-E, Moscow 103009
Tel/Fax: (095) 202-2787;

Roald Nestorovich Lebedinskiy,
Dir., Registration/Accreditation (information in English)
Tel: (095) 132-0500

Tatyana Kuzminichna Nikanorkina, Expert
for Registration of Companies with Foreign Capital
(information in Russian)
Tel: (095) 202-4042

St. Petersburg City Administration:
Gennady I. Tkachev, Chairman, External Relations Committee
1, Smolniy, St. Petersburg 193060
Phone: (812) 276-1204; Fax: (812) 276-1633

Ilya I. Klebanov, First Vice Governor
Chairman, Cmte. on Economy and Industrial Policy
16 Voznesensky Prospect, St. Petersburg, Russia 190000
Phone: (812) 315-5152; Fax: (812) 319-9292.

Igor Yu. Artemiev, First Vice Governor
Chairman, Committee on Finance
16 Voznesensky Prospect, St. Petersburg, Russia 190000
Phone: (812) 319-9308; Fax: (812) 319-9967.

Leninrad Oblast Administration:
Inna L. Bigotskaya, Chief of Protocol Department
External Relations Committee,

67, Suvorovskiy Prospekt, St. Petersburg 193311
Phone: (812) 274-4859; Fax: (812) 274-2463.

Mark A. Vybornov, Chairman,
Committee on Foreign Economic Relations and Investments
67, Suvorovskiy Prospekt, St. Petersburg 193311
Phone: (812) 278-5587 or 274-4742; Fax: (812) 274-5986.

Yekaterinburg Oblast Administration:
Igor Ivanovich Arzyakov, Dir., Foreign Relations Department
1, Oktyabrskaya Ploshchad, Yekaterinburg 620031
Phone: (3432) 51-54-97, 58-96-56; Fax: (3432) 51-98-70

Yekaterinburg City Administration:
Vladimir I. Lomovtzev, Dir., Foreign Relations Department
1, Oktyabrskaya Ploshchad, Yekaterinburg 620031
Phone: (3432) 51-13-07, 51-43-83; Fax: (3432) 51-90-05

Primorskiy Territorial Administration:
Andrey Gennadyevich Zagumyonnov, Chairman
Committee for Foreign Economic Relations and Regional Trade
of the Dept. for Foreign Economic Relations and Tourism
22 Svetlanskaya ulitsa, 690110, Vladivostok
Phone: (4232) 22-08-52
Fax: (4232) 22-10-19

Khabarovsk Territorial Administration:
Sergey I. Lopatin, Chief, Foreign Economic Relations Dept.
56 ul.K.Marksa, Khabarovsk
Phone/fax: (4212) 32-41-21

Sakhalin Regional Administration:
Vitaly Nikolaevich Elizariev, Director
Department of Foreign Economic Relations
32 Kommunisticheskiy prospect, "Sakhincenter", office 236
693000 Yuzhno-Sakhalinsk 693000
Phone: (4242) 72-74-94
Fax: (4242) 72-74-93; International fax: 7 509-95-1236

State Duma (Lower chamber of Parliament

--Cmte. on Budget, Taxes, Banking and Finance:
Alexander Zhukov, Chairman
2, Georgiyevskiy Pereulok, Moscow
Tel: (095) 292-3618; Fax: (095) 292-5601

--Cmte. on Property, Privatization and Economic Activity:
Pavel Grigoryevich Bunich, Chairman
2, Georgiyevskiy Pereulok, Moscow
Tel: (095) 229-9559; Fax: (095) 229-6996

--Cmte. on Industry, Construction, Transport and Energy:
Vladimir Kuzmich Gusev, Chairman
2, Georgiyevskiy Pereulok, Moscow
Tel: (095) 292-0365; Fax: (095) 292-3763

TRADE ASSOCIATIONS/CHAMBERS OF COMMERCE IN RUSSIA:

American Chamber of Commerce in Russia (Amcham)
Scott M. Blacklin, President
Kosmodamianskaya Nab. 52, Building 1, 8th floor, Moscow
Phone: (095) 961-2141; Fax: (095) 961-2142

American Chmbr. of Commerce in Russia, St. Petersburg Chapter:
Slava Bytchkov, Executive Director
25, Nevsky pr., St. Petersburg, 191186
Tel: (812) 326-2590; Fax: (812) 326-2591

St. Petersburg International Business Association (SPIBA)
Anna Kessner, Executive Administrator
27, Naberezhnaya Moiki, 5th Floor, St. Petersburg, 191186
Tel: (812) 325-9091; Fax: (812) 325-9933

Vladivostok International Business Association (VIBA)
Andrew Wilson, President
c/o U.S. and Foreign Commercial Service, Vladivostok
32 Pushkin Street, Vladivostok, Russia 690000
Phone: (4232) 300-093; Fax: (4232) 300-092
e-mail: csvlad@online.ru

Council for Trade and Economic Cooperation (CIS-USA)
Boris Petrovich Alekseyev, President
3, Naberezhnaya Shevchenko, Moscow 121248
Phone: (095) 243-5514, -5470; Fax: (095) 230-2467

Russian Chamber of Commerce and Industry
Stanislav Alekseyevich Smirnov, President;
Yuriy Nikolayevich Denissenkov, Head,
Sergey B. Kulyba, Expert on Accreditation, Protocol Department
6, Ilyinka Ul., Moscow 103684
Phone: (095) 929-02-86,-60,-61,-62,-63; Fax: (095) 929-0356

Primorskiy Territory Chamber of Commerce
Vladimir Borisovich Brezhnev, Chairman
13a Okeanskiy prospekt, Vladivostok
Phone: (4232) 26-96-30

Fax: (4232) 22-72-26

Khabarovsk Territory Chamber of Commerce and Industry
Mikhail Kruglikov, President
113, Shevronova Ulitsa, Khabarovsk 680000
Phone: (4212) 33-03-11, 33-11-30; Fax: (4212) 33-03-12

U.S. GOVERNMENT PERSONNEL HANDLING BUSINESS ISSUES IN RUSSIA:

U.S. EMBASSY IN MOSCOW:

--John Peters, Minister Counselor for Commercial Affairs
U.S. and Foreign Commercial Service
Bolshaya Molchanovka 23/28, Moscow 121019
Phone: (095) 967-3414; Fax: (095) 967-3416
Satellite phone: 7 (502) 224-1105;
Satellite fax: 7 (502) 224-1106

--Michael Matera, Minister Counselor for Economic Affairs
21, Novinskiy Bulvar, Moscow 121099
Phone: (095) 956-4220; Fax: (095) 956-4146

--Asif Chaudry, Minister Counselor for Agricultural Affairs
21, Novinskiy Bulvar, Moscow 121099
Phone: (095) 956 4103; (502) 221 1245
Fax: (095) 975 2339; (502) 224 1356

--James Waller, Treasury Attache
21, Novinskiy Bulvar, Moscow 121099
Phone: (095) 956-4258; Fax: (095) 956-4146

--U.S. Agency for International Development
Office of Privatization and Economic Restructuring
U.S. Embassy, Moscow
21 Novinskiy Bulvar., Moscow 121099
Phone: (095) 956-4281

U.S. and Foreign Commercial Service, St. Petersburg
James McCarthy, Principal Commercial Officer
25, Nevsky prospekt., St. Petersburg, Russia 191186
Tel: (812) 326-2560; Fax: (812) 326-2561/62

American Business Center, St. Petersburg
Zhanna Agasieva, Assistant Manager
25, Nevsky prospekt, St. Petersburg, Russia 191186
Tel: (812) 326-2570; Fax: (812) 326-2571

U.S. and Foreign Commercial Service, Vladivostok
Richard Steffens, Principal Commercial Officer
32 Pushkin Street, Vladivostok, Russia 690000
Satellite phone/fax: (509) 851-1211
Phone: (4232) 300-093; Fax: (4232) 300-092
e-mail: csvlad@online.ru

American Business Center, Vladivostok
Inna Nazarova, Assistant Manager
2, Batareynaya Ul., Vladivostok
Satellite phone/fax: (509) 851-1212
Phone: (4232) 25-46-25; Fax: (4232) 25-46-61

U.S. Consulate-General in Yekaterinburg
Alexander Deyanov, Commercial Assistant
15A Gogol Street, Third Floor
Yekaterinburg, Russia
Phone: (3432) 564-619; Fax: (3432) 564-515
Phone: (3432) 564-736 (Foreign Commercial Service)

Federal Aviation Administration (FAA)
Dennis B. Cooper, Senior Representative
American Embassy, Brussels
27 Boulevard du Regent, B-1000 Brussels, Belgium
Phone: 322 508-2700; Fax: 322 230-06428
Phone: (095) 956-4036; Fax: (095) 956-4293

WASHINGTON-BASED U.S. GOVERNMENT CONTACTS FOR RUSSIA:

Business Information Service
for the Newly Independent States (BISNIS)
Anne Grey, Director
U.S. Department of Commerce, Rm.7413,
Washington, D.C. 20230
Phone: (202) 482-4655; Fax: (202) 482-2293

U.S. Export-Import Bank
David Fiore, Loan Officer
811 Vermont Avenue, N.W., Washington, D.C. 20571-0999
Phone: (202) 565-3815; Fax: (202) 565-3816

Overseas Private Investment Corporation
Peter Ballinger, Manager, NIS Investment Development
1100 New York Avenue, N.W., Washington, D.C. 20527
Phone: (202) 336-8618; Fax: (202) 408-5145

U.S. Trade and Development Agency
Daniel Stein, Regional Director
U.S. Department of State, SA-16, Rm.301
Washington, D.C. 20523-1602
Phone: (703) 875-4357; Fax: (703) 875-4009

U.S. Department of State, Office of Russian Affairs
Thomas K. Huffaker, Chief Economist
2201 C Street, N.W., Washington, D.C. 20520

Phone: (202) 647-6747; Fax: (202) 736-4710

U.S. Department of Commerce -- Market Access and Compliance
Russia and Independent States Division
Jack Brougher, Director,
U.S. Department of Commerce, Rm.3318,
Washington, D.C. 20230
Phone: (202) 482-3952; Fax: (202) 482-3042

U.S. Agency for International Development
Office of Privatization and Economic Restructuring
Washington, D.C. 20523
Phone: (202) 736-4410

U.S. Department of Agriculture
Russian Area Officer
14th St. and Independence Avenue S.W.,
Washington, D.C. 20250
Phone: (202) 720-3080

U.S. Bureau of Export Administration
Export Counselling Division
U.S. Department of Commerce, Rm.3898,
Washington, D.C. 20230
Phone: (202) 482-4811; Fax: (202) 482-3911

Special American Business Internship Training Program (SABIT)
Liesel Duhon, Director
U.S. Department of Commerce, Rm.3006,
Washington, D.C. 20230
Phone: (202) 482-0073; Fax: (202) 482-4098

U.S.-Based Multipliers and International Organizations
with Interests in Russia:

U.S.-Russia Business Council
Eugene K. Lawson, President
1701 Pennsylvania Ave., N.W. Suite 650,
Washington, D.C. 20046
Phone: (202) 956-7670; Fax: (202) 956-7674

Russian-American Chamber of Commerce
Deborah Palmieri, President
6200 South Quebec St., Suite 210, Englewood, Colorado 80111
Phone: (303) 689-8642; Fax: (303) 689-8762

Foundation for Russian-American Economic Cooperation
Carol Vipperman, President
1932 First Avenue, Suite 803
Seattle, WA 98101
Tel: (206) 443-1935; Fax (206) 443-0954

National Association of State Departments of Agriculture
Richard Kirchhoff, Executive Vice President
1156 15th Street, N.W. Suite 1020, Washington, D.C. 20045
Tel: (202) 296-9680; Fax: (202) 296-9686

The World Bank
Thomas Kelsey, U.S. Department of Commerce liaison
1818 H Street, NW, Washington, DC, 20433
Phone: (202) 458-0118; Fax: (202) 458-0118

International Finance Corporation (IFC)
Mark Constantine
1850 Eye Street, NW, Washington, DC 20433
Phone: (202) 473-9331; Fax: (202) 676-1513
Moscow Office: Roger Gale
6, Neglinnaya St., Moscow
Tel: 7-095-928-5328; Fax: 7-095-927-6832

International Bank for Reconstruction and Development
U.S. Department of Commerce Liaison
to the U.S. Executive Director's Office
1818 H Street, N.W., Room D-13004
Washington, D.C. 20433
Phone: (202) 458-0118; Fax: (202) 477-2967

Office of Multilateral Development Banks,
U.S.& Foreign Commercial Service
U.S. Department of Commerce, Room H-1107
Washington, D.C. 20230
Phone: (202) 482-3399; Fax: (202) 273-0927

European Bank for Reconstruction and Development (EBRD)
One Exchange Square, London EC2A 2EH, United Kingdom
Dean Peterson, U.S. Department of Commerce Liaison
Tel: 011-44-171-338-6569; Fax: 011-44-171-338-6487

MARKET RESEARCH

A comprehensive and up-to-date listing of market research reports
prepared by the U.S. & Foreign Commercial Service in Russia is
available on the NTDB (National Trade Data Bank). The following
listing is of key publications from 1998, and publications under
consideration for 1999:

SECTOR ANALYSES (ISAS

Advertising
Agricultural Machinery and Tractors
Automotive Aftermarket
Aviation Industry
Computer and Office Equipment
Construction Equipment in Northwest Russia

Construction Materials and Services on Sakhalin Island
Construction Materials in the Urals Region
Consumer Goods (General)
Consumer Appliances
Cosmetics
Electronic Components
Financial Services and Insurance
Food Processing and Packaging Equipment
Food Processing Equipment in the Urals Region
Furniture Manufacturing in the Urals Region
Hotel and Restaurant Equipment
Internet Services
Laboratory Diagnostic Equipment
Metallurgy in the Urals Region
Meters and Controls for Heating and Ventilation
Mining Equipment Interior Building Products
Packaging Equipment
Petroleum Markets (Retail)
Pharmaceuticals
Satellite Equipment and Services
Transportation Services
Travel and Tourism Services (Russian Far East)

COMMODITY REPORTS AND MARKET BRIEFS:

Annual Marketing Plan Information Report (annual)
Livestock (annual and semi-annual)
Poultry (annual)
Fresh Deciduous Fruit (annual)
Agricultural Situation Report (annual)
Seafood (annual)
Sugar (annual and semi-annual)
Foreign Buyer List Annual Report
Dairy (annual)
Planting Seeds (annual)
Forest Products (annual)
Grain & Feed (annual)
Oilseeds and Products (annual)
Cotton (annual)

GOLD MINING IN RUSSIA: STRATEGIC INFORMATION AND OPPORTUNITIES

Proven reserves of gold Russia ranks third in the world after South Africa and the United States and has sufficient resources to increase gold production . The share of gold ore in stockpiles in Russia is 80 % , placer - 20%, while at the placers for 85% of the total production of the metal , and mineral deposits - only 15%.

All the world's gold industry has faced in recent years with the problem of depletion of gold and is forced to work with a low metal content in the rock. This problem is closely related to the sharp increase in the cost of gold production , which in turn leads to lower profitability of gold mining companies and the deterioration of their financial condition.

In Russia , after years of intensive development of the richest placer sharply deteriorated economic geological and mining- technical conditions of their operation - the average gold content of the sands has decreased by 2-3 times , the depth increased and the cost of treatment have increased dramatically. As a result, the cost of gold production at some of the alluvial deposits is now higher than in the processing of native gold deposits . According to expert estimates extraction of gold from placer deposits has reached its limit, and by 2000 will be reduced to 70 tons per year.

Gold mining in Russia is currently being implemented in 28 regions . The industry employs about 700 enterprises entities of different ownership forms (joint stock companies , Artel , state-owned enterprises , private enterprises) , acting as independent mining companies . Total employment in the industry is about 350 thousand people.

The largest gold mining regions in the Russian Federation are the Republic of Sakha (Yakutia) , the Chukotka Autonomous District , Amur , Irkutsk and Magadan Oblast. In Yakutia, 79 are engaged in gold mining businesses , the annual production of only the companies of the holding " Sahazoloto " and its related companies have agreed to centralized supply of gold is about 25 tons. According to forecasts , the reserves of gold ore in South Yakutia reach 350 tons. Of these, more than 100 tons stored in the storerooms of natural deposits of "The Dark tabor " - this pearl of South Yakutia. 35 tons of these stocks today, geologists have confirmed. In the Altai region are 10 mining communities , producing about 130 kg . of gold.

Gold production in almost all regions of gold fell , but at the end of the year due to the rise in the dollar , when the ruble price of gold has increased by three to four times , cutting off his most high costs , many businesses have been able to stabilize the level of output and exit a positive rate of return . A number of enterprises were not only able to pay the salaries of its people, but also to pay off some debts to the federal and local budgets . For example, in the I quarter of Yakutia first time in years, a marked increase in production in the gold mining industry , amounting to 49.3 %. This was mainly due to intensive care unit of one of the largest enterprises of the republic - " Aldanzoloto ."

THE PRODUCTION PERFORMANCE OF THE INDUSTRY

Over the past 5 years, the level of gold production decreased by 12%, and production - by 27%. The global fall in the "yellow metal" by 25 %, and also due to the under- pricing of its purchase Gohran and the Central Bank , increased costs for material resources , prospectors lose 40% for refining , leading to failures and reduce the allocated funds for the development production.

Commercial bank loans to support the industry can not save the situation, because basically issued for the short term and high interest rates . Another factor that is of great importance to the industry is the decline in world gold prices. If , as of December 1, 1998 the price of gold on the London Stock Exchange was $ 194 per troy ounce by the beginning of 1999 for about $ 288 , and by the end of April fell to U.S. $

281 note in the beginning of 1997 . the price of 1 troy ounce of gold on the London Stock Exchange was more than $ 350

The problem of the deterioration of the situation in the industry and reduce the production of gold is acute not today , and for many years has been the focus of the government. Despite this, in 1995, when the decline in production was the most prominent, the situation has changed little in the industry .

In order to maintain gold production at current levels and further development of the industry was Roskomdragmetom the Federal target program of the production of gold and silver in Russia for the period up to 2000. The program included to build 21 new gold mining company total annual capacity of production and processing 17.3 million tons of ore to reconstruct seven active companies with increasing their capacity by 3.2 million tonnes of ore. Today, it has become clear that the main provisions of the program have remained only on paper. According to experts, is largely to blame , and the legislators who passed the Law " On Precious Metals and Precious Stones " did not provide a mechanism for its implementation.

Currently, the extraction of gold in Russia is used only half the capacity of the industry. According to the Committee on Natural Resources of the State Duma , to date, producers can sell about 60 tons of gold is mined . According to most experts , the only way out of this situation may be to attract serious investors in the sector who are interested in further development of gold mining. However, an obstacle for investors remains imperfect legislation , including tax .

As of today - mostly because of the August crisis and the actual failure of the state to purchase gold from the manufacturers - the industry has created a situation that may result in the termination of funding research and gold mining in general and the bankruptcy of many cooperatives .

One of the most significant problems in the industry is the depreciation of fixed assets . The average age of equipment used in the industry is about 15 years old and abroad bought machinery previously used . Currently, often used techniques that were used with 30 - 40's , and not surprisingly , they are morally and physically obsolete. The following picture : the natural monopoly in the face of the gold mines gold , spending on production of one gram of gold more money than the cost of one gram of gold on the world market and as a result of moving to bankruptcy. At the same time, to ensure the normal development of the resources of any enterprise sector may increase gold production by 50-100 %.

With the privatization of state enterprises collapsed all the industrial unions , which organized all the activities of the enterprises of the regions . At that lost almost all of the auxiliary complex industry (sectoral engineering , transport , supply , construction , project organization, etc.) .

In the same period in the industry , a large number of new entities on the basis of equity and private equity. State ownership remains only 30 companies , of which 11 mines and mines , which account for about 1% of gold production in Russia . Among the 30 companies that remain in public ownership - 4 refining plant , 6 exploration expeditions.

Deteriorated socio- economic situation of enterprises, their financial situation , which led to the closure and liquidation of enterprises, the miners' settlements and social and cultural spheres . Continuing serious brain drain of gold mining areas .

Excessive fragmentation of previously existing structures has led to the creation of a huge number of low-power companies are not able to solve the serious production problems , living with little or no prospect that does not contribute to the normal functioning of the industry.

The largest volumes of gold occur in Yakutia. In Yakutia, more than 100 low-volume , but rich in content of gold deposits .

FPK " Sahazoloto ." " Sahazoloto " - one of the major gold producers in Russia , which provides 25 % of gold production in Russia and more than 50 % - in the Republic of Sakha (Yakutia). The company was founded in 1995 with the purpose of financial and economic support of gold-mining complex in the Republic of Sakha (Yakutia) in the period of restructuring and the transition to the development of cost effective mineral resource base of the ore deposits of precious metals , creating the conditions for growth. The authorized capital of the company is formed of controlling stakes in former state-owned processing plants (GOK) , formed the basis for adjustment to the national gold-mining complex .

" Aldanzoloto " - one of the largest gold mining companies in the Republic of Sakha (Yakutia). The company is a holding company " Sahazoloto ." Results of the enterprise in the I quarter of this year show that the company is beginning to overcome a severe crisis in which it had been in recent years. Exceeded of the volumes of production : for three months produced more than 700 kg of gold produced and sold jewelry worth more than 55 million rubles (reference 38 mln.) . This significantly exceeded production volumes compared to the same period last year : the extraction of gold by 1.35 times, jewelry is 3.6 times .

" Yuzhuralzoloto " - the main gold mining company , Chelyabinsk region. In recent years the company was on the verge of bankruptcy , and in August of last year for the first time in the last few years, came to a zero level of profitability. Monthly gold production exceeds 80 kg. In 1998 JSC " Yuzhuralzoloto " (Chelyabinsk region) has extracted 490 kg of gold and reached a positive level of profitability. Currently, the average return on gold is about plus 5 %. In 1999 is planned to produce at least 1 ton of gold. Most of the metal prior to the stage of refining Company sells a large Moscow banks for 180-190 rubles. per gram.

Bashkir gold mining company .

The company was established 4 years ago Bashkortostan . Initially, 40 % of the shares owned by the state enterprise " Bashkirzoloto " and 60 % - Interregional Scientific and Production Association " Polymetal " from St. Petersburg. After the bankruptcy, " Bashkirzolota " MSIA " Polymetal " has become a 100 - percent owner of the company. In 1998, the company produced 600 kg of gold and 400 kg of silver . According to experts, the gold reserves in the Uchalinski district of Bashkortostan , where are being developed , it remains for two years , the profitability of energy-intensive production does not exceed a few percent.

Gold reserves of the Bank of Russia are currently 520 tons. The Central Bank buys annually from the Russian mining companies about 100 tons of gold to replenish the reserves of Russia . In 1999, the Central Bank of Russia plans to purchase 90 tons of gold from the Ministry of Finance of the Russian Federation, as well as from commercial banks authorized to trade in gold. In 1998, there was a trend to an increase in the proportion of gold in the international reserves of the country. For example, if the share of foreign currency in the total amount of foreign exchange reserves declined from 72.5 % to 63.8 %, the proportion of gold for the year increased from 27.5 % to 36.2 %.

However, not a secret that the federal budget is not always on time and in full, calculated for the miners surrendered gold, which puts them in a difficult financial situation. Correct the situation could only establishment in Russia of a civilized market of gold and allowing commercial banks to buy gold directly from the manufacturers .

The creation in Russia of a civilized market of precious metals began in 1995, this market was necessary in order to encourage commercial banks in lending to unprofitable gold mining industry . In accordance with the Government of the Russian Federation in 1995 , the sale of gold to commercial banks. At present , work continues on creating the conditions for the normal functioning of the spot market gold. It is, above all, on the treatment of gold coins and gold bullion dimensional . It is planned to create conditions for gold transactions for individuals, with the intention that they should be similar to those transactions in foreign currencies. In addition , the Ministry of Taxes and Levies proposes to allow trading in gold not only banks but also other financial institutions.

So, in Yakutia , more than half of all gold mined in the past year have been sold directly to commercial banks. On mutually beneficial agreements with banks worked 46 subjects gold . This year, that number will increase obviously . In any case, it is known that a number of reputable mining communities which have already been "under the roof" FPK " Sahazoloto " now abandoned this house and work directly with the banks.

Currently, many Russian banks are seriously interested in placing their free ruble funds in gold mining , and therefore the Bank of Russia took the advance of gold mining. According to experts, this provides the best opportunity to participate in the lending of banks with state participation , namely, Sberbank, Vneshtorgbank and Vnesheconombank . At this point, the volume of applications to the commercial banks lending industry is 1.5 times higher than the level projected gold production of not more than 106 tons.

In early 1999, the Savings Bank of the Russian Federation in Moscow was the first Russian banks began to exhibit two-way prices for transactions with gold bars . At the end of April 1999 Russian Sberbank signed with the operators of more than 80 contracts for the purchase of more than 20 tons of gold bullion . In total, according to the results of 1999 , Sberbank plans to buy more than 50 tons of gold, 100 tons of silver and 10 tons of platinum bullion .

Discount price set by the Savings Bank , established on the basis of the price of gold on the London Stock Exchange quotations of the Central Bank of the Russian Federation and , of course, to the U.S. dollar exchange rate against the ruble . Limits the demand for gold is the fact that when buying bullion to pay VAT . And the most potential buyers of gold bars deters extremely low liquidity of the market.

Russian jewelry industry uses only about 10 % of gold . For example , last year, the needs of the jewelry industry , only about 10 tons. For comparison , in the world last year were produced 3.8 tons of gold , of which the production of jewelry has gone 80 %. Thus, the Russian Federation , which occupies the 6th place in gold production is on the 36th place on its use in jewelry purposes. State support for the jewelry industry can contribute to the economic recovery of the country as a whole, the annual consumption of about 50 tons of gold will improve the financing of gold mining and the need to reduce the sale of raw materials abroad at low prices.

Not all the gold mined in Russia remains in the country. Currently, the license of the Central Bank on gold exports have more than 100 commercial banks.

PROBLEMS OF RUSSIA'S GOLD INDUSTRY

Gold mining in Russia is currently being implemented in 28 regions. The industry employs about 700 enterprises entities of different ownership forms (joint stock companies, Artel, state-owned enterprises, private enterprises), acting as independent mining companies. Total employment in the industry is about 350 thousand people.

The largest gold mining regions in the Russian Federation are the Republic of Sakha / Yakutia / Chukotka, the Amur, Irkutsk and Magadan Oblast.

Proven reserves of gold Russia ranks third in the world after South Africa and the United States and has sufficient resources to increase gold production. The share of gold ore in stockpiles in Russia is 80 percent, 20 percent of stream, while at the placers account for 85 percent of the total production of the metal, and mineral deposits - only 15 percent.

After many years of intensive development of the richest placer sharply deteriorated economic geological and mining-technical conditions of their operation - the average gold content of the sands has decreased by 2-3 times, the depth increased and the cost of treatment have increased dramatically. As a result, the cost of gold production at some of the alluvial deposits is now higher than in the processing of native gold deposits.

According to expert estimates extraction of gold from placer deposits has reached its limit, and by 2000 will be reduced to 70 tons per year.

Exploration for gold in the past year were 5 and 2 public joint-stock companies and specialized in more than 190 offices in the mining companies.

For the period 1991-1995, the amount of exploration for gold has declined, a large number of geological organizations eliminated. In such a situation, many gold mining companies in 3-4 years will have nowhere to run, according to Roskomdragmete Russia. A total of 1995 in the gold mining industry in Russia mastered 1.125 billion rubles of investments, including 343.8 billion rubles from the funds of the "golden credit", 562,950,000,000 rubles falls on companies' own funds 218 250 000 000 rubles - on foreign investment. However, investment in the sector hunger exacerbated to the limit. The volume of investments do not provide even simple reproduction with reduced capacity.

In order to stabilize the financial situation of the Russian gold mining companies in 1995 was carried out pre-payment products. For these purposes, gold mining companies, organizations have been allocated through the refiner 1.5 trillion rubles.

In accordance with the Government of the Russian Federation in 1995, the sale of gold by the specially authorized commercial banks. A total of 1995 were considered and recorded 43 transactions of purchase and sale of gold and silver bullion through specially authorized commercial banks.

The share of payments to the budget and extra-budgetary funds in the gold price in 1995 was 60 percent. However, many gold mining companies include on their balance social infrastructure, spending on its content up to 8 percent of the estimated price of gold. In these circumstances, income from the sale of precious metals do not allow gold mining companies is able to settle with the budget and suppliers, accounts payable have a chronic phenomenon.

In the ongoing throughout 1995 rising material and energy resources and reducing by 13.5 percent in the period from June to September, precious metals prices declined substantially revenues remaining at the disposal of gold mining companies, and their financial situation has worsened.

Overall, in 1995, in relation to the level of 1994 while reducing the production of precious metals sales at current prices increased by 76 percent, and the cost of consumable material and energy resources increased by 2.2 times.

According to the available data for January-September 1995, 19 gold mining companies were unprofitable / size of losses ranging from 325 million to 87 billion rubles /, including 5 - in the Magadan region and 3 - in the Khabarovsk Territory.

The main cause of loss of a number of gold mining companies is a significant increase in the cost of gold.

By gold mining companies Magadan cost of 1 gram of gold for the first 9 months of 1995 ranged from 52 thousand rubles / mine im.Matrosova / up to 75 thousand rubles / Open Company "PRIISK PILOT '/, in the Primorsky region - from 59 thousand / JSC" PRIMORZOLOTO "/ up to 76 thousand rubles / Open Company" IMKAR "/. The estimated price of gold in September was 54.5 thousand rubles per 1 g

The manual payable to the gold mining enterprises repaid. In order to maintain gold production at current levels and further development of the industry Roskomdragmetom draft federal target program for the production of gold and silver in Russia for the period up to 2000. The program envisages to build 21 new gold mining company total annual capacity of production and processing 17.3 million tons of ore to reconstruct seven active companies with increasing their capacity by 3.2 million tonnes of ore.

Proven reserves of gold Russia ranks third in the world after South Africa and the United States has sufficient reserves to increase gold production.

The share of gold ore in stockpiles is 80 percent, and placer - 20 percent, while mined from alluvial deposits 85 percent, as of ore deposits - only 15 percent.

Placer gold deposits have a limited resource base, which through many years of intensive development of the richest placer deteriorated sharply geological and mining conditions and economic / average gold content in the sands decreased by 2-3 times the depth of the groundwater has increased and the cost of processing increased sharply /, resulting in the production cost of one gram of gold on some of the alluvial deposits is now higher than in the processing of native gold deposits.

According to expert estimates extraction of gold from placer deposits has reached its limit, and by 2000 will be reduced to 70 tons per year.

As a result of the implementation of the federal target program is expected by 2000, compared with 1994, to increase gold production by 145 percent and silver - more than 2 times.

The implementation of this program will require about 5.47 billion U.S. dollars.

Under these circumstances, the possibility of Roskomdragmeta in the management sector, including state-owned, is very limited. RF Government Decree of 10 February 1994 N 96 Committee is empowered only to approve the statutes of state enterprises and contracting with the leaders of these enterprises.

In this case, the big powers, in accordance with applicable law, submitted to the Administration of the Federation, and the property rights of the state share in the joint-stock companies and property of state-owned enterprises are at the Russian State Property Committee.

With the privatization of state enterprises collapsed all the industrial unions, which organized all the activities of the enterprises of the regions. At that lost almost all of the auxiliary complex industry / sectoral engineering, transport, supply, construction, project organization, etc. /. In the same period in the industry, a large number of new entities on the basis of equity and private equity. State ownership remains only 30 companies, of which 11 mines and mines, which account for about 1 percent of gold mining in Russia. Among the 30 companies that remain in public ownership - 4 refining plant, 6 exploration expeditions.

Deteriorated socio-economic situation of enterprises, their financial situation, which led to the closure and liquidation of enterprises, the miners' settlements and social and cultural spheres. There is a serious brain drain of gold mining areas.

Excessive fragmentation of previously existing structures has led to the creation of a huge number of low-power companies are not able to solve the serious production problems, living with little or no prospect that does not contribute to the normal functioning of the industry.

Dramatically weakened the state's role in the gold mining industry, Russian State Property Committee has failed to ensure the management of public property, and could not do it, taking on the function of the asset management of the entire national economy. State property should work to generate income. As noted, the State Property Committee of the Russian Federation was engaged only in its distribution and sale.

"Under the current system of taxation is inevitable crisis of the gold mining industry and the trend of decline can be predicted with confidence, and for 1996 is not excluded that in the beginning of the new millennium legal gold mining in Russia will be stopped," - said in a research note of the State Duma in precious metals and precious stones presented to the parliamentary proceedings. In the recommendations made at the hearings are exempted from VAT revenues from the supply of gold to the State Fund to allow the Central Bank and the authorized banks to offset the costs incurred VAT on gold production at the expense of other payments to the budget.

It is also proposed to establish the size of royalties for gold at the rate of 2.4 percent instead of the current 10.4 percent.

When these conditions are gold mining companies will be able to achieve the level of profitability of 25-30 percent, provide expanded reproduction at their own expense and to be attractive to investors. The share of budget payments to the selling price is reduced from 60 to 30-35 percent, which will be offset by the increase in production, reduction of budget expenditures on advancing metal purchases for conservation and liquidation of unprofitable mines and the evacuation of the northern towns.

However, the tax breaks will not provide output branch of the impasse, if the only buyer of gold will remain a state with a budget deficit. Creating a functioning market of precious metals remains a key problem, which determines the output of the industry crisis, highlighted in the recommendations.

INVESTMENT IN GOLD MINING

Projects for the extraction of gold in Russia are implemented through the following sources of investment:

public funds (mostly in the form of "gold loans and budget development);

own funds (profit and depreciation);

Russian banking capital;

foreign investment in the gold mining industry.

For the implementation of the federal program, "Gold and silver production in Russia up to 2000", provides for the construction and reconstruction of the gold mining companies expected more than 5 billion dollars in the 1996-1999 reality. has invested 706 million dollars, including the federal budget $ 192 million, equity companies $ 170 million, borrowings -112 banks, foreign investment - 232.

From 1991 to 1997, the volume of public investment in the gold mining industry in Russia has fallen steadily. In 1991, the state capital investments in the construction of the gold mining companies were $ 475 million, in 1996 total investment amounted to 281mln. U.S. total for 1992-1996,. in the gold mining industry has invested 1,782 million

The amount of government loans repayable (in the form of "gold" credit), directed during this period on the development of the gold mining industry accounted for $ 358 million in 1997 for the construction and reconstruction of the gold mining industry was allocated only $ 18 million in 1998 public investment in the gold mining industry have not been made. At present, the role of government is to regulate the flow of investment and the creation of conditions to motivate Russian and foreign investors to invest in long-term projects. Regions even in the absence of investment resources could also have investment support to businesses in the form of tax relief, debt restructuring Gold "credit or offsets in the calculation of the local budget. Such support will ease the tax burden on businesses that can direct the released funds for its development.

The legal basis of the gold market is developing in Russia. Adopted, federal laws № 2395-1 "On Subsurface", № 41 "On Precious Metals and Precious Stones", № • 2615-1 "On Currency Regulation and Currency Control", № 3941-1 "On the Central Bank of the Russian Federation," Resolution of the Government of the Russian Federation, departmental regulations relating to precious metals.

However, the imperfection of the legislation affects the increase in investment in the gold mining industry in Russia, for example, requires a clear definition of the term pre-emptive right of the state to purchase precious metals, gold exclusion from the list of currency values as well as around the world, it is only a commodity or financial instrument, permit extraction of the metal to individuals, the liberalization of exports, etc.

The high level of taxes and obligatory payments are also not conducive to the development of the gold mining industry. In 1998-1999. the share of taxes and payments in Russia accounted for almost a quarter of the cost of goods sold.

List of taxes and charges are constantly revised and supplemented. Introduction of the export duty (at the rate of 5%) for precious metals at low domestic demand severely limited budget of gold mining companies.

Of the total funds invested in 1996-1999. in the gold mining industry, 24% of companies have made money. In the Magadan region of extractive industry at its own expense provide 25-35% of the financial needs of the project for the extraction of gold ore. In Russia there are already companies doing production only at their own expense. Their experience, their acceptance of the development strategy, the parameters field, the technology to extract gold in each case are critical in the search for an investor and an investment vehicle of choice.

Prior to 1997, all gold mined in Russia is the State Fund of Precious Metals and Stones of the Russian Federation (Goskhran). In 1998, the state has refused to invest in the gold mining industry and acquire the metal. Vacuum emerged in the gold market began to fill the commercial banks who had previously worked mainly in the oil and gas industry. In 1998, they invested more than 80 tons of production of the metal (in 1996 only 6m.). In 2000, already 159 commercial banks were licensed to conduct operations with precious metals (in 1996 only 5).

Increased competition among commercial banks leads to cheaper credit. With the participation of banks in 1999-2000. in Russia produced more than 75% of the gold. Russian commercial banks have decided the issue of investing seasonal work the alluvial deposits and began to work with companies that implement the projects of ore deposits, moving from a "short" vacation to the "long" investment component. Commercial banks were the main intermediaries between mining companies and all other stakeholders of the gold market, ie between the sphere of production (output) and the sphere of its circulation in the economy.

There are examples of direct investment (Lanta Bank, Gazprombank, Bank "Zenit", JSC "Oil Financial Company"). Carried out and project financing "golden" loans. So, on the development of the fields Olympics. Kubaka, Even. Dukat, Vassilyevskoe, Val infusion, School, Juliet, Lunar banks extended "gold" loans. The "golden" development loans in the gold mining regions were also made available by the Government of the Russian Federation subjects in the amount of 26 tons of gold including -10 Tons of Yakutia, Buryatia - 0.75 m

Traditional form of raising funds in the gold mining industry is direct (strategic) investments. Direct investment in the gold mining industry can be implemented in three ways: in the form of a loan, to purchase shares of enterprises (in the case of joint-stock companies) and in the form of foreclosure (when it comes to business partnerships, limited liability companies, cooperatives or cooperatives). By purchasing a stock or share company engaged in the production of gold, the investor acquires a share of its property that is the object of investment serves the company (its tangible and intangible assets, liabilities, income). When an investor acquires a bond or issue a credit, then the object of investment serves only liability company.

Lending processes inherent in a gold-mining companies, is a gold loan (credit). The essence of the "gold" credit is that the mining company takes a certain amount of gold in the loan and sells it, and uses the proceeds for his own needs.

An additional possibility of investing gold mining companies, which on the one hand reduces the tax burden on businesses, and on the other - credit risk of banks is a financial lease (leasing) of fixed assets for production purposes. Leasing is a kind of investment for the acquisition of property and transfer it to legal persons for a fee for a certain period of time and under certain conditions, under the contract, with the right of redemption of the property by the lessee.

Another form of portfolio investments are attracting money (speculative) investments, where the investor acquires marketable securities business for profit in stock trading. Strategic investors are more willing to contribute their money to the charter capital of the joint-stock companies, the securities of which are the subject of portfolio investments.

In the fight for major subsoil banks are trying to provide additional services (factoring, cash management services, maintaining metal invoices, etc.) in the early 90s in Russia were high expectations for foreign investment in the gold mining industry. In the framework of the Federal Program "Gold and silver production for the period up to 2000" provided for 5 years in the commissioning of new facilities and renovation of existing attract 1,246 million, however, according to the Ministry of Economic Development for the period 1996-1999. instead of the $ 842 million has managed to attract only 232 million

Noteworthy are two successful projects with foreign investments, realized of "Omolonskaya Gold Mining Company" and JSC "BuryatZoloto." JSC "Omolonskaya Gold Mining Company" attracted to the project processing Kubaka $ 142 million investment from large foreign financial institutions (EBRD, OPIC, ABN, AMRO Bank). The project involves foreign mining companies Kinross Gold (Canada) and Cypros Amax (USA) with more than half of the shares. The project of "BuryatZoloto" (deposits Zun-Holba and Irokanda) involved a Canadian company High River Gold; raise funds for the Bank. In the implementation of the project involved 25 million dollars of foreign investment, securities companies listed on the Berlin and Frankfurt stock exchanges (portfolio investments).

Foreign investment in the gold mining industry may be in the form of direct investments (in the form of loans or equity), on the basis of production sharing agreements (PSAs), as well as in the form of portfolio investment (purchase of securities of companies). The projects of the production sharing agreement on Kuranahskry group of gold deposits in Yakutia and Maisky field in the Chukchi Autonomous District. Under the PSA is expected to develop as Nadezhdinskoye deposit in Yakutia and Taseevskoe in the Chita region. The right to enter into PSAs in Russia on gold deposits with reserves of up to 50 tons and placer deposits with reserves of up to 1 ton is made possible by a decision of the federal and regional executive authorities without the involvement of the legislature.

RESERVES IN RUSSIA

According to the Central Bank of Russia monetary gold reserves to Russian international reserves as of January 1, 2012 amounted to 883,34 tonnes for the 2011 increase in the gold reserves of the Russian Federation amounted to 11.8% and increased by 93.31 m (from 790.03 to 883.34 m). The share of monetary gold during the year increased from 7.5 to 9%. By the volume of gold reserves, Russia still ranks seventh in the list of the World Gold Council (World Gold Council, WGC), after the U.S., Germany, Italy, France, China and Switzerland. Exports of precious metals in 2003 to 2011.

Most of the companies profiled in this report on top of the already known Russian resource classification statistics. Although many investors still doubt the veracity of the Russian classification system, in fact it has been quite good and rarely diverges wildly from Western audit results for the same ore field. The main difference between the systems is the gray area of “modifying factors” that in the Western system gives more leeway to the judgment of the group performing the geological analysis. In simple terms, however, Russia’s “B” reserves could be roughly considered as proved or measured; “B+C1” reserves are roughly equivalent to proved and probable or indicated; and “C2” is inferred. Furthermore, a combination of the B and C1 categories is roughly equivalent to the Western definition of “reserves,” while B+C1+C2 is roughly equivalent to “resources.”

SOVIET GEOLOGY: DATA MINING ISSUE

The former Soviet government funded geological expeditions throughout Russia and so collected extensive information on the country’s metal resources. Key statistical thresholds were set in place, and if met these would result in further, more detailed exploration. This Soviet-era data forms the bulk of current information on Russian gold reserves. Importantly, many Russian industry veterans who took part in inventorying gold reserves for the Soviet Union have since moved to private mining companies, and their wealth of experience provides them and their employers with unparalleled competitive advantages. Additionally, it is generally not a coincidence that gold companies have more than one site in a region, as the ties and contacts built up through a project naturally lead to other projects.

Russian reserve/resource classification is based on a strict regime of statistical probability, while Western reserve classification methods are much more open to case-by-case interpretation. The disadvantage of the Russian system is that it applies a blanket approach to everything, which does not allow for ore body nuances to influence the final result. The advantage is that the results are consistent, making the comparison between different ore bodies throughout the former Soviet Union easier.

THE ABCS OF RUSSIAN GEOLOGICAL DATA

The Russian system has set guidelines as to how much exploration and study work is required at a site before each resource or reserve category can be awarded. The main reserve/resource categories for gold sites are B, C, and P, and each category has subcategories.

The basic premise behind the rating system is the statistical probability of finding a certain amount of gold in a given area. The B category – the highest used by gold companies – is defined by a statistical confidence level of 75%. Roughly put, there is a 75% probability that the reserves suggested by collected geological data actually do exist.

Next comes the C category; reserves given as C1, the highest rating in the group, have a statistical confidence level of 50%. The C1 classification requires at least 350 tons of ore to be tested and processed, with test drillings no more than 40 meters apart, and underground sampling to verify geological inferences.

C2 is the next rating, carrying a significantly lower statistical confidence level than C1, with drilling no more than 80 meters apart and only 0.5 tons of ore to be tested. Additionally, a preliminary feasibility study has to be performed and approved by the government.

Below C2, the P classification group carries the most assumptions and is most fraught with uncertainty. At best, only the P1 classification can be considered as having enough data for a company to begin thinking of a site as an asset. P2 and P3 are more like educated guesses based on limited data, which is usually limited to a few drill holes and soil samples. The statistical certainty of P2 and P3 findings is extremely low.

Of course, Western classification also has a set of parameters for rating geological information. However, the main difference between the Russian and Western systems is the gray area of “modifying factors” that in the Western system gives more leeway to the judgment of the group performing the geological analysis. In simple terms, however, Russia’s “B” reserves could be roughly considered as proved or measured; “B+C1” reserves are roughly equivalent to proved and probable or indicated; and “C2” is inferred. Furthermore, a combination of the B and C1 categories is roughly equivalent to the Western definition of “reserves,” while B+C1+C2 is roughly equivalent to “resources.”

In the hands of competent geologists, this leeway can give more scope for experience to factor into the equation, with a site that may look modest in a strict statistical context actually revealed to be exceptional and given a corresponding classification. Likewise, the opposite can apply, with incompetence and lack of experience reducing the accuracy of the Western system.

Basic outline of the parameters of Western classification

Source: JORC

LICENSES AND GOLD SALES REGULATION

According to Russian law, all subsoil resources are state property and their use is controlled and regulated by several state organs through a complex system of federal and local licensing laws and regulations. In general, the current subsoil licensing regime is not very efficient, as there are significant overlaps between federal and local regulatory power.

Licenses usually follow two steps. The first step is the exploration license, which is granted for a term of five years with a certain minimum exploration spend required to maintain the license. At some time before the end of the five year period, the exploration license holder can submit the results of exploration to the government GKZ bureau, which certifies the results, resulting in an "official" resources classification of C1, C2 or P. This process also results in the conversion of the five-year exploration license into a 20-year exploitation license. We note, however, that the exact terms of this process do vary from region to region and from ore body to ore body, and the terms of license can be modified extended or changes subject to the approval of the issuing body. For ore bodies that already have extensive exploration work done and are being sold off by the state, the license is usually a straight exploitation one with set parameters for development.

For brownfield sites, owning just a license is not enough, as there are often significant above and below ground infrastructure and assets to exploit a given resources that are not included. As such, many companies acquire these assets first and then bid for the license – a process that deters other bidders.

It is important to note the state has the preemptive right to purchase any gold extracted in Russia. Before the legal reforms of precious metal sales in 1998, which lifted state control over all sales, this was a serious problem, as not only did the state have preemptive purchasing rights, but it also fixed prices. Today, although the state has preemptive rights, the market sets the price for gold sales. If the state does not purchase the gold, the seller can then freely sell it to either domestic or foreign customers.

Largest increase gold production in 2011. provided by:

- GC "Petropavlovsk» (Petropavlovsk PLC) - more than 7 tonnes due to increased production at the mines and Malomyr pioneer in the Amur region, as well as by an increase in gold mining;

- OJSC "Polyus Gold» (Polyus Gold International Ltd) - more than 3 tonnes by entering recovery project and increase recycling at Blagodatnoye GOK, and the modernization of the mill-1 Olympiadinskoye Mining for processing ores with Titimukhta in Krasnoyarsk;

- Nordgold (formerly a subsidiary of JSC "Severstal") - 1.3 tonnes due to increased production in the fields beresite (OOO "Rudnik Berezitoviy" in the Amur region) and tabor (LLC "Neryungri Metallic") in the Republic of Sakha (Yakutia) ;

- Of "highest" - 0.7 tons of "Yuzhuralzoloto CC" - 0.34 m, LLC "Congo" - 0.22 m, Ltd. "Status" - 0.19 m, and others making the entries new facilities in Kamchatka (Asachinskoe field, the British Trans-Siberian Gold), in Irkutsk (Verninskoye field, OAO "Polyus Gold") and Amur regions (mine Albyn, SC "Petropavlovsk"). decline in production due to the deterioration of raw materials took place on companies: JSC "Chukotka Hydropower" (mine Dome), OAO "Rudnik Karalveem" and OOO "A / V" Chukotka "in Chukotka, LLC" Cupid Gold "in the Khabarovsk region, etc. In comparison with 2010. by 7% to 422, the number of gold mining companies. This trend was for the first time after a 10-year reduction. The growth was due to small enterprises with annual production of up to 100 kg (up 10%) and large enterprises with annual production of 2 to 5 tons (up 23%). Large enterprises with an annual production of more than 2m secured 90% (9.6 out of 10.6 tonnes) increase in gold production in 2011.

GOLD MINING IN THE RUSSIAN REGIONS

Results of the gold-mining regions, and individual com-panies Russia in 2011.

Krasnoyarsk region

in 2011. compared with the previous year gold production in the Krasnoyarsk region increased by 9.6% to 39.547 tons including from ore deposits were mined more by 17.6% to 36.899 tons and from alluvial deposits - by 24.4% to 2,648 m (Table 17).

Dynamics of the leading gold mining companies of the Krasnoyarsk Territory in 2007-2011. * - JSC "Vasilevsky Rudnik" in view of JSC "Gerfed." ** - in 2011, LLC "FCA Gold Star" has extracted only 549.1 kg of They 159.1 kg - the Krasnoyarsk Territory and 390 kg - in the Republic of Khakassia. *** - Since 2006, ceased to exist a / c "Angara". Its assets are transferred to the LLC "A / V" Angara-North, "united with" Sisim. "

Company "ZDK" Polyus "(part of the Polyus Gold) in 2011. increased production by 11.2% to 32.242 tons company develops in the region Olimpiada, Beneficial and Titimukhta. Production growth is due mainly to the project output extraction and processing volumes increased by Blagodatnoye GOK. On fertile field completed pit (South and North), and the gold recovery plant (ZIF-4) with the achievement of project performance - 6 million tons of ore and 12 tonnes of gold a year. On Titimukhta was increased ore extraction in connection with the modernization of the gold recovery plant (ZIF-1). Among the negative factors hindering the expansion of production, still remain technological challenges of Olimpiada. The problem of processing of sulphide ore, which began in 2010., Not overcome. In the IV quarter of 2011. Gold recovery from sulphide ore was about 71% (for the whole year - 69.1% versus 66.4% a year earlier). By the end of 2012. the company expects to increase this to 78%.

Besides, the issue negatively impacted by the lower gold content in the ore processed at the Olympics (from 3.77 g / t to 3.43 g / t). CJSC "ZDK" Polyus "plans in 2012. compared with last year to increase gold production in the Krasnoyarsk region of 8.9% - up to 35.6 tons will develop the project to expand the Blagodatnoye Mining and 8 million tonnes of ore per year.

On Titimukhta expansion will be completed by 20% to 2 , 4 million tons of ore, and 4 tons of gold per year capacity ZIF-1. Planned recovery was 86%, as part of a new project to increase the capacity of ZIF-1, will not be affected. LLC "Sovrudnik" - this is the second in the province in terms of gold mining company that implements a 2007 investment project to expand production capacity and increase the volume of gold production. In 2011. gold production increased by 0.2% as compared to 2010. - Up to 3,464 tons of mining operations increased by 18.5% - up to 9.6 million cubic meters. m ore processed by 7% - to 1.84 million tons of construction of the new tailings North Yenisei mill. According to the plan of modernization factory replaced the outdated equipment, improved ore processing circuit - all allowed to raise its capacity to process ore from 1.5 to 2 million tons per year. In 2011. completed exploration work in the fields of Proletarian, Mace and the tips. On the first two put on government balance sheet 6 tons of gold reserves. Also managed to increase its gold reserves at the field Eldorado by 13.8 tons in 2012. the company intends to increase gold production by 8% to 3.7 tons, compared with 2011.

Growth is planned due to start production in the field of Alexander Ageevskoe. In 2013. plant can produce up to 4 tons of gold annually. For exploration in 2012. planned to be about 200 million rubles. protiv180 mln. in 2011. Will continue exploration work on Noybinskoy area where the expected increase in reserves may reach 5 m in the field of good. Total reserves Noybinskoy area will grow to 8.5 m JSC "Vasilevsky Rudnik" (owned by Gazprombank) in 2011. continued refinement of Basil and Nicholas gold deposits and subsequent processing of extracted ore at the existing processing plant (400 thousand tons of ore per year.) In the long term development of the company planned to launch a set of heap leaching (VHF) on ore deposits of the Archangel, and the construction and commissioning of the second queue processing plant with an annual capacity of 1 million tonnes per year for processing ores Gerfed. According to the regional program "Development of the production of mining organizations in the Krasnoyarsk Territory in 2011 2013." gold production in the Krasnoyarsk region in 2013 may be increased to 49 tons Amur region by the end of 2011. Gold mining in the Amur region increased compared with 2010. by 47% - up to 29.111 tons At the same time production has increased: from ore deposits - by 62% to 22,027 tonnes and from alluvial deposits by 14% to 7,084 t (Table 18).

On the territory of the bulk of gold production (about 70%) carries a British company Petropavloysk plc. It is industrial development of gold deposits Pokrovsky, Pioneer, Malomyr, at the end of 2011 was launched fourth project - Albyn. Intercession on the field in 2011. continued decline in gold production due to depletion (up to 2.8 tons, compared to 4.5 tons in 2011.). In 2012. existing ore processing capacity will be used by 81% (at full processing capacity of 2.1 actual capacity will be 1.7 million tonnes per year). Planned to reduce production to 2.1 tons of gold. Pioneer at the field at full capacity, there are three factories with a total capacity of 4.6 million tonnes of ore per year. In 2012. plans to commission the fourth stage of the Pioneer mine, designed for processing neupornoy 2 million tons of ore a year. The total design capacity of the mine will be 6.6 million tonnes of ore per year. Gold production is planned for 11-12 tons annually. Malomyr involved at two stages of the mine a total design production capacity of 2.6 million tonnes of ore per year. In 2011.

The mine has been increased gold production by 2.5 times to 2.8 tons in 2012. planned to release 3.7 tons of gold at the existing facilities. in 2011. were put into the first stage of Albynskogo mine design capacity of 1.8 million tonnes of ore per year. The company reports that the second phase of the mine production capacity of 1.8 million tonnes per year is planned to introduce in the third quarter of 2012. (Instead of 2014. As previously planned) due to increase in reserves at the field. In 2012. Gold production at the field Albyn could reach 3.6 tons started large-scale construction autoclave production at Pokrovsky mine. Since 2013, there will concentrate processing refractory ore from the mines and deposits Pioneer Malomyr.

According to the plans of the company, in 2012. refining capacity in the fields of Pokrovsky, Pioneer and Albyn Malomyr will take to the level of 14.9 million tonnes of ore per year. LLC "Berezitoviy Mine" (a subsidiary of the Russian international company Nordgold) in 2011. increased gold production compared to 2010. 1.5 times to 3,258 tonnes increase was made possible thanks to the improvement of the quality of planning and ore mining optimization, construction of the second stage of career and modernization of the mill. in 2012. the company plans to increase gold production to 3.6 tons of "Mine Soloviev" - the oldest enterprise of the region, whose history dates from the time of opening in 1866. mining engineer N.P.Anosovym rich alluvial deposits in the valley r.Dzhalinda. Currently, it is one of the most successful and fastest growing companies of alluvial gold mining in Russia. It has been working off of deep alluvial deposits, accumulating experience and gold ore is developing a classic small placer prospecting method. In the near future detailed exploration of the mine and the construction of a mine at Dzhalindinskom gold deposit. According to our estimates, in 2012. Gold mining in the Amur region may exceed 30 tonnes due to increased production at Albynskom and Malomyrskom fields (Petropavloysk plc.), as well as the increase in gold production Company "Berezitoviy mine." Chukotka Chukotka Enterprises in 2011. produced 20,057 t gold and 216.2 tons of silver, respectively - by 19.4% and 2.5% less than in 2010. Gold mining of ore deposits decreased by 20.3% to 18,438 tonnes of gravel - by 7.3% to 1,619 tons of silver production decreased by 2.5% to 216.2 m

In 2012. Kinross Gold plans to complete a feasibility study on the deposit and Double commencement of commercial production of gold in 2013. The field will be developed by underground mining capacity of about 900 tons of ore per day. The average gold grade is expected to be 17.5 g / t, the starting amount of capital investment - $ 300 million The ore will be delivered for processing into gold factory Dome (90 km to the south of the Double.) According to the results of prospecting and exploration in the SRC approved balance sheet reserves in the amount of 46 tons of C1 + C2 reserves of the deposit Kekura within Karalveemskogo ore unit. further prospects of development of precious metals in the Chukotka generally assessed as positive. The region plans to begin production at large fields gold and silver ore: Maisky (part of JSC "Polymetal"), Double (Kinross Gold) and Kekura (JSC "Base Metals").

In 2012. in Chukotka expected to produce 20 tonnes of gold and silver that is about 200-210 Republic of Sakha (Yakutia) Gold production in the Republic of Sakha (Yakutia) in 2011. compared with the previous year increased by 4.3% to 19.378 tons, including production of ore deposits increased by 0.9% to 10,299 tonnes and from alluvial deposits - by 8.3% to 9,079 t (Table 20).

LLC " Aldanzoloto GRK "(part of the Polyus Gold) - the largest gold mining company of the republic in 2011. reduced gold production by 9.7% to 3.63 tons due to difficulties encountered modernization project Kuranakh mine and processing project-balance and off-balance ore dumps Kuranakh ore field by heap leaching. In 2011. failed to complete the industrial tests on the separation of ore sludge and crystalline fractions and their subsequent processing on the reconstructed mill and installation of heap leaching / VHF /, respectively. In the case of projects, the company by 2014. increase the extraction of ore and 8 million tonnes, with an additional gold production at the expense of the factory is about 2.2 tons and through VHF - about 1.8 tons, which will almost double increase compared to 2011. Holding Company "Seligdar" (one of the key shareholders of the holding - IG "Russian Funds") in 2011. compared with the previous year reduced the production of gold ore at 1% to 2,539 tons

The company is working off of gold deposits Samolazovskoye, Garbuzovskoe, Mezhsopochnoe and Hope and Upper Nizhneyakokitskoye ore field. in 2012. She has completed the construction Nizhneyakokitskoye factory with capacity of 2 tons of gold per year and plans to launch a deposit is adjacent to the 2.6 tonnes of gold reserves relating to Nizhneyakokitskoye ore field. Previously, the company acquired a license to mine Podgolichnoe examined in the evaluation work with reserves of about 7 tons gold at a ratio of C2: P1 equal to 1:2, ie field, which required a significant investment for exploration. For a license at the auction company spent 20.4 million rubles. (1.5 times higher than the starting price). After spending in 2010 to 2011. exploration, the company adopted a short-circuit current of Sakha (Yakutia) of the deposit Podgolichnoe reserves cat. C1 + C2 in the amount of 1 million tons of ore (about 2.8 tons of gold) and commenced their commercial development, while continuing exploration activities. The project includes the construction of the quarry 350 thousand tons of ore and heap leach plant to produce 700 kg of gold per year.

Production will start in 2012. Also, in 2012. expected to launch the first phase of mining complex (GAD) production capacity of 200 thousand tons of ore and the production of 500 kg of gold in gold-uranium deposit in the Lunar Elkonsky mining district. By 2014. the project envisages the expansion of GAD to 400 tons of ore and 720 kg of gold per year. prepares to apply for industrial development field Ryabinovoye with balance reserves cat. C1 + C2 in the amount of 18,576 tons of gold. development plans of the company "Seligdar" may increase gold production in the republic in 2015. up to 5 tons per year. CJSC "GDK Aldgold" (the owner of "Very High") in 2011. put into commercial production gold mining dredge number 135 on the deposit of alluvial gold placer Buried r.Bolshoy Kuranah capacity of 400 kg of gold per year. This is the second in a unique Russian dredge with a bucket capacity of 400 liters and a digging depth of 30 m total reserves and resources of the deposit on the JORC Code more than 160 tons of gold. in 2012. compared to 2011. planned to double the production of placer gold and

400 kg at the expense of a new dredge. The old dredge in accordance with the program of development of the enterprise to be phased out of service for modernization. In the next 2 years the company intends to build a new onshore processing plant for the processing of raw ore by the scheme and reconstruct the existing enrichment capacity and dredge. In the long term production from the field is expected to grow to 1.5-2.0 tonnes per year. According Nezhdaninskoe field in 2011. conducted pilot tests on bio-oxidation process technology "BIOKS" with the participation of "Gold Fields Group Services LTD. ' Research on the optimization of production schedules will continue.

Throughout the Republic in 2012, 13gg. increase gold production is not expected, as the increase in production of ore deposits will be offset by lower production from alluvial deposits. The growth of gold can only be known after experiencing problems at Kuranakh ore field. Irkutsk region in 2011. compared with the previous year gold mining in the region increased by 5.9% to 16.99 m, including of ore deposits - 4.5% to 5.31 tons of alluvial deposits - 6.6% to 11 , 68 ppm (Table 21).

Dynamics of mining of gold leading enterprises of the Irkutsk Region in 2007-2011. * - LLC "friends" together with "A / V" Siberia "and LLC" Daksib. " ** - of "first-born" on the basis of which the consolidated gold- assets of OJSC "Polyus Gold" in the Irkutsk region.

OAO "Lenzoloto" (part of the Polyus Gold) - one of the oldest gold-mining companies in Russia dates back to the second half of the 19th century, with the beginning of the "gold rush" in Siberia. In 1921. more than 400 mines were nationalized by the partnership, combined, and are called "Lenzoloto." in 2011. compared to 2010. the company increased production of placer gold by 7.8% to 6,594 tons merit of management is to sustainable development of the company over the last five years. In the future, it can produce up to 7-7.5 tonnes of placer gold annually. of "first-born" on the basis of which from 2011. consolidated gold mining assets of OJSC "Polyus Gold" (part of the Polyus Gold) in the Irkutsk region, in particular, the fields of the western (temporarily canned) Verninskoye, entering into service which took place at the end of 2011., and exploration projects in the field Ferris trough and Mukodekskoe and portions of the adjacent, Bear (western part), Illigirskaya area. Initially, prior to installation of flotation and hydrometallurgical equipment Verninskoye mine will produce a gravity concentrate, sending it to the mill of the Western Mining.

The output on a designed capacity (2.2 million tonnes of ore per year) is expected in the second half of 2012. Expected annual production of gold in the processing of 2.2 million tonnes of ore - 5.7 m at a rate of extraction of 86.9%. The company plans in 2012. produce 1.9 tons of gold ore. considered in the future expansion project Verninskoye GOK to 3.6 million tonnes per year, which will by 2013. increase gold production of 4.4 tonnes, bringing total gold production to 9 tons per year. Proved and probable (proven + probable) reserves at the field Verninskoye JORC make 179 tons of gold at an average grade of 2.7 g / t of " Highest »(GV Gold) in 2011. relative to the previous year, increased gold production by 20.6% to 4,207 tonnes due to output at full capacity in the field of Mill Brook 3 highest. Ykanskoye at the field in 2011. the company started developing the technology of extracting ore in the mode of pilot operation at Mill-4, which has produced about 70 kg of gold.

Necklaces are held on deposit exploration in order to calculate the possibility of building a factory. Geologists have calculated that the recoverable reserves amount to at least Necklaces 10 tons of gold. At the same time the field is preparing for the construction of the first stage of Mill No. 5. At the end of 2012. the company plans to increase gold production in the region up to 4.8 tonnes will also increase the extraction of alluvial gold in 2011. CJSC "A / s Vitim" (0.6%), OOO "SAM Grain-Star" (in 40,3,2%), OOO "Ugakhan" (19.5%), A / V "Lena" (66.5%), etc. In general, the Irkutsk region in 2012. gold production is expected to reach 17.5 tons

According to experts of the prospects for exploration and development of gold deposits in the Irkutsk region is quite high. Only Dry Valley can provide annually 56 tons of gold ore. primary directions for this area is to provide a power generating facilities on the basis of the associated gas and gas condensate fields in the construction of power lines and Bodaybinskiy Mama Chuy areas. Magadan Gold mining in the area in 2011. compared to 2010. decreased slightly by 0.1% to 15,607 tonnes, including from ore deposits - increased by 1% to 4.46 m, and from alluvial deposits - fell by 0.6% to 11,147 tonnes major contribution made by the enterprise of "Sysymanzoloto ", JSC" GAD "Berelekh", JSC "Concern" Arbat ", JSC" Omolonskaya SAM ", JSC" Omsukchanskaya Hydropower ", LLC" Status ", etc. (Table 22).

"Sysymanzoloto" - the holding in which the parent company owns 50 licenses for exploration and mining of gold deposits, the owner of 10 dredges, 120 units of modern earth-moving equipment and various mining equipment. Exploration and production of gold mining on the basis of the contracts involved in 15 subsidiaries in the form of LLC. At the end of 2011. Enterprise "Sysymanzoloto" reduced production by 12.5% to 3.26 tons in 2012. all the conditions for increasing the volume of ore and placer gold mining. On mine "Vetrenskoye" in 2011. Ltd. "RADOS" (Krasnoyarsk) put into commercial operation a new Ore-picking equipment on the same field. plant capacity X-ray radiometric separation (URS) for processing 200-250 tons of ore per year. With the use of URS removed up to 40% of the volume of waste rock ore mass, which will increase in 2012. extraction of gold ore to 920-1000 kg. In addition, the development will involve new horizons of the deposit, where the gold content (averaging 7.6 g / t) of 1.5 times the ore extracted earlier.

CJSC "Magadan Silver" (part of JSC "Polymetal") - the largest a Russian producer of silver. Production is from Dukat gold-silver, Moon, and Arylakh Goltsovoye processing - on Omsukchan mill and factory on the field the Moon. In 2011. completed the reconstruction of Mill Omsukchan design capacity of 1.5 million tonnes of ore per year (actually processed 1.432 million tonnes of ore containing 0.7 g / t gold and 383 g / t silver). At present, the security of its raw materials for 12 years - until 2024. Mining of ore mined in an open pit and underground. At the beginning of 2012. commissioned quarry at the site of the initial-2. in 2011. on Omsukchan mill was put into operation a new line of gravity concentration, designed for the processing of silver-containing ore with a high concentration of lead produced at Goltsovoye, 80 km from the factory and 40 km of all-weather roads.

Power underground mine at Goltsovoye 200 tons of ore per year (actually produced 126 tons of ore containing 467 g / t silver). Concentrate sales are based in Kazakhstan. OAO "Omolonskaya SAM" (part of JSC "Polymetal") has completed the construction and launch site on the Merrill-Crowe Kubaka mill for processing high-grade ore from Sopka. Mill provided by raw materials for a period of up to 2023g. This period may be extended by 5-6 years due to the results of exploration work in the fields and Predictive Burgali. Ore production in 2011. carried out in the fields and Birkachan Sopka. Ore processing is conducted on VHF Birkachan capacity of 500 thousand tons of ore with a gold content of about 1.6 g / t and at the Kubaka mill capacity of 550 tonnes per year with a gold grade of 2.4 g / t Since 2012. will yield a Kubaka mill at full capacity. In the future ore production is expected to Kubaka mill cap on deposits, and the Far Oroch. In 2013, the design of the construction site will heap leaching at Sopka for the processing of low-grade ores.

JSC "mine them. Matrosov "(part of Polyus Gold) in 2011, completed the preparations for the construction of the first stage of the enterprise output of 10 million tons of ore a year. Rosnedra extended up to 2036g. the license for the Natalka deposit. Polyus Gold has entered into a contract with CEMTEC to supply mills - SAG and ball - for the Natalka deposit. The contract amount - 36.2 million euros. The capacity of mills - at 1,228 tonnes per hour. predicts Polyus Gold, capital investments in the development of the Natalka deposit in 2012 will amount to 594 million dollars., and by 2014 it will rise to 738 million dollars. following planned timing of the project : in the 4th quarter of 2013. - Completion of construction of the 1st stage, in December 2013. - Commissioning, in 2014.

- Output at full capacity with an annual output of ore processing in a volume of 10 million tons per year in 2016. - To enter the second stage output of 20 million tons / year in 2020. - Entering the third stage output of 40 million tons of ore and 50 tonnes of gold per year. decision to begin implementation of each new line will be made on the basis of security GOK electric power at reasonable rates, economic conditions, above all, inflation and the gold price. increased extraction of alluvial gold in 2011. JSC "Concern Arbat" (by 39% to 0,962 t), LLC "Status" (by 22.6% to 1.02 tons), OOO "Grand Prix" (by 8.2% to 0,252 tons), LLC "Dnipro Gold "(up 44.9% to 0,226 tonnes) and others in 2012. possible increase in production: gold - up to 17 tons and silver - up to 800 tons Khabarovsk Territory in 2011, gold mining in the province over the previous year decreased by 11.4% - up to 13,486 tons of which extraction of ore deposits decreased by 14% to 9.83 tons, and from alluvial deposits - by 3.6% to 3,656 tons (Table 23).

On the flanks of MNV field exploration work carried out in order to increase reserves. Currently, proven reserves can provide field service for a period of 6 years from the decline in gold production from 5 tons to 2.7 tons in 2016. At the White Mountain mine ore extraction was performed with the aim of transporting and processing at Mill MNV field. In 2010. was recovered 31.1 kg, and in 2011. planned - about 340 kg of gold. Commissioning a separate processing facility is planned for 2012. HF power of the future enterprise will reach 1.5 million tons of ore (3-3.5 t gold) per year. OAO "Okhotsk Mining and Geological Company" (included in the JSC "Polymetal") in 2011. led production at the fields Hakadzhinskoe, Yurievskoe and Avlayakan and ore processing mill at Khakanja. There were extracted and processed more than 600 million tons of ore and recovered nearly 2.5 tons of gold and 80 tons of silver, including Avlayakan - produced 128 thousand tons of ore with a grade of 17 g / t in 2012. planned construction of an underground mine at Khakanja. Construction of a factory on Avlayakan-Kirankane will depend on the results of exploration work.

LLC "Albazino Resources" (part of JSC "Polymetal") in 2011. processed at the processing plant 620 tons of ore containing 4.3 g / t gold. Produced 43.1 million tonnes of concentrate containing gold. Implemented in China 1,006 kg of gold in concentrate. expected first melting gold at the factory in Amursk POX (AMMC) design capacity of 12-14 tons of gold a year. In 2012. expected to start processing albazinskogo concentrate (about 6 tons of gold annually). Full design capacity AMMC is reached in 2013. from two sources (Albazino and May.) In the future, the implementation of exploration projects in the East and Yuzhnoalbazinskih squares and on the field Kutyn. Kutyn license covers 120 square meters. km Tuguro-Chumikansky district, 113 kilometers north-west of Albazino and 10 km from the Sea of Okhotsk. Probable reserves and probable reserves are estimated in the amount of 12.67 million tons of ore containing 3 g / t gold (38 tons of gold). Subsoil users of Khabarovsk Territory in 2012. may increase gold production by 10-11% to 15 tonnes due to ore deposits. Sverdlovsk Region

Gold mining in the area in 2011. increased compared to 2010. by 2.4% to 8,279 tons, including: due to mineral deposits - fell by 4% (to 5,714 m) and from alluvial deposits - increased by 20% (to 2,565 m).

bulk of gold production provided (relative to 2010.): ZAO "Northern Urals Gold" (part of JSC "Polymetal") - 5405kg (1.7% increase); "Uralelectromed" - 799kg (3.6% more), a / c "Neiva" - 908kg (by 2.7%), OOO "Berezovskoye RU" - 452kg (23.8% less), CJSC "Ural Mining Company" - 266kg (up 7%), a / c "Ural-Nord" - 76kg (31% less), etc.

JSC "Northern Urals Gold" in 2011. led mining ore deposits Voro, Degtyarskoye and February. Ore processing was carried out on Vorontsovskaya CIP plant ("CIP") capacity of 0.9 million tons and VHF output of 1 million tons of ore a year. in 2011. area will keep the gold production at the level of 8.2-8.5 tons Buryatia gold production in the country in 2011. compared to 2010. increased by 8% to 6,506 tonnes, including from ore deposits - by 5.2% to 5,241 tons, and from alluvial deposits - by 21.6% to 1,265 tonnes major contribution to the production of gold made (with respect to 2010).: JSC "BuryatZoloto" (part of Nordgold) - 4106kg (1.5% less), LLC "A / V" Western "- 927kg (22.8% more), CJSC" Vitimgeoprom "- 151kg (50% less) , LLC "A / V" Sininda-1 "- 232kg (down 11.2%), OOO" A / V "Kurba" - 208kg (up 4.5%) and "Mine Tsipikansky" - 405kg (on 34.1% more), and others in 2011. Ltd. "Huzhir Enterprise" has commissioned Konevinskoe gold deposit in the Eastern Sayan Mountains (Oka District of Buryatia) and 207.8 kg of gold mined. The design capacity to process 100 tons of ore, 800-1000 kg of gold per year. Stocks cat. C2 - 9.3 m gold (containing about 10 g / t). There are prospects for growth stocks. mining gold in Buryatia in 2012 may increase to 7 tons Trans-Baikal Territory Gold mining in the province in 2011. compared to 2010. increased by 14.8% to 8,426 tonnes, including from ore deposits - by 6.3% to 4,147 tons, and from alluvial deposits - by 24.4% to 4,279 t The bulk of provided (relative to 2010).: JSC "Mine Aprelkovo" (part of Nordgold) - 955kg (up 7.8%), OOO "Daura" - 725kg (up 7.9%), OOO "Balci" - 458kg (5.7% less) Ltd. "Ildikanzoloto" (part of White Tiger Gold Ltd) -

526kg (11.7% more), LLC "HRE number 324" (part of Central Asia Gold) - 260kg (36% less), LLC "Gazimur" - 364kg (3.3% less), LLC "Uryumkan" (part of "The mine Soloviev) - 691kg (84.3% more), JSC" Ust-Kara Mine "- 332kg (up 4.4%) , JSC "Kamensky careers" - 266kg (14.2% more), LLC "Nergeoprom" - 200kg (59% more), LLC "Darasunsky Mine" (part of "Uzhuralzoloto Group of Companies") - 191kg (8 , 5 times), JSC "Ksenevskaya mine" - 148kg (26.2% less), OOO "Taiga a / c" - 143kg (30.9% increase), and others

in 2012. Gold mining in the Trans-Baikal region will remain at 8.5 tons Chelyabinsk Region Gold mining in the area in 2011. increased to 5% (up to 3,747 tons). Including placer mined 76 kg of gold. OAO "Uzhuralzoloto group companies" (UGC) has commissioned a reconstructed mill production capacity of 4 million tonnes of ore per year. After upgrading the UGC plans to stably produce 3.5 tonnes of gold per year. The construction of the VHF power of 800 tons of ore per year and 3-mill capacity of 400 thousand tons per year (production of 1.5 tonnes of gold per year) on Bereznyakovskaya field (Etkulsky district) and VHF capacity of 600 thousand tons of ore per year (release of 0.5 tonnes of gold per year) from the field West Kurosan (Verkhneuralsk district.) in 2012. area may increase gold production to 5-5.5 tonnes Kamchatka By the end of 2011. compared to 2010. Gold mining in the region has increased by 7% to 2,489 tons at the Aga mine (of "Kamchatka Gold," a member of the group "Renova") produced 2,027 kg (2.7% less than in the previous year.) in 2011. entered commercial operation Asachinskoe gold-silver deposit (Trans-Siberian Gold) and received 24 kg of gold. After reaching the design capacity of the plant will process 150 tons of ore per year. JORC resources at the field are estimated at 21.7 t gold and 53.2 tonnes of silver at an average grade of gold, 17 g / t silver and 41.5 g / t Development Strategy mining region until 2015. planned construction of five new mines: Baranevsky, Amethyst, Kumroch, spring and Ozernovskiy a total capacity of up to 16 tonnes of gold a year.

in 2012. Gold mining in the Kamchatka region may reach 3-3.6 m Tuva Republic in 2011. in the country produced 1,367 tonnes of gold - 5.5% less than in 2010., while on the Tardan gold mine production fell to 0,094 tonnes from alluvial deposits - by 1% to 1,273 tonnes leading enterprise of the Republic is the artel "Ojna" , dobyvshaya 1175 kg of alluvial gold - 4% less than in 2010. Ltd.

"Tardan Gold" (part of the Central Asia Gold) at the end of 2011 launched the first factory for the processing of ores by heap leaching and started commercial production of gold. In 2012, the expected production of 700 kg of gold production in the future can grow up to 1 ton

Mining Construction continues on the Kyzyl-Tashtyg ore deposit (LTD "Longxing Temple of Shijiazhuang» - is a Chinese corporation Zijin Mining). The field is located 120 km north-east of Kyzyl. Main components of the ore deposit: zinc, lead, copper, barium, sulfur, passing - gold, silver, cadmium, selenium. Stocks of ores cat. B + C1 + C2 reserves amount to 12.9 million tonnes of copper ore per category. C2 -2 million tons of ores sernokolchedannyh cat. C1-6, 2 million tons in 2012. Gold mining in the country may be about 2 tons of Khakassia Republic of gold mining in the country in 2011. amounted to 1,182 tons, including 1,007 tons - from ore deposits and 0,175 tons - from alluvial deposits. OAO "Kommunarovskiy Mine" (part of "Yuzhuralzoloto GC") has reduced gold production compared to 2010. 25% up to 487 kg. CJSC ZDK "Gold Star" on VHF in the field Elovoe removed the 390 kg of gold (26% more than in 2010.). JSC "NPO Irion" in the field Juzik on pilot plant heap leaching reduced gold production up to 130 kg (30% less than in 2010.). In 2012.

Gold mining in the country will remain at 1.2-1.3 tons of other gold mining regions of Russia should be noted Altai region, where production in 2011. almost doubled to 0,862 tonnes of gold mining in the region are: LLC "Search" (included in OAO "Seligdar") on the field Murzinskoe - 281 kg (20% less than in 2010.) Ltd. "Gold Kuryi" on Novofirsovskom field - 534 lbs. According to the JSC "Seligdar" on Murzinskoe field was discovered in the mine, from which, probably, the first gold was mined in Russia.

According to the results of dendrochronological and radiocarbon analysis determined that the structure was built in the years 1772-1789. OAO "Siberia-Polymetal" (part of UMMC) on Rubtsovskaya concentrator produces concentrates of polymetallic ores containing precious metals. In 2011. Climb gold production was about 0.8 m (30% more than in 2010.). in 2012. in the Altai Territory gold production may exceed 1 m, excluding the associated production of gold from concentrates containing precious metals. State of the world silver market.

The results of production and produc-tion of silver in Russia in 2011. World production of silver in 2011. compared to 2010. increased by 1.3% to 23.7 thousand tons Ranking of countries in terms of production of silver led Mexico, Peru, China, Australia and Chile. Sale of state stocks fell nearly 4 times to 370 tonnes mainly due to decrease in sales of silver from Russia. use of silver in industry decreased by 2.5% to 15.13 million tons Jewelry demand declined by 4.5% to 4 , 97 thousand tons of annual average price of silver in 2011. compared with the previous year increased by 74%, from 20.19 to 35.11 dollars. / oz. Spot silver prices rose sharply, reaching 49.831 dollars in April. / Ounce, and then in September, they rapidly decreased to 26.1 dollars. / Oz. Historical record silver futures reached in January 1980 - 50.35 dollars. / Oz. According to analysts Bloomberg, the silver will continue to rise in price in 2012, the cost may exceed the average in 2011 to 26% on rising investment demand for this metal. According to GFMS forecast the average price of silver in 2012. may be 45 dollars. / oz.

in Russian mining and production of silver in 2011. compared with the previous year increased by 2.4% to 1,590.9 tons (about 6-7 in the world). In this case, the actual production grew by 8.6% to 883.2 tonnes, extraction and secondary production declined by 5.3% to 314.4 tonnes and 3.6% to 393.3 tons, respectively. 's largest Russian mining company Silver - JSC "Polymetal" - in 2011. compared to 2010. Silver production increased by 15% to 619 tons in 2012. the company plans to increase production up to 653-715 tons of JSC "Chukotka GGK" takes second place to the volume of production in 2011. - 207.4 ppm (Table 24).

State of World Platinum and Palladium Market. The results of exploration and production of platinum and palladium in Russia in 2011.

Average price of platinum and palladium in 2011. compared with the previous year increased by 6.9% to 1,720 dollars. / oz. and by 72.4% to 734 dollars. / oz respectively. However, the spot price of platinum and palladium in the IY quarter of 2011. fell to the level of 1400 and 650 dollars. / oz. respectively (Fig. 1). According to the forecast Royal Bank of Scotland Group (RBS), the average price of platinum in 2012. may remain at the level of 2011. due to the expected increase in physical demand from Asian investors. predicts RBS in 2012, the average price of palladium will increase. The market went from a state of surplus arising out of the supply end of the Russian reserves, which previously accounted for 15% of global supply. Gokhran in 2011 almost completed the export of palladium due to the depletion of reserves, the latter supplies probably occurred in January and February 2012. According to experts, the cessation of exports of palladium Gohran can lead the world market to a shortage of the metal used in the manufacture of catalytic converters. Russia ranked first in the world in the production and manufacture of palladium and a second place for the extraction and production of platinum after South Africa. extraction and production of platinum in 2011 . compared to the previous year increased by 7.4% to 32,552 tons increase was due to growth in secondary production by 40% to 6,789 tonnes, and production growth of alluvial platinum by 7.8% to 3,774 tons (JSC "A / V" Cupid " in the Khabarovsk Territory) (Table 25).

Mining and palladium in 2011 compared with the previous year increased by 8.4% to 99.67 ppm

Extraction and production of palladium in Russia in 2008-2011. (Source: Ministry of Finance of Russia, messages Companies)

MMC "Norilsk Nickel" - a leading manufacturer of platinum and palladium in Russia - in 2011. produced 20.9 tons and 84.1 tons of platinum-palladium-platinum and 20.62 against 86.22 tonnes of palladium in 2010. in 2012. MMC "Norilsk Nickel" plans to produce in Russia 20,2-20,5 t platinum and palladium 80,86-82,4 t. diamond production in Russia in 2011, diamond production in Russia in 2011. amounted to 35.140 million carats, which is 0.8% more than 2010. In value terms, the increase was 12.3% to 2.675 billion (Table 27).

at OJSC "AK" ALROSA "for 98 % of Russian diamond production. According to the company in 2011 was produced 34.438 million carats of diamonds is 0.4% more than in 2010. In 2012, the company plans to produce 34.6 million carats of diamonds. According to experts, the demand for diamonds in 2015 may reach 25 4 billion U.S. dollars, compared with 15.1 billion in 2010. The share of China and India in world consumption of diamond jewelry will increase to 28% by 2015. (21.5% currently). Union of Gold. Published in "Gold & Technology» № 2 (16) / June 2012

A LOW-COST PRODUCTION GROWTH

Russia's gold mining sector is the fastest-growing in the world, with a six-year output CAGR of 8.4%. Several companies are directly plugged into this trend and have high future growth potential. This report focuses on these companies, with a review of Highland Gold, Peter Hambro Mining and Celtic Resources, and initiation of coverage for Centerra Gold, Bema Gold and High River Gold.

Russia is one of the world's lowest-cost producers, with its average cash cost of $220/oz coming in 14% below the world average ex-Russia. These low costs are attributable to a complete shift in mining activity since 1998, with the focus now on lode ore, and new high quality projects offering favorable economics coming on line. Moreover, low Russian labor and energy costs also help to make mining in the country very competitive.

Poor information flow creates an opportunity. All the public Russian gold mining companies are traded outside of Russia, and are usually followed by investors with a mining focus but little Russia/CIS expertise. Conversely, Russia market specialists have generally ignored these companies as they are neither domiciled in Russia nor a part of any Russia-related market index. This inefficient information exchange results in a lack of appropriate investor awareness, which in turn represents an opportunity to profit.

Valuations appear attractive, particularly on an asset basis. Although on financial multiples Russian/CIS companies trade at or above established global players, their expected growth explains this. On an asset basis, they trade at an average $66 per EV/oz of resource, which is 48% lower than international junior mining peers and 41% lower than global majors. With gold prices rising and growth plans becoming reality, we expect investors to take a second look at Russian gold miners' huge, cheaply valued resources. However, execution risk is still a major company-specific issue, as the businesses profiled here do not have the scale and balance sheets to easily absorb development mistakes.

Gold is up 9% y-t-d and It is possible to estimate that our forecast average 2006 gold price 13% to $450/oz, although our long term $400/oz forecast remains unchanged. This should provide additional support to earnings, though we make a particular point that Russian/CIS gold stocks are plays on low-cost production growth rather than simple gold plays.

Our top picks in the sector are Bema Gold and Highland Gold due to their high growth potential based on world-class asset portfolios. With this report we also initiate coverage of High River Gold with a Buy. Peter Hambro Mining, Centerra Gold and Celtic Resources appear to be fully valued at current levels. However, It is possible to note that that relative to junior gold miners active in other parts of the world, all the companies profiled here appear cheap.

Timothy McCutcheon atonres@aton.ru Vladimir Katunin 7 (095) 777-8877

RUSSIA'S GOLD SECTOR EXPANSION

Russia's gold mining industry is moving to the forefront of the business globally, as new companies emerge with fundamentally attractive, large-scale projects – all only made possible by the liberalization of the sector in 1998. At the same time, leading global producers are seeing a fall in output from developed country mines, prompting them to go where the gold is to replace depleted resources, develop new mines and maintain revenues. In the past this hunt for gold focused on places such as Peru, Indonesia and even Uzbekistan, while Russia received only tepid interest, not least because of country risk perception. However, Russian output growth of 8.4% over the past six years, which is set to accelerate in the future as the country's large resource base is further developed, is too impressive to ignore in the current environment, and multinationals cannot afford to stay on the sidelines for much longer.

A NEW ENGINE OF GLOBAL SECTOR GROWTH

Russia is currently the world's fifth largest gold producer with about 8% of total global production. This is a massive jump from 1999, when the country accounted for only 4.8% of output. Most importantly, no other country is growing at a pace to match Russia's, so that while the industry is already big on a global scale, it will expand even further as undeveloped ore sites start coming on line in the next several years. From 1998-2004 Russia's gold industry had a production CAGR of 8.4%, while the world overall posted zero output growth. In this short timeframe the country has gone from being an opaque marginal player to representing one of the most exciting growth opportunities.

Much of this growth has been fueled by a complete change in the domestic industry operations due to a shift from the exploitation of placer ore to that of lode ore. Previously known but undeveloped lode ore sites have started to come on line. Also, several greenfield projects that had close to zero exploration work done when started, have been developed. Indeed, in 1999 only 20% of all gold produced in Russia was from lode ore mines, while in 2004 this had reached 50%. Lode ore mines are more permanent, year-round operations that are capital intensive but relatively predictable and usually much bigger than their placer ore counterparts.

LOW COSTS ARE RUSSIA'S COMPETITIVE ADVANTAGE

Russia is one of the world's lowest cost gold producers, with its 2004 average cash cost of about $220/oz coming in 14% below the $256/oz world average ex-Russia. The country's low overall costs are due to low labor and energy expenses. Additionally, with the shift to lode ore mining, new projects that come on stream in Russia feature high-grade ores with high silver content, which is netted against production costs. Although wage pressures and inflation will erode some of this competitive advantage in the future, the main source of production growth in Russia is the

introduction of new, modern mines that employ the latest technologies, implying that efficiency gains will partially offset other cost increases.

Russia has massive untapped gold resources, and its giant greenfield ore bodies mean it is one of the few places where major new mines are possible. The country's total estimated gold resources are almost 500mn oz while output was only 5.9mn oz in 2004, implying a resource life of 85 years at the current extraction rate. With the exception of South Africa, resource lives for major producers (US, Canada and Australia) are between 15 and 20 years. This implies there is considerable potential for raising output in Russia, and indeed this is exactly what we have seen.

Limited information flow between companies and markets

All the public Russian gold mining companies are traded outside of Russia, and are usually followed by investors with a mining focus but little Russia/CIS expertise. Conversely, Russia market specialists have generally ignored these companies as they are neither domiciled in Russia nor a part of any Russia-related market index. This inefficient information exchange system creates a lack of appropriate investor awareness, which in turn represents an opportunity to profit from.

KEY INDUSTRY TRENDS: POSSIBLE CONSOLIDATION, SHIFT TO LODE ORE

Despite having the world's fifth largest output, Russia's gold industry remains fairly unconcentrated, with the largest producer, Polyus, accounting for only 18% of total domestic production. Additionally, many of the major gold mining companies active in the country are foreign domiciled and often headquartered outside Russia. Because of this, the country's industry does not have a flagship business outside of Polyus, nor a budding domestic junior mining scene that could serve as a development base for the most risky projects. In short, Moscow is not set to be a world gold mining capital in the way that Toronto, London or Vancouver are. The implication is that if an investor wants to see the future of Russian gold, he should look outside Russia's borders.

Russian gold output by company: low concentration, ripe for M&A

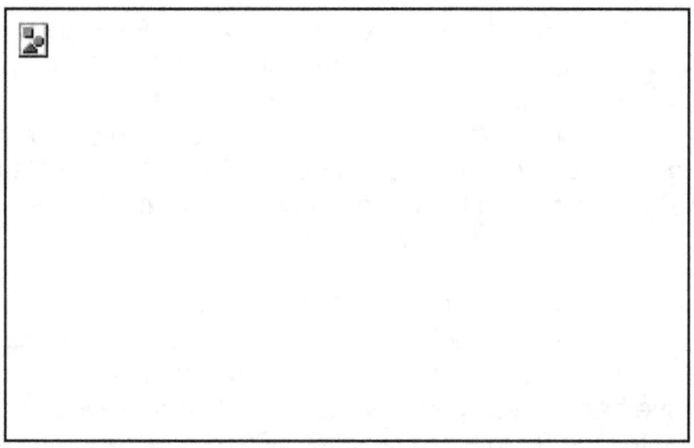

The largest gold producer in Russia is Polyus, the gold mining division of Norilsk Nickel that is set to be spun off on Jan. 1, 2006. It is forecasted that that the company's market share of domestically produced gold was slightly over 18% last year. The next largest player is Polymetal, with a much lower market share of 3.6% – although rapid expected growth should see this increase in the next several years. Additionally, Polymetal is the world's sixth largest silver producer. Peter Hambro and Highland Gold were almost tied last year in gold output, while High River's Buryatzoloto subsidiary was Russia's fifth largest producer. Norilsk Nickel ex-Polyus is also a major gold producer, as the metal is a by-product of its core nickel smelting operations. Kinross's Russian mine, with a 2.2% market share, has nearly depleted its resource base and represented only about 8% of total company output last year. Bema's Julietta is a similar story although it represents 36% of total company output.

The rest of Russia's production – or almost 63% – consists of smaller operations, placer mining cooperatives and by-product material. Despite being a major part of current production, the most likely source of M&A activity is not to be found here, but in greenfield ore deposits that are in need of development funds.

SHIFT FROM ALLUVIAL TO LODE ORE DRIVES GROWTH

Gold mining can roughly be split into two types of operations based on the type of ore exploited. **A lode deposit** is a large mineral deposit in which the metal is either disseminated throughout the ore body or is in a widespread network of narrow veins. This kind of deposit can be either refractory or non-refractory. In simple terms, refractory ore is mineralized rock in which much of the gold is encapsulated in sulfides or other minerals and is not easily dissolved by cyanide solutions (unlike non-refractory or oxidized ore), even with fine grinding. Non-refractory ore (oxidized ore) is mineralized rock that has been subjected to weathering and oxidation of primary minerals. This tends to make an ore more porous, allowing better permeation of cyanide solutions so the minerals can be readily dissolved. Lode ore is mined either underground or by open pit. In both cases, lode-mining operations tend to be capital-intensive.

Alluvial, or placer, deposits are essentially the result of erosion on a lode deposit, leading to a build-up of gold in the delta riverbeds of existing and former water flows. These deposits can be so rich in gold content that in some cases the gold can be "panned" out manually. However, they are usually relatively small and operations are seasonal. Additionally, with a placer deposit it is difficult to predict the volume of reserves at a site due to the haphazard way the gold arrived there in the first place.

Of the two basic types of gold ore, lode operations are those that usually involve big projects with long-term, predictable operations and require financing from the capital markets.

Increasingly more of Russia's gold output coming from lode ore mining

Part of Russia's gold output growth is due to the dramatic shift in mining operations from placer to lode ore exploitation. Clearly, the government legal reform of 1998 opened up the gold industry to market prices and paved the way for investment in the sector. With large, undeveloped but well-explored lode ore sites suddenly economically viable, investors jumped at the chance to get involved and this period saw the development of such mines as Peter Hambro's Pokrovka, Bema's Julietta, and the turnaround for Highland Gold's MNV.

RESOURCE BASE AND EXPLOITATION LEVELS

Russia has the world's largest gold resource base after South Africa. However, despite this massive national asset, current mining rates imply a resource life span of 85 years at current mining rates, which shows both the low development of the industry and the potential for growth.

Resources by country: Russia has lots of gold...

RUSSIAN GOLD DEVELOPMENT MATH: RELATIVELY EASY TO ADD VALUE

Russian gold development is relatively straightforward. On average, the cost of buying a P1 and above resource from the government, or in a few cases private owners, is about $7.7/oz (or $5.3/oz pre-Polyus/IG Alrosa deal). In general, the replacement cost for gold for a global major, in terms of the cost of exploration that results in the placement of a new ounce of gold on a company's reserve balance sheet, is about $20/oz. Granted, there is a difference between statistically implied, but economically unproven, P1 gold resources and an audited Western-standard figure that is actually booked. Nonetheless, P1 number usually does have a fair amount of exploration work behind it, and an interesting field with a competent geological team can turn that P1 resource into something more certain fairly quivckly. Therefore a P1 resource (and particularly C2) in a global context is worth closer to $20/oz than $7.7/oz. Finally, the average EV valuation of gold resources in Russia/CIS is $66/oz.

While we acknowledge that exploration expense can be considerable and time consuming, we argue that the value spread between the acquisition cost and capital market valuation for Russian gold in the ground is so wide as to dwarf the funds needed to develop a site.

Selected recent gold resource M&A transactions: Cheap to buy gold in ground in Russia

Asset Acquirer Deal date Deal size, $mn Implied price for Resources, Price to resources, 100%, $mn mn oz $/oz

Matrosov Norilsk Nickel 8/03 34.1 89.7 7.8 4.3 Mayskoye Highland Gold 9/03 34.9 34.9 3.7 9.4 Titimukhta Norilsk Nickel 12/03 10.1 10.1 1.1 9.2 Yamalzoloto Peter Hambro 4/04 5.0 5.6 1.0 5.5 Avlayakan/Kirankan Vostok 6/04 0.1 0.1 0.2 0.4 Tophor Minco 7/04 0.5 1.0 0.8 1.2 Western Kurasan Yuzhuralzoloto 9/04 0.2 0.2 0.1 1.6 Southern Kurasan Yuzhuralzoloto 9/04 0.2 0.2 0.1

2.5 Taseevskoye Highland Gold 9/04 25.5 25.5 1.7

15.0 Bogunay Trans Siberian 11/04 0.1 0.1 0.3

0.3 Chyortovo Koryto Norilsk Nickel 12/04 31.7 31.7 4.8

6.6 Bamskoye Norilsk Nickel 2/05 0.9 0.9 2.8

1. Sredne-Golgotayskoye Highland Gold 2/05 0.4 0.4 0.3
2. Malomir Peter Hambro 2/05 0.8 0.8 1.5

0.5 Bodaibo Norilsk Nickel 3/05 0.1 0.1 0.0

2.5 Tokichanskoye Norilsk Nickel 5/05 0.6 0.6 0.9

0.7 Bolshoi Patom Norilsk Nickel 6/05 0.1 0.1 0.1

1. Upper Aliinskaya Peter Hambro 6/05 2.1 2.1 0.6
2. Bessonov Tera Gold 7/05 0.2 0.2 0.1

3.3 IG Alrosa fields Norilsk Nickel 9/05 285.0 N.M. 28.0

10.2 Baley gold tailings Highland Gold 10/05 0.6 0.6 0.3

1.8

Weighted average 7.7

Source: Company data; Prime-Tass; Aton estimates

Existing data helps reduce exploration risk, capital markets fund development. In general, a major project risk for Russia gold developers is removed due to the large geological database collected during the Soviet era. If one considers the biggest risk of gold companies, particularly high growth developers, is the core issue of finding gold, then armed with Soviet data, geologists begin their hunt relatively well-informed – suggesting less money spent on fruitless exploration.

Assuming a company finds gold that is economically feasible to extract, the next step is raising capital to build a mine. In general, the entry barrier to the gold business relative to other metals extraction industries is quite low. So while around $100mn would be needed to contemplate a fairly modest nickel operation, a heap leach gold operation with 100,000 tons of ore processed per annum can cost about 10% of that sum. Indeed, a respectable 400,000 ton per annum mill and smelter could cost $40mn-$60mn, which is well within the range of a wide investor audience from private equity players to small-cap portfolio investors. So with a 1mn oz resource, one could be pretty sure of finding capital for development through to actually generating cash from gold extraction. And this development is possible because of the wide discrepancy between the cash needed to develop a gold mine and the valuation the capital markets assign to it because of gold's "special status" as an alternative asset class. As mentioned above, the market is currently paying an average EV/oz valuation of $66. Many companies are taking advantage of this opportunity, with several Russia/CIS-focused IPOs a year on foreign exchanges.

OUTSIDE RUSSIA: CIS AN EXPANDING AREA OF INTEREST

Many of the nuances of the Russian gold mining industry apply equally to the entire CIS space, particularly in terms of licensing, resource classification, cost competitiveness and growth potential. The scale of the industry in these countries is much smaller, although relative to their economy gold mining in some cases is actually a major source of government revenue. This is the main challenge for gold companies operating in the post-Soviet space since any significant development in a small country is likely to be a major part of the local economy, which makes the company an indispensable partner, but also the potential target of high-level politics. For example, Centerra's Kumtor mine in Kyrgyzstan accounts for about 10% of that country's GDP. The same situation applies to the company's Boroo mine in Mongolia.

Output in Russia's neighbors: much smaller, with one mine usually bulk of total

Tajikistan Kazakhstan Mongolia* Kyrgyzstan Uzbekistan Russia

**Mongolia is not part of the CIS*

Source: Multiple media sources; Aton estimates

The key difference in CIS countries relative to Russia is that because mining represents such an important growth engine and major employer, governments are keener to attract foreign mining companies through legislative and tax incentives. The Uzbek and Kyrgyz governments, for example, have opted to become major partners to foreign mining companies, with the best example being the state-owned Kyrgyz gold company, the second largest shareholder of Centerra. The Uzbek government, meanwhile, is the direct JV partner in the country's massive Zarafshan open pit mine with Newmont, the world's largest gold company.

GOLD PRICE FORECAST: NEAR TERM UPGRADE, LONG TERM UNCHANGED

The gold market continues to attract attention as prices have broken out of the range to exceed $470/oz, a level not seen since 1987. The average price of gold in 2004 was $410/oz, while the average year-to-date price in 2005 is $436/oz. So far for this year, gold prices have risen 8.7%.

The previous tug of war between believers in dollar weakness and monetary tightening seems to have finally turned a corner, with the weaker dollar side winning out. With a new focus on the role of gold as a store of wealth and the rising global liquidity, the investor audience that follows the metal has dramatically widened, which of course has helped to improve its pricing and trading liquidity. It is possible to note that that although there is much debate on the actual worth of gold, as it has limited industrial application, the overriding factor is market perception. As long as the market, particularly major sources of demand such as India and China, view gold as valuable, it will remain so.

Although we are bullish on gold prices, we believe the investment case for Russian gold miners is not simply "the gold price is to go higher" and/or "it will be high long/term," as there are far more liquid companies with longer track records to satisfy such demand. Simply put, there are less risky ways to gain exposure to gold than by buying high growth Russian gold miners.

FINANCIAL REVIEW AND FORECAST

The main driver for our financial models is future production levels, both from currently operating mines and mines that are forecast to open within the forecast period. Development pipelines are key here, and where there was no company guidance on which fields will be developed, the overall timeframe, cost of development and indications of when operations will start, we have simply assumed an exploration value of the resources involved. It is possible to note that the companies profiled here operate in various countries, with different domestic dynamics for inflation, cost structure, business stability and outlook. Because of this we have used company guidance for mine costs adjusted where we thought necessary.

Revenue and costs

Our revenue estimates for each company are based on mine-by-mine production forecasts. Unless there is an obvious lack of resources to support mine activity, we assume that mines maintain constant production after reaching the target peak, although with adjustments for ore grade declines. We then consolidate the performance of all mines owned by the company. Regarding attributable production, we consolidate all ownership over 50% and then account for minority interest in the consolidated income statement. For less than 50%, It is forecasted that the proportional share in the bottom line.

As there is no product mix for gold miners, forecasting revenue involves the simple task of calculating gold produced and sold and multiplying this by the forecast gold price. Indeed, one of the advantages with gold mining is that the end product has a very deep and liquid market that does not require extensive market penetration, marketing or sales effort. None of the companies profiled here have a gold hedging program that would affect revenues.

Costs have been determined by using company guidance for each mine, adjusted for our perception of mine particulars that may make company guidance too optimistic. Depreciation and amortization are both a function of the useful life of assets and a product of mining levels itself, and for the sake of simplicity we have forecast this cost item as yearly gold output as a percentage of total reserves per mine in operation, using our own forecasts as to the book value of each mine based on historical valued and expected capex.

Capital structure

We have made few assumptions regarding future capital structure changes. Debt levels have been based on the last known results. However, companies' stated development timelines and

financing needs required us to make assumptions about future capital structure, in particular project financing to bring new mines into operation. We have also assumed that all free cash flow accumulates on balance sheets as none of the companies profiled have a set dividend policy.

Financial forecast

The companies profiled in this report are forecast to have high output growth in the near- to medium term (with the exception of Centerra) and as a result our financial forecasts only begin to show significant improvements in revenue and profitability once this expansion begins. The key external variable is the gold price, which It is forecasted that at $445/oz in 2005 and $450/oz in 2006, falling back to our long-term average of $400/oz by 2007.

In terms of company specifics, It is forecasted that Highland Gold and High River Gold to have a strong 2006, as the former recovers from this year's difficulties and the latter opens two new mines. Also in 2006, Celtic Resources is forecast to continue growing output at its Kazakhstan assets, which will have a positive effect on the company's financials. Finally, in 2006 Bema Gold will have had a full year of production from its Refugio mine, which will bolster its results.

We expect 2008 to be the critical year for our top picks as Bema's massive Kupol project and Highland's Mayskoye project are due to come on line, while Peter Hambro is forecast to begin production at its Pioneer property.

Strong 2006 seen on volume growth, strong prices; after weaker 2007 (due to lower gold price forecast), banner 2008

VALUATION REVIEW

We have used our standard DCF-based model to value the companies profiled in this report; however, we made a slight adjustment to the CAPM inputs we use. Clearly, Russia risk is present in our gold universe, but given all of the companies profiled are foreign domiciled and listed and "Russia risk" is company-specific rather than systemic, we have not used the RTS Index's excess volatility factor in calculating our cost of equity.

Base cost of equity calculation Assumptions Comment

Long-term risk free rate, % 5.5 Based on 5-yr. trailing average yield of LT US Govt. bond Russian country risk premium, % 1.5 Based on the expected spread of LT Russian Eurobonds over US Govt. bonds (end-2005)

Russian risk-free rate, % 7.0

Standard equity premium, % 4.0 Historic differences between stocks and bonds

Base cost of equity, % 11.0

Source: Aton estimates

We then adjusted individual companies' cost of equity to reflect company-specific risks, such as liquidity and leverage. Our cost of debt was taken from the historical borrowing rates at each individual company. In terms of terminal growth rates, gold mining companies generally use the cash flows from one mine to finance the opening of another, repeating this process ad infinitum. The result of our CAPM calculations was an EV valuation, which was then adjusted for the amount of net debt or cash a company had in its capital structure, as well as minority interest. The resulting figure is the target market capitalization of the company's equity, which divided by shares outstanding gave us our fair value target.

DCF valuation summary						
	Bema Gold	Highland Gold	Peter Hambro Mining	Centerra Gold	High River Gold	Celtic Resources
Beta (unlevered)	1.00	1.25	1.25	1.25	1.25	1.25
Cost of equity	11.5%	12.6%	12.5%	12.0%	12.8%	13.1%
Cost of debt (after tax)	6.8%	6.5%	5.8%	6.0%	6.1%	5.9%
WACC	10.8%	11.8%	11.7%	12.0%	11.6%	11.5%
DCF EV value, $mn	1504	947	738	1080	270	176
Terminal as % of total	65.1%	77.1%	58.1%	43.8%	46.3%	76.5%
Fair value per share, $	3.53	5.92	11.97	18.77	1.22	3.52
Upside	32.9%	44.0%	-14.1%	-5.3%	15.7%	-2.8%
Recommendation	Buy	Buy	Hold	Hold	Buy	Hold

Source: Company data; Aton estimates

On a DCF basis our top picks are Highland Gold and Bema Gold, which are the most undervalued of the companies profiled in this report. Additionally, High River Gold has upside to its fair value from current levels and we also rate it a Buy. Our recommendation on Centerra Gold, Peter Hambro and Celtic Resources, which are currently trading in the vicinity of our target prices, is Hold.

Peer group comparison

None of the companies profiled in this report is on the same scale as sector giants like AngloGold Ashanti or Barrick, and the most appropriate peer group for them is international junior gold producers, which incorporates a wide array of companies producing anything from 100,000oz to 1mn oz per annum in various parts of the world. Additionally, given most of the profiled companies are forecast to deliver high growth, the financial multiples for our universe are relatively high – and that in a sector that already has some of the highest multiples in the market. As a result, we have also undertaken an asset-based valuation comparison, which shows what the market is currently paying for gold resources in Russia and internationally.

Comparative valuation on financial multiples: inconclusive results

As of Nov. 8, 2005	Price, $	Mcap, $mn	EV, $mn	EV/EBITDA 2004	2005F	2006F
Russia / CIS						
Centerra Gold	19.98	1,440	1,205	10.9	10.0	8.0
Bema Gold	2.55	1,149	1,277	N. M.	48.0	31.9
Peter Hambro	13.93	1,100	1,060	30.3	19.5	16.4
Highland Gold	4.09	650	711	27.8	58.4	12.1
High River Gold	1.03	222	247	17.4	12.7	5.5
Celtic Resources	3.75	178	187	28.4	30.0	18.0
Weighted average				21.2	28.9	16.6
Majors						
Newmont	42.5	18,977	20,452	10.7	11.9	10.5
Barrick Gold	24.9	13,387	16,249	25.0	20.1	13.2
Anglogold Ashanti	39.4	10,434	12,594	19.6	16.3	12.3
Placer Dome	19.3	8,428	7,824	14.6	16.5	13.2
Goldcorp	19.8	6,667	4,952	49.1	9.7	9.4

Gold Fields	13.3	6,545	5,394	17.5	13.3	8.1
Harmony	10.4	4,084	3,418	290.1	38.2	13.4
Weighted average				36.4	16.2	11.5
Juniors						
Glamis Gold	20.8	2,744	2,964	76.4	34.8	15.9
Kinross Gold	6.90	2,383	2,512	15.7	10.4	8.0
Meridian Gold	18.5	1,850	1,938	23.9	23.3	19.6
Lihir Gold	1.31	1,676	1,102	14.8	18.1	8.7
Iamgold	6.89	1,014	1,051	28.7	23.4	15.6
Randgold Resources	13.9	932	856	41.3	15.5	22.6
Yamana Gold	3.86	734	511	78.6	51.6	7.9
Weighted average				38.9	23.8	13.8
Russia / CIS relative to Majors				-41.8%	78.4%	44.3%
Russia / CIS relative to Juniors				-45.6%	21.4%	20.3%

Source: Bloomberg; Company data; Aton estimates

Asset/output based comparison: Russian/CIS companies look cheap vs juniors, expensive to majors

As of Nov. 8, 2005 2004 Reserves Resources Total cash Life EV/ Mcap/ EV/ Mcap/ EV/ Mcap/

output				cost	span	output	output	reserves	reserves	resources	resources
000 oz		000 oz	000 oz	$/oz	years	$/oz	$/oz	$/oz	$/oz	$/oz	$/oz
Russia / CIS											
Centerra Gold	610	4362	10834	189	7	1976	2361	276	330	111	133
Bema Gold	230	8392	21896	332	36	5554	4994	152	137	58	52
Peter Hambro	209	2651	17449	135	13	5071	5263	400	415	61	63
Highland Gold	195	8000	18288	215	41	3649	3335	89	81	39	36
High River Gold	107	2079	6942	257	19	2308	2074	119	107	36	32
Celtic Resources	32	3550	9600	240	111	5848	5568	53	50	19	19
Weighted average				215		3720	3683	220	233	66	70
Majors											
Newmont	6989	92400	135400	231	13	2926	2715	221	205	151	140
Barrick Gold	4958	89056	109514	212	18	3277	2700	182	150	148	122
Anglogold Ashanti	6407	78900	218200	268	12	1966	1629	160	132	58	48
Placer Dome	3652	59917	113999	241	16	2142	2308	131	141	69	74

Goldcorp	628	12490	24060	115	20	7885	10616	396	534	206	277
Gold Fields	4254	75552	178033	302	18	1268	1538	71	87	30	37
Harmony	3428	54100	528600	360	16	997	1191	63	75	6	8
Weighted average				259		2961	3062	186	188	111	110
Juniors											
Glamis Gold	234	6300	20992	192	27	12669	11727	471	436	141	131
Kinross Gold	1616	19410	27596	250	12	1555	1475	129	123	91	86
Meridian Gold	315	4355	6375	50	14	6153	5872	445	425	304	290
Lihir Gold	599	21000	40000	279	35	1839	2799	52	80	28	42
Iamgold	432	4000	8000	248	9	2434	2347	263	254	131	127
Randgold Res.	510	2510	12530	184	5	1679	1828	341	371	68	74
Yamana Gold	101	4072	11795	218	40	5059	7265	125	180	43	62
Weighted average				225		5354	5353	281	277	127	125
Russia / CIS relative to Majors						25.6%	20.3%	17.8%	23.8%	-41.0%	-36.0%
Russia / CIS relative to Juniors						-30.5%	-31.2%	-21.9%	-15.9%	-48.4%	-43.6%

Source: Bloomberg; Company data; Aton estimates

Although a comparative valuation of Russia/CIS companies with foreign peers on a financial performance basis suggests they are expensive on an EV/EBITDA and P/CF basis, they appear cheap on a P/E basis. As a result, the comparative valuation data based on financial multiples is inconclusive. However, from an asset-based perspective it appears that Russia/CIS miners are undervalued relative to their junior peer group. EV/Resources multiple for Russia/CIS miners is 48.4% below foreign junior peers, while EV/output is 30.5% lower.

RISKS: ALL ABOUT SCALE AND EXECUTION

Gold can be a handy issue in populist politics, as it is easy for the public to grasp, and political posturing on who mines and sells Russian gold resonates with the electorate. However, given the way Vladimir Putin's presidency and state-building has developed it appears to us that the political risk of gold mining in Russia is actually quite low. Ultimately, the value discrepancy between the actual cash flows a gold company generates and the market valuation of that cash flow is vast. So while the market may see a large source of value, the government sees relatively limited cash flows. Since the political risk of an asset depends on the leverage it provides the government, either in terms of global influence or cash flows, gold miners in this context should be considered quite low risk. Russia will not be able to influence world gold markets by controlling any or all of the country's gold output. And in terms of cash flows, 1mn oz producer Polyus had operating cash flow last year of only $127mn (by way of comparison, Yukos's 2004 operating cash flow was more than $4bn).

The exception to this may be Centerra Gold, because the Kyrgyz economy is so small that Centerra actually makes up a large proportion of GDP, 10% at last count. Indeed, the company was a government target immediately after the April political unrest that replaced President Askar Akayev with Kurmanbek Bakiyev. However, the questionable tax claims involved were quickly settled with no practical effect on the company.

Operational risks for gold miners, on the other hand, are high because most of the companies profiled in this report are projecting high growth from new mines. Inevitably, mistakes will happen: costs will overrun and delays in execution of plans occur. Thus, investors should be willing to pay a premium for lower execution risk, which can only be assessed by companies' track records and project development profiles. If a company's new project is a massive low-grade complex metallurgy site in a remote area run by a management team that has never built a mine, then the execution risk is understandably high; unfortunately bullish investors sometimes brush such factors aside. Global giants have the luxury of scale, which means any one project does not influence the total picture too much. However, for our profiled companies, one mine may be the entire source of value and any disappointment could have serious negative consequences for the share price.

Share Price Performance Review

After a strong rally in 2004 on the back of rising gold prices, most of the gold producers profiled in this report have had a rather lackluster 2005. Costs have accelerated and various problems, from political unrest to mine troubles, have held share prices back – and none of the companies in our gold universe has outperformed the Russian market in 2005. Having said that, two factors are beginning to move share prices upward again:

1) Growth plans are coming closer to fruition as project development progresses; and

2) The inexorable rise in the gold price is becoming difficult to ignore.

Bema Gold and Highland Gold have both underperformed the RTS Index this year by around 60%. Bema's performance is based on two points: 1) Investors' belief in the company's ability to deliver growth was dented by ownership issues at its Cerro Casale project; and 2) Due to its diverse shareholder base and share liquidity, Bema has represented a volatile alternative for retail investors to play on future gold prices. Highland's performance is mainly the result of operational problems that have plagued the company for the past year. Only when it became clear that the company's growth plan was back on track, albeit with a delay, did investors begin to push the stock price higher.

High River and Centerra have also underperformed the RTS Index for the past year. Here the main issue is catalysts – as neither company, although solid, has had a headline deal or news event that could drive the stock higher. High River completed the consolidation of its Russian subsidiary and increased its presence in Africa, although neither of these events represented a paradigm shift for the company. Centerra had negative news flow from Kyrgyzstan due to the April political revolution there, although by 3Q05 the market had forgotten this and again priced the company as a steady state annuity.

Celtic and Peter Hambro have followed two very different trajectories. Celtic suffered because of the breakdown of negotiations with its long-targeted strategic partner, IG Alrosa, as Polyus stepped in as the deal breaker. On top of that, the company's Kazakh operations have not been running as smoothly as expected, which has also put downward pressure on the stock price. In contrast, Peter Hambro stands out as the only stock in our coverage universe to have matched the RTS Index's performance over the past year, with steady share price growth on the back of good operating and financial performances.

Conclusion and Recommendation: Go for Growth

Russia's gold sector continues to make its way in the global arena, with an average six-year CAGR of 8.4% and a good future growth story to tell. Transparency in the sector is high and there are several projects that are truly world class. Given Russia has the world's second largest resource base but extremely low extraction rates relative to the reserve base, this implies major growth potential.

The growth will be complemented by the low cost of producing gold in Russia. This competitive advantage is due to high cost efficiency and low energy and labor costs, as well as the change in ore field development to lode ore, with the best (ie most economically attractive) sites currently being developed. And while inflation and the strengthening ruble are set to erode the cost competitiveness somewhat, new mines being built – which are the source of Russia's output growth – are set to be very modern and efficient, thus offsetting the effect of these projected rising energy and labor costs.

High company-specific risk due to start up nature of operations. It is possible to note that that none of the companies profiled here is an established player and all are relatively young. While the companies profiled have the advantage of new assets that are modern and not burdened by Soviet legacy costs, the flip side is that these new assets are not tried and tested, and there have been (and will continue to be) development disappointments due to budget overruns, problems in construction and errors in mine planning.

Our top picks in the sector are Highland Gold and Bema Gold due to the low valuation of their resource base and their high growth potential. We have Buy recommendations on these companies, with 44% and 33% upside respectively to their fair values. High River Gold is also a Buy with a more modest 15.7% upside to fair value. We believe that Centerra Gold is fairly priced and initiate coverage of it with a Hold recommendation. Peter Hambro is fairly priced given the company's current development program, although It is possible to note that that details on further growth from its wide resource base may change our fundamental view. Celtic Resources is in the midst of a stand-off with domestic giant Polyus, news of which is the main driver for the stock at present; however, fundamentally the stock is fairly valued and we rate it Hold.

Recommendations: Go for growth, clear development plan						
In $	Bema Gold Highland		Peter Hambro	Centerra	High River	Celtic
As of Nov. 9, 2005	Gold		Mining	Gold	Gold	Resources
End-2006 target price	3.53	5.92	11.99	18.77	1.22	3.52
Current price	2.66	4.11	13.93	19.82	1.05	3.62
Upside	32.9%	44.0%	-14.1%	-5.3%	15.7%	-2.8%
Recommendation	Buy	Buy	Hold	Hold	Buy	Hold

Source: Company data; Aton estimates

SITUATION IN THE GOLD MINING SECTOR

CHEAP RESOURCES

The Russian/CIS gold sector trades at a premium to global and junior market peers on average forward EV/EBITDA multiples, with a ratio of 28.9X for our universe compared to 16.2X and 23.8X for major and junior peers respectively. However, Russian/CIS gold trades at a discount on P/E multiples, with our profiled companies having a forward P/E of 36.3X compared to 51.9X and 62.3X for global and junior peers. On an asset basis, relative valuations diverge further. The market is paying an EV/Resource ratio of $66/oz for Russian/CIS gold, while for major companies the figure is $111/oz and for juniors it is $127/oz. Our top Buy recommendations are Highland Gold and Bema Gold with 44% and 33% upside to fair value respectively. High River Gold is also rated a Buy, although with smaller upside. Centerra Gold, Peter Hambro and Celtic Resources are rated Hold as they appear to be fully valued.

COMPARATIVE VALUATION: JUNIORS COMPARE TO OTHER JUNIORS

Gold miners in general are grouped into three categories: global majors, junior producers and exploration plays. All of the businesses profiled in this report are junior producers with at least some cash flow being currently generated from mining and selling gold. Nonetheless, they are all dwarfed by the global majors such as Barrick and AngloGold Ashanti, which each make more gold than all of Russia combined. Therefore, the most relevant peer group for Russia/CIS miners is international junior gold producers, which includes a wide array of companies producing from 100,000oz up to 1mn oz annually in various parts of the world. We also note that junior gold miners are often growth stories, and which is also true for Russia/CIS gold companies.

FINANCIAL MULTIPLES

In general, financial multiples for gold companies are high, due partially to gold's special status as an asset class. This is a result of the metal's counter-cyclical nature and its use as a form of insurance and store of wealth. Aside from high multiples, many junior companies – and those profiled here – are forecast to deliver strong future growth, even though some currently operate in the red. Therefore, in order to provide more information on relative value than is available from financial multiples, we have included asset and operating multiples, giving additional insight into how our profiled companies compare relative to their peer group.

Comparative valuation on financial multiples: inconclusive results

As of Nov. 8, 2005	Price, $	Mcap, $mn	EV, $mn
Russia / CIS			
Centerra Gold	19.98	1,440	1,205
Bema Gold	2.55	1,149	1,277
Peter Hambro	13.93	1,100	1,060
Highland Gold	4.09	650	711
High River Gold	1.03	222	247
Celtic Resources	3.75	178	187
Weighted average			
Majors			
Newmont			42.5
Barrick Gold			24.9
Anglogold Ashanti			39.4
Placer Dome			19.3
Goldcorp			19.8
Gold Fields			13.3
Harmony			10.4
Weighted average			
Juniors			
Glamis Gold			20.8
Kinross Gold			6.90
Meridian Gold			18.5
Lihir Gold			1.31
Iamgold			6.89

Randgold Resources	13.9
Yamana Gold	3.86
Weighted average	

EV/EBITDA				P/E			P/CF	
2004	2005F	2006F	2004	2005F	2006F	2004	2005F	2006F
10.9	10.0	8.0	28.5	22.6	14.3	16.3	13.2	10.3
N. M.	48.0	31.9	N. M.	N. M.	N. M.	N. M.	75.9	41.8
30.3	19.5	16.4	73.3	37.0	29.7	84.6	28.0	23.5
27.8	58.4	12.1	129.8	N. M.	27.0	62.2	74.0	28.3
17.4	12.7	5.5	N. M.	36.8	9.4	15.1	16.4	7.0
28.4	30.0	18.0	63.7	142.5	64.3	N. M.	20.6	N. M.
21.2	28.9	16.6	64.5	36.3	23.5	47.0	40.6	23.8
10.7	11.9	10.5	42.8	51.1	35.8	11.3	15.0	13.1
25.0	20.1	13.2	54.0	46.5	34.5	26.4	18.7	14.1
19.6	16.3	12.3	118.5	45.1	27.6	23.1	15.9	13.0
14.6	16.5	13.2	29.7	79.2	61.9	22.4	21.5	15.7
49.1	9.7	9.4	129.8	29.2	28.6	126.0	16.7	16.3
17.5	13.3	8.1	58.6	64.0	28.1	26.9	18.3	11.0
290.1	38.2	13.4	N. M.	N. M.	47.9	N. M.	14.7	12.8
36.4	16.2	11.5	66.3	51.9	36.8	31.3	17.1	13.7
76.4	34.8	15.9	131.3	94.1	29.8	59.9	34.4	17.3
15.7	10.4	8.0	N. M.	38.8	20.9	14.8	11.6	9.7
23.9	23.3	19.6	50.5	44.8	44.1	26.5	25.6	22.7
14.8	18.1	8.7	5.1	91.5	25.3	55.4	29.9	18.4
28.7	23.4	15.6	87.4	50.8	31.0	74.3	20.8	15.9
41.3	15.5	22.6	46.3	23.0	19.2	217.4	15.6	14.3
78.6	51.6	7.9	263.7	N. M.	33.4	86.0	57.6	13.8
38.9	23.8	13.8	88.0	62.3	29.1	60.2	26.2	16.1
-41.8%	78.4%	44.3%	-2.6%	-30.0%	-36.1%	50.3%	137.2%	73.8%
-45.6%	21.4%	20.3%	-26.6%	-41.7%	-19.0%	-22.0%	54.8%	47.5%

Source: estimates

Financial multiples for Russian/CIS gold companies are not conclusively higher or lower than those in either the major or junior peer group. Relative P/E ratios suggest our universe is cheaper than peers, while on an EV/EBITDA and P/CF basis Russia/CIS gold miners look expensive.

Asset-based valuation

Russia/CIS miners look inexpensive relative to peers on an asset basis, as the average EV/Resource ratio is $66/oz, while for majors it is $111/oz and for juniors it is $127/oz. As mentioned earlier, junior mining companies tend to have strong growth outlooks and therefore are the best peer group for our profiled companies. Here we see that despite the strong growth outlook and fairly good profitability of Russia/CIS gold miners, the market has valued their production below that of junior peers.

Asset/output based comparison: Russian/CIS companies look cheap to juniors, expensive to majors

As of Nov. 8, 2005 2004 Reserves Resources Total cash Life EV/ Mcap/ EV/ Mcap/ EV/ Mcap/ output cost span output output reserves reserves resources resources

000 oz		000 oz	000 oz	$/oz	years	$/oz	$/oz	$/oz	$/oz	$/oz	$/oz
Russia / CIS											
Centerra Gold	610	4362	10834	189	7	1976	2361	276	330	111	133
Bema Gold	230	8392	21896	332	36	5554	4994	152	137	58	52
Peter Hambro	209	2651	17449	135	13	5071	5263	400	415	61	63
Highland Gold	195	8000	18288	215	41	3649	3335	89	81	39	36
High River Gold	107	2079	6942	257	19	2308	2074	119	107	36	32
Celtic Resources	32	3550	9600	240	111	5848	5568	53	50	19	19
Weighted average				215		3720	3683	220	233	66	70
Majors											
Newmont	6989	92400	135400	231	13	2926	2715	221	205	151	140
Barrick Gold	4958	89056	109514	212	18	3277	2700	182	150	148	122
Anglogold Ashanti	6407	78900	218200	268	12	1966	1629	160	132	58	48
Placer Dome	3652	59917	113999	241	16	2142	2308	131	141	69	74
Goldcorp	628	12490	24060	115	20	7885	10616	396	534	206	277
Gold Fields	4254	75552	178033	302	18	1268	1538	71	87	30	37
Harmony	3428	54100	528600	360	16	997	1191	63	75	6	8
Weighted average				259		2961	3062	186	188	111	110
Juniors											
Glamis Gold	234	6300	20992	192	27	12669	11727	471	436	141	131
Kinross Gold	1616	19410	27596	250	12	1555	1475	129	123	91	86
Meridian Gold	315	4355	6375	50	14	6153	5872	445	425	304	290
Lihir Gold	599	21000	40000	279	35	1839	2799	52	80	28	42
Iamgold	432	4000	8000	248	9	2434	2347	263	254	131	127
Randgold Res.	510	2510	12530	184	5	1679	1828	341	371	68	74
Yamana Gold	101	4072	11795	218	40	5059	7265	125	180	43	62
Weighted average				225		5354	5353	281	277	127	125
Russia / CIS relative to Majors						25.6%	20.3%	17.8%	23.8%	-41.0%	-36.0%
Russia / CIS relative to Juniors						-30.5%	-31.2%	-21.9%	-15.9%	-48.4%	-43.6%

Source: Bloomberg; Company data; Aton estimates

DCF VALUATION

Our DCF-based models are based on the financial forecasts presented in the company profiles that follow in this report, as well as the key CAPM/discount rate assumptions outlined in the following table.

Base cost of equity calculation Assumptions Comment Long-term risk free rate, % 5.5 Based on 5-yr. trailing average yield of LT US Govt. bond Russian country risk premium, % 1.5 Based on the expected spread of LT Russian Eurobonds over US Govt. bonds (end-2005)

We believe a capital asset pricing model (CAPM) is the best of the limited number of choices available to price an asset, though we recognize that statistically it is only as good as the inputs used. In addition to our standard cost of equity calculation, we have used a forecast unlevered beta, which is based on the companies' trading liquidity and our perception of risk relative to the rest of the market. Since all of the companies profiled here are incorporated outside Russia and with the exception of Peter Hambro and Highland Gold, all of the companies profiled also have assets outside of Russia, the "Russian risk" as pertains to trading, politics and corporate governance is company-specific and not systemic. Therefore, we have not used our standard upward adjustment for the excess RTS volatility premium as no company profiled here trades domestically in Russia.

Forecast beta and WACC for our profiled companies

Bema Gold Highland Peter Hambro Centerra High River Celtic Gold Mining Gold Gold Resources

Beta (unlevered)	1.00	1.25	1.25	1.25	1.25	1.25
Cost of equity	11.5%	12.6%	12.5%	12.0%	12.8%	13.1%
Cost of debt (after tax)	6.8%	6.5%	5.8%	6.0%	6.1%	5.9%
WACC	10.8%	11.8%	11.7%	12.0%	11.6%	11.5%

Source: Company data; Aton estimates

We have estimated companies' after-tax cost of debt from the financial data presented in their 2004 reports and have assumed that the income tax rate applied is in line with the statutory Russian rate of 24%. Granted, the companies here operate in various jurisdictions. However, past financial results suggest that a 24% tax rate fairly captures what the companies pay on a consolidated basis.

Most of the companies profiled in this report are growth stories, which means that the terminal value makes up a significant portion of our fair value. Additionally, with these companies changing so quickly, it is difficult to determine what the "steady state" business operations would resemble. However, we do believe that by being in Russia/CIS now, these companies will have an advantage in picking up new ore sites in the future and have an easier time in their future development as they establish operating track records with local governments. Therefore, we have given our profiled companies a terminal growth rate of 5% to reflect their growth opportunities over and above what they already own. The one important exception here is Celtic Resources, to which we have given a lower 3% growth rate because the company's current difficulties may hinder its ability to line up new projects for growth in the future.

The result of our CAPM calculations is an EV valuation, which is then adjusted for the amount of net debt or cash a company has in its capital structure, as well as minority interest. Additionally, where applicable we have added an exploration value component to our DCF-based fair value estimates to give companies that have large, but as yet undeveloped, resources credit for the likely value to be gained from this asset in the future. Our standard approach is highlighted in the table below.

The resulting adjusted figure is the target market capitalization of the company's equity, which divided by the number of shares gives us our fair value target price.

On a DCF basis Highland Gold and Bema Gold are the most undervalued of our six companies profiled here and we have Buy recommendations on both names. High River Gold is also rated a

Buy. The rest of our universe seems to be fairly valued although for different reasons. Centerra lacks growth beyond its two massive mines, Celtic is in the midst of a corporate battle, and Peter Hambro has yet to disclose development plans for its various licenses throughout Russia. Our fundamental value of these three companies is near the current market levels and we rate all of them as Hold.

Fair values based on our DCF forecasts

As of Nov. 9, 2005	Bema Gold	Highland Gold	Peter Hambro Mining	Centerra Gold	High River Gold	Celtic Resources
End-2006 target price, $	3.53	5.92	11.99	18.77	1.22	3.52
Current price, $	2.66	4.11	13.93	19.82	1.05	3.62
Upside	32.9%	44.0%	-14.1%	-5.3%	15.7%	-2.8%
Recommendation	Buy	Buy	Hold	Hold	Buy	Hold

Source: Company data; Aton estimates

CONCLUSION

With the value of Russian/CIS gold miners so inexorably tied to their growth plans, near term financial multiples are of limited use as a valuation metric. Therefore, we believe the core focus in valuing Russian/CIS gold miners should be on their resources and the growth outlook these imply. Relative to international peers, Russian/CIS gold mining companies look cheap on an asset basis. Although we understand that investors may discount some of the future growth as they require more confirmation that development execution is proceeding apace, the discount the market assigns to Russian/CIS companies vs. junior gold miners in other parts of the world seems excessive. On the other hand, assets have only limited value without sound management and a development plan. As such, we believe the key criteria for picking attractively priced stocks in this sector is to look for cheap resources first, and then examine how sound the management team is and the development plan to turn those resources into cash. Based on this, we believe Bema Gold, Highland Gold and High River Gold have the best potential for share price appreciation and we rate them as Buys.

LARGEST COMPANIES OVERVIEWS

RUSSIA/CIS BASED, FOREIGN LISTED

This report profiles six public companies that are major players in the gold mining sector in Russia/CIS. Each company has a uniquely attractive mix of assets, although with so much anticipated growth in the picture it is essential for investors to pick through the promotional hype to find the players that can capitalize on the opportunities in the Russian gold industry today.

Investors' options for exposure to the Russian/CIS gold story are, ironically, all foreign as every company profiled is technically domiciled overseas and traded in London or Toronto. This seems unlikely to change in the future as the start-up capital for new development and the entrepreneurs driving exploration and development are all non-Russian. The advantage of this is that it implies a certain level of transparency and corporate behavior.

In this report, we have updated our coverage of Highland Gold, Peter Hambro and Celtic Resources and initiated coverage of Bema Gold, High River Gold and Centerra.

In terms of pure, large Russian exposure, Polyus, Norilsk Nickel's gold mining subsidiary, is due to be spun off at the beginning of next year, creating a multibillion-dollar company that is unquestionably the Russian leader in domestic gold mining (see our Oct. 4, 2005 report: *Norilsk Nickel – Polyus: Free gold anyone?* for more details). However, we believe that the smaller companies profiled here should not be ignored and with the growth potential that many have in the pipeline, some could ultimately become major players in Russia.

BEMA GOLD: A GROWTH STORY

Canadian-based Bema Gold is one of Russia's largest gold companies by market capitalization, which operates the Julietta mine in Magadan region and is developing the vast Chukotka-based Kupol deposit, projected to produce more than 500,000oz per annum and come on line in 2008. Bema currently has three major areas of operation: Russia, South Africa and Chile, though its high-cost South African operation is more an option on high gold prices and its Chilean operation is only just coming on line. In this context, Bema's Russian projects represent the cornerstone of its value.

OVERVIEW: GLOBAL ASSETS BUT RUSSIAN GROWTH BASE

Bema Gold has three operating mines in Russia, South Africa and Chile, with three major development sites in Russia, Chile and Canada. The company produced 229,545 oz in 2004 and according to its development plan will have about 1mn oz of output by 2009. Bema has 16mn ounces of reserves and resources, more than 38% of which are located in Russia. However, we argue that the bulk of company value is sited in Russia, for while representing only 38% of total resources, Russia's resources are profitable whereas the South African assets are at best breakeven and the Chilean ones are so far only a small part of total value.

OPERATIONS AND ASSETS

Bema currently has three operating mines in three different countries. The Julietta mine in Russia's Magadan region; the Petrex mine in South Africa; and the Rufugio mine in Chile. Bema's Russian assets are modern and efficient while its South African ones are average.

Bema built the Julietta mine (and mill) – a lean operation employing just 320 people – from scratch. As a successful greenfield project the mine has none of the legacy cost issues of many Russian assets inherited from the former Soviet Union. Indeed, Bema has established a strong reputation as a foreign company with operational and asset development experience in Russia. As a result, the company's Russian development project, Kupol, so far no more than drill holes and exploration support facilities, is likely to be an efficient, modern operation once completed, in line with the Julietta experience.

Bema's South African mine, Petrex, is a different story, as it was purchased as an ongoing concern in 2003. Bema has put Petrex through an extensive operational reshuffling, including shutting down its open-pit operations as it sought to turn around the mine, a process complicated by the strengthening South African rand, which raised costs. However, progress has been made on improving efficiency by changing management, raising employee training and better operational conditions (namely mine water pumping).

Bema owns 50% of the Refugio mine in Chile, which is set to be a very modern operation that is forecast to be cost competitive despite low ore grade of 0.8g/ton. The mine will be operated by Kinross, which owns the other 50%. As an open pit heap leach operation, Refugio is rather simple operationally and unlikely to be a source of problems for the company in terms of operational surprises.

In 2004, Julietta contributed 83,317oz to Bema's gold output, or 36% of total, while the remaining production came from Petrex, at 146,228oz; Refugio only came on line this year and is forecast to produce 50,000oz for total estimated 2005 output for Bema of 309,000oz.

Share of total output: Julietta and Petrex the sole contributors in 2004

Bema has a long pipeline of development projects aside from its three active mines. The most significant of these is Kupol, which is a massive high-grade gold and silver deposit in Russia's remote Chukotka region. In addition to Kupol, the company also has a minority 24% stake in Cerro Casale, a large low-grade copper/gold deposit in Chile. In October the former controlling owner (51%) of Cerro Casale, Placer Dome, agreed to relinquish its stake in return for future cash or gold payments. It is not yet clear how Bema can move the project forward (in terms of financing development) and in the absence of details we have not included this in our forecasts, although we give the company value for the resources at the site. Aside from Kupol and Cerro Casale, Bema also owns several exploration projects, the most promising of which is Monument Bay in Canada. But Kupol is clearly the key driver for the company's value for the near- to medium term.

Reserves and resources: a wide base

Although a breakdown of resources provides broad pointers to the sources of Bema's future growth, It is possible to note that that its large South African resource base can be interpreted in two ways:

1) As a drain on resources given the mine is not competitive due to high production costs associated with the strong South African rand; or

2) As a leveraged operation that turns a profit in a high gold price environment with a disproportionately positive effect on the company's financials.

KUPOL: HIGH GRADE GOLD WITH A SILVER LINING

Kupol is one of the world's most exciting new gold fields and, as mentioned, is the primary driver for Bema's future value. The field currently has more than 5.3mn oz of gold and silver equivalent resources and exploration work is consistently finding new veins which will likely result in an increase in resources going forward. Even more impressive is the average grade of the ore body: 18.1g/ton, or 3.5X higher than the global average. Bema owns 75% of the project and the Chukotka regional government the remaining 25%. It is possible to note that that the governor of Chukotka is Roman Abramovich, a former core shareholder of Sibneft and very much pro-business.

The current development plan for Kupol envisions the construction of a mine and mill with annual throughput of 1.3mn tons of ore and a recovery rate of 90%. This puts forecast annual output at more than 700,000oz. The project is forecast to come on line in 2008 and is set to be the second largest gold mine in Russia after Polyus's Olimpiada. Additionally, with the silver credits included, Kupol is set to be Russia's lowest cost mine, which is even more impressive given that Russia is already the world's lowest-cost gold producer.

CERRO CASALE: VAST CHILEAN FIELD IN LIMBO

Cerro Casale is one of the world's largest undeveloped gold-copper deposits and located in Northern Chile. Although the ore grade of the site is low, at 0.26% copper and 0.7g/ton gold, the actual metal content is vast, with a total resource base of 6.9mn oz of gold and 0.8mn tons of copper. Until October, the site was jointly owned by Placer Dome, one of the world's largest gold mining companies, Arizona Star and Bema Gold. Arizona Star is partially owned by Bema and in the past the latter has had significant management control over it, although Arizona Star has recently become more autonomous in its activities.

In September, Placer Dome announced that the development of Cerro Casale was not economically feasible, which was greeted with incredulity by its partners and immediately challenged by Bema and Arizona Star. In October, Placer Dome agreed to sell its interest in the site for $10mn at the start of mine construction and subsequent payments of either 190,000oz of gold over 12 years or a lump sum of $70mn. Bema management has a more optimistic view than Placer Dome about the economic viability of the project, although development will come at a price, with the estimated cost of construction estimated at well over $1bn. Given the uncertainty, we have only incorporated Cerro Casale in our valuation of Bema as exploration value.

OWNERSHIP

Bema's shares are listed in Canada (BGO CN), the US (BGO US), on AIM (BAU LN) and in Frankfurt (MDG GR). Surprisingly, little of the company is owned by management and Bema's stock is very liquid: average daily trading volume is regularly above $5mn and the entire company's market capitalization is turned over in less than a year.

SUBSIDIARIES AND EQUITY INVESTMENTS

Bema owns stakes in smaller companies that are either potentially complementary to its core business or the result of opportunistic acquisitions. However, instead of keeping these projects in-house, the company has dropped these projects into separate vehicles, allowing Bema to gain exposure while disbursing risk and not clouding its core focus. In this way Bema acts as an incubator for smaller, high-risk projects. This is particularly true for Puma Minerals (CPW CN, Not rated). Puma is an early stage exploration-development PGM company that owns a very prospective ore field in Russia's Murmansk region. Bema holds 55% of Puma. So far the company has spent $3.6mn on exploration and has identified a very high-grade PGM deposit, which has to date 400,000oz of C2 resources and total P2 resources of near 4mn oz. The company plans to continue its exploration to hopefully prove a multi-million oz deposit in the C2 category and above in the next several years.

Subsidiaries and equity investments

Ownership Note

Puma Minerals 55% PGM development in Russia Victoria Resources 32% Aggressive gold exploration in US Westview Resources 44% Aggressive nickel/PGM exploration in Canada Arizona Star 5% Owns 25% of the Cerro Casale project

Source: Company data

Victoria Resources (VIT CN) is active in Nevada exploring for gold at sites that have been exploited in the past, but with significant potential for gold strikes.

Westview Resources (CWS.H CN) is active in Ontario, Canada, exploring for copper, nickel and PGM deposits.

Finally, Arizona Star (AZS CN), which used to be managed by Bema and is now more autonomous, shares ownership with the latter in the Cerro Casale project.

FINANCIAL REVIEW AND FORECAST

Bema's current revenue breakdown is the same as for production, with Russia accounting for 36% and South Africa the remainder. Refugio's coming on line this year will give the company a third top line contributor, while Kupol is still three years away from generating revenue. The key issue for Bema is how well it manages the interim period before Kupol begins production, in terms of keeping costs in check, particularly in relation to SG&A.

Revenue

We assumed that Petrex would continue to operate for the forecast period and indeed the mine has the resources to do so. However, Julietta is projected to run out of resources by the end of 2009 and It is forecasted that the mine to be closed at that time. Refugio is projected to be a stable producer of more 100,000oz per annum for our entire forecast period. The main driver for Bema, however, is Kupol. Our financial forecasts assume the company is able to bring the Kupol project on line under the current development plan, namely with the first gold pour in late 2007. Bema's total output volume is expected to rise from 229,545oz in 2004 to 1mn oz in 2010. On the costs side, the key drivers are the volume of ore processed and the average cash cost for each mine. In the case of Kupol, we expect the silver netback to play a significant role in lowering costs and have used the company's feasibility study as guidance for our forecasts.

Costs

Bema's high average costs are a function of its low Russian production costs being inflated by its high-cost South African operations. For 2004, net of various put options, Bema's average cash cost was $315/oz, which was 25% higher than the global average of $253/oz. In the near term the key issue concerning costs is how the company manages Petrex, although efficiency improvements and management changes made in 2004 seem to be turning around this troubled asset. Bema's cash costs are forecast to fall as the Refugio mine comes on line and as the improvement at Petrex takes hold. As with everything else about Bema, though, the true change in the company will not happen until Kupol is up and running, as its scale should result in a substantial lowering of the company's average cash cost.

We have used Bema's projected cash costs for each of its mines though It is possible to note that a full breakdown of COGS was not available. Aside from cash costs, depreciation and amortization are a function of the useful life of an asset and the mining process itself. And for the sake of simplicity we have forecast this item as yearly gold output as a percentage of total reserves per mine in operation, using our own forecasts for the book value of each mine based on historical values and forecast capex.

SG&A costs are projected to be driven by inflation and the overall scale of Bema's business. Further down the income statement is income expense, which is a function of the balance sheet from year to year and It is possible to note that that Bema Gold is forecast to have significant project financing debt mainly due to Kupol. Although Bema operates in many different jurisdictions, It is possible that it will pay the Russian statutory income tax rate of 24%.

It is forecasted that Bema to spend about $200mn this year in capex, and over $200 in the next two years in order to develop Kupol, restart Refugio, maintain current operations at Julietta, and reform Petrex.

However, most of this investment will be used to construct the Kupol mine and ore processing facility, while the rest will be for maintenance.

Bema's near-term capex bill will be a major cash drain and significant leverage will be needed (and is already lined up) in order to bring the company's growth plans to fruition.

Massive capex for growth in near term, returns to maintenance level in 2008

Balance sheet and cash flow

Bema's balance sheet is forecast to build up leverage and this is only projected to decline as Kupol begins to generate free cash flow in 2008. As with most gold companies, working capital is not anticipated to be an issue for Bema and so receivables and payable are likely to be minor balance sheet items.

Although we cannot forecast it, Bema is likely to seek equity cash infusions to complement project financing as there is a three-year lag before the company is forecast to turn a profit with the opening of Kupol; indeed, Bema placed $121mn in equity in October. It is possible to note that that due to heavy capex in the near- to medium term there is no scope for dividend payments from the company.

Operating cash flow: long term average to stabilize above $100mn

Bema's 1H05 US GAAP results were poor but brought no surprises as both the company and market are geared towards future developments. Bema produced 114,411oz of gold in 1H05, up 7.1% y-o-y, and sold 105,216oz, up 1.2% y-o-y, while a 7.3% rise in revenue was mostly due to higher gold prices. Despite total cash costs being kept under control at $337/oz (vs. 1H04's $332/oz), COGS rose 13.6% due to expenses associated with the restarting of operations at the Refugio mine. Bema's South African operations had an overall negative impact on the company's financials due to very high total cash costs and the fact the mine had not yet been turned around by the end of 1H05.

SG&A expenses were kept very kept firmly under control at $6mn. The company's net loss more than doubled to $27mn due to one-off derivative events: in 1H04 Bema recorded unrealized derivative gains of more than $18mn vs. a $3mn derivative loss in 1H05.

The company's net debt position at the end of 1H05 widened substantially to $162mn from $47mn at the end of 2004. This was mostly related to hefty capex and exploration expenses amounting to $94mn in the period, with more than $66mn spent on the Kupol project alone. More capex at Kupol and Refugio is expected in 2H05; however, an equity placement of $12mn in October should help ease the company's leverage and fund development.

1H05 income statement highlights of limited importance

In $mn, CA GAAP	1H04	1H05	Y-o-y %
Revenue	41	44	7.3%
COGS	-52	-59	13.6%
Gross profit	-11	-15	36.9%
Gross margin	-26.8%	-34.2%	
SG&A	-6	-6	1.0%
Operating profit	-17	-21	24.7%
EBITDA	-7	-12	63.2%
EBITDA margin	-17.4%	-26.5%	
Interest income	-4	-3	-40.4%
Other non-operating expense	8	-6	-177.5%
Income tax	-1	3	-605.0%
Minority interest	0	0	-70.6%
Net income	-13	-27	102.5%

Net margin	-32.9%	-62.0%

CONCLUSION: STRONG GROWTH OUTLOOK FROM LARGE-SCALE ASSETS

Bema Gold is one of the largest gold mining companies in Russia by market capitalization and has a world-class asset in Kupol that is attracting increasing attention. Given the company's growth is set to come from Russia, we have included Bema in our gold universe. Additionally, It is possible to note that that while the Cerro Casale project in Chile is only included in our model as exploration value, it could be a major catalyst for the company once there is more detail on who will own the mine and how it will be developed.

The key issue for Bema is to execute its development timetable, as the company is projected to be in constant need of new cash. To date, Bema has adhered to its development plans and its track record suggests it can bring Kupol into operation as scheduled in 2008. With this report we initiate coverage of Bema Gold with a Buy recommendation and end2006 target price of $3.53, providing 32.9% upside to the current market price.

SUMMARY FINANCIAL FORECAST

Income statement									
In $mn, CA GAAP	2002	2003	2004	2005F	2006F	2007F	2008F	2009F	2010F
Total revenues	36	87	92	135	162	144	293	439	346
COGS	-15	-72	-99	-94	-104	-104	-136	-166	-138
Gross profit	22	15	-6	41	58	40	157	273	208
SG&A	-4	-7	-10	-15	-18	-18	-20	-20	-21
EBITDA	17	8	-17	27	40	22	137	253	188
Depreciation	-12	-18	-20	-23	-32	-32	-69	-88	-59
Operating income	5	-10	-37	4	8	-11	68	165	129
Net interest expense	-8	-7	-7	-9	-14	-22	-23	-18	-11
Other expense/income	0	-7	-35	0	0	0	0	0	0
Pre-tax income	-3	-24	-80	-5	-6	-33	45	147	118
Income taxes	-1	-6	0	1	1	8	-11	-35	-28
Minority interest	0	0	0	0	0	0	-23	-46	-36
Net income	-3	-31	-80	-4	-4	-25	11	66	54

Balance sheet									
In $mn, CA GAAP	2002	2003	2004	2005F	2006F	2007F	2008F	2009F	2010F
Cash and liquid assets	17	31	87	50	5	10	10	81	184
Inventories	10	15	16	17	19	19	29	36	28
Accounts receivable	2	6	8	11	13	12	24	36	28
Other current assets	4	8	10	10	10	10	10	10	10
Total current assets	33	60	122	88	48	52	74	163	251
Fixed assets	149	304	419	605	682	749	690	613	563
Investments	0	0	0	0	0	0	0	0	0
Other non-current assets	24	69	53	53	53	53	53	53	53
Total non-current assets	173	373	471	657	735	801	743	666	616
Total assets	206	433	593	745	783	853	816	829	867

Short-term debt	11	46	4	1	38	133	67	0	0
Accounts payable	4	23	32	32	37	37	56	70	54
Other current liabilities	0	0	0	0	0	0	0	0	0
Total current liabilities	15	69	36	33	75	170	123	70	54
Long-term debt	18	7	130	175	175	175	175	175	175
Other non-current liabilities	6	83	92	92	92	92	92	92	92
Total non-current liabilities	25	90	222	267	267	267	267	267	267
Minority interest	1	1	3	3	3	3	3	3	3
Total shareholders' equity	165	273	333	443	439	413	424	491	544
Total liabilities and equity	206	433	593	745	783	853	816	829	867
Cash flow statement									
In $mn, CA GAAP	2002	2003	2004	2005F	2006F	2007F	2008F	2009F	2010F
Net income	-3	-31	-80	-4	-4	-25	11	66	54
Depreciation	12	18	20	23	32	32	69	88	59
Changes in working capital	0	6	4	-4	0	2	-3	-6	0
Other	1	15	48	0	0	0	0	0	0
Operating cash flow	10	8	-8	15	27	9	77	148	113
Capex	-16	-57	-128	-209	-109	-99	-11	-11	-9
Acquisitions	0	0	0	0	0	0	0	0	0
Other	-6	23	-4	0	0	0	0	0	0
Investing cash flow	-22	-34	-132	-209	-109	-99	-11	-11	-9
Change in debt	-	24	81	42	37	95	-66	-67	0
Dividends	0	0	0	0	0	0	0	0	0
Other	24	16	115	114	0	0	0	0	0
Financing cash flow	24	40	196	156	37	95	-66	-67	0

Source: Company data; Aton estimates Source: Company data; Aton estimates

DCF valuation of Bema Gold

In $mn	2004	2005F	2006F	2007F	2008F	2009F	2010F	2011F	2012F	2013F	2014F	2015F
Revenue	92	135	162	144	293	439	346	325	326	327	328	329
Operating expenses	-109	-108	-122	-122	-156	-186	-158	-154	-155	-157	-158	-159
EBITDA	-17	27	40	22	137	253	188	171	171	169	170	171
Depreciation	-20	-23	-32	-32	-69	-88	-59	-51	-52	-54	-56	-59
Operating income (EBIT)	-37	4	8	-11	68	165	129	120	119	115	114	111
Less: Income taxes		-1	-2	3	-16	-40	-31	-29	-29	-28	-27	-27
Less: Capex		-209	-109	-99	-11	-11	-9	-9	-7	-7	-7	-7
Less: Changes in WC		-4	0	2	-3	-6	0	0	0	0	0	0

Plus: Depreciation	23	32	32	69	88	59	51	52	54	56	59
Free cash flow	-187	-71	-73	107	197	148	133	136	135	136	137
Discount factor (WACC)		1.00	1.11	1.23	1.36	1.51	1.67	1.85	2.05	2.28	2.52
Present value of future FCF		-71	-66	87	144	98	79	73	66	60	54
Total PV of future FCF 525											

Calculation of terminal value		Cost of equity calculation		Forecast beta calculation	
Terminal free cash flow, $mn	137	Long term risk free rate	5.5%	Avg monthly trading volume*	Forecast
Terminal growth rate	5%	Russian country risk premium	1.5%	(com. + pref.), $mn	beta
Terminal discount rate	10.8%	Russian risk free rate	7.0%	> 100	1.00
Terminal value, $mn	2,470	Standard equity premium	4.0%	10-100	1.25
PV of terminal value, $mn	979	Excess RTS volatility factor	1.00	1-10	1.50
		Russian equity market premium	4.0%	0.1-1	2.00
		Forecast beta	1.00	< 0.1	3.00
Target price calculation		Levered forecast beta	1.13	*Based on trailing 3 month total dollar	
PV of terminal value + future FCF, $ mn	1,504	Cost of equity	11.5%	volume on RTS, MICEX and ADR markets	
Less: Net debt (cash), $mn (end 05F)	126				
Less: Minority interest, $mn	3	WACC calculation		Capital structure, $mn	
Exploration value	215	Gross debt as % of capitalization	15.0%	Gross debt (end 05F)	176
Total equity value, $mn	1,591	Cost of debt (after-tax)	6.8%	MV of common	1,000
		Equity as % of capitalization	85.0%		
		Cost of equity	11.5%	Total MV of equity	1,000
Common shares outstanding, mn	451	WACC	10.8%	Total capitalization	1,176
Fair value per common share, $	3.53				

PETER HAMBRO MINING

Peter Hambro Mining is currently Russia's largest public gold mining company with a variety of assets spanning from producing mines to early stage exploration projects. Since going public four years ago, Peter Hambro has developed operations without interruption or mishap and has laid the foundation for future growth through license acquisitions, some of which have high synergetic potential with existing operations. However, there are scant details on what that growth will look like, so while the company has the assets to support higher production, investors have no information on how growth would be financed, which ore bodies would be used and how much it would cost. As a result, investors have to take the company's statements at face value, which they have been prepared to do to date.

OVERVIEW: GOOD GROWTH POTENTIAL BUT DETAILS SCANT

Peter Hambro was listed on London's AIM in 2002 and since then has seen its share price rise almost 5X. This success has been underpinned by good, low cost operations at the company's main mine, Pokrovsky, as well as the promotional skills of the company's namesake and executive chairman, Peter Hambro, who has successfully conveyed a vision of a low cost, growth-oriented Russian gold miner. Since going public, the company has acquired a number of interesting licenses, although development plans have been scant, aside from the company flagging an output target of 1mn oz by 2009. Nonetheless, exploration continues and it appears from operational developments that news should be forthcoming on a timetable for opening new mines in the near future, particularly on the very prospective Malomir deposit. In terms of existing production, Peter Hambro produced 209,000oz of gold in 2004, up 40.4% y-o-y.

In general, the company has built up a very large inventory of P2 and P3 resources, which have the lowest certainty and require extensive exploration to raise their classification to a level that could justify mining. By drilling out and proving new resources in a manner akin to just-in-time inventory management, the company has a unique business model with many positive points, like lowering exploration costs; however, the risk is that the underlying assumptions on resource abundance to grow production may turn out to be wrong.

The key issue for Peter Hambro is that no matter what one's view on its resource base is, with only three years until 2009 the 1mn oz output goal is looking increasingly overoptimistic (unless there is an intention to buy a producing company).

OPERATIONS AND ASSETS

Peter Hambro's main asset is the Pokrovsky mine, a large open-pit operation that has very low costs and scope for further growth. This mine is the backbone of Peter Hambro and has been in operations for six years, with the bulk of its initial startup kinks long ago resolved. Adjacent is the Pioneer mine, with an ore body similar in scale and expected to capitalize on its proximity to Pokrovsky. Peter Hambro also has a JV in the Magadan region, which is primarily placer ore mining. Total gold output for the company last year was 209,000oz.

In addition to its operating assets, Peter Hambro also has a portfolio of exploration licenses. The Malomir license in the Amur region, which contains 19% of the company's resources, is likely to be the first developed, as the company had long targeted the site through the acquisition of adjacent license concessions and has scheduled an intensive drilling program to further identify ore bodies. Additionally, preliminary work has begun on building infrastructure (roads, telephone lines etc) to the site. Peter Hambro is exploring the Tokur license area, also in the Amur region, which was an operating mine in the past and has the potential to be a solid, if not particularly large, operation; however, Malomir seems to have higher priority here. Peter Hambro also owns Yamalzoloto, which has a small, high-grade ore field in Russia's Far North-West.

Given Pokrovsky and Pioneer are so close, they could be considered one operation representing 45% of Peter Hambro's ore resources. Despite already constituting the bulk of production, the area also holds the most promise for near term growth. Magadan, the company's second area of current production, represents 18% of total resources and we do not expect any change in its production schedule.

In terms of long-term growth, Malomir, representing 19% of total resources, is the most obvious candidate, although as mentioned Peter Hambro has not provided any details on the potential scale of operations there. Tokur and Yamal are at present no more than an option on future growth for the company.

Pokrovsky/Pioneer: company's bread and butter

The Pokrovsky mine was opened in 1999 and has shown very good results since then. Despite its low grade, the ore has been easy to process – keeping expenses very low, at an operating cash cost of $107/oz in 2004. Peter Hambro intends to expand the mine by raising milling capacity at its smelter from the current 1.5mn tons of ore throughput to 2.2mn tons by the end of 2006. Additionally, given the mill facility is very scalable the company estimates the cost of adding capacity will be very low; at just $4mn. In addition to the milling operation Peter Hambro also has several heap leach pads, which process low grade ore.

Pioneer, only 40km from Pokrovsky, is the company's most immediate source of output growth. Similar in type and scale to Pokrovsky, Pioneer is essentially an add-on ore body that is likely to have similar operating results. Peter Hambro is currently preparing a feasibility study and we do not expect any production before 2008; however, what is clear is that the adjacent infrastructure and regional operating experience should reduce the Pioneer mine's start-up costs.

Malomir: a source for growth

Earlier this year Peter Hambro won the auction to the Malomir deposit in the Amur region. The company had long coveted this license and bought adjacent exploration licenses several years ago, thus heading into the auction well prepared. In addition to its 1.5mn oz of C2 resources, Malomir has 4.3mn oz of P1 classified gold, which with additional exploration could be confirmed at a higher level and form the basis of a very large mining operation. Although the company has yet to detail a development plan for the ore body, we suspect that an operation not unlike Pokrovsky (large open-pit) is the most likely outcome.

OWNERSHIP

Peter Hambro has a significant management presence in its shareholder structure, with deputy chairman Pavel Maslovsky the largest single shareholder at 25%, followed by Peter Hambro with 8%. The company also has a wide institutional investor shareholder base and is quite liquid.

Shareholder structure: management has sizeable stake in company

FINANCIAL REVIEW AND FORECAST

Peter Hambro has enjoyed significant share price growth due to a smooth operational record, which has earned the company investor confidence. The key issue now is how it moves with the development of its various ore bodies, such as Malomir, which so far has no development plans. We have not included the development of Malomir or any other ore body in our valuation, as there is simply not enough information on which to base assumptions. Instead, the assets are assigned a per oz value based on the level of ore classification at each site.

Revenue

We assume that the Pokrovsky mine will continue to expand its operations although It is forecasted that its ore grade to begin to deteriorate as the company mined the best ore first. Despite the lack of established plans for Pioneer, due to the likely synergies with Pokrovsky and ongoing development, we have included it in our valuation and project the mine to open in 2008. It is forecasted that placer output at the Magadan operation to stay fairly constant throughout the forecast period, while the small amount of lode mining will exhaust its resources by 2010.

Total output for the company is forecast to increase from 209,000 oz in 2004 to about 660,000oz by 2009 and then slowly decline as ore grades continue to deteriorate at Pokrovsky.

Costs

Peter Hambro's costs have historically been very low and the company has achieved the necessary mine scale to keep them low at Pokrovsky; we anticipate Pioneer will replicate this performance. Cash costs for the company's main mine were $135/oz or 38.6% below the Russian average. The company's placer mining in Magadan, however, is not as competitive, as cash costs there were $307/oz in 2004 (which is not consolidated due to the JV nature of Peter Hambro's participation in Magadan). This operation brings in marginal revenue and income and so there is no reason to close it, but It is possible to note that that Peter Hambro does not plan to increase output from placer mining. We believe that while inflation and a strengthening ruble will put pressure on cost, the expansion of Pokrovsky (through Pioneer) will yield strong economies of scale that should help keep expenses in check.

Depreciation and amortization are forecast as yearly gold output as a percentage of total reserves per mine in operation, using our own forecast of the book value of each mine based on historical value and forecast capex. We note, however, that with resource levels increasing through exploration to extend the ore body, depreciation is set to remain low.

SG&A costs are forecast to be driven by inflation and the overall scale of the business, while interest expense are based on the company's debt level, which are quite low and on a net basis falling due to Peter Hambro's cash generation.

Gross margin: high and steady profitability

Source: Company data; Aton estimates

Capex

Peter Hambro's Pokrovsky mine has a lot of scalability, which reduces the need for capex to expand capacity. For example, the company plans to raise ore throughput at the mine by 46% from the current 1.5mn tons per annum to 2.2mn tons for only $4mn. It is forecasted that the entire cost of building the Pioneer mine at $130mn and project it to be completed in 2008. In relation to the Magadan operations, we envisage no expenditure beyond maintenance for the forecast period.

As we have noted before, without company guidance future capex is unknown beyond Peter Hambro's core operating assets. It is possible to note that that the total cost to bring a mine like Malomir into production will likely be in the vicinity of at least $100mn, due to its size and remote nature.

Balance sheet and cash flow

Peter Hambro's balance sheet is very lean with a net cash position of $13mn at the end of 1H05 boosted since then by a $140mn convertible bond issuance. Working capital for the company, as with most gold miners, is minimal. Given the lack of future development guidance from the company we have no way of forecasting future capex and therefore possible capital borrowing needs; however, we believe that the company has plenty of borrowing capacity plus the possibility of equity issuance to fund construction of a mine at Malomir, likely the next big ticket item. Operating cash flow is forecast to be $100mn from 2010F onward in our model.

1H05 results look good

Peter Hambro's 1H05 UK GAAP results showed strong revenue growth, up 56.6% y-o-y to $36mn, and a 58.3% y-o-y rise in operating costs to $28mn, resulting in a 50.9% y-o-y rise in operating income to $8mn. No further breakdown of operating costs was provided; however, we estimate that EBITDA was $12mn for the period, up 58% y-o-y.

Encouragingly, the company has significantly reduced its debt load, causing interest expenses to fall 53.6% y-o-y. Finally, 1H05 net income nearly doubled y-o-y to $6mn.

The company's balance sheet remained very lean, with a net cash position of $13mn, or roughly the same as at the start of the year.

Peter Hambro's total 1H05 attributable output was 102,178oz, up 37.5% y-o-y. The main driver of the growth was the Pokrovsky mine, whose output rose 40.9% y-o-y to 84,600oz. Additionally, Peter Hambro managed to keep down expenses, with cash operating costs of $149/oz, which is very low and makes the company one of the most cost effective miners in Russia today.

CONCLUSION: STABLE AND PROFITABLE; DETAIL ON FUTURE PLANS NEEDED

Peter Hambro is a solid company that has a proven track record of keeping costs low and increasing output. However, despite the company's success it has remained fairly unspecific on how it intends to grow in the future, despite the very broad goal of 1mn oz of output by 2009. Clearly the company has enough assets to move beyond the core Pokrovsky / Pioneer mining operation, and we believe Peter Hambro is far from exhausting its balance sheet in terms of debt raising opportunities, not to mention using equity. However, we have not yet seen this potential materialize in the form of new mine development plans or significant upgrades of the resource base to reserves. In the absence of this type of news flow, it appears that the market has priced Peter Hambro at its fair value. We have reviewed our model for the company and raised our end–2006 target price from $11.21 to $11.99. Our recommendation remains Hold.

SUMMARY FINANCIAL FORECAST

Income statement									
In $mn, UK GAAP	2002	2003	2004	2005F	2006F	2007F	2008F	2009F	2010F
Total revenues	23	44	62	90	108	111	195	240	233
COGS	-4	-24	-23	-28	-33	-39	-77	-97	-95
Gross profit	19	19	39	62	74	72	118	143	138
SG&A	-4	-7	-9	-13	-16	-19	-19	-24	-23
Other operating costs	0	4	5	6	6	3	3	3	3
EBITDA	14	16	34	54	65	57	102	122	118
Depreciation	-4	-5	-7	-8	-11	-9	-14	-18	-17
Operating income	10	10	28	46	54	48	88	104	100
Net interest expense	-1	-2	-2	-6	-4	-3	-5	-3	1
Other expense/income	0	1	-1	0	0	0	0	0	0
Pre-tax income	9	9	24	40	50	45	83	101	101
Income taxes	-1	-5	-8	-10	-12	-11	-20	-24	-24
Minority interest	-4	-1	-1	-1	-1	-1	-2	-2	-2
Net income	5	3	15	30	37	33	61	74	75
Balance sheet									
In $mn	2002	2003	2004	2005F	2006F	2007F	2008F	2009F	2010F
Cash and liquid assets	1	15	26	186	198	162	198	276	368
Inventories	8	11	16	18	18	16	30	39	37
Accounts receivable	5	14	18	15	18	18	32	39	38
Other current assets	0	0	0	0	0	0	0	0	0
Total current assets	14	40	59	219	233	196	260	354	443
Fixed assets	46	39	61	82	111	185	195	184	173
Investments	1	12	19	33	33	33	33	33	33
Other non-current assets	23	73	90	90	90	90	90	90	90
Total non-current	69	124	169	205	233	308	318	307	295

assets									
Total assets	83	164	228	424	466	504	578	661	739
Short-term debt	18	38	9	0	0	0	0	0	0
Accounts payable	1	2	2	3	4	4	7	9	9
Other current liabilities	3	2	4	4	5	5	10	13	12
Total current liabilities	23	42	16	7	9	9	17	22	21
Long-term debt	12	4	4	144	144	144	144	144	144
Other non-current liabilities	0	2	7	7	7	7	7	7	7
Total non-current liabilities	12	6	11	151	151	151	151	151	151
Minority interest	1	1	2	2	2	2	2	2	2
Total shareholders' equity	48	116	200	264	305	342	408	486	565
Total liabilities and equity	83	164	228	424	466	504	578	661	739
Cash flow statement									
In $mn, UK GAAP	2002	2003	2004	2005F	2006F	2007F	2008F	2009F	2010F
Net income	5	3	15	30	37	33	61	74	75
Depreciation	4	5	7	8	11	9	14	18	17
Changes in working capital	-8	-13	-7	1	-1	2	-20	-11	2
Other	5	9	-2	0	0	0	0	0	0
Operating cash flow	6	5	13	39	47	44	56	81	94
Capex	-12	-8	-20	-30	-39	-84	-24	-7	-6
Acquisitions	0	0	0	-14	0	0	0	0	0
Other	-1	-16	-25	4	4	4	4	4	4
Investing cash flow	-14	-23	-45	-40	-35	-80	-20	-3	-2
Change in debt	-	12	-29	131	0	0	0	0	0
Dividends	0	0	0	0	0	0	0	0	0
Other	8	20	98	30	0	0	0	0	0
Financing cash flow	8	32	69	161	0	0	0	0	0

Source: Company data; Aton estimates ***Source: Company data; Aton estimates***

DCF valuation of Peter Hambro Mining												
In $mn	2004	2005F	2006F	2007F	2008F	2009F	2010F	2011F	2012F	2013F	2014F	2015F
Revenue	62	90	108	111	195	240	233	226	220	213	207	201
Operating expenses	-28	-35	-43	-54	-93	-118	-115	-114	-111	-109	-107	-103
EBITDA	34	54	65	57	102	122	118	113	109	105	100	98
Depreciation	-7	-8	-11	-9	-14	-18	-17	-17	-18	-18	-18	-18
Operating income (EBIT including JV)	28	46	54	48	88	104	100	95	91	87	82	79
Less: Income taxes		-11	-13	-12	-21	-25	-24	-23	-22	-21	-20	-19

Less: Capex	-30	-39	-84	-24	-7	-6	-6	-6	-6	-6	-6
Less: Changes in WC	1	-1	2	-20	-11	2	1	1	1	1	1
Plus: Depreciation	8	11	9	14	18	17	17	18	18	18	18
Free cash flow	15	12	-37	37	79	89	85	82	79	76	74
Discount factor (WACC)		1.00	1.12	1.25	1.39	1.56	1.74	1.94	2.17	2.42	2.71
Present value of future FCF		12	-33	30	57	57	49	42	36	31	27
Total PV of future FCF	309										

Calculation of terminal value		Cost of equity calculation		Forecast beta calculation	
Terminal free cash flow, $mn	74	Long term risk free rate	5.5%	Avg monthly trading volume*	Forecast
Terminal growth rate	5%	Russian country risk premium	1.5%	(com. + pref.), $mn	beta
Terminal discount rate	11.7%	Russian risk free rate	7.0%	> 100	1.00
Terminal value, $mn	1,159	Standard equity premium	4.0%	10-100	1.25
PV of terminal value, $mn	428	Excess RTS volatility factor	1.00	1-10	1.50
		Russian equity market premium	4.0%	0.1-1	2.00
Target price calculation		Forecast beta	1.25	< 0.1	3.00
		Levered forecast beta	1.39	*Based on trailing 3 month total dollar	
PV of terminal value + future FCF, $ mn	738	Cost of equity	12.5%	volume on RTS, MICEX and ADR	
				markets	
Less: Net debt (cash), $mn (end 05F)	-42				
Less: Minority interest, $mn	2	WACC calculation		Capital structure, $mn	
Exploration value, $mn	126	Gross debt as % of capitalization	12.6%	Gross debt (end 05F)	144
Total equity value, $mn	904	Cost of debt (after-tax)	5.8%	MV of common	1,000
		Equity as % of capitalization	87.4%		
Common shares outstanding, mn	75	Cost of equity	12.5%	Total MV of equity	1,000
		WACC	11.7%	Total capitalization	1,144
Fair value per common share, $	11.99				

HIGH RIVER GOLD: AT A BEND IN RIVER

High River Gold is a Canadian-based medium-sized gold miner with assets in Russia and Burkino Faso (formerly Upper Volta) in West Africa. The company's core asset is an 84% stake in Buryatzoloto, one of Russia's largest gold mining operations. The company also has two late stage development projects that will start generating cash next year, as well as a pipeline of exploration projects in Russia and Burkino Faso. Despite High River lacking a major headline asset to act as a catalyst, the company has solid operations that appear to be attractively valued.

OVERVIEW: SOLID, IF UNINSPIRING, ASSETS

High River Gold is a Canadian company that has operations in Russia and Burkino Faso (formerly Upper Volta) in West Africa. The company is listed in Canada under the ticker HRG CN and its main asset is an 84% stake in Buryatzoloto, which operates in Russia's Buryat region. High River's Canadian operation was closed at the end of last year due to resource depletion and a similar fate awaits Buryatzoloto in several years time. To replace this lost output, High River will open two new mines next year and has a pipeline of exploration projects that are promising, but still in the early stage. By 2007 the company is forecast to have annual output of more than 300,000oz.

OPERATIONS AND ASSETS

High River currently has only one operating asset since its Canadian mine was closed down at the end of last year. As a result, Buryatzoloto will contribute all of the company's gold output for 2005 and the key year is shaping up to be 2006, when it brings two new mines, one in Russia and one in Burkino Faso, on line.

High River's total 2004 output was 178,905oz, with Buryatzoloto making up 87% of that and the remainder coming from the since-closed New Britannia mine in Canada. The company's growth is due to come from two sources

1) Burkino Faso, where High River has gained significant exposure and which should produce results in 1H06 with the opening of the Taparko mine, with forecast output of 140,000oz per annum when it hits full production capacity in 2009.

2) The Berezitovy mine in Russia's Chita region, due to begin operating in 2H06, which should produce about 100,000oz per annum. Although Berezitovy is slated to replace the output from Buryatzoloto in Russia, High River's main source of growth moving forward is set to be from Burkino Faso.

Output: New Britannia closed; HRG to rely solely on Buryatzoloto to 2006

Source: Company data

The company's reserves and resources at its Berezitovy and Burkino Faso projects have been audited to Western standards, while its existing Buryatzoloto mine uses the Russian classification system. At the end of 2004, Russia was clearly Highland River's main exposure in terms of resource base. However, in terms of the exploration activities High River has lined up, most new projects are in Burkino Faso, and the picture of resource location could change significantly in the event a new find to resource classification standards.

High River is currently establishing the Taparko-Bouroum mine in Burkina Faso, which is set to begin operating in 1H06 with projected annual gold output of 140,000oz when it hits full capacity in 2009. Aside from being a major growth driver for the company in the short term, the mine is also expected to be the core asset of expanding operations in the country. To this end, High River acquired the Jilbey Gold Exploration company in Burkina Faso this summer, which at this stage has gold resources of 150,000oz in a neighboring area.

However, High River plans to increase exploration work at the Jilbey site to prove more resources and the preliminary findings are highly prospective. Additionally, the acquisition makes High River the premier mining company in the country and a key local partner for any potential newcomers.

Total reserves and resources: Russia the company's main exposure

Source: Company data

Buryatzoloto: leading producer, consolidation to continue?

High River's mainstay asset is Buryatzoloto, which is already a mature gold producer that operates two mines: Irokinda and Zun-Holba. Both of these mines have been producing for more than 10 years and It is forecasted that Ironkinda to run out of resources by 2007 and Zun-Holba by 2011. Due to the age of the mines and resulting lower grade ore that is processed, output has been declining and costs rising. The average cash cost for Buryatzoloto was $174/oz in 2003, $223/oz in 2004 and the company reported 1H05 cash costs of $239/oz.

Over the course of 2004 the company conducted two equity swaps to consolidate control over Buryatzoloto, which raised its equity stake from 54% to 84%. The swap ratios used imply that the shareholders performing the swap were diluted in value, although It is possible to note that that there were several classes of Buryatzoloto equity used, so a straight one for one valuation probably overestimates the true value of the Russian mine's equity; additionally, High River is a more liquid security than Buryatzoloto. Currently, there remains a 16% minority stake in Buryatzoloto that has not been offered swap terms and although the company has mentioned it wants to continue with consolidation, no proposals have been made to date. The future really depends on the intent of High River management, since the life span of Buryatzoloto's operations is limited, meaning its equity is losing value with time.

Arbitrage between HRG, Buryztzoloto on past swap ratios: not enough liquidity

Deal date	HRG price, US$	BRZL price, US$	Deal swap ratio	Implied value of BRZL from swap, US$	Value dilution
24.8.04	1.03	16.85	11.76	12.15	-27.9%
9.12.04	1.23	16.65	11.76	14.43	-13.3%
Current price (9.11.05)	1.05	12.00	11.76	11.43	-4.8%

Source: Company data; Bloomberg; Aton estimates

Other Russian assets: Berizitovy to provide near term growth

To replace the declining production at Buryatzoloto, High River has been developing the Berezitovy ore field, with production slated to begin in 2H06 and projected annual output of about 100,000oz. Berezitovy is in the Amur region in Eastern Siberia, and gives High River a foothold in a major gold growth area alongside names like Peter Hambro and now Polyus, which recently entered the region. We would not be surprised if High River expanded its presence in the region by buying further licenses, as the company seeks to expand on a mill operation due to be opened in 2006.

Finally, earlier this year High River acquired the license to the Novophirskoye deposit in the Altai region. Novophirskoye is an early stage exploration project with P2 resources of 1.6mn oz (including silver as gold equivalent). Currently High River is exploring the area.

OWNERSHIP

High River's shares are listed in Canada (HRG CN) and the company has not been averse to using equity as an acquisition currency, putting it ahead of its Russian peers in capital markets sophistication. In 2005, High River raised its ownership in Buryatzoloto from 54% to 84% through a share swap and the company also bought out 100% of Jilbey using shares. Management owns just 2% of the company, but despite the large free float, High River is not particularly liquid due to its relatively small size.

Shareholder structure: insiders do not own much

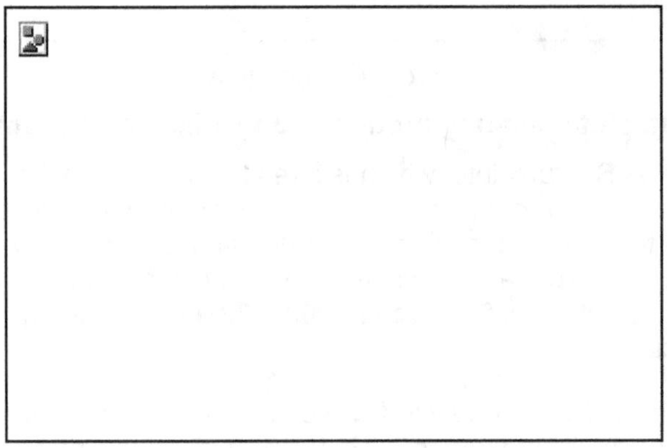

Source: Company data

FINANCIAL REVIEW AND FORECAST

High River's 2005 revenue will be exclusively from Buryatzoloto and by 2006 we project this to widen to include Berezitovy and Taparko. The key issue for the company is managing the short period of complete reliance on one revenue source. So far there has been no problems; however, significant company risk will be removed once the two new mines come on line next year.

Revenue

We assume that Buryatzoloto will run out of resources and its last contribution to the top line come in 2011. Therefore there is a "hump" of revenue between now and then, as the company's two new mines come on line before Buryatzoloto is depleted. Total output volumes are expected to rise from the 178,905oz attributable in 2004 to a peak of 330,000oz in 2007. Rising output at Tapako will then help maintain output levels at approximately 300,000oz for the company as a whole. Given the small size of High River's assets, there is no single large ore field that will fundamentally shift the company's profile.

Production by mine: projected major boost from Africa

mn oz

Buryatzoloto

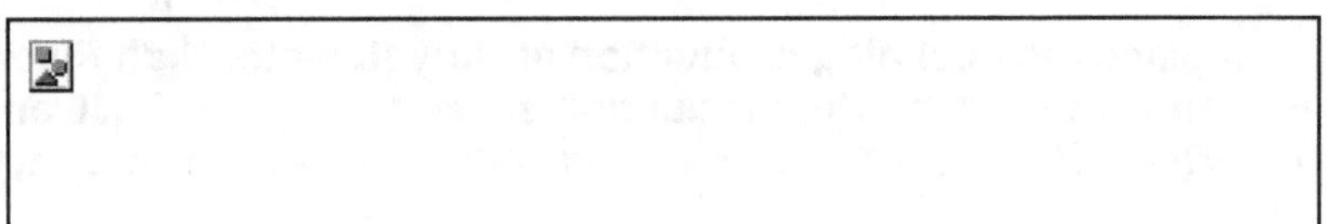

Berezitovy

Taparko

New Britannia

Source: Company data; Aton estimates

Costs

High River's costs are forecast to be higher y-o-y in 2005 due to the maturity of the company's operating mines in Buryatzoloto. This cost situation will not be helped in 2006, as It is forecasted that that the first year of operations for both Taparko and Berezitovy to see higher costs, as is usual with new mines.

For 2004 the company's average cash cost was $257/oz, while in 2005 it is forecast to be $270/oz, high due to ore grade deterioration at Buryatzoloto, the company's only producing asset for this year.

We have used High River's cash costs for each of its mines; It is possible to note that that the company's cost forecast for Berezitovy is conservative and in line with average costs in Russia. Depreciation and amortization, not included in cash costs, are based on the amount of golf produced relative to the total resource of the mine as a proportion of the capitalized value of each mine.

SG&A costs are forecast to be driven by inflation and the overall scale of the business. It is possible to note that that High River has very low SG&A costs, especially considering that the company operates in two countries that are far from corporate headquarters. Income expense is set to be modest as the company's capital needs are also modest, implying low debt levels, which are a function of the forecast balance sheet and cash flow from year to year. Although High River operates in many different jurisdictions, It is possible that the company will pay Russia's statutory 24% income tax rate.

Capex

It is forecasted that High River to spend $68mn in capex this year and given its long term projects are due to come on line next year, projected capex in the near- to medium term is low, as most of the development cost for the two mines will have been spent by the end of this year. Going forward, investment depends on whether the company can find and develop an economically-feasible ore field from its exploration pipeline. We suspect that it will, with the most likely area for expansion being new ore fields in Burkino Faso adjacent to Taparko. As such, future capex for this potential growth should be small, as existing infrastructure could be harnessed.

Balance sheet and cash flow

High River's balance sheet is forecast to be small as it has low levels of debt and little working capital (common to most gold producers). Given the current slate of development projects and new mine openings, combined with the company's existing cash and expected cash flows, we do not see a need for the issuance of new equity or debt in the near future as High River has the financial resources it needs. Therefore, operating cash flow is expected to rise steadily throughout the forecast period from $15mn in 2004 to a forecast $32mn in 2010.

1H05 results bring no surprises

High River's 1H05 results showed revenue fell 13.3% to $33mn due to a decline in production following the closure of the Canadian operation late last year. EBITDA came in at $9mn, down 12.8% y-o-y and the company posted a small $1mn loss. Buryatzoloto's output was virtually flat at 73,802oz gold produced at a total cash cost of $265/oz, or 5.2% higher than its 1H04 level. High River's full year results are set to be mediocre as the key catalyst events for the company is the opening of the Berezitovy project in Russia and Taparko-Bouroum project in Burkina Faso, which are slated for 2006.

High River had a net cash position of $18mn at the beginning of the year, which turned into a $16mn net debt position on the back of large $40mn capex. We project capex to be of roughly the same magnitude in 2H05 as Berezitovy and Taparko are nearing completion.

1H05 income statement highlights are of limited importance			
CA GAAP, $mn	1H04	1H05	Y-o-y %
Revenue	38	33	-13.3%
COGS	-30	-27	-10.9%
Gross profit	8	6	-22.0%
Gross margin	21.0%	18.9%	
SG&A	-1	-2	118.1%
Operating profit	7	4	-44.6%
EBITDA	10	9	-12.8%
EBITDA margin	26.1%	26.2%	
Interest income	-1	-1	-5.4%
Other non-operating expense	-1	-2	157.0%
Income tax	-2	-2	7.8%
Minority interest	-2	0	-81.1%
Net income	2	-1	-159.0%
Net margin	5.2%	-3.6%	

Source: Company data; Aton estimates

CONCLUSION: SOLID, IF MODEST, COMPANY WITH CLEAR FOCUS

High River has chosen a path of small- to medium sized projects that have lower execution risk; this strategy that has paid off operationally with steady progress in developing new mines. However, High River also lacks a headline project that could capture investor attention in an increasingly crowded universe of small gold mining companies. The company is at a turning point as it closed down one of its two operations in 2004 and will only start its new mines in 2006. Although we do not envision any problems with this period of exposure to one revenue source, It is possible to note that that there does not appear to be a pipeline of new development projects to complement and support the two new mines once they begin operations.

The key events to look for will be any significant discoveries of new gold, particularly in Burkino Faso, where High River has been adding to its already extensive license portfolio. What we like about the company is a clear development plan that has taken projects from the exploration to production phase. High River's business model is simple and its growth demonstrable. With this report we initiate coverage of High River Gold with a Buy recommendation and an end-2006 target price of $1.22.

SUMMARY FINANCIAL FORECAST

Income statement									
In $mn, CA GAAP	2002	2003	2004	2005F	2006F	2007F	2008F	2009F	2010F
Total revenues	53	69	74	70	127	143	120	130	130
COGS	-33	-46	-53	-43	-71	-89	-73	-79	-79
Gross profit	20	23	21	28	56	55	47	51	51
SG&A	-2	-4	-4	-4	-7	-7	-7	-8	-8
Other operating costs	-4	-3	-2	-4	-4	-4	-4	-4	-4
EBITDA	14	16	14	20	45	44	36	39	39
Depreciation	-8	-8	-7	-10	-12	-12	-9	-10	-11
Operating income	6	8	7	9	33	32	26	29	28
Net interest expense	-2	-3	-3	-1	-2	-2	-1	0	1

Other expense/income	0	-10	0	0	0	0	0	0	0
Pre-tax income	5	-5	5	8	31	30	26	29	29
Income taxes	-2	-4	-2	-2	-7	-7	-6	-7	-7
Minority interest	-2	-3	-2	0	0	0	0	0	0
Net income	1	-12	0	6	23	23	19	22	22

Balance sheet

In $mn, CA GAAP	2002	2003	2004	2005F	2006F	2007F	2008F	2009F	2010F
Cash and liquid assets	6	13	31	40	41	69	91	118	146
Inventories	10	11	10	11	17	20	16	18	18
Accounts receivable	4	5	6	6	10	12	10	11	11
Other current assets	1	1	0	1	1	1	1	1	1
Total current assets	22	31	47	57	69	102	119	148	176
Fixed assets	57	53	50	107	117	110	109	104	98
Investments	0	0	0	0	0	0	0	0	0
Other non-current assets	15	24	60	82	82	82	82	82	82
Total non-current assets	72	77	110	189	199	192	191	186	180
Total assets	94	107	156	246	267	294	309	333	356
Short-term debt	9	0	0	9	0	0	0	0	0
Accounts payable	5	6	11	9	14	17	14	15	15
Other current liabilities	0	5	3	4	6	8	6	7	7
Total current liabilities	14	11	14	22	20	24	20	21	22
Long-term debt	29	12	9	44	44	44	44	44	44
Other non-current liabilities	3	26	26	26	26	26	26	26	26
Total non-current liabilities	31	38	35	70	70	70	70	70	70
Minority interest	22	28	32	12	12	12	12	12	12
Total shareholders' equity	26	30	75	142	165	188	207	230	252
Total liabilities and equity	94	107	156	246	267	294	309	333	356

Cash flow statement

In $mn, CA GAAP	2002	2003	2004	2005F	2006F	2007F	2008F	2009F	2010F
Net income	1	-12	0	6	23	23	19	22	22
Depreciation	8	8	7	10	12	12	9	10	11
Changes in working capital	0	4	5	-3	-4	-1	1	-1	0
Other	1	9	3	0	0	0	0	0	0
Operating cash flow	10	9	15	14	31	34	30	32	33
Capex	-12	-22	-37	-68	-22	-5	-8	-5	-5
Acquisitions	0	0	0	0	0	0	0	0	0
Other	0	0	0	-5	0	0	0	0	0

Investing cash flow	-12	-22	-37	-73	-22	-5	-8	-5	-5
Change in debt	-	-25	-3	44	-9	0	0	0	0
Dividends	0	0	0	0	0	0	0	0	0
Other	9	45	43	24	0	0	0	0	0
Financing cash flow	9	20	40	68	-9	0	0	0	0

Source: Company data; Aton estimates

DCF valuation of High River Gold

In $mn	2004	2005F	2006F	2007F	2008F	2009F	2010F	2011F	2012F	2013F	2014F	2015F
Revenue	74	70	127	143	120	130	130	121	102	103	103	104
Operating expenses	-60	-51	-82	-100	-84	-91	-91	-85	-73	-74	-75	-75
EBITDA	14	20	45	44	36	39	39	36	29	29	29	29
Depreciation	-7	-10	-12	-12	-9	-10	-11	-11	-9	-10	-12	-14
Operating income (EBIT)	7	9	33	32	26	29	28	25	20	19	17	15
Less: Income taxes		-2	-8	-8	-6	-7	-7	-6	-5	-4	-4	-4
Less: Capex		-68	-22	-5	-8	-5	-5	-4	-4	-4	-4	-4
Less: Changes in WC		-3	-4	-1	1	-1	0	1	1	0	0	0
Plus: Depreciation		10	12	12	9	10	11	11	9	10	12	14
Free cash flow		-53	11	30	23	27	27	27	21	20	21	21
Discount factor (WACC)			1.00	1.12	1.25	1.39	1.55	1.73	1.93	2.16	2.41	2.69
Present value of future FCF			11	27	18	19	18	15	11	9	9	8

Total PV of future FCF 145

Calculation of terminal value		Cost of equity calculation		Forecast beta calculation	
Terminal free cash flow, $mn	21	Long term risk free rate	5.5%	Avg monthly trading volume*	Forecast
Terminal growth rate	5%	Russian country risk premium	1.5%	(com. + pref.), $mn	beta
Terminal discount rate	11.6%	Russian risk free rate	7.0%	> 100	1.00
Terminal value, $mn	336	Standard equity premium	4.0%	10-100	1.25
PV of terminal value, $mn	125	Excess RTS volatility factor	1.00	1-10	1.50
		Russian equity market premium	4.0%	0.1-1	2.00
Target price calculation		Forecast beta	1.25	< 0.1	3.00

		Levered forecast beta	1.46	*Based on trailing 3 month total dollar	
PV of terminal value + future FCF, $ mn	270	Cost of equity	12.8%	volume on RTS, MICEX and ADR	
				markets	
Less: Net debt (cash), $mn (end 05F)	13				
Less: Minority interest, $mn	12	WACC calculation		Capital structure, $mn	
Exploration value, $mn	18	Gross debt as % of capitalization	18.1%	Gross debt (end 05F.)	53
Total equity value, $mn	263	Cost of debt (after-tax)	6.1%	MV of common	240
		Equity as % of capitalization	81.9%		
Common shares outstanding, mn	216	Cost of equity	12.8%	Total MV of equity	240
		WACC	11.6%	Total capitalization	293
Fair value per common share, $	1.22				

HIGHLAND GOLD

Highland Gold has a massive resource base with high grade gold ore, but the AIM-traded company has until now failed to demonstrate its cash flow/output growth potential due to a run of management and operational problems. However, a management reshuffle has restored investor confidence in the battered business, and it appears that the problems of the past are over, paving the way for steady growth and improved financials. With resources second only to Polyus, and good quality ore, it now appears to be only a question of time before Highland Gold starts assuming its rightful place in the Russian gold universe.

OVERVIEW: REBUILDING CREDIBILITY, OVERHAULING OPERATIONS

Since we initiated coverage of Highland Gold in July 2004, the company has had its share of troubles, from faulty mill construction to poor mine planning and even extreme weather conditions. Now, it seems that the UK registered company, which trades on AIM under the ticker HGM LN, is finally back on its feet again and is set to realize growth plans set out over two years ago. A key development is a reshuffling of management, which has brought in experienced personnel from other gold miners to replace the old team, which was relatively new to business development and prone to making mistakes. Highland Gold hired key personnel from Kinross and Fleming Partners, as well as shuffling the BoD to help turn the company around and build confidence with investors. This move seems to have been embraced, as the stock is up 53.7% since the full damage for 1H05 was announced in August.

The company's main strategy has been to acquire cheaply brownfield sites that still have significant resources left unmined. While in theory this appears a wise and low-cost way to enter the business quickly and ramp up production in a short time, in practice the brownfield sites have been problematic due to past neglect and unforeseen start-up costs. The real incongruity of the company's business model, however, is that while near term cash flow is based on these types of projects, real output growth hinges on a huge greenfield site, Mayskoye, which rivals Bema's Kupol deposit.

OPERATIONS AND ASSETS

All of Highland Gold's assets are in Russia and the company has aggressive plans to raise production from the current 200,000oz level to a forecast 700,000oz by 2011. Highland's core operating mine is MNV, which is located in the Khabarovsk region and produced 195,026oz in 2004 – or 98% of the 199,896oz total. MNV's cash costs for 2004 were $187/oz, up 17.6% y-o-y, while 1H05 cash costs rose to $318/oz due to operational problems. With the new management team and better mining practices, we expect 2H05 cash costs to revert back to 2004 levels. The company also started its second mine, Darasun, in 2004 but faulty mill engineering essentially halted operations soon after opening and this was only fully fixed by the end of summer 2005. It is forecasted that that the company will make 197,000oz of gold in 2005, thus losing any growth that was earlier planned and falling far short of its original goal of 270,000oz.

Highland Gold has a well ordered basket of projects to complement its core MNV. Darasun opened last year and the company's third mine, Novoshirokinskoye, is set to open in 2006. At full capacity these two assets should add about 145,000oz of production to Highland's total. Additionally, Highland Gold, together with strategic partner Barrick is set to develop the Taseevskoye deposit on a 50/50 basis. This brownfield asset has 3.4mn oz of JORC audited gold resources and potentially could produce 200,000oz annually, although an exact timeframe for development has yet to be announced.

2004 output: MNV was the key mine, and is set to remain so moving forward

Source: Company data

Highland Gold has an impressive portfolio of ore fields, each of which is large and fairly high grade, although the company's key project is Mayskoye, which accounts for 52% of the total resource base.

Total reserves and resources: waiting for Mayskoye

MNV: company workhorse

MNV is the company's core asset and has been the main cash generator for the company. The mine was developed during the Soviet period, although throughout the 1990s it was almost inactive due to a lack of management at the site. Highland Gold acquired the asset and turned it around, raising production from 48,625oz in 1999 to 194,000oz by 2003. The cash flow generated from this mine financed the development work of the company's two near-term projects, Darasun, which went into operation in 2004 and Novoshirokinskoye, scheduled to begin gold output in 2006.

MNV produced 195,026 oz in 2004 but due to operational problems in 1H05 (extremely bad weather and higher than expected stripping) output for full-2005 is forecast to be 150,000oz. Fundamentally, the mistakes of the first half that can be attributed to company management appear to have been fixed, and output going forward should be around 200,000oz annually.

Chita: Highland Gold's main asset base

Highland Gold has taken the sensible step of acquiring several assets all in one region and all relatively close to one another, making administration easier and cheaper. The assets in question are Darasun, Novoshirokinskoye and Taseevskoye, all located in the Chita region in Eastern Siberia and all brownfield projects. Darasun was originally slated to be a fairly easy project that would contribute 120,000oz annually. The site has been mined for over 100 years and there is significant infrastructure already in place both above ground and below.

However, the construction of a new mill at the mine encountered significant problems, and although the asset went into operation in the summer of 2004, it was a year before it began to work near its planned capacity. Novoshirokinskoye, a short distance from Darasun, was originally planned as a lead/zinc mine before Highland Gold acquired it, having realized the high gold content at the site. The site is expected to become operational in 2006. Taseevskoye was acquired in late 2004 and is split on a 50/50 JV basis with strategic partner Barrick. The site was previously owned by a junior mining company that completed a feasibility study in 1997 but ran out of money before it could begin operations. To date, however, no announcements detailing expected development time for this project have been made.

Mayskoye: cornerstone of planned growth

Mayskoye is a greenfield ore site located in the Chukotka region. The site is a key company driver and the main source of the excitement about Highland Gold's growth potential. With a high 11.5 g/ton grade of gold and about 9mn oz of resources, Mayskoye is about 70% larger than Bema's Kupol, making it Highland Gold's crown jewel and the cornerstone of its planned future growth. Mayskoye has difficult metallurgy, and there is only minimal silver, so there will not be large byproduct credits to reduce gold cash costs. However, there are few +9mn oz greenfield sites in the world and the market has yet to appreciate the size of this deposit.

The development plan for Mayskoye calls for the construction of the mine and mill by the end of 2007 with production beginning in 2008. The mill will have a planned throughput of 1mn tons of ore annually, which should result in an average annual output of 325,000oz of gold.

OWNERSHIP

Highland Gold has a diverse shareholding structure. Although free float at 45% is enough to ensure market liquidity, we believe that minority investors benefit from having a large financial investor in the form of Fleming Family and an industry giant in the form of Barrick as the key shareholders.

Shareholder structure

Management

FINANCIAL REVIEW AND FORECAST

Highland Gold's financial performance for 2005 is expected to be lackluster due to the problems of the first half, as essentially an entire year of potential growth has been lost. However, the key determining factor will be how much the company has managed to recover in 2H05. Considering that both MNV and Darasun have been running at full capacity since the beginning of the second half, It is forecasted that that the company has adequate cash and financial stability to realize its interrupted growth plans

Revenue

For 2004 almost all of the company's revenue came from MNV, a situation that should change somewhat in 2005 as Darasun is set to produce about 50,000oz on top of MNV's 150,000oz forecast. Revenue diversification should continue in 2006 with Novoshirokinskoye coming on line. However, the real boost to the top line in our forecast occurs when Mayskoye is up and running – which we expect in 2008 – at which point the company is expected to produce 535,000oz.

Costs

Highland Gold's cash costs for 2004 were $215/oz, and though this rose 70% to $318/oz in 1H05, we expect a decline in 2H05 due to operational improvements to put average cash costs for the year at $320/oz. As Highland Gold consists of a collection of new mines that have staggered opening dates across our forecast period, production cash costs for the company as a whole vary from year to year. MNV, Darasun and Novoshirokinskoye are expected to have the same cash cost as the Russian industry in general at around $220/oz$240/oz over the course of their mining life. The company should see a fall in costs once the low cost Mayskoye mine comes on line in 2008. We expect Mayskoye to have a cash cost of $164/oz when it is running at full capacity in 2011.

SG&A costs are expected to rise with inflation and overall company growth, although It is possible to note that that Highland Gold already has a substantial management staff, which should be able to run the development projects the company has once they go into production.

Capex

Due to Highland Gold's high growth profile, significant levels of capex will be needed in the future, particularly as Mayskoye progresses. The capex spend for 2005 is forecast to be $66mn, and though this rises to $91mn in 2006 in our model, total spend should decline significantly as mine development progresses. Maintenance capex based on existing asset development plans should be in the neighborhood of $11mn annually.

Balance sheet and cash flow

Highland Gold's balance sheet is one of the most highly leveraged among the businesses profiled in this report. The company issued ruble denominated debt in 1H05 (which has been hedged into dollars), and has a large credit facility for financing mine development. Total gross debt was $85mn at end-1H05, although the company had a cash position of $79mn due to equity issuance. It is possible to note that that given Highland Gold's capex plans to fund growth, internally generated cash flow will not be sufficient for its needs; we thus forecast the use of project financing to fund the gap, which we list as long term debt.

As Highland Gold progressively opens more mines, operating cash flow is expected to rise as well. Additionally, since the company is incurring development costs without revenue to offset it from these mines, once the projects do open the net effect is an acceleration of cash flow.

Highland Gold's 1H05 UK GAAP results showed revenue slumped 25.9% y-o-y to $28mn due to a decline in production that was partially offset by higher gold prices, averaging $425/oz in 1H05 vs. $395/oz in 1H04. EBITDA plummeted 88.1% to $2mn due to a slight increase in COGS and lower revenue. On a brighter note, SG&A items fell 5.7% y-o-y, suggesting the company was at least able to rein in management costs for the period.

Interest expenses rose 35.2% y-o-y to $3mn amid rising debt at the company. Highland Gold posted a $7mn loss in 1H05 vs. net income of $7mn in 1H04.

Income statement reflects difficult 1H05

In $mn, UK GAAP	1H04	1H05	Chg. y-o-y %
Revenue	38	28	-26.0%
COGS	-23	-25	11.4%
Gross profit	15	3	-81.4%
Gross margin	40.3%	10.1%	
SG&A	-5	-4	-5.7%
Operating income	11	-1	N.M.
EBITDA	14	2	-88.1%
EBITDA margin	36.4%	5.8%	
Interest expense	-3	-3	35.2%
Other non-operating expense	0	-1	N.M.
Income tax	-2	-1	-20.8%
Net income	7	-7	N.M.
Net margin	18.1%	-24.3%	

Source: Company data

On the balance sheet, Highland had net debt of $38mn and a cash position of $79mn, with no looming liquidity issues. Capex actually fell 17% y-o-y in 1H05 to $25mn, due to feasibility study problems at Mayskoye and Novoshirokinskoye (expected to be resolved by the year-end), but remained at a significant level.

Highland sold 63,333oz of gold in 1H05, down 32.7% y-o-y due to operating issues at its key MNV mine – mainly extremely bad weather combined with higher than expected stripping costs due to poor operational planning. The result was a rise in cash costs of 64.6% to $349/oz. The interim report notes that the problems encountered at MNV have been addressed, and there has been a management reshuffle, as outlined above.

Highland Gold 1H05 operational highlights			
1H04		1H05	Y-o-y %
Gold sold, oz	94,055	63,333	-32.7%
MNV cash cost	212	349	64.6%

CONCLUSION: TURNAROUND APPEARS TO BE COMPLETE

Highland Gold has faced a series of problems over the past year that have severely dented both the company's growth plans and overall management credibility. However, new key professionals have replaced the old team and it appears that company has turned a corner. Granted, an entire year of growth has been lost, but Highland appears to have learned from its mistakes and we believe it is better suited to tackle problems in the future. Although the near term development projects in the Chita region are substantial, clearly all eyes are on Mayskoye, which has the potential to vault Highland Gold into position as a premier global mining company from its status as a niche Russian player.

We are raising our end-2006 target price for the company from $5.43 to $5.92, with current implied upside of 44%. Our recommendation remains unchanged at Buy.

SUMMARY FINANCIAL FORECAST

Income statement									
In $mn, UK GAAP	2002	2003	2004	2005F	2006F	2007F	2008F	2009F	2010F
Total revenues	27	72	82	88	158	146	230	230	249
COGS	-16	-31	-45	-65	-84	-89	-119	-122	-132
Gross profit	11	41	37	23	74	56	111	108	117
SG&A	-3	-8	-11	-11	-15	-15	-18	-19	-19
EBITDA	8	32	26	12	59	41	93	89	98
Depreciation	-1	-4	-7	-9	-19	-24	-37	-39	-40
Operating income	6	28	19	3	40	18	55	50	58
Net interest expense	-1	-4	-6	-5	-8	-13	-14	-12	-8
Other expense/income	2	0	1	0	0	0	0	0	0
Pre-tax income	7	25	14	-2	32	5	42	38	50
Income taxes	-2	-7	-9	1	-8	-1	-10	-9	-12
Minority interest	0	0	0	0	0	0	0	0	0
Net income	5	18	5	-2	24	3	32	29	38
Balance sheet									
In $mn, UK GAAP	2002	2003	2004	2005F	2006F	2007F	2008F	2009F	2010F
Cash and liquid assets	27	5	41	30	5	10	10	10	23
Inventories	13	28	42	49	52	56	78	81	86
Accounts receivable	8	17	21	21	38	35	55	55	60
Other current assets	4	8	18	15	26	24	38	38	41
Total current assets	51	59	122	115	121	126	182	184	211
Fixed assets	52	146	224	286	358	390	374	356	327
Investments									

Other non-current assets	0	-8	-9	-9	-9	-9	-9	-9	-9
Total non-current assets	52	138	215	277	349	381	365	347	318
Total assets	103	196	337	392	470	507	547	531	529
Short-term debt	16	67	66	65	65	97	90	44	0
Accounts payable	4	4	11	14	20	22	30	31	33
Other current liabilities	5	6	7	9	14	14	20	21	22
Total current liabilities	24	77	84	88	99	133	141	96	55
Long-term debt	9	31	23	25	69	69	69	69	69
Other non-current liabilities	9	12	20	20	20	20	20	20	20
Total non-current liabilities	17	43	43	45	88	88	88	88	88
Minority interest	0	1	0	0	0	0	0	0	0
Total shareholders' equity	61	76	210	258	282	286	318	347	385
Total liabilities and equity	103	196	337	392	470	507	547	531	529
Cash flow statement									
In $mn, UK GAAP	2002	2003	2004	2005F	2006F	2007F	2008F	2009F	2010F
Net income	5	18	5	-2	24	3	32	29	38
Depreciation	1	4	7	9	19	24	37	39	40
Changes in working capital	0	-27	-20	1	-20	2	-41	-1	-10
Other	-4	13	18	0	0	0	0	0	0
Operating cash flow	2	8	10	9	23	29	28	67	69
Capex	-8	-57	-69	-66	-91	-56	-21	-21	-11
Acquisitions	-2	-12	-39	-5	0	0	0	0	0
Other	0	0	0	0	0	0	0	0	0
Investing cash flow	-10	-68	-108	-71	-91	-56	-21	-21	-11
Change in debt	-	73	-8	1	43	32	-7	-46	-44
Dividends	0	-3	-3	0	0	0	0	0	0
Other	25	-21	151	50	0	0	0	0	0
Financing cash flow	25	50	140	51	43	32	-7	-46	-44

Source: Company data; Aton estimates ***Source: Company data; Aton estimates***

DCF valuation of Highland Gold												
In $mn	2004	2005F	2006F	2007F	2008F	2009F	2010F	2011F	2012F	2013F	2014F	2015F
Revenue	82	88	158	146	230	230	249	288	295	302	309	317
Operating expenses	-56	-76	-99	-104	-137	-141	-151	-168	-173	-179	-184	-189
EBITDA	26	12	59	41	93	89	98	120	122	123	125	127
Depreciation	-7	-9	-19	-24	-37	-39	-40	-49	-52	-44	-43	-44
Operating income	19	3	40	18	55	50	58	72	70	79	82	83

(EBIT)											
Less: Income taxes	-1	-10	-4	-13	-12	-14	-17	-17	-19	-20	-20
Less: Capex	-66	-91	-56	-21	-21	-11	-11	-11	-11	-11	-11
Less: Changes in WC	1	-20	2	-41	-1	-10	-20	-4	-2	-3	-4
Plus: Depreciation	9	19	24	37	39	40	49	52	44	43	44
Free cash flow	-53	-62	-17	17	55	64	72	90	91	91	92
Discount factor (WACC)		1.00	1.12	1.25	1.40	1.56	1.74	1.95	2.18	2.44	2.72
Present value of future FCF		-62	-15	14	39	41	41	46	42	37	34
Total PV of future FCF	217										

Calculation of terminal value		Cost of equity calculation		Forecast beta calculation	
Terminal free cash flow, $mn	92	Long term risk free rate	5.5%	Avg monthly trading volume*	Forecast
Terminal growth rate	5%	Russian country risk premium	1.5%	(com. + pref.), $mn	beta
Terminal discount rate	11.8%	Russian risk free rate	7.0%	> 100	1.00
Terminal value, $mn	1,424	Standard equity premium	4.0%	10-100	1.25
PV of terminal value, $mn	730	Excess RTS volatility factor	1.00	1-10	1.50
		Russian equity market premium	4.0%	0.1-1	2.00
Target price calculation		Forecast beta	1.25	< 0.1	3.00
		Levered forecast beta	1.39	*Based on trailing 3 month total dollar	
PV of terminal value + future FCF, $ mn	947	Cost of equity	12.6%	volume on RTS, MICEX and ADR	
				markets	
Less: Net debt (cash), $mn (end 05F)	61				
Less: Minority interest, $mn	0	WACC calculation		Capital structure, $mn	
Exploration value	54	Gross debt as % of capitalization	13.1%	Gross debt (end 05F)	90
Total equity value, $mn	940	Cost of debt (after-tax)	6.5%	MV of common	600
		Equity as % of capitalization	86.9%		
Common shares outstanding, mn	159	Cost of equity	12.6%	Total MV of equity	600
		WACC	11.8%	Total capitalization	690

Fair value per common share, $	5.92

CELTIC RESOURCES

Celtic Resources is an Irish-based gold miner with assets in Russia and Kazakhstan. The company's operating assets are two medium sized mines in Kazakhstan that deploy cutting-edge technology. Celtic's Russian asset is a 50% stake in the Nezhdaninskoye gold field, one of the country's largest undeveloped ore bodies, which has significant infrastructure already built above ground. At this point, however, the main driver of the company is how it navigates the situation with Polyus, the recent buyer of the remaining 50% of Nezhdaninskoye and the spoiler of the long awaited Celtic-IG Alrosa merger deal. Until this issue is resolved, we believe fundamentals will play only a minor role in company's share price.

OVERVIEW: A WILD RIDE WITH NO END IN SIGHT

Celtic Resources has had the full gamut of experiences that can accompany a massive headline project, from laying plans that only possession of an in-place infrastructure story with high grade, massive resources can prompt, to the nightmare scenario of time lost, a change in development partner and predatory lawsuits. The project in question is Nezhdaninskoye, one of Russia's largest undeveloped ore fields, with an estimated resource base of 28mn oz. The site also has $400mn of built infrastructure that is waiting for a workforce and working capital to be put into operation.

Celtic Resources, which owns 50% of Nezhdaninskoye, negotiated for several years with the other 50% owner, IG Alrosa, to perform an asset for equity swap, thus bringing full control of the Russian site under one roof, easing development issues and ultimately helping garner a higher valuation for the asset. However, in a surprise move, Polyus, Norilsk Nickel's gold mining subsidiary and emerging domestic giant, acquired IG Alrosa's stake in Nezhdaninskoye together with other assets for $285mn in September, 2005. With Polyus in the picture and not Alrosa, we believe Celtic is unlikely to have anything more than a minor role in Nezhdaninskoye, certainly not operational control of the mine. Moreover, Polyus will soon be a publicly traded company that – unlike IG Alrosa – will not need Celtic as a capital market platform. Although both sides have made tepid comments about joint development of Nezhdaninskoye, there remains significant doubt about how they can work together. Although Polyus may try to force Celtic out by a combination of stalling development while at the same time requesting capital for the project, It is possible that in our model that the two will end up cooperating, although development will be delayed by several years.

OPERATIONS AND ASSETS

Celtic Resources operates in both Russia and Kazakhstan, and although the company has received most attention for its Russian asset, it has had the greatest operational success in Kazakhstan. The company brought into operation two greenfield mines, Zherek and Suzdal, and these now produce about 65,000oz a year. Furthermore, Suzdal employs some of the most advanced technology in the business, using biological elements to process gold ore. Total 2004 output for the company was 31,809oz and cash costs were $240/oz. The Kazakh assets are still in a transition stage due to new mines being opened, and It is forecasted that that they will hit full capacity output of 160,000oz annually by 2008. Nezhdaninskoye, Celtic's Russian asset, is potentially a major mine with its large resource base. However, It is possible to note that that the site was producing in the 1980s but was closed down. We suspect that the task of bringing Nezhdaninskoye into operation with a major capacity is formidable, with many unresolved issues that neither Celtic nor Polyus is ready to tackle.

The company's reserves and resources at Nezhdaninskoye under the Russian classification system total 15.4mn oz at C2 and above. According to JORC standard audits, which have not been performed on the entire ore body, resources are 7.4mn oz. Either standard indicates a very large ore body. At the end of 2004, Russia was clearly the company's main exposure in terms of resource base. Celtic's exploration pipeline is limited to further defining gold resources at existing sites, and considering the size of Nezhdaninskoye it had not focused on exploration when there was already so much proven gold in the ground.

Total reserves and resources: Nezhdaninskoye is company's major asset

Nezhdaninskoye potentially a great asset, but little clarity for now

Nezhdaninskoye, owned 50% through a vehicle called SVMC, is Celtic's core asset and the main reason why the company has been able to attract investor interest for the better part of a decade. Briefly, the Nezhdaninskoye gold field is located 440km east of Yakutsk in Russia's Sakha region. The site is extremely remote and home to the coldest temperature ever recorded in an inhabited region, -75° C. However, despite its inhospitable location the site is well worth the effort involved in mining it, as 15.4mn oz of C2 gold resources are located in fairly rich ore not far underground. In addition to gold, the Nezhdaninskoye site has significant silver content, with an average grade of 20.7g/ton. Because of this and the solid average gold grade level of 5.1g/ton, Nezhdaninskoye is expected to be a very cost competitive mine. The site was actually producing from 1975 to the late 1980s, although operations were limited as there were problems with low recovery rates, which modern technology in trial operations has raised to acceptable levels. Despite lying dormant from the late 1980s, there remains significant infrastructure, including a town, at the site. Celtic Resources estimated the replacement value of the assets in place at Nezhdaninskoye at $400mn, as the mine is essentially set to begin production with some working capital and a workforce.

After several years of negotiations with 50% partner IG Alrosa, the investment arm of the diamond mining giant of the same name, it seemed an equity swap to consolidate control over Nezhdaninskoye was imminent in 1H06. However, Polyus, Norilsk Nickel's gold mining subsidiary, acquired IG Alrosa's 50% stake in September, thwarting plans of bringing full control over the ore site under Celtic's roof. The deal was a major blow to Celtic, as it meant years of negotiations were wasted and also cast the future of the company's main asset in doubt. Despite a preliminary announcement that both companies were exploring how to bring Nezhdaninskoye forward, Norilsk Nickel has no history of joint development and does not need Celtic to bring the mine into operation. Ultimately, the most logical choice for Polyus is simply to stall development of Nezhdaninskoye, which it can afford to do considering its project pipeline at present, and wait for Celtic to sell.

In the meantime, the key issue is ownership, as Celtic Resources does not want to give up its stake to this prime asset and its strategic partner, Barrick, is keen to have exposure to the mine. Additionally, a past loan collateralized with part of Celtic's stake in the mine (30% of the company's 50% stake), has been at the center of several recent lawsuits, as Celtic is fighting against a Russian bank that claims the collateral is now its property. We believe this legal action will be resolved in favor of Celtic, but nonetheless it is an additional headache attached to the company's prime asset and the source of much of its value.

Ownership Celtic Resources has a wide shareholder base among institutional investors and the current management team owns 11% of the company. Barrick is Celtic's strategic partner and became a minority shareholder in January 2005, with the goal of securing the right to operate and own 51% of the Nezhdaninskoye mine in the event of the IG Alrosa deal outlined above. Now that the IG Alrosa deal is off, it is unclear what Barrick's position is vis-à-vis Celtic, although the company's Kazakh assets are probably too small for the global giant to go to the trouble of increasing its equity stake. Nonetheless, Barrick continues to own 8% of Celtic.

Legal problems: likely not a threat, but worrisome nonetheless

Celtic recently announced a lawsuit against Russia's Zenit bank concerning a loan taken out in 2001. The loan was collateralized with a 30% stake in SVMC (holder of 100% of Nezhdaninskoye) owned by Celtic, which has 50% of SVMC in total. Although Celtic repaid the loan on time and in full, the 30% SVMC stake used as collateral was never released back to the company. The result was that while Celtic had title to the 30% stake, it was not under full management control. Celtic's lawsuit claims that this condition resulted in damages and it is suing Zenit Bank in London for $200mn.

Ultimately, we believe Celtic will prove its rights to 50% of SVMC as we find it hard to believe that both Barrick and Deloitte & Touche (Celtic's strategic partner and auditor respectively) have not already undertaken a serious analysis on the issue. However, the lawsuit is likely to take time and money, further diverting management attention away from expanding the business.

FINANCIAL REVIEW AND FORECAST

Celtic has been almost completely dependent on its Kazakhstan assets for revenue, and current developments suggest that will remain the case for the near to medium term. Obviously, the key issue is the resolution of Nezhdaninskoye's ownership so that development can begin, preferably with Celtic's participation. However, given the small scale of the Kazakhstan operations, it appears that the company's value is not driven by financial performance at this point, but rather by news on Nezhdaninskoye.

Revenue

Despite all of the problems and uncertainty surrounding Nezhdaninskoye, It is possible that in our model that development of the mine will begin in earnest in 2007-2008, with the first full year of operations in 2009. Granted, this assumes that Celtic is able to come to an agreement with Polyus and maintain a 50% stake in the project. But, in the absence of alternative scenarios, we believe this is an appropriate assumption that gives the company value for the asset but recognizes the problems of owning it. Our 2005 forecast output is 65,000oz, which with the exception of minor gold from ongoing testing at Nezhdaninskoye, all comes from Celtic's Kazakh operations.

Costs

Celtic's costs have varied significantly over the years due to operational problems at new facilities. In 2004, the company's average cash cost was $240/oz, and this year It is forecasted that cash costs to be $261/oz, up 8.8% due to previously announced problems at the Suzdal mine. The company plans to ramp up output at both Zherek and Suzdal in the next several years, which should provide some scale to operations and lower costs. Additionally, the grade of ore at Zherek has been lower than the mine average, and we expect this to rise, thus further lowering costs at this operation. Our model assumes that Nezdaninskoye will not be as cost competitive as Celtic has announced in the past (a cash cost of under $100/oz), simply because the ore body is a difficult mining project in an extremely hostile operating environment. Our forecast is for the site to have cash costs around $250 per oz.

Depreciation and amortization, not included in cash costs, are based on the amount of gold produced relative to the total resource of the mine as a proportion of the capitalized value of each mine.

Celtic Resources has done an admirable job of keeping SG&A costs low, although given the multiple legal battles the company is fighting, this item will likely increase in the near term. Moving forward, SG&A costs are forecast to be driven by inflation and business size using gold output as a rough proxy.

Capex

With the uncertainty surrounding the ownership of Nezhdaninskoye, capex plans for Celtic are at best indicative at this stage. It is possible that the company's own previous capex estimates for the giant Russian field but pushed the spend dates out in the future, as we have with that asset's development.

The company's Kazakh mines, however, are over the hump of the major capex spend, and so for them future capex is forecast to be quite modest.

Balance sheet and cash flow

Celtic's balance sheet is rather small, and the company recently decided to account for its stake in 50% of Nezhdaninskoye as a financial asset, which simplifies the balance sheet further but also decreases transparency. The company's total debt at the end of 1H05 was $26mn, while it had a cash position of $9mn. Celtic raised $10mn in equity finance in October, although it seems that unless it is able to raise significant equity or debt capital or manages to expand income from the Kazakh assets, it will have a difficult time waiting out the period of Nezhdaninskoye's development.

So far, Celtic's cash flow generation has been poor, although the increase in output for 2005 should help add to the company's cash position. Real cash flow generation will begin when Suzdal and Zherek are operating at full planned project size in 2008, while Nezhdaninskoye starts in earnest in 2009.

1H05 UK GAAP results were poor

Celtic's 1H05 UK GAAP results were poor, as revenue declined 16.6% y-o-y to $2.6mn despite a 4.5% y-o-y increased in gold output to 8,859oz and higher average spot prices in 1H05.

Celtic reported an operating loss of $2.9mn due to a large foreign exchange loss on dollar borrowing by its subsidiary in Kazakhstan, though this was partially offset by interest income and income tax gains. The company posted a net loss of $2.4mn for the period.

Celtic Resources 1H05 results disappointing

In $mn, UK GAAP	1H04	1H05	Change y-o-y
Revenue	3	3	-16.6%
COGS	-2	-2	-3.9%
Gross profit	1	1	-39.4%
Gross profit margin	35.9%	26.1%	
SG&A	-1	-4	260.0%
Operating income	0	-3	NM
EBITDA	1	-2	NM
EBITDA margin	15.4%	-66.0%	
Interest income (expense)	0	0	NM
Other non-operating expenses	0	0	NM
Income taxes	0	0	NM
Minority interest	0	0	NM
Net income	-1	-2	NM
Net income margin	-16.4%	-76.1%	

Source: Company data, Aton estimates

It is possible to note that that the bulk of Celtic's revenue comes in the second half due to seasonality factors in production. However, the results highlight Celtic's relatively small scale in terms of its income statement. Additionally, the company's valuation is clearly driven by its growth potential, as its financial results are too minor to be considered a major share price driver.

CONCLUSION: A HOLD FOR NOW, BUT BUYER BEWARE

Celtic Resources has an interesting portfolio of assets, and the company's two active mines in Kazakhstan are set to be low cost producers using very modern technology. However, clearly all eyes are elsewhere, as investors await news on the fate of Nezhdaninskoye. The Russian asset is worth fighting for, as it represents 80% of Celtic's resources and is one of the largest undeveloped gold sites in both Russia and the world. However, after a drawn out negotiating process with IG Alrosa, and now the prospect of a similarly long process with Polyus, the company will clearly have a difficult time keeping focus and achieving the best deal possible. Additionally, with so much attention concentrated on Nezhdaninskoye, the task of expanding the business and seeking new opportunities is at the periphery of management's attention. As such, we believe Celtic will miss growth opportunities that other gold miners will capitalize on.

It is possible to estimate that our end-2006 target price for Celtic Resources from $3.44 to $3.52 and our recommendation stays unchanged at Hold.

SUMMARY FINANCIAL FORECAST

Income statement									
In $mn, Ir GAAP	2002	2003	2004	2005F	2006F	2007F	2008F	2009F	2010F
Total revenues	9	12	14	26	36	53	66	71	71
COGS	-2	-5	-6	-15	-20	-28	-33	-33	-34
Gross profit	7	7	8	11	15	25	33	37	37
SG&A	-3	-2	-1	-5	-5	-5	-6	-6	-6
EBITDA	4	4	7	6	10	20	28	37	38
Depreciation	-2	-1	-2	-1	-2	-6	-9	-10	-11
Operating income	2	3	5	5	8	14	19	27	27
Net interest expense	0	0	0	-2	-3	-4	-5	-5	-5
Other expense/income	0	12	1	-1	-1	0	0	0	0
Pre-tax income	2	14	6	2	4	11	14	22	22
Income taxes	-1	-1	-2	-1	-1	-3	-3	-5	-5
Minority interest	0	0	-1	-1	0	-1	-1	-2	-3
Net income	1	13	3	1	3	7	10	15	14
Adjustments		-12							
Adjusted net income	1	1	3	1	3	7	10	15	14
Balance sheet									
In $mn, Ir GAAP	2002	2003	2004	2005F	2006F	2007F	2008F	2009F	2010F
Cash and liquid assets	2	8	30	33	33	16	10	10	10
Inventories	2	3	7	8	11	13	17	17	18
Accounts receivable	4	7	5	6	8	9	11	12	12
Other current assets	0	8	47	47	47	47	47	47	47
Total current assets	9	26	90	94	100	85	85	86	86
Fixed assets	6	12	28	49	68	96	127	137	147
Investments									
Other non-current assets	41	63	20	20	20	20	20	20	20
Total non-current assets	47	75	48	69	88	116	147	157	167
Total assets	55	101	138	163	187	201	232	243	253
Short-term debt	0	1	7	13	13	13	29	25	20
Accounts payable	6	8	4	9	6	9	11	12	12
Other current	5	1	4	6	8	12	15	16	16

liabilities									
Total current liabilities	11	10	15	28	28	35	56	52	48
Long-term debt	2	20	28	28	50	50	50	50	50
Other non-current liabilities	0	0	0	0	0	0	0	0	0
Total non-current liabilities	2	21	28	28	50	50	50	50	50
Minority interest	4	3	0	0	0	0	0	0	0
Total shareholders' equity	38	67	95	106	109	116	126	141	155
Total liabilities and equity	55	101	138	163	187	201	232	243	253
Cash flow statement									
In $mn, Ir GAAP	2002	2003	2004	2005F	2006F	2007F	2008F	2009F	2010F
Net income	1	13	3	1	3	7	10	15	14
Depreciation	2	1	2	1	2	6	9	10	11
Changes in working capital	0	-13	-44	6	-6	4	0	0	0
Other	-1	-10	24	0	0	0	0	0	0
Operating cash flow	2	-9	-15	9	0	16	19	24	25
Capex	-19	-25	-29	-22	-21	-34	-40	-20	-20
Acquisitions									
Other	0	0	0	0	0	0	0	0	0
Investing cash flow	-19	-25	-29	-22	-21	-34	-40	-20	-20
Change in debt	-	19	14	6	22	0	15	-4	-5
Dividends	0	0	0	0	0	0	0	0	0
Other	21	20	43	10	0	0	0	0	0
Financing cash flow	21	39	57	16	22	0	15	-4	-5

Source: Company data; Aton estimates ***Source: Company data; Aton estimates***

DCF valuation of Celtic Resources												
In $mn	2004	2005F	2006F	2007F	2008F	2009F	2010F	2011F	2012F	2013F	2014F	2015F
Revenue	14	26	36	53	66	71	71	71	71	71	71	72
Operating expenses	-7	-20	-25	-33	-38	-34	-33	-25	-27	-27	-28	-29
EBITDA	7	6	10	20	28	37	38	46	44	44	43	43
Depreciation	-2	-1	-2	-6	-9	-10	-11	-11	-12	-13	-14	-16
Operating income (EBIT)	5	5	8	14	19	27	27	35	32	31	29	27
Less: Income taxes		-1	-2	-3	-5	-6	-7	-8	-8	-7	-7	-6
Less: Capex		-22	-21	-34	-40	-20	-20	-7	-7	-7	-7	-7
Less: Changes in WC		6	-6	4	0	0	0	0	0	0	0	0
Plus: Depreciation		1	2	6	9	10	11	11	12	13	14	16
Free cash flow		-11	-18	-14	-17	10	12	31	30	30	30	30

Discount factor (WACC)	1.00	1.12	1.24	1.39	1.55	1.72	1.92	2.14	2.39	2.66
Present value of future FCF	-18	-12	-14	7	8	18	15	14	12	11
Total PV of future FCF 41										

Calculation of terminal value		Cost of equity calculation		Forecast beta calculation	
Terminal free cash flow, $mn	30	Long term risk free rate	5.5%	Avg monthly trading volume*	Forecast
Terminal growth rate	3%	Russian country risk premium	1.5%	(com. + pref.), $mn	beta
Terminal discount rate	11.5%	Russian risk free rate	7.0%	> 100	1.00
Terminal value, $mn	359	Standard equity premium	4.0%	10-100	1.25
PV of terminal value, $mn	135	Excess RTS volatility factor	1.00	1-10	1.50
		Russian equity market premium	4.0%	0.1-1	2.00
Target price calculation		Forecast beta	1.25	< 0.1	3.00
		Levered forecast beta	1.51	*Based on trailing 3 month total dollar	
PV of terminal value + future FCF, $ mn	176	Cost of equity	13.1%	volume on RTS, MICEX and ADR markets	
Less: Net debt (cash), $mn (end 05F)	8				
Less: Minority interest, $mn	0	WACC calculation		Capital structure, $mn	
Exploration value, $mn	0	Gross debt as % of capitalization	21.7%	Gross debt (end 05F)	42
Total equity value, $mn	167	Cost of debt (after-tax)	5.9%	MV of common	150
		Equity as % of capitalization	78.3%		
Common shares outstanding, mn	48	Cost of equity	13.1%	Total MV of equity	150
		WACC	11.5%	Total capitalization	192
Fair value per common share, $	3.52				

CENTERRA GOLD

Centerra is a very well run company spun off in 2004 by uranium mining giant Cameco, which retains a 53% stake. Centerra's core asset is the enormous Kumtor mine in Kyrgyzstan, which has been in operation since 1997, while the company also has substantial operations in Mongolia and an interesting development project in the US. The key issue for Centerra is output growth, and although it has mentioned the possibility of an M&A deal to achieve this, there has been little news on this front so far. Therefore Centerra falls into an odd position vis-à-vis its peers as it is a major Russia/CIS producer but has a limited growth outlook.

OUTLINE: TWO BIG MINES IN TWO LITTLE COUNTRIES

Centerra Gold was a 100% subsidiary of uranium mining giant Cameco before the business went public on Canada's TSE in 2004. Producing assets include the Kumtor mine in Kyrgyzstan and the Boroo mine in Mongolia, and in 2004 Centerra produced 903,030oz of gold. The company's activities account for 10% of GDP in both Kyrgyzstan and Mongolia, a factor that endows it with a certain amount of political authority while also carrying responsibility and liabilities. Clearly, such a leading position gives Centerra advantages in terms of securing new licenses and access to the top levels of government. However, there is the risk that the company's high profile will be assailed in populist politics.

Centerra's main growth driver has been the commencement of operations at Boroo in 2004, and so far there are few development projects owned by the company. The one exception is the REN property in the US, but it will be many years before this is likely to crystallize into real output. And this is the core issue for Centerra: it has big mines that are competitive and capture headlines, but nothing new in the pipeline with which to use profits from these mines and move forward. So a major catalyst for the company will be any announcement on the acquisition of new licenses or producing companies. Given that Centerra's end 1H05 net cash position was $204mn and growing, this is certainly possible.

OPERATIONS AND ASSETS

Centerra's Kumtor mine started operations in 1997 and has literally buoyed the Kyrgyz economy since the years leading up to its launch. The mine was a massive headline development project for Kyrgyzstan, with major participation from the EBRD to help finance its $450mn development cost. Having been in operation for eight years the mine's original reserve base is significantly diminished, although ongoing exploration seems to be increasing resources at an acceptable rate. Centerra's second mine, Boroo in Mongolia, began operations in 2004, and although it too has limited resources these are set to be bolstered by the company's adjacent license area, Gatsuurt. Lastly, Centerra's only development project, REN in Nevada US, is jointly owned with Barrick. It is still in the exploration stage although drilling results have been impressive.

In 2004 Centerra made 903,030oz of gold, although only 68% of that was attributable to the company. With the consolidation of minority interests, Centerra is set to make close to 800,000oz this year.

Centerra's combined reserves and resources broadly reflect the production picture: Kumtor has 61% of the total and Boroo and Gatsuurt (located next to each other) have another 27% of the 10.8mn oz total. However, it is clear the company currently does not have a wide development pipeline to support future organic growth, with only REN in the lineup.

Total reserves and resources: correspond to production

Source: Company data

Centerra needs to convert more resources to reserves Mn. oz Reserves Resources Total

Kumtor: stable, profitable mine and likely to be plenty of reserves

Kumtor is 100% owned by Centerra, as an innovative part of the company's spin-off was to consolidate full mine ownership in return for giving equity to the Kyrgyz state-owned gold agency, Kyrgyzaltyn, which used to be a direct owner of Kumtor. The mine is open pit at extremely high altitude, more than 4,000m above sea level, and despite this challenge has consistently put in a good operating performance, with 2004 cash costs of $202/oz.

The mine has been in the operation since 1997 and has produced 500,000oz-750,000oz annually, which has left the ore site with 3.2mn oz of reserves and an additional 3.4mn oz of resources. Despite investor fears to the contrary, we do not believe that the mine will run out of ore in the near to medium term. We point out that when Centerra was only a minority shareholder in the mine (before 2004) there was little incentive to perform exploration work around the main ore body. This is not the case now and the company has a large exploration program in place, which spent $6mn in 2004 and is set to spend $11mn in 2005. Moreover, the company now has adjacent license areas to the main Kumtor pit and drilling results have demonstrated good ore grade over significant core intervals. In short, although the main mine resource may be soon depleted there appear to be offshoots that will support the site mill, although costs are likely to rise due to transportation.

Mongolian assets are ready to perform

Boroo open pit mine commenced operations in 2004 and immediately posted impressive operating results with low cash costs of $149/oz and output of 246,000oz. Boroo singlehandedly increased Mongolia's gold output by 75% in 2004. As with Kumtor there have been concerns that the mine life of the deposit is too short, since there are only 1.1mn oz of reserves and an additional 0.4mn oz of resources. However, the company is confident it will find gold resources to support the mine, and the adjacent Gatsuurt exploration property, only 35km away, has a large resources base of 1.5mn oz that through exploration is being proven to a reserve classification that can be mined. The company is still studying the possibility of developing Gatsuurt separately, but given the very close proximity of the property, we assume that ore will simply be trucked over to the Boroo mill.

The company's Mongolian assets are all set to continuously deliver over 260,000oz over the life of the forecast period, and It is possible to note that that the legal mining environment in Mongolia is very favorable, with no income tax in the first three years of operations, only 15% in the next three years and 30% thereafter.

SHAREHOLDER STRUCTURE

Centerra Gold went public in 2004 when Canada's Cameco decided to sell equity of its gold mining subsidiary on the open market. The company's stake in Kumtor was increased to 100% from 33% at the time of the IPO and in Boroo to 95%.

Cameco currently holds a 53% interest in Centerra, and Kyrgyzaltyn – a company wholly owned by Kyrgyz government – owns 16%. Kyrgyzaltyn's stake was received as an equity swap to consolidate full control over Kumtor. The remaining 31% of company is free float.

Cameco makes the decisions, Kyrgyzaltyn is a good partner and free float is large

Source: Company data; Aton estimates

FINANCIAL REVIEW AND FORECAST

We have built a model for Centerra based on the company's plans regarding the development of its two operating mines. The company has a very competent management team that is well respected in the mining world, and what it lacks in promotional panache, it more than makes up for in experience. Our key issue is that costs are set to rise as the company's mines move increasingly far from its mills and smelters. Additionally, with a small development pipeline, output growth is likely to come through acquisitions, a major unknown for investors.

Revenue

Centerra's output and revenue was dependent on Kumtor until the opening of Boroo early in 2004. In addition to this, the company consolidated control over its mines last year so that it gets the full benefit of ownership with minimal minority expense.

Centerra's attributable gold output was 610,287oz in 2004, which is forecast to rise to 800,000oz in 2005 due to the effects of consolidation. However, company guidance for this year's output by mine actually suggests an 11% drop y-o-y due to declining ore grades at Kumtor. It is possible that that the major drop in ore grade from 2004-2005 will not be repeated, although It is possible that a slight deterioration of grade.

As Centerra's two mines are already opened and have an operating history, while there is no schedule for opening new mines, we do not envision any one-off events that will alter cash costs significantly. Last year, the total cash cost for the two mines was $189/oz, which is 34% below the world's average of $253/oz. This is even more impressive considering that Kumtor operates in an extremely difficult environment, has only average ore grade and relatively low recovery rates from the mill. We expect costs to rise slightly as lower ore grade is mined, especially at Kumtor, but the company is still forecast to show good cost performance.

Based on the past total cash cost at the two mines and using Centerra's guidance for future operating costs we have constructed our own costs forecast, shown below.

Depreciation and amortization are both a function of the useful life of assets and a product of mining itself; they are not included in total cash costs. We have forecast this item to equal yearly gold output as a percentage of total reserves per mine in operation, using our own forecasts as to the book value of each mine based on historical value and expected capex.

Exploration expenses are reported under SG&A. This is very conservative on the company's part, as management has decided to expense exploration, instead of capitalizing it as an asset with the danger of future write-downs. By choosing this method, management has depressed near term profitability but clearly has taken the path of shunning promotional accounting opportunities. Other SG&A costs are forecast to be driven by inflation and gold output.

Gross margin set to stabilize at 40%

Centerra has very modest capex plans, which revolve only around maintenance at the two mines. The $24mn expense in 2005 is associated with investment in new machinery at Kumtor, which is expected to increase the efficiency of the operations and help keep cash costs down. As most of the big capex events are behind us, and there is no forecast mine opening, capex costs are set to be very modest throughout the forecast period.

Balance sheet and cash flow

Centerra has a very clean balance sheet with a cash position of $204mn at the end of 1H05 and no debt. Additionally, the company has high inventory turnover, meaning that working capital requirements are practically zero. Given that the company has two stable, cost-efficient mines without any drain on operating cash in the future, it is a prime candidate to leverage, which could be used for M&A.

Operating cash flow is likely to be high due to low costs, low capex and low working capital needs. In this sense Centerra is set to be the only company profiled in this report to behave like an annuity.

1H05 results look good

From the financial point of view Centerra's interim results show excellent growth in revenues, EBITDA and net income – primarily due to the company increasing its stake in Kumtor from 33% to 100%, Boroo mine operating at full capacity in 2005 and higher gold prices.

Total production of the two mines was 426,675oz in 1H05, actually 1.8% lower y-o-y, but the amount of gold sold by Centerra was 445,202oz vs. 197,161oz in 1H04. Coupled with a higher average gold spot price of $420/oz compared to $360/oz previously, revenues were up 157.4% at $187mn. COGS, however, increased even faster on top of a $216/oz total cash cost, rising 35% y-o-y. The gross margin thus shrunk by 8.2% y-o-y to 28.3%.

A big increase in SG&A came from an increased exploration program and a much larger administration expense, which we hope can be kept under control in the future. EBITDA was up 85.6% to $66mn and net income almost quadrupled to $27mn, giving a net margin of 14.7%.

The increase in cash costs was expected as grades at Kumtor were falling and the company is on target to meet the 2005 forecast of $233/oz. The output target was exceeded in 1H05 and the company should easily meet the forecast production of 800,000oz for the year. An increase in inventory turnover is another bonus to the cash flow. The company's net cash position is at $204mn, up from $153mn at the end of 2004, but more capex and exploration expenses are to come in the remainder of 2005.

1H05 income statement highlights show growth across board

In $mn, CA GAAP	1H04	1H05	Y-o-y %
Revenue	73	187	157.4%
COGS	-46	-134	190.6%
Gross profit	27	53	99.6%
Gross margin	36.5%	28.3%	
SG&A	-6	-21	233.8%
Operating profit	20	32	59.1%
EBITDA	36	66	85.6%
EBITDA margin	49.2%	35.4%	
Interest income	0	0	68.2%
Other non-operating expense	-9	0	-100.0%

Income tax	-1	-4	648.2%
Minority interest	-4	-1	-65.2%
Net income	7	27	284.7%
Net margin	9.7%	14.7%	

Source: Company data; Aton estimates

CONCLUSION: WAITING FOR A CATALYST

Centerra Gold is a well run large-scale operation that has been a pioneer at successfully developing big projects in countries that have little experience with multinationals. The company has a clean balance sheet and more financial flexibility than any other business profiled in this report, although it has yet to take advantage of this. Granted, it is barely more than a year since Centerra went public – so judgment on this point may be premature

– but unless the company buys new growth opportunities there is not much for investors to get excited about beyond potential dividend payouts. We believe Centerra is fully valued at current levels and our end-2006 target price is $18.77. We initiate coverage of the company with a Hold recommendation.

SUMMARY FINANCIAL FORECAST

Income statement									
In $mn, CA GAAP	2002	2003	2004	2005F	2006F	2007F	2008F	2009F	2010F
Total revenues	55	82	247	354	358	317	313	312	311
COGS	-37	-47	-110	-191	-173	-170	-168	-169	-168
Gross profit	18	35	137	163	185	147	145	143	143
SG&A	-5	-4	-12	-18	-19	-19	-20	-20	-20
Other operating costs	-6	-7	-15	-24	-15	-15	-15	-5	-5
EBITDA	7	25	111	121	151	113	111	118	118
Depreciation	-13	-15	-54	-52	-42	-33	-26	-22	-20
Operating income	-5	9	57	69	108	80	85	96	98
Net interest expense	0	-1	8	6	10	15	19	23	27
Other expense/income	0	0	-9	1	0	0	0	0	0
Pre-tax income	-6	8	56	76	118	95	104	119	125
Income taxes	2	-1	0	-9	-15	-18	-20	-23	-28
Minority interest	1	2	-5	-3	-3	-3	-3	-3	-3
Net income	-3	9	51	64	100	74	81	94	95
Balance sheet									
In $mn, CA GAAP	2002	2003	2004	2005F	2006F	2007F	2008F	2009F	2010F
Cash and liquid assets	20	10	153	238	371	477	577	686	793
Inventories	5	2	22	30	27	25	24	24	24
Accounts receivable	7	6	3	5	5	4	4	4	4
Other current assets	68	48	48	59	59	53	52	52	52
Total current assets	100	66	225	331	462	559	657	766	873
Fixed assets	91	142	268	239	204	178	160	144	132
Investments	0	0	0	0	0	0	0	0	0
Other non-current assets	45	33	168	168	168	168	168	168	168

Total non-current assets	136	176	436	407	372	346	328	312	300
Total assets	236	241	660	739	834	906	985	1,078	1,172
Short-term debt	4	38	0	0	0	0	0	0	0
Accounts payable	12	19	32	47	41	39	37	37	36
Other current liabilities	0	0	0	0	0	0	0	0	0
Total current liabilities	16	58	32	47	41	39	37	37	36
Long-term debt	28	18	0	0	0	0	0	0	0
Other non-current liabilities	7	7	24	24	24	24	24	24	24
Total non-current liabilities	35	25	24	24	24	24	24	24	24
Minority interest	11	9	2	2	2	2	2	2	2
Total shareholders' equity	174	150	602	665	766	840	921	1,015	1,110
Total liabilities and equity	236	241	660	739	834	906	985	1,078	1,172
Cash flow statement									
In $mn, CA GAAP	2002	2003	2004	2005F	2006F	2007F	2008F	2009F	2010F
Net income	-3	9	51	64	100	74	81	94	95
Depreciation	13	15	54	52	42	33	26	22	20
Changes in working capital	0	31	-4	-7	-3	6	0	0	0
Other	6	-31	-12	0	0	0	0	0	0
Operating cash flow	16	24	88	109	140	113	107	116	115
Capex	-21	-61	-12	-24	-7	-7	-7	-7	-7
Acquisitions	0	0	0	0	0	0	0	0	0
Other	25	0	24	0	0	0	0	0	0
Investing cash flow	5	-61	13	-24	-7	-7	-7	-7	-7
Change in debt	-	24	-56	0	0	0	0	0	0
Dividends	0	0	0	0	0	0	0	0	0
Other	-1	2	98	0	0	0	0	0	0
Financing cash flow	-1	26	41	0	0	0	0	0	0

Source: Company data; Aton estimates ***Source: Company data; Aton estimates***

DCF valuation of Centerra Gold												
In $mn	2004	2005F	2006F	2007F	2008F	2009F	2010F	2011F	2012F	2013F	2014F	2015F
Revenue	247	354	358	317	313	312	311	310	309	308	307	306
Operating expenses	-137	-233	-207	-204	-203	-194	-194	-192	-193	-193	-193	-192
EBITDA	111	121	151	113	111	118	118	118	116	115	115	114
Depreciation	-54	-52	-42	-33	-26	-22	-20	-17	-17	-19	-21	-23
Operating income (EBIT)	57	69	108	80	85	96	98	101	99	97	94	91
Less: Income taxes		-8	-13	-15	-16	-18	-22	-22	-22	-21	-21	-20

Less: Capex	-24	-7	-7	-7	-7	-7	-7	-7	-7	-7	-7
Less: Changes in WC	-7	-3	6	0	0	0	0	0	-3	0	0
Plus: Depreciation	52	42	33	26	22	20	17	17	19	21	23
Free cash flow	82	128	97	88	93	89	89	88	84	87	87
Discount factor (WACC)		1.00	1.12	1.25	1.40	1.57	1.76	1.97	2.21	2.48	2.77
Present value of future FCF		128	87	70	66	57	50	44	38	35	31
Total PV of future FCF 607											

Calculation of terminal value	2015	Cost of equity calculation		Forecast beta calculation	
Terminal free cash flow, $mn	87	Long term risk free rate	5.5%	Avg monthly trading volume*	Forecast
Terminal growth rate	5%	Russian country risk premium	1.5%	(com. + pref.), $mn	beta
Terminal discount rate	12.0%	Russian risk free rate	7.0%	> 100	1.00
Terminal value, $mn	1,310	Standard equity premium	4.0%	10-100	1.25
PV of terminal value, $mn	472	Excess RTS volatility factor	1.00	1-10	1.50
		Russian equity market premium	4.0%	0.1-1	2.00
Target price calculation		Forecast beta	1.25	< 0.1	3.00
		Levered forecast beta	1.25	*Based on trailing 3 month total dollar	
PV of terminal value + future FCF, $ mn	1,080	Cost of equity	12.0%	volume on RTS, MICEX and ADR markets	
Less: Net debt (cash), $mn (end 05F)	-238				
Less: Minority interest, $mn	2	WACC calculation		Capital structure, $mn	
Exploration value, $mn	39	Gross debt as % of capitalization	0.0%	Gross debt (end 05F)	0
Total equity value, $mn	1,353	Cost of debt (after-tax)	6.0%	MV of common	1,270
		Equity as % of capitalization	100.0%		
Common shares outstanding, mn	72	Cost of equity	12.0%	Total MV of equity	1,270
		WACC	12.0%	Total capitalization	1,270
Fair value per common share, $	18.77				

STRATEGIC INFORMATION ON RUSSIAN GOLD MINING INDUSTRY

GOLD MINING IN RUSSIA: IMPORTANT DEVELOPMENTS

This report will focus on the following two issues:

- Examination of the prospect and variants of the development of the Russian gold mining industry in a global context

AN INTRODUCTION TO THE CLOSED JOINT STOCK COMPANY "GOLD MINING COMPANY POLYUS" AND ITS DEVELOPMENT STRATEGY.

Section 1: Russia and the Global Gold Mining Industry

The Russian gold mining industry has a history over 300 years long. The first gold bullion was poured following metallurgical processing of complex ores at Nerchinsky mines in 1702.

About 16.2 thousand tonnes of gold have been mined in the Russian Empire, Soviet Union and Russian Federation, approximately 11.3% of the total amount of gold that has been produced historically (about 143.2 thousand tonnes).

In contrast to other countries, Russia has very specific raw material sources: about 70% of gold has been mined from alluvial deposits, 23% from hard rock ones and 7% at composite deposits. Gold is now simultaneously extracted from hard rock and composite deposits worldwide.

Until recently, gold mining in Russia was a completely state monopolised industry. The process of privatisation, mergers and redistribution of mining companies began during the 1990s. The rapid reorganisation and privatisation of the Soviet gold mining industry initially resulted in the breakdown of one large production association into more than 600 small, poorly equipped alluvial producers with an annual production of the first hundred kilos of gold. This disintegration of the industry had a long-term negative effect: small producers had no access to long-term financial resources, and the sharp decrease in investments became an obstacle to the development of hard rock deposits.

The sharp devaluation of the national currency in 1998 and a lack of effective investment instruments fuelled the interest of Russian banks to fund alluvial gold production. The increased activity of national banks resulted in increased gold production.

The correlation between placer and alluvial deposits began to change in the middle of the 90s. The increase of production costs and taxes led to a situation where the profitable share of alluvial deposits was reduced to 60% of balance reserves. Nevertheless, experts believe that the potential of alluvial deposits in Russia could provide the extraction of 60-70 tonnes of gold annually during a period of 10-15 years. This period would be enough for the re-orientation of the gold mining industry to hard rock deposits.

As regards the allocation of gold mining in the Russian territories, the most productive region is Magadan (33.5 tonnes in 2002), Krasnoyarsk Territory (29.3 tonnes), Yakutia (17.5 tonnes), Irkutsk Territory (16.3 tonnes), Khabarovsk Territory (15.3 tonnes) and Amur region (12.7 tonnes).

Section 2: The Current State of the Gold Mining Industry in Russia

Today the world gold mining industry faces the following long-term challenges:

- The depletion of reserves and the absence of new prospects and highly remunerative deposits

- An increase in the cost of financial resources due to a negative public opinion of the gold mining sector

- A decrease in countries and provinces that welcome large-scale gold mining operations

- Fears of political and social instability in the leading gold producing regions.

Gold Mining in Russia German Pikhoya

MINE PRODUCTION (TONNES)

Country	2000	2001	2002E
S. Africa	431	402	395
U. S.	353	335	300
Australia	296	285	280
China	180	185	175
Peru	133	138	140
Soviet Union-Russia	126	152	170
Canada	154	160	160

Source: US Geological Survey

RUSSIAN GOLD MINING INDUSTRY: A NEW STAGE OF DEVELOPMENT

- Thanks to improved macroeconomic and political conditions, Russia has once again joined the group of the five leading gold producing countries

- This trend will have a long-term effect if it is supported by a strong gold price increase and the commencement of new mines

- Experts believe that Russia's unique resource potential can enable annual production of about 300 tonnes of gold (9.6 million ounces)

- Today Russia has a highly skilled labour potential and advanced technology in the mining and processing of gold ore

-There is a stable increase of extraction volume.

Russia is among the few countries that have stably increased gold mining during the last four years. In 2002, gold production increased 21.1% to 158.7 tonnes. About 35 tonnes of gold are consumed for the needs of jewellery. Gold is also used in electronics and additionally, it is an important export item: Russian banks sell abroad more than 60 tonnes per annum.

The increase in extraction is attributed primarily to the launch of several new hard rock projects:

- The largest deposit in Eurasia, *Sukhoy Log,* (398 million tonnes, average content – 2.6 g per ton, reserves – 1100 tonnes) is still unavailable for development. This deposit can provide an additional 30 tonnes of gold annually and will be among the world's largest gold operations

- The principal modernisation of the deposit *Natalka,* which is licensed to the joint-stock company "Rudnik Imeni Matrosova", (243 million tonnes, average content is 2.85 g per tonne, probable reserves are 1,000 tonnes or more), will provide an increase in output of 24 tonnes a year

- Aldan group of deposits *Kuranakh* (240 tonnes, average contents is 2 g per tonne)

- The development of such deposits as *Sukhoy Log* and *Mayskoye* will replenish alluvial reserves and help Russia obtain a leading position in the global gold mining industry.

THE IMPROVED INVESTMENT CLIMATE

Economic and political stabilisation, tax reform and a thorough improvement of the investment climate during the previous two years have strengthened the position of Russia in the world economy. During last two years, the Russian state worked hard for the liquidation or, at least, the lowering of the so-called "Russian discount". The cancellation of a 5% export duty for refined gold contributed to increased investment in the industry and a rise in precious metal output.

THE CONSOLIDATION OF THE INDUSTRY

The Mining and Metallurgical Company Norilsk Nickel has taken a 100% stake in the largest Russian gold mining company, Polyus. The new corporation will rank amongst world's first-rate gold mining companies.

This event inaugurated a new stage in gold mining industry development in Russia; the industry can meet the requirements of today's reality and market. The example of Norilsk Nickel is typical of the consolidation process. Polyus is an effective company; its net profit can be directed to the development of production. In addition, aiming to expand activities, the high financial and international prestige of Norilsk Nickel can contribute to capital formation.

POSITIVE PUBLIC PERCEPTION AND PERSONNEL POTENTIAL

The positive public perception of this industry favourably distinguishes Russia from other gold mining countries. Gold mining is of exceptional importance for budget revenues in some regions, for example, Magadan, Irkutsk, Amur and Chita, which is why its development enjoys the support and approval of local authorities and public opinion.

Russian gold mining regions are the most distant from economically developed regions and noted for their extreme climate. In fact, gold mining determines the industrial potential of these territories. Besides that, Russian gold miners never forget the tremendous social significance of this industry: every one tonne of gold mined directly or by implication ensures employment for one thousand people. The development of machinery, construction industry, prospecting and jewellery depends on gold mining. It is of principal importance to us that the gold mining industry should provide life for the territories where it is carried out.

Gold Mining in Russia German Pikhoya

Thanks to the special position historically held by qualifications of Russian geologists and mining gold mining in the Soviet Union, the industry engineers are recognised around the world and today has exceptionally trained and experienced are never in doubt. personnel at its disposal. The first-rate

THE LARGEST RUSSIAN GOLD MINING COMPANIES OUTPUT OF GOLD IN 2002

(in kg)

Company	Region	Basic deposits	Volume of output		
			2000	2001	2002
					29,600

Omolon Gold Mining Co.	Magadan	Kubaka	13,900	13,502	12,500
Lenzoloto	Irkutsk	Alluvials	5,700	7,053	9,200
Susuman Zoloto	Magadan	Alluvials	4,000	4,526	5,800
Mnogovershinnoye	Khabarovsk	Mnogovershinnoye	3,200	4,799	5,700
Buryatzoloto	Buryatia	Zun-Kholba, Barum-Kholba	3,954	4,578	4,700
Polymetal	Ural	Vorontsovskoye, Ducat	917	2,584	4,200
Amur	Khabarovsk	Alluvials	800	2,966	4,000
Pokrovsky Rudnik	Amur	Pokrovskoye	1,600	2,814	2,300

Russia today is one of few countries where the dynamic development of gold mining companies is possible due to:

- Unique high quality long-term gold ore reserves

- Improved investment climate and tax regime stabilisation

-Positive authorities' and non-governmental organisations' attitude to industry development.

PROSPECTS FOR GOLD MINING IN RUSSIA

Russia's extremely favourable competitive position in today's world markets can only be preserved by:

- Setting world class deposits – *Sukhoy Log*, *Natalka*, *Aldan* Group – into industrial operation

- Executing effective exploration programmes and replenishing gold reserves

- Financing prospective research efforts

-Having available a skilled and well-trained labour force.

Only a mining company with the proper financial and technical resources can achieve all these goals.

The independent geological prospecting of gold is an important direction of Russian gold mining companies' investment policy. During the last ten years, the overwhelming majority of Russian enterprises were developing deposits explored during the Soviet period. The state, and, therefore, all taxpayers, cannot and should not assume the risks related to exploration, construction and financing of R and D programmes of commercial significance.

The gold mining company Polyus is facing the task of developing exploration in the Krasnoyarsk Territory and other regions and has enough potential to do that. The company will increase output in this region by 10-15 tonnes of gold due to prospecting works. Several licensed districts for exploration are at the disposal of Norilsk Nickel in Taimyr. Polyus is about to receive some new prospecting licenses in other regions.

CLOSED JOINT VENTURE GOLD MINING COMPANY POLYUS TODAY

Polyus is the largest gold mining company in Russia and has abundant experience in construction works and the exploitation of large-scaled mining complexes. Some details:

- output of gold came to 25,000 kg. in 2002; together with Norilsk Nickel, it was 29,600 kg.

- revenues amounted to $250 million a year

- a complex able to process refractory goldsulphide ores by means of bio-leaching has been constructed for the first time in Russia

- the company self-finances exploration works and has an in-house geological service

-together with the main shareholder, Norilsk Nickel, Polyus has enough financial resources to develop large gold deposits.

The company has the following strategic tasks on agenda for the next four to five years:

- preserve and strengthen its leading position in Russian gold mining

- maintain high profitability of production

- form a horizontally-integrated gold mining company

- provide long-term competitive advantages

- become one of the world's largest mining companies.

Taking into account the above-mentioned tasks, it is expected to:

- increase economic output up to 100 tonnes of gold within four – five years

- increase the reserve base up to two thousand tonnes in two – three years

- construct three to four new mining complexes.

The above-mentioned tasks and targets can be achieved by:

- further development of the Olimpiada deposit and increasing the processing facility

- acquisition of prospective gold mining companies and promising exploration licenses

- participation in tenders and auctions for the subsoil use

- development and accomplishment of an effective exploration programme.

Achieving the above-mentioned goals will allow the company to:

- increase and diversify its reserve base to secure control over deposits of long-term importance for the gold mining industry in Russia

- eliminate its dependence on conditions and peculiarities of one-deposit exploitation

- enter into new regions, creating a platform for further corporation development on a countrywide scale

- secure leading position in process of gold mining consolidation

- position itself in the world market as one of the largest gold producers in Eurasia.

Polyus has every reason to participate in the exploitation of the largest Russian deposits, *Sukhoy Log*, *Natalka* and *Kuranakh*. In the event that Polyus receives the right to develop the above-mentioned projects:

- approximately $1 billion will be invested in their development

- they will be run by a first-rate company armed with the necessary manpower, financial and technical resources

- short-term speculation and change of owners will be impossible

- three new world standard mining complexes will be constructed in a timely manner

- putting the largest Russian deposits into operation will raise Russia's output of gold to 230 tonnes.

Gold still plays its special "reserve" or "stabilising" role in the world economy.

The Russian gold mining industry is restoring its formerly lost competitive position and is becoming one of the mostly inviting and dynamically developing industries within the world mining community.

A new stage of industry development is connected with the consolidation of companies, projects and the foundation of large national gold-mining companies of world-class level.

Only large national mining companies will have the ability to let Russia preserve its competitive advantages and solve new tasks, such as geological subsoil study, R and D work and manpower training.

INDUSTRY OVERVIEW

After almost a decade of depression, the gold-mining industry in Russia has started to recover and develop. Two-thirds of Russian gold mining is located in Eastern Siberia and The Russian Far East (RFE). The recent statistics show a steady growth in gold production in the RFE. Considerable wear-and-tear of existing equipment and the necessity of introducing new technologies, combined with better access to financial resources provide improved business opportunities to U.S. exporters of mining machinery. This report provides an overview of the gold-mining industry in the RFE, and an insight into prospects for U.S. businesses.

History: Gold-mining has always been one of the traditional and leading sectors in the Russian Far East (RFE) economy. In Soviet times, the gold-mining industry was a total government monopoly, although in the 1970s the first non-government enterprises (the so-called artels) started to appear. But the government still was strictly regulating the extraction, production, and sale of precious metals.

Before Russia started to go through reforms in the 1990s, the largest gold-mining enterprise in the RFE was SeveroVostokZoloto which covered Kolyma (Magadan), Chukotka, and Kamchatka, and produced up to 50 tons annually. Yakutzoloto from Sakha (Yakutiya) manufactured up to 30 tons per year, Amurzoloto (Amur Oblast) - 10-12 tons and Primorzoloto (Primorskiy and Kahabrovskiy Krais, and Sakhalin) - 8-10 tons.

Outdated labor-consuming technologies and equipment, low capital investments, turmoil in the Russian economy, and drop in the gold prices on the world's market nearly resulted in the industry's collapse in the mid 1990s.

The reserves of gold in Western Russia are almost exhausted. But in Eastern Russia (Eastern Siberia and the RFE) there are at least 5 deposits with estimated reserves of over 300 tons, as well as a number of 100-300 ton deposits.

After Russia began shifting to a market economy and the government stopped supporting the gold-mining industry, most of the companies were experiencing considerable financial constraints during 1991-1997. Besides, the seasonal nature of gold production made it very challenging to find financial resources in advance to prepare for the mining season. Banks were very reluctant to provide loans and credit lines, and the interest rates were outrageous – 40-45% in hard currency. The government support through Komdragmet (The State Committee for Precious Stones) was more nominal than practical. Most of the gold-miners found themselves in financial deadlock - - they kept on borrowing money to pay back loans and interest.

Current Situation: The situation in the industry improved in 1998. Like many other export-oriented industries, gold mining has benefited from Russia's August 1998 financial crisis. The ruble devaluation and resulting decreased production costs, improved the development of the RFE's gold-mining industry. Most of the loans taken by gold-miners were in rubles, so with the ruble's collapse and with the world's market prices starting to stabilize, the gold-mining companies were able to pay them back very easily. As a result, the profitability of the gold-mining industry and its attractiveness for the investors grew significantly by the end of 1998.

Also in March 1998 the Russian government adopted a Federal Law "On Precious Metals and Gemstones", and in December 1998 Decree #1419 was issued. These new regulations released the government's strict control over the gold industry and gold exports. Commercial banks started to export Russian gold. For the first time in the history of modern Russia, its gold market became a part of the global market. Another positive factor was that gold prices on the world market started to stabilize and increase after a two-decade period of decreases (in 1998 the lowest price for 20 years was registered).

Extraction of placer gold (which is a seasonal process) always significantly prevailed over mining of ore gold. Over the last few years, however, the structure of the gold-mining industry has been changing, and has started to shift from extraction of placer gold to lode gold mining. Lode gold mining is much more attractive to investors because it is not seasonal and is economically more effective.

Investors and banks started to more extensively finance gold-mining projects and companies. Sberbank became an absolute leader in providing loans and credit lines to gold-miners. Together with Vneshtorgbank it accounts for almost 50% of commercial loans given to the domestic gold-miners. Among other banks, the most active were Moscow-based Alfa-Bank, MDM, Zenit, NOMOS-Bank and Menatep, as well as regional and local banks - - Dalkombank, Regiobank, Neryungri Bank, and Kolyma-Bank. In 2000 the average loan interest rate for gold-miners ranged from 15-22% in rubles, and 15-17% in hard currency. Some banks even provided 3-5-year credit lines.

There are some negative factors impeding development of Russia's gold industry. The gold-mining enterprises still lack sufficient capital to update equipment and technology as required.

The introduction of a 5% customs duty on gold exports in April 1999 disappointed the Russian gold-producers, as well as commercial banks involved in the gold exports. To get around this tax, the Russian gold is now being exported via "gray routes", i.e. through countries that are members of the customs union with Russia. The major route is through Belarus (according to the Russian State Customs Committee estimates, in the first half of 2001 96.5% of the total commercial banks' exports was made via this former Soviet Republic).

Although the current world trend in the gold-mining industry is the merging of smaller gold manufacturers into larger corporations, the rate of small companies and artels in Russia is still very high - - about 70% (although they produce only 11% of the total gold output). Such small entities fail to attract investments and are often unable to maintain financial sustainability. But there is already emerging an understanding in the industry of the necessity for amalgamation to better adapt to the existing situation. The latter requires decreasing production costs, introduction of new technologies, and attraction of domestic and foreign investments. Another reason for merging is the on-going shifting from the placer to lode gold production, which needs considerable initial capital investments.

Recent Gold Production Statistics: In 2000 Russia produced 143 tons of gold, 13.2% more than in 1999. In the first 5 months of 2001 (before the active season started) the growth was already 13.9% more than in the same period of 2000.

In the RFE the most successful was **Sakha Republic (Yakutiya)**, where gold production increased by 150%. One of the reasons for such impressive growth was the 1-ton "golden loan" given to Aldanzoloto by Komdragmet of the Sakha Republic (Committee of Precious Metals, a state agency), and used for purchasing new equipment. Other leading enterprises in Sakha are Bamskaya, Drazhnik, Zolotinka, Zapadnaya, Nirungan, Ingali, Poisk, Zoloto Yinykchana, and Zoloto Neryungri.

Annual gold production growth in **Chukotka** was over one ton in 2000. Among the leaders are Ruda (35% growth in ore gold mining), Chukotka (300 kg increase), Arctica, Polyarnaya, and Shakhtyor. Severniye Rudniye Tekhnologii produced 600 kg versus 80 kg during the previous year.

According to the statistics of the **Magadan Oblast** Administration, the volume of gold produced in 2000 was 30 tons, which is 650-kg growth compared to 1999, and the highest results within the last 7 years. There is a slight shrinkage in gold production in 2001.

Amur Oblast also increased gold production, which reached 11.86 tons in 2000. The best results were achieved by Solovyovskiy Priisk (1.8 tons), Maya, Vostok-1, Zeya, Rassvet, Dalnyaya, Khergu, and Petrovskoye. In the first 7 months of 2001 the region produced 5.18 tons (1.29 tons of lode gold, and 3.89 tons of placer gold). It is 7.4% more than in the same period of 2000. By the end of this year Amur Regions plans to mine about 13 tons.

The growth rate of the gold-mining industry in **Khabarovskiy Krai** increased 10 times, and was 35% (In 1999 it was 3.5%). In 2000 Kahabrovskiy Krai was in 6th place among the leading gold-mining regions of Russia, and produced 9.2 tons of gold. The projected growth in 2001 is 9%, and the territory plans to mine over 10 tons of gold. Such dramatic increase was the result of the growth of ore gold mining, which now prevails over placer gold extraction. The largest deposits of ore gold are Monogovershinnoye (mined by the company with the same name, which produced 3 tons in 2000), and Ryabinovoye (mined by Amur, which is also one of the largest Russian platinum producers). Other companies with growing production are Vostok, Sever, Zarya, Pribrezhnaya, and Ros-DV.

The results in **Primorskiy Krai** were much less impressive - - 460 kg. It was mainly because last year was the first for several start-up companies. But in 2001 some growth is expected. Nevada Manhattan, a U.S. license holder for mining Glukhoye lode has not started any site operations yet.

MAJOR DEPOSITS, PROJECTS, AND KEY-PLAYERS

The JV Omolonskaya Zolotorudnaya Kompaniya, the second largest gold-mining company in Russia mines the Kubaka lode in Northeast Magadan. Initially the 50% share belonged to the US company Cyprus Amax, and another 50% was distributed between several local companies (Dukatskiy GOK, Magadanskaya Zolotoserebryannaya Kompaniya, Geometall, Elektrum, and the North-Evenk regional association of Evenk tribes). In 1996 Geometall and Elektrum merged into Geometall Plus, and their mutual share grew up to 28%. Later Cyprus Amax sold its share in the JV to the Canadian Kinross Gold Co., while 85.6% of Geometall Plus was acquired by another Canadian firm Western Pinnacle. Now it is a project with major Canadian participation. A total investment of $250 million resulted in extraction of over 50 tons of gold since 1997. In 2000 the company mined 13 tons of gold.

The Kuranakh gold deposit (about 300 tons) in Yakutiya was expected to be mined by Kuranakh Gold Mining Company - - a JV between the local Aldanzoloto, Sakhazoloto, and Canada's Echo Bay Mines. But now the US Newmont Gold is in the process of purchasing shares from Echo Bay Mines. The Kuranakh is included into the list of deposits that are to be mined under PSA, but the parties have not yet agreed about the terms and conditions (note: the PSA process can be very lengthy, and Echo Bay has been involved in this process for several years).

The Nezhdaninskoye lode was discovered in 1961 and is located 800 km to the east from Yakutsk (Sakha Republic/Yakutiya). Projected reserves are 95 million of ore (494 tons of gold with the content of 5.1 grams per 1 ton of ore). It is the second largest gold deposit in Russia. In 1996 the Irish Celtic

Resources Holding PLC together with the Russian companies Finansovo-Promyshlennaya Kompaniya and Sakhazloto formed the JV Yuzhno-Verkhoyanskaya Mining Company. But the gold production can start only after the Russian Duma and the government adopts the PSA on this deposit. Without a PSA specifying favorable terms for foreign investors the low initial profitability and delayed returns on investments make this project unattractive.

The Pokrovskoye gold lode is one of the largest in the Amur Oblast. It is mined by Pokrovskiy Rudnik company, which became famous throughout Russia for its unique experience of year-round production by the method of glomeroblastic leaching, and mined 1.5 tons in 2000. This year the company started to build a new gold-extraction plant with annual production capacity of 4 tons. The company already has produced 1.23 tons of gold in 7 months of 2001. One of the largest deposits in the region deposit Bamskoye (over 150 tons of projected reserves) is being exploited by Apsakan company. In 1-2 years it plans to produce 2-3 tons annually.

The Mayskoye deposit in Chukotka (about 300 t of gold in reserves) has already passed three readings, but was not signed by the president because, according to his advisors, it must go through additional editing to better meet the existing legal requirements. The license belongs to the Fund of Chukotka's Development, Fund of the Development of the Chukotka's Economy, artel Chukotka, and Chaunskiy Mining-Geological Enterprise. If the PSA is adopted, several international investors are interested in participating in this project.

The Mnogovershinnoye lode is located in the north of Khabarovskiy Krai near the city of Nikolayevsk-on-Amur. Its reserves are 105 tons of gold with an average content of 9 grams per ton. Mnogovershinnoye is mined by the Mnogovershinnaya Company. It started development of the lode in 1999, and mined 3 tons of gold in 2000. The company plans to reach projected annual capacity of 5 tons in 2002.

BUSINESS OPPORTUNITIES

The major share of local gold-mining equipment is outdated, with a high wear-and-tear rate. There is substantial demand for a broad range of machinery for mining both placer and lode gold, as well as ore-dressing and engineering equipment. Due to political, and then economic, reasons, U.S. equipment was rarely imported in the past. Both political and economic changes as well as growing gold production in the RFE present business opportunities for U.S. exporters of mining equipment.

Among the best sales prospects are: trucks, bulldozers, excavators, drilling machinery, ore-dressing equipment, ore-crushing/milling machinery, and ore-recovering equipment.

Further Assistance for U.S. Companies

This information is being provided by the U.S. & Foreign Commercial Service in Russia, which offers its services to U.S. companies wishing to sell U.S. products and services in Russia, including identifying distributors and arranging meetings with prospective buyers during business visits. Commercial Service Russia has offices in Moscow, St. Petersburg, Vladivostok and Yekaterinburg.

Contact: For further information you are welcome to contact the author of this report at CS Vladivostok:
Yana Tselikova
U.S. Commercial Service Vladivostok
32 Pushkinskaya Street
Vladivostok, Russia, 690000
Tel.: (7-4232) 300-093
Fax: (7-4232) 300-092
Int'l Fax: (7-509) 851-1211
E-mail: Yana.Tselikova@mail.doc.gov or Vladivostok.office.box@mail.doc.gov
www.cs.vladivostok.com

Since 2000, Russia's gold production has been steadily increasing with 154 t being produced in 2001 (of which 142t represented mine production, the highest in Russia's history). Russia has a variable gold production industry with only 14% of its gold producers (about 78 companies) producing 74% of Russia's gold. It is estimated that 69% of Russia's 389 gold producers mined less than 100kg of gold, accounting for only 11% of Russia's total production. This has led to no consolidation and therefore stagnation of the industry. Production from these mines are sold exclusively to the Gokhran (State reserve). Similar to South Africa, Russia is thought to employ approximately 400 000 people in its gold mining industry. "Artels" or private entrepreneurial brigades of gold prospectors produce nearly half of Russia's gold production.

Canadian companies have been the largest foreign investors in Russia's gold industry, although investment has dropped almost 90% since 1995. Canada's Bema Gold, Western Pinnacle and High River Gold Mines are among the main investors, with Placer Dome and Barrick appraising the development of the giant Sukhoi Log gold lode in Irkutsk region, which has an estimated $1.5 billion start up cost. Apart from having a potential 43 Moz resource base, Sukhoi Log also has significant PGM potential.

The Irkutsk region produced just over 12 t of gold in 1999, with production stemming from two main producers, the Lenzoloto gold company (producing more than half) and the Vitim artel producing 2 t.

Most production is from placer deposits in the eastern parts of Russia, with most identified resources (60%) located in the Russian Far East and in eastern Siberia. Nearly half of Russia's gold is produced from the Magadan Oblast (30t), Krasnoyarsk (15t) and the Yakut – Sabkha Republic (11t) regions. Hard rock deposits are generally low grade at around 4g/t. Due to the fact that most of Russia's production is sourced from placer deposits, the reserve base is being diminished rapidly. Emphasis is to be placed on the delineation of new mines, which is going to require major investments.

The Russian banks are still purchasing large amounts of gold for stockpiling and investments with the State Precious Metals and Gold Reserve (Gokhran) planning to buy 60 t of gold in 2000.

The Magadan Region in Russia's Far East produced 29 t of gold in 1999 and intends to increase production to 35 t in 2000. Nearly 60% of gold production from this region was derived from lode deposits, with the remainder from placer deposits.

Kinross Mining has a 54.7% share in the high grade (average grade of 24 g/t) Kubaka mine in the Russian Far East in the Magadan Oblast area. Kubaka produced 450 000 oz in 2000 (at cash costs of $139/oz) and plans to produce only 391 000 oz in 2001, possibly as a result of decreasing grade.

Western Pinnacle's subsidiary, the Omolon Gold Company is Russia's second largest gold producer, after the Polyus artel from the Krasnoyarsk territory. Omolon produced 15.4 t in 1999, with the Polyus artel producing 15.7t. of gold. The Omolon gold mine in the Magadan area was constructed in the late 1990's with a planned production of around 300 000 ounces gold and 200 000 oz silver annually. The Krasnoyarsk territory, whose gold production is sourced mainly from lode gold deposits (totalling 33 out of 190), aims at producing between 25 – 27t gold by 2005.

The Urals have traditionally been Russia's main gold producing region, with ZAO Yuzhuralzoloto being the major producer, producing its quota of 1.5 t in 1999. The focus of Yuzhuralzoloto's operations is on the Svetlinskoye gold lode in Plast, which is estimated to contain 100 tonnes of gold and 80 tonnes of silver. Yuzhuralzoloto were also carrying out a feasibility study to develop the Mikhailov placer deposit, thought o contain just over 1t of gold. However, production from Yuzhuralzoloto's operations should be as much as 4.5 t/year.

High River Gold Mines has a 54.5% interest in JSC Buryatzoloto, one of Russia's largest gold producers. It currently has two operational lode gold mines in southern Siberia (the Zun-Holba and Irokinda gold lodes) which produced just over 127 000 oz in 2000 (with average cash costs of $160/oz). Buryatzoloto has total estimated reserves and resources totaling nearly 12 Moz gold. The company's previous heavy reliance on hedging books is decreasing with a small hedging programme in place for the years 2000 through 2004, consisting of annual forward sales of 7 200 oz declining to 4 800 oz, at prices approximating US $401 per ounce. This means that more than 95% of production will be sold at current bullion prices. Production in 2001 is expected to be 10% higher at 140 000 oz gold. In mid 2002, High River Gold acquired the Berezitovoye Au-Ag-Zn-Pb project, located in the Amur region of southern Siberia. The deposit has estbalished reserves estimated at containing 1.38 Moz gold and 6.5 Moz silver.

Canadian Bema Gold Corporation has completed the construction and development of the $45 million high grade Julietta gold and silver project situated in the Magadan Oblast region. Bema has a 79% interest in the Julietta gold mine through its 79% owned Russian subsidiary Omsukchansk Mining Geological Company ("OMGC"). The remaining 21% is owned by local Russian partners. Initial annual production of some 140 000 oz gold and 2.4 Moz silver are anticipated. Total operating cash costs (including royalties and taxes) of less than $100/oz are expected at Julietta. Full production is expected to begin in late 2001.

The mineral rich internal province of Yakutia produced approximately 15 t of gold in 1999, with this total expected to increase to over 20 t with the development of the Nezhdaninzkoye gold lode, which has been estimated to contain over 340 t of gold. Celtic Resources has a 50% interest in a joint venture to develop Nezhdaninzkoye and have set up a joint stock company, South Verkoyansk Mining Company to develop the mine.

Gold production in Russia goes back many centuries.

Rich alluvial deposits in the Ural mountains yielded gold that passed down ancient trade routes to the Black Sea and the Mediterranean. And a quartz outcrop found at Ekaterinburg in the Urals in 1774 stimulated the Czars to greater exploration. Over the next century prospectors moved steadily east into the Altai mountains and into Siberia along the tributaries of the Yenisei river, locating many alluvial deposits. By the 1840s Russia had become the world's leading producer. In 1847, the year before gold was discovered in California, Russian output was between 30 and 35 tonnes, out of a world total of about 75 tonnes. California, then Australia and later South Africa, changed the perspective, but Russian production continued to rise and in 1914 was about 60 tonnes.

After the Revolution Stalin saw gold mining as one way of opening up the vast wastes of Siberia, having noted the effect California had on the development of the American West. He even recruited an American mining engineer, John D. Littlepage, who supervised the birth of a more modern mining industry in the Soviet Union in the 1920s and 1930s. Output, essentially in Russia itself, increased rapidly to around 155 tonnes annually, almost on a par with Canada and the United States. Thereafter no hard information was available before the early 1990s, but until then the Soviet Union was the second biggest producer (after South Africa), helped by the opening of the giant Muruntau mine in Uzbekistan in 1969.

In Russia itself most production has always been alluvial, coming mainly from placer deposits in Siberia. These are concentrated in an area embracing the Lena and Aldan rivers, the province of Magadan, and the Kamchatka and Chukotsk peninsulas, opposite Alaska, where very similar gold deposits are encountered. The harsh climate means the mining is seasonal; even in summer extracting gold from terrain locked solid by the

permafrost is difficult. Much of the gold is won by huge dredges excavating gold-bearing sands in the rivers once they thaw. The heart of the system is over 200 artels, or co-operatives, each managing their own affairs and employing between 30 and 1,000 people.

Since the collapse of the Soviet Union production within Russia itself has declined steadily, beset not just by problems of lack of fresh investment, but in the mid-1990s by a virtual breakdown in the payments system to the artels, so that not only were advance payments not forthcoming, but serious delays occurred in payment for gold. And while inflation sent production costs soaring, official prices scarcely rose. In 1996 output fell in all but two of Russia's 30 gold producing regions to a modest 130 tonnes, ranking Russia sixth in the world league, behind China.

The outlook, however, is that gold mining in Russia will stabilise if the economy can be put on a firmer footing and the political, legal and tax position of foreign investors confirmed. Plenty of unexploited alluvial deposits exist but the initial experiences of Australian and North American companies to establish joint ventures were often fraught. However, Amax Gold's Kubaka mine came on stream in 1997 with potential output of 10 tonnes annually and by the millennium Russia's production should be rising again, especially if Sukhoi Log can be developed.

GOLD IN FAR EAST

The Russian Far East accounts for the largest share of gold mined in Russia (almost 70%). The richest gold deposits are located in the Amur, Kamchatka and Magadan regions and the Republic of Sakha. Not long ago, the gold-mining industry in the Far East was composed of four large state-owned organizations: "Amurzoloto," "Primorzoloto," "Yakutzoloto," and "Severovostokzoloto," all under Moscow ministry control. Each organization consisted of lower-level operating units and ore-dressing complexes (Russian term GOK: gorno-obogatitelniy kombinat). Under each GOK, were individual mining operations: placer mines (priisk) or bedrock mines (rudnik). There also existed independent mining teams (the Artel). These teams constituted an important part of the gold-mining industry even in Tsarist Russia. The distinguishing feature of independent Artels was that they worked without the state support. At present, these pyramid-like organizations have split up into many separate parts that now act independently. The main problems of the gold-mining industry are high fuel costs, high taxes and Moscow's inability to provide loans or other forms of capital for the industry. Therefore, foreign capital is highly sought-after to contribute to the development of gold mining.

Relevant Laws, Decrees and Regulations: Demand for gold on the Russian domestic market accounts for no more than 15% of supply. In order to stimulate the demand for gold, the Russian government issued a directive which allows the sale of gold bullion to members of the public. Bullion can be purchased:

--Directly: The purchaser pays 20% VAT at bank's stock exchange site; purchaser pays a 3% commission to the exchange.
--In addition, the Finance Ministry is drawing up regulations to permit individuals to take gold into and out of Russia. Rules under which banks and credit organizations may trade precious metal bullion with members of the public came into effect in June, 1997. All transactions must be accompanied by receipts containing detailed descriptions of the deal and the origin of the metals.

The Administration of Magadan Region recently signed a decree on "Extraction of Gold by Individuals." The decree gives permission for licensed individuals to extract precious metals without using heavy machinery. To obtain the license, an individual must file an application with the district where he intends to extract gold, and pay the associated licensing fees. The extracted gold is sold to specialized agencies, after deduction of 12 % income tax.

FUTURE DEVELOPMENT OF THE GOLD MINING INDUSTRY:

Yakutia (Sakha): During the last five years Yakutia produced 25% of Russia's gold output. Gold is mined in the Tsentralno-Aldanskiy, Verkhne-Indigirskiy, Allakh-Yunskiy and Kularskiy gold fields. The gold mining industry of the republic is looking for ways to expand the output of vein gold mining and buried placers. The cost of gold produced in Yakutia is higher than the world market price, due to high transport and energy costs (often in the Far East, electricity supplies to mines are disrupted completely for several hours at a time). Sakha Republic government experts say that profit margins of gold production are continuing to contract and will not pick up until current economic policy with respect to the gold industry is adjusted. But despite all of this, the Republic is hoping to export raw materials abroad and to attract foreign capital to develop large resource-extraction projects.

A U.S. company, Echo Bay Mines (Englewood, Colorado) maintains a 50% stake in a joint venture with Russian partners Aldanzoloto (30%) and Sakhazoloto (20%) formed for development of the Kuranakh deposit project near the town of Aldan. They are drilling at the deposit to verify and augment existing

Russian data. Under Russian federal legislation, the Kuranakh project is now eligible for a production sharing agreement, which holds the promise of favorable (stable) tax treatment and a gold marketing agreement. Though the project is still at a very early stage and must clear additional hurdles, it has received endorsements from the Sakha government as well as the Russian Federation government.

Magadan Region: The Magadan economy is based upon the extraction and processing of raw materials. The mining industry has undergone many changes and dislocations, but still accounts for more than 70% of the region's industrial output. Regional and local officials believe that for the industry to get out of its present crisis, it must come to terms with its real costs of production and with the declining quality of its ore base. New deposits are mostly hard rock, and exploitation of these requires substantial capital. The region hopes and expects to see more business groups bringing financial capital to enterprises that are seeking to expand into hard rock mining.

The Kubaka project would produce an average of more than 300,000 ounces of gold and 200,000 ounces of silver annually. The Kubaka mine has gold reserves of 2.5 million ounces. A joint venture, the Omolon Gold Mining Company, was established to carry out construction for future development of the Kubaka lode gold deposit. Puget Sound International (Seattle, WA), one of the companies supporting the Kubaka project, supplied electrical and pluming equipment. Current problems facing the project are: difficulty in selling the output profitably (due to low world market prices for gold) and the needs to explore new mine deposits, as known resources of the Kubaka mine will be fully depleted within 9 years.

Arian Resources (U.K.) holds the licence to develop the Julietta gold-and-silver deposit in the Magadan Region. The Arian Resources Corporation secured a USD 40 million project loan from Standard Bank (London) for the development of the project operated by Omsukchan Mining and Geological Company. This is the first commercial loan from a western bank for a mining project in Russia. Arian Resources announced a USD 6.5 million nonbrokered placement in September. Public offerings by prospectus were planned for early 1998. The Julietta deposit contains initial reserves and resources of 866,000 gold equivalent ounces. The mine is scheduled to produce 127,000 gold equivalent ounces per year during its first three years of operation.

The Kamchatka Region: Prospects for the mining industry in Kamchatka are tied to the development of the gold mining industry. The development of Kamchatka's mining industry began in 1994 when the Kamchatka Geology Committee announced international tenders for exploration of two gold reserves: the Aginskoye reserve in central Kamchatka and the Asachinskoye and Rodnikovoye reserves in southern Kamchatka. According to rough estimates, these deposits contain 198 tons of gold and 650 tons of silver. There are many placer gold deposits in the south of Kamchatka, where extract ion of gold with the help of heavy machinery is not permitted for ecological reasons. The most efficient alternative may be to give permission to individuals to extract gold as has been done in the Magadan Region (see "Relevant Laws, decrees and regulations" above). The main factor impeding Kamchatka's mining industry is lack of detailed geological exploration surveys of most of the deposits. The federal and regional government hope to attract foreign partners to invest in the carrying out of the necessary surveys.

A potentially significant gold-mining project in the region, the Aginskoye project is perhaps the most controversial project in the Russian Far East. Foreign partners in the Kamgold Joint venture have unsuccessfully sought financing and USD 50 million in political risk insurance from the Overseas Private Investment Corporation, with opposition of U.S. and other Western and Russian environmental groups and activists as the key obstacle (among other opposition, several American non-governmental organizations lobbied intensively and successfully to have volcanic areas of Kamchatka, including the Aginskoye project location, designated as "World Heritage Sites" by the United Nations in 1996, over the objections of Kamchatka authorities). Kamgold cannot begin the project without such risk insurance. More recently, it is reported that the Aginskoye project has managed to receive political risk insurance from the International Union for Conservation of Nature. Project developers are also seeking a credit from Dresdner Bank. The project is being undertaken by Kamgold, a joint venture originally formed between Russian partner Kamgeo (itself a consortium of local government, Kamchatnedra - the local Committee on Surface Mineral Use - and private Russian companies Desi Holdings, Kamchatipex, Kon and Pobedit) and U.S. partners Asarco (New York, NY) and Grynberg Resources (Cranford, NJ). In April, 1995, Asarco was replaced by Kinross Gold (Toronto, Canada) which purchased Asarco's interest in the Aginskoye project.

THE GOLD MINING INDUSTRY IN KRASNOYARSK KRAI, RUSSIA

by Azim Mamanov, BISNIS Network Representative, Novosibirsk, Russia

The Krasnoyarsk Krai is one of Russia's richest areas with natural resources. The most important resources are natural gas, oil, hydroelectric power, timber, manganese, copper, mercury, rare earth metals, ferrous and non-ferrous metals, coal, platinum, high-quality marbles, and precious and semiprecious stones.

Another important natural resource is gold. Approximately 20% of all of Russias gold is located in the Krasnoyarsk Krai, which makes it the richest Russian region for gold.

Currently, twenty seven enterprises are involved in gold mining. One hundred and thirty nine deposits of gold are being explored, including 16 ore and 126 loose deposits. Mainly loose deposits are being explored, even though resources of ore deposits amount up to 89 percent of the gold found in the Krai. Meanwhile, the majority of the gold extracted is coming from loose deposits, and the Program of Development of the Gold Mining Industry in the Krasnoyarsk, with the estimated cost of US$ 1 million. Krai priorities extraction of gold from ore deposits. Up to 25-27 tons of gold are planned to be mined annually during 50 years, which will make the Krai a leading gold-mining region in Russia. Implementation of the Program stipulates maintaining of the existing gold mining enterprises (for instance "Zoloto" JSC, "Severo-Angarsky GMK" JSC, "Artemovsky Rudnik", etc.), as well as establishing new gold-mining sites. The sites are mainly located in Nizhneye Priangarie (Low Angara) and their development is stipulated in another program called the Federal Program for the Development of Nizhneye Priangarie (http://www.rmi.net/racc/Krasnoyarsk.html). The following table shows the planned dynamics of the gold mining in the Krasnoyarsk Krai:

Location

GOLD MINING, TONS

	1996	1997	1998	1999	2000	2005
For entire Krai, including:	8.13	12.67	16.19	18.43	20.02	21.31
ore gold	2.68	6.76	10.42	13.12	15.23	19.55
loose gold	5.45	5.91	5.77	5.31	4.79	1.76
I. Eniseysky Mining & Industry Region, including:	6.40	10.05	13.45	15.87	17.41	19.50
ore gold	2.35	5.93	9.39	12.09	14.20	18.52
loose gold	4.05	4.12	4.06	3.78	3.21	0.98
1. Bolshemurtinsky sub-region, loose gold	0.26	0.12	0.12	0.12	0.12	0.07
2. Eniseysky sub-region, loose gold	-	-	-	-	0.05	0.05
3. Motyginsky sub-region,	1.43	2.50	2.77	3.46	3.80	3.26

including						
ore gold	-	0.8	1.10	1.90	2.50	2.80
loose gold	1.43	0.70	1.67	1.56	1.30	0.46
4. Rybinsky sub-region, inluding	0.03	0.03	0.03	0.23	0.23	0.20
ore gold	-	-	-	0.20	0.20	0.20
loose gold	0.03	0.03	0.03	0.03	0.03	-
5. Severo-Eniseysky sub-region, including	4.29	7.15	10.38	11.49	13.10	15.92
ore gold	2.35	5.13	8.29	9.99	11.50	15.52
loose gold	1.94	2.02	2.09	1.95	1.60	0.40
6. Sukhobuzimsky sub-region, loose gold	0.26	0.12	0.07	0.07	0.07	-
7. Turukhansky sub-region, loose gold	0.13	0.13	0.08	0.05	0.04	-

----

II. South and Center of the Krai, including	1.73	2.62	2.74	2.56	2.61	1.81
ore gold	0.33	0.83	1.03	1.03	1.03	1.03
loose gold	1.40	1.79	1.71	1.53	1.58	0.78
8. Balakhtinsky sub-region, loose gold	0.21	0.24	0.15	0.09	0.07	-
9. Emelyansky sub-region, loose gold	-	-	-	-	0.05	0.05
10.Ermakovsky sub-region, loose gold	0.16	0.30	0.33	0.30	0.26	-
11. Irbeysky sub-region, loose gold	-	-	-	-	0.15	0.15
12. Karatuzsky sub-region, loose gold	0.25	0.35	0.35	0.35	0.35	0.35
13. Kuraginsky sub-region, including	0.72	1.35	1.68	1.58	1.55	1.21
ore gold	0.33	0.83	1.03	1.03	1.03	1.03
loose gold	0.39	0.52	0.65	0.55	0.52	0.18
14. Partizansky sub-region, loose gold	0.19	0.19	0.19	0.20	0.14	0.05
15. Sayansky sub-region, loose gold	0.20	0.19	0.04	0.04	0.04	-

For American companies and investors it's extremely important that they find highly qualified local partners that can help develop their business more successfully. One such potential partners is the "KrasnoyarskGeologia" JSC.

The main activities of the company are: all types of geological and prospecting works connected with prospecting and exploring solid natural resources, coal and underground water resources; engineering and geological research; environment protection.

For the last few years the company's activity is mainly concentrated in the regions with existing gold and iron mines. Furthermore, the geology prospecting works were mainly concentrated in searching for gold deposits.

Besides the work conducted for the state, the company provides its services to private companies. Particularly, the company is designing the work plan on the Ayakhtinsky ore field for the Canadian gold-mining company "Barrik Gold Corporation".
The company has been involved in the loose gold mining mainly since 1993. Within that period of time the company mined 210 kilograms of gold. In 1996, the revenue from the gold mining was 11 percent from the total revenue of the company. In 1997, the revenue from the gold mining was 2.6 million rubles, which is about 10 percent from the total revenue of the company. The company has technology, equipment and highly qualified staff for the gold mining. For today, the company has 6 licenses for the loose gold mining in the Krasnoyarsk Krai. Reserves of the gold in these deposits are estimated 1.2 tons. In addition, the company applied for licenses for other 30 deposits. Prognosticated reserves of the deposits being licensed total 1.3 tons.
The company is seeking American partners to prospect and mine solid natural resources, including gold. The company can provide its wide range of services connected with prospecting and exploring natural resources.

Contact: Anatoly Khokhlov, Director General
Karl Marx St., 62
Krasnoyarsk, Russia 660049
Phone: 7-3912-272906
Fax: 7-3912-272906
E-mail: krasgeolog@vsptus.oilnet.ru

RUSSIAN GOLD PRODUCTION 1991-1997

This table can be sorted by column. Just click on the column heading.

Unit: kilograms							
Area	1991	1992	1993	1994	1995	1996	1997
Karelia	n/a	n/a	n/a	n/a	31	8	12
Komi Republic	218	350	350	850	106	46	41
Bashkortostan	305	320	515	788	566	321	44
Orenburg oblast	55	86	85	130	n/a	n/a	n/a
Sverdlovsk oblast	3877	3302	3712	3514	3267	2182	1049
Chelyabinsk oblast	1945	1714	1769	2175	1609	1149	662
Altai krai	48	54	200	350	n/a	n/a	n/a
Altai Republic	235	287	319	650	259	418	146

Khanty-Mansii Autonomous okrug	n/a	n/a	n/a	n/a	125	96	114
Kemerovo oblast	922	608	1050	1550	873	796	336
Novosibirsk oblast	295	117	143	205	387	280	259
Republic of Khakasiya	1195	1483	2218	2665	1343	1873	715
Irkutsk oblast	11000	7232	11925	11800	11649	11876	11221
Chita oblast	7800	8470	8167	7900	7228	6110	4630
Buryat Republic	2600	2745	3370	2700	4293	4370	4126
Republic of Tyva	70	462	750	900	775	1002	729
Krasnoyarsk krai	6535	6369	7057	7250	7047	8774	17481
Primorskii krai	240	244	455	450	421	272	31
Khabarovsk krai	7795	7514	7702	8580	8358	8275	7091
Amur oblast	10800	10222	11200	12990	12418	11805	9651
Jewish Autonomous oblast	n/a	n/a	n/a	n/a	n/a	156	92
Koryak Autonomous okrug	n/a	n/a	n/a	n/a	421	413	333
Sakhalin oblast	165	190	144	160	n/a	n/a	n/a
Republic of Sakha	32800	30515	33358	31000	28759	22946	19988
Magadan oblast	30388	29156	28600	32900	22343	20775	26074
Chukotka AO	14412	14417	13068	13500	9790	9231	9083
Other	n/a	n/a	75	170	n/a	n/a	n/a
Total (as published)	133700	126021	136232	144057	122118	113630	114129
Total (as calculated)	133700	125857	136232	143177	122068	113174	113908
Difference	0	164	0	880	50	456	221

UZBEKISTAN

The largest gold mine in the former Soviet Union opened at Muruntau (meaning "hilly place") in the Kyzyl-Kum desert of Uzbekistan in 1969.

After nearly three decades it still produces close to 55 tonnes annually, ranking Uzbekistan second in the new Commonwealth of Independent States gold league and accounting for almost one-quarter of all CIS output. The mine is still worked as an open pit, now over 3.5 kms long, 2.5 kms wide and over 300 metres deep.

The deposit resembles a tree with branches spreading out near the surface and the trunk plunging into the earth. The gold, originally graded up to 4 g/t (0.12 oz/t), but by the 1990s declined to 2.6 g/t (0.08 oz/t). Work at depth in the pit had become increasingly difficult due to poor air circulation which causes summer temperatures to rise to 50 degrees centigrade. Underground mining of the 'tree trunk' may eventually be necessary if the investment needed is available. Meanwhile Muruntau's life is being extended by a joint project between the Uzbekistan government and Newmont Mining from the United States to heap-leach low grade stockpiles around the mine, recovering up to 1 g/t.

Operations started late in 1995 and are set to yield 1 tonne per month for several years. Gold output has also risen as a by-product of copper mining at Almalyk, pushing Uzbekistan's output to 71 tonnes in 1996, ranking the republic eighth in the world league.

KAZAKHSTAN

Kazakhstan, the CIS republic stretching from the Caspian Sea to the borders of China, has immense mineral reserves in oil, natural gas, base metals and gold.

Under the Soviet regime the gold was primarily a by-product of lead and zinc mining, but two new projects, Aksu and Bakyrchik Gold, developed as joint ventures with the help of Australian and Canadian mining groups, despite poor local infrastructure and a harsh climate, lifted production to just over 20 tonnes by 1996.

Initially all gold had to be offered to the central bank, which would pay in dollars.

COMMONWEALTH OF INDEPENDENT STATES (CIS)

Taken together the Commonwealth of Independent States (the former Soviet Union) rated fourth in world production in 1996 with output of 223 tonnes. However, that reflected a decline of 20 per cent on a decade earlier when the Soviet Union was in comfortable second place behind South Africa, a position it had held for most of the twentieth century. (gold production 1840 -1996)

In the meantime, output in most other countries rose inexorably with the United States and Australia easily outstripping it. A diverse pattern has evolved, however, within the individual states: while production in Russia itself (historically the main gold region) fell, it increased elsewhere, especially in Uzbekistan and Kazakhstan with new projects also going ahead in Tajikistan. (CIS gold production 1989 - 1996)

The story of gold mining in each of these states is covered in their own entries, but what has emerged in recent years with respect to the old Soviet Union is that overall gold mine production during the communist era, which was a secret, never reached the levels forecast by some western analysts. The peak output was 285 tonnes in 1989, and suggestions that production was regularly over 300 tonnes in the 1970s and 80s proved false. The immediate consequence of this over-optimism was that when the Soviet Union collapsed its gold reserves were much less than anticipated.

The received wisdom was that Soviet reserves were 1,500 to 2,500 tonnes; actually in 1988, as the Soviet Union entered its crisis period, they were only 850 tonnes. Most of this modest reserve was soon swapped for foreign exchange, and then sold out during the early 1990s. The inheritance of the new CIS, therefore, was neither a high level of production nor reserves. While the CIS possess extensive mineral wealth, investment in development, which calls for western finance and technology, has been slow in forthcoming, especially in Russia itself, because of the political, legal and economic uncertainties of the new regimes.

Several promising gold projects have fallen foul of governments moving the legal or tax goal posts, amid some reluctance to permit foreigners access to rich resources. Taking a longer view through the twenty-first century, however, the Commonwealth of Independent States will ultimately have significant gold deposits to be mined

THE CURRENT STATE OF PRECIOUS METALS MARKET IN RUSSIA

V. Fadeev, Bank MENATEP, St. Petersburg

Despite a series of dramatic in periods in the development of world economy and financial market, gold has not lost its appeal as a financial instrument.

Over the last 25 years of the development of the global exchange trade, demand for gold has almost doubled, especially in the private sector. A number of central banks successfully use reserve gold assets for obtaining supplementary incomes. Mining and technological companies due to gold have new sources of financing which depend on the cost of their capital and the price of precious metals. Private (individual) investors are able to make decisions on favorable investment of their savings owing to the availability of a set of financial tools associated with gold.

Current flourishing of the jeweler industry is a consequence of the developing exchange trade in futures and forwards contracts for the supply of physical gold. Gold is a basic elements of investment portfolios of various funds stabilizing their cost volatility.

Financial instruments

Financial instruments based on the use of gold are a form of gold mining financing. Development of new markets of both physical and paper gold has quickly adapted for the needs of the gold mining industry traditionally financed via loans and issue of shares. Forwards, option and futures contacts are used for mining financing and simultaneously help producers to optimize their balance sheet structure. This enables them to satisfy growing requirements of investors to business solvency of producers.

The technique of work with derivative financial instruments allows gold producers to reduce the value of financing, optimize volumes of borrowings and payments caused by business recession, secure themselves against sharp price changes, i.e. level up fluctuations of cash flows.

Gold producers, unfortunately, often have no clear understanding of the current state of the Russian financial market. This takes place against the background of depleting commercial reserves of placers gold which accounts for the bulk of Russia's total gold output.

A great many large and medium gold producers start seeking for opportunities of realizing their potentials on ore objects financing of which requires quite other orientations from participants in the bullion market. First of all, financial institutions should understand that the bullion market being not temporary business needs more serious assessment of its share and place in the total volume of banking business.

The financial analysis of work of mining enterprises shows that for the last ten years their turnover has reflected no major costs, which among other factors determine the trading cost of precious metals and money supply required for it. This took place with the active participation of banks which granted loans adjusting to the situation.

Unlike trade where capital turns over and redistributes much quickly, in mineral mining the bulk of resources are in fixed assets (capital is considerably less mobile). In this connection, banks financing gold mining projects often face problems from their unawareness of the necessity to finance production adequately to its cycle and input pattern. Ore gold mining projects cause particularly great difficulties. The main problem of the in this case is to make "short" money "long" and then secure its return. There are no changes for better in this sphere. A number of banks see a way out of the situation in transference of debts to property (when granting credits they demand corresponding pledges). However, prospects of their auction sale look unattractive taking into account the level of liquidity of assets in the gold mining sector of economy. The imperfect procedure of bankruptcy disable creditors to claim for property from defaulters.

To date, the issue of securities against accumulated debts and their sale on the open market is a new instrument that has recently emerged on the capital market. The use of the instrument may lead to the appearance of new owners of enterprises enabling them to avoid the formal procedure of bankruptcy of the debtor as transformation of debts into newly issued securities is determined by the Ministry of Finance of Russia and appropriate bodies of the Federation subjects. However, the development of the market of industrial enterprises' debts depends on the activity of banks and their understanding of its prospects.

The current state of the financial market

When appraising the prospects of commercial banks' participation in and will grow in the near two-three year, one should bear in mind that from the data of the Association of Russian Banks (ARB), capitalization of the whole bank system of Russia comes to about $4 billion, i.e. aggregate banking capital is below 3% of GDP. At the same time short money prevails in structure of banks' liabilities. Long-term financial resources of banks account to only 9% of the total sum of monetary resources and are mainly deposits of the population with more that 1 year fixed periods. "Long" money of banks is, as a rule, of foreign origin.

Contributions of the population and, to a lesser extent, corporate clients are, naturally, the most affective source of long money. According to the data of the ARB, three leading bank (SberBank, Vneshtorgbank and Gazprombank) account for over 30% of corporate clients, SberBank – for 86% of private contributions. However, short-term deposits prevail even in SberBank. The situation will hardly change soon as it depends on the solution of such a large-scale problem as gaining the population's confidence in the Russian bank system and the state after the 1998 crisis.

Besides, the situation is aggravated by strict norms of the Central Bank limiting, in particular, risks per one borrower and reservation of credit funds. Thus, banks are to reserve in the Central Bank sums sums sometimes equal to credit ones. This not only exhausts their resources but also leads to an automatic downturn in the class the bank's reliability complicating its work with foreign partners. And this takes place when gold mining projects estimated at not less than $150-200 million are ready for consideration for the attraction of investments.

In addition, banks which seriously desire to develop precious metals business face not only the problem of selecting a mining object, but also the necessity of preparing the client to the reception if investment resources. To achieve this, the bank should master the cycle of banking technologies to ensure project financing and control risks of corporate management during the whole period of realization of the project. It should be able to lead the client through all the stages of preparation for the acceptance of investments starting from the primary audit up to listing on the stick exchange on the bullion market.

Thus, with Russian banks having not only limited resources, but also experience in investing in the real sector of economy related to precious metals mining and project financing, let us turn to the appraisal of possible source of investments.

Market mechanisms of attracting investments

Direct (strategic) investments are the most conventional form of attracting financial resources in the gold mining industry. The readiness of Russian bank to hold shares depends on the features of the form of property of mining enterprises (artel, limited company, etc.) and their capitalization (which is low a; a rule) and capitalization of banks themselves (which is also comparatively low in most banks and in regional ones in particular). Rates of refinancing have been reducing over the last two years. This is to the advantage of gold producers but decreases the profit-making capacity of banks' assets. Most large barks capable of direct investing are interested mainly in the oil or gas branches and disregard the gold mining industry. In case they show strategic interest in gold mining, properly would be redistributed towards its consolidation. This will reserve as a redistributed for making the bullion market in Russia and may lead to the loss by the existing gold producers of their positions with all the ensuing consequences. Such examples already exist.

The other form of attracting money is the above mentioned portfolio (speculative) investment (the investor buys securities of the enterprise on the market to obtain profit from exchange trade). Unlike state securities with receipts from their trade spent for closing the budget gap, receipts from portfolio investment obtained from purchase and sale of shares already circulating on the market go to their former owner (seller), and from purchase of new shares directly to the enterprise which may invest them in its development. In Russia, there are a few enterprises ready to attract portfolio investment. However, their management is not quite prepared for working in this sphere of the attraction of money, and this juts bounds to realization of their opportunities. The task of banks working with these enterprises is to explain potentialities of the share market professionally and assist in the organization of issue of shares. Unfortunately, such banks nave other interests – drawing of profit from sale contracts.

Banks working with large gold producers should make themselves responsible for organization of the market of portfolio investment in corporate securities explaining to them the reason of their appeal for the share market. Moreover, strategic investors readily invest in authorized capitals of those joint-stock companies shares in which are objects of portfolio investments.

In case mining producers are unwilling to revise their shares in capital being sure of their ability to implement a project using their equities, banks ready to finance gold mining projects should pay attention to such financing instrument as corporate bonds. The latter may be not only the subject of the pledge, but also a means of replenishing the share market related to gold mining attracting additional or lacking resources. Issue of bonds is an alternative to bank credit (possibly at a lower interest rate). Projects of bond issue may stipulate for their retirement in gold. Bonds will be more attractive if their retirement in gold is effected at the price fixed on the date of issue (a dollar equivalent) thus protecting the investor from inflation. In Russia, this is possible only in case bonds have a gold backing. The advantage of bonds over shares can conciliate the interests of the borrower and creditor, since issue of liquid bonds allows to involve long-term resources, and the investor can receive investments at any moment through their selling on the secondary market. It is worth noting that banks engaged in the îil-and-gas sector widely use potentials of corporate bones as financial instruments.

Besides, condition of gold mining bank financing may be improved due to the use of regional resources.

In Russia traditionally there are practically no investment funds in resource regions though large investments are budgeted in the federation subjects. In this situation, the pledge value of guarantees even provided for in the line in the budget is doubtful for banks. If the best happened, the region can render investment support to enterprises by granting tax credits or offsetting mutual claims with the local budget. Such support reduces the tax burden on enterprises enabling them to allocate released funds for their development.

Financial leasing of fixed industrial assets is an additional instrument of banks, which reduces the tax burden on the enterprise on the one hand and the risk of crediting on the other hand. According to Russian legislation, leasing is a form of Investment activity related to the purchase of property and its transference to legal persons for the determined fee, certain period and on certain conditions specified by the contract, with the right to purchase this property by the lessee. Financial leasing used for investment purposes calls for the leased property use period comparable with or exceeding its full depreciation period. From the financial point of view, the leasing transaction is generally an alternative to the attraction of credits that the enterprise needs to purchase capital assets. In addition, banks become able to insure commitments. In case a leasing company belongs to a bank or keeps up long-term credit relations with it, the subject or leasing can be a reliable guarantee of this part of investment. The creditor cannot simply take the pledged assets, and the leasing company retains the possession of leased property. This gives it the indisputable right to return the property in its possession in case of the lessee's failure to perform obligations under the contract. This gives it the indisputable right to return the property in its possession in case of the lessee's failure to perform obligations under the contract.

It is necessary to note that intensive attention of representatives of many West gold-mining companies to Russian gold fields observed in 1990s before the crisis in the year of 1998, was connected with total gold price fall and necessity to search for high profitable gold fields. Besides, Russian working fields license-holders got the possession without any expenses. Low capitalization of gold-mining enterprises allowed foreign investors, whose companies' stocks quoted on the exchange, to increase first of all their capitalization without additional expenses.

However, inability of Russian license-holders to work with foreign investors, complicated law base and tax system for use of mineral resources and, finally, financial crisis in Russia and Russia's rating fall down almost to default – all that decreased possibilities to attract foreign investors.

To revive investment process in gold-mining industry, banks should lobby creation of regulatory base of corporative (syndicated) financing of gold-mining enterprises with foreign investor's participation.

Before the crisis in the year of 1998 banks were using this kind of financing as borrowers, but not as partners. At present time syndicated credits could solve the problem of "long" money to invest in projects with recoupment period of 2–3 years.

Besides, Russian banks that have been working with gold-mining sector for a long time, could attract foreign investments from venture funds for financing of gold-placer mining, where production cost is low.

Finally, there necessary mutual steps on development of technology of project financing of mining industry, where Russian banks could play considerable role in the way of operative work, information search and enterprises circulating capital crediting both in money and bill form, organization of finance leasing.

EXPLORATION FOR AND MINING OF GOLD AND PLATINUM METALS ON THE NIMENGSKAYA AREA

ZAO (closed joint-stock company) Severzapmetall is a holder of license ARKh 00632 BR for the right to conduct geological study and mine gold and platinum metals on the deposits revealed within the Nimengskaya area.

The Nimengskaya area promising for the discovery of gold and platinum metals deposits is located 200 km south-west of Arkhangelsk and links to its by a railway line and motor roads. A project area is characterized by developed infrastructure. Gold occurrences revealed within the area are of the following three types studied to different extents and requiring different methodical approaches:

- gold and platinum metals manifestation of the buried ancient placers formation in Vendian basal horizons;
- gold and platinum metals manifestation of the Quaternary placers formation;
- gold veins and vein deposits of the gold-quartz and gold-sulfide-quartz formation of the Archaean – Lower Proterozoic.

Five gold manifestations discovered on the Nimengskaya area are associated with a formation of ancient placers in gold-bearing conglomerates of the Vendian age and recent alluvial placers. The belt of development of gold-bearing conglomerates within the area is about 60 km long and from 0.5–1.0 to 4.0–5.0 km wide (2 km on the average). Expected gold resources in ancient conglomerates to a depth of up to 70 m are estimated at 87 t with average metal contents being 4–8 g/m3. Expected gold resources in alluvial quaternary placers are 7 t with ultrabasic and basic rocks are also of commercial importance. Discovery of platinum metals in quaternary placers (up to 15–20% of total metal in heavy concentrate of the sample) is a particularly important result of work in 2000 (Figs. 1, 2).

ZAO Severzapmetall invites Russian and foreign investors to participate in joint activity aimed at conduction of searches and exploration as well as development of revealed commercial deposits of gold and platinum metals through establishment of a joint enterprise. Allotment of shares in the enterprise and terms of cooperation will representatives of interested organizations.

ZAO Sevzapmetall
Russia, 162061 Arkhangelsk,
Ul. Loginova, 17 off.52
Phone/Fax: (+7-8182)64-14-68
E-mail: kraton@arh.ru

GOLD RESOURCES OF SEVERNAYA ZEMLYA

A.V. Cherepanov, *General Geologist, SGP CAPGE*
A.G. Listkov, *Severnaya Zemlya Group, SGP CAPGE*
M.I. Bentza, *Chief Geologist, Severnaya Zemlya Group*

Bolshevik hardrock & alluvial goldfield is located at the northern extremity of Russia washed by Arctic Ocean (Severnaya Zemlya Islands, at latitudes of 76–78° north), in poorly developed region of Taimyr autonomous district. The goldfield belongs to Taimyr- Severnaya Zemlya gold-bearing province. Mineral resource potential of the province has to be discovered yet; as the exploration cycle here is at a very early stage.

- Some 70–80% of the area have been covered by regional geological surveys;
- Large-scale surveying along with reconnaissance exploration program (GGS-50, geographic-geological survey) has been performed for separate sites. Exploration program didn't involve any mechanized sampling procedures like drilling, channeling or test mining. Up to date only 0.2% of the area have been surveyed, that is ten times less than in current gold producing regions;
- No exploration targeting primary gold and correspondent resource estimation had been carried out up till 1995.

So, while Bolshevik goldfield is the most explored area within Taimyr district, its total resource potential can be just vaguely outlined. Alluvial deposits have been well explored and resource/reserve calculation has been done (proved and probable reserves of Ñ1+Ñ2 categories are estimated at 9.5 mt of gold, or 38% of total resources, with probable increase of mineable reserves by further 2.5–5 mt). At the same time, primary gold resources can be just roughly estimated. According to various experts, they may contain from 150 mt (that is equivalent of US $1.4 billion) to 2,446 mt (US $23.2 billion).

Such a fundamental geological factor of a global nature as a consistent pattern of occurrence of large hardrock goldfields on the rim of the Siberian platform gives solid ground for the assumption of discovering here a new major goldfield.

- In the east the Siberian platform is flanked by Yano-Indigirskaya and Kolymskaya gold-bearing provinces with widely renowned hardrock and alluvial deposits. Since 1940th and up to early 1990th these provinces had been the main gold producing territory of the USSR. Its gold resources are estimated as containing well over one thousand tonnes;
- In the south the platform is bordered by Aldanskaya and Leno-Viluiskaya gold bearing provinces, where the major Russian gold deposit – Sukhoi Log – is located. Since the end of 19th century

both provinces have been important Russian gold producing regions (Lena gold placer mines). Their gold resources are estimated as containing several thousand tonnes;

- Along the west edge of the platform lies Yeniseiskyi gold-bearing region, which has been known for its industry potential for more than 150 years.
- In the north this gold-bearing ring encompassing the Siberian platform is closed by the Taimyr – Severnaya Zemlya gold-bearing province. The province industry potential has not been recognized yet due to an inadequate available exploration data. Nevertheless, close resemblance between the province and Yeniseiskyi region in geological structure, geological development, basic metalogenic and gold mineralization particularities makes the high industry potential of the province an indisputable issue. Even rather humble primary gold search efforts on Bolshevik island during the last three years have resulted in discovering some promising ore occurrences with gold grades from several dozens to several hundreds g/t.

It has been discovered that 2 out of 7 mineralization zones within Golyshevskiy gold ore field contain separate contiguous carbonate-quartz veins and quartz vein zones with grades over 20 g/t. In 1997, for example, in the Nizhnelitkinskaya zone of hardrock mineralization a group of steeply inclined veins was found with grades up to 257 g/t (an average grade 27 g/t with separate veins thickness of 0.4 m) and traced continuously over 720 m.

Surface churn drilling and trenching in the central part of the Primorskiy zone of hardrock mineralization has shown that mineable ore zone is over 800 m along the strike and 3–10 m in outcrop width; grading up to 23 g/t according to the results of the applied sampling techniques. The ore zone was traced to the depth of 70 m. In addition to intensive quartz veining, carbonate-quartz ore bodies 5.5 m thick were intersected (at the total thickness of quartz zones of more than 9 m) with grades over 40 g/t.

The results of this exploration program conducted with insufficient financing give ground to the conclusion that the first commercial reserves might be estimated within the next 2 to 3 years. Metallurgical ore properties allow for gold production during exploration phase with estimated yield of several dozens kilos. The ores are amenable to low-cost & energy-efficient gravity concentration methods, while even not requiring fine grinding stage (milling).

Currently, there is a scoping study for a complex development of the island and its gold resources. It provides for \$4 to \$5 million as a loan facility with payback time of 3–4 years at interest rates of 4–5 % against production facilities available at the island (base camps, pneumatic equipment, fuel storages, workshops, energy and heat supply infrastructure etc.), licenses for developing alluvial deposits with resources sufficient for achieving annual production level of 250–350 kg/y for a mine life of 6 to 7 years; a license for exploration with uncompleted work scope estimated as 196 million roubles (at rouble/dollar exchange rate as of 1999).

The project provides for:

- 3 year payback time;
- 25–30% profits;
- prospects of discovering a whole new rich goldfield;
- priority rights for obtaining licenses for discovered gold hardrock deposits.

Intensive development of mineral resources would transform Bolshevik region into a 21th century new Russian gold producing region.

MINERAL RESOURCES OF KURIL ISLANDS

M.I. Lopatnikov, *Cand. Sci. (Geogr.)*

The economic development of a region and its importance for the state as a whole depends largely on the presence of mineral resources. During the discussions on the importance for Russia to retain its sovereignty over the Kuril Islands, two aspects are usually emphasized, their strategic position and importance as fishing grounds. Without denying this obvious fact, it should be noted that the Kuril Islands are also promising for mineral resources.

During the period of the Japanese sovereignty over the Kuril Islands, according to the available data, sulfur, gold, and base-metal ores were produced and transported to Japan, and concrete was produced from local sands and gravel mostly for military constructions.

Systematic geologic surveys and exploration activities targeted at various minerals in the Kuril Islands are under way since 1946.

Of mineral fuels, only peat is found. Three deposits have been explored, the largest of which is located on Kunashir Island in the immediate vicinity of Yuzhno-Kurilsk.

No direct signatures of oil or gas have been reported on the Kuril Islands or in adjacent offshore area. However, the Sakhalin scientific institutions and production companies consider the petroleum potential of the so-called Mid-Kuril interarc trough as fairly high. It extends over 600 km from Hokkaido Island in the south to Simushir Island in the north with a width of 40 to 60 km. The offshore oceanic area adjacent to Iturup and Urup islands is considered as promising for mostly gas/condensate discoveries with total reserves of more than 1 billion tons.

Of ferrous metals, vanadium-titanomagnetite placers widely developed on the coasts of almost all large Kuril islands are interesting. The placers on Iturup Island are best known. On this island, the Reydovskoye, Vetrovoye, Rucharskoye, and Zerkalnyy Plyazh placers have been explored. The length of the explored placers along the sea coast ranges from 4.6 to 6.7 km; average thickness ranges from 3.5 m in the Rucharskoye to 6.7 m in the Reydovskoye placer. Average metal concentration is 15 to 21% Fe and 2.1 to 3.5% Ti. In addition, the sands contain vanadium in small amounts.

Most placers obviously extend offshore. Pilot recovery of sands with only 8% Fe from the seafloor in the Prostor Bay (offshore extension of the Reidovskoye deposit) with a further immediate magnetic separation on the barge yielded a concentrate with 51% Fe and high Ti and Va concentrations.

Also, the Kuril Islands are promising for nonferrous metal ores, base metal ores in particular. The Valentinovskoye and Dokuchayevskoye deposits with 2 to 18% Pb, 5–16% Zn, and 1-4% Cu in the ores were exploited in northern Kunashir Island during the Japanese sovereignty.

Urup Island is rich in base metal ore manifestations, which are also known in Iturup (Chistorechenskoye, Gorbushinskoye), Paramushir (Rifovoye), Shumshu, and Onekotan islands.

Cassiterite-rich rocks have been discovered in central Iturup Island. Tin manifestations have been discovered on Urup and Shikotan islands. These and a number of other geologic indications enabled the geologists to postulate the possibility of commercially significant tin discoveries on Kuril Islands.

Indications of the possible occurrence of the ores of some other metals are also available: mercury shows have been discovered on Kunashir, Paramushir, and Urup islands; molybdenum shows, on Iturup Island; and arsenic ore shows, on Paramushir and Shumshu islands.

The greatest expectations in terms of metallic minerals are presently imposed on the possible discoveries of gold-silver ores. Thus far, only one Prasolovskoye gold deposit on Kunashir Island is known. It was discovered and exploited by the Japanese during their sovereignty over the islands. At present, the deposit is reappraised and exploited. The produced ore is sent away for concentration.

At least ten gold and silver shows have been discovered on Paramushir Island, of which the ore shows near Cape Rifovyy, Kruzenshtern, and Vasilyev are most favorably located. On Shumshu Island, the northwestern sector is the most promising for gold-silver mineralization.

The Kuril Islands are unique in the Russian Federation in terms of native sulfur occurrence. Sulfur manifestations here were known as far back as the 18th century. During the Japanese sovereignty, a number of deposits were exploited on Kunashir, Iturup, and Paramushir islands, and the produced sulfur was transported to Japan.

At present, 12 deposits have been explored to a varying degree, including 5 deposits on Iturup Island; 5, on Paramushir Island; and 2, on Kunashir Island. Numerous sulfur shows are known on other islands.

Among other minerals, noteworthy are barite manifestations on Kunashir Island and alunite, in the Zaozernoye sulfur deposit on Paramushir Island and near Lake Krasivoye 50 km to the southwest of the Burevestnik village on Iturup Island. The latter can be utilized as a raw material for potash manure, aluminum, and sulfuric acid production.

Thus far, a great number (at least 80) of industrial mineral (sands, gravel, rubble) deposits have been discovered on almost all large islands; 23 of them have been appraised with reserves calculation. The other deposits are unexplored, and their resource estimates are prognostic. However, the available data suggest that the demand for industrial minerals will be fulfilled from local sources in practically all parts of the islands, and the possibility to produce concrete using sulfur from local deposits as the binding agent, established by scientists, eliminates the necessity to bring cement to the islands.

The problem of energy supply for utility and industrial sectors of the islands is a restricting factor of the socio-economic development of the Kuril Islands, mineral exploration and production inclusive. However, the Kuril Islands possess of a source of energy capable of covering the present-day and future local heat and power demand. This source are the thermal water and steam-water springs linked to hydrothermal water reservoirs discovered or predicted on almost all of the Kuril Islands.

Predicted thermal water and steam-water mixture resources of the Kuril Islands are estimated as great, and some deposits have already been explored. On Iturup Island, the Okeanskoye deposit has been explored near the town of Kurilsk; its reserves are sufficient to completely cover the existing and future heat and power demand in the town. On Paramushir Island, a geothermal water deposit in the immediate vicinity of the town of Severo-Kurilsk is being explored since 1992, but exploration activities are presently stopped for the lack of finance.

To summarize, the available data on the mineral potential of the Kuril Islands suggest that they are potentially rich in many commercially important minerals, whose resources are sufficient to cover the power and industrial mineral demand of the islands and which can be utilized in many industries in Russia or exported to other countries.

MINERAL RESOURCES OF CHITA REGION (RUSSIA)

Yu. Proshin, *Deputy Head of the Representation Office of the Chita Oblast Administration in the RF Government*

The Chita Oblast with an area of 432,000 km2 is located in the eastern and south-eastern part of the Trans-Baikal region. It has huge mineral resources and is potentially capable to meet the long-term requirements of many sectors of the Russian industry. As to the variety and the economic value of the mineral resources the Trans-Baikal region is comparable with the Urals Mountains.

The economy of the region has been based for many decades on the use of its mineral resources.

The extent of the geological exploration of the region is very high. There are abundant deposits of copper, copper-zinc, gold-containing, molybdenum and iron ores (the iron ores contain also Ti, V, and platinum group metals), as well as ores of rare metals (Ta, Nb, Zr, Y, Li, Be, Ge), rare-earth metals, fluorite, coal, zeolite, phosphates, synnyrite, magnesite and graphite. The complex ores contain in commercial amounts Ag, Co and Ni.

Of special importance is the northern part of the Chita Oblast with its high industrial potential. It is located adjacent to the Baikal-Amur Railroad line. There is a large number of ore deposits and two major coal fields, which can serve as a source of energy in the process of the development of the ore deposits. Most deposits have large ore reserves and a significant part of reserves can be extracted by open-pit mining.

The economic efficiency of the development of mineral resources under the harsh conditions of the mountainous Trans-Baikal region is greatly dependent on the proper selection of advanced technologies for ore processing and integrated utilization of minerals.

The southern part of the region extends for about 1,000 km along the Trans-Siberian Railroad Line and has good prospects for production of many metals.

Main ore deposits of Chita Oblast

Ore deposit; Mining or licensed company	Type of ore	Degree of commercial development	Ore grade, %	Economic reserves, x 1000t	Prognosticated resources, x 1000t
		Iron, titanium and vanadium			
Chineyskoye (Magnitny area); "ZabaikalStalinvest"	Iron.titanium & vanadium ore	Prospecting and appraisal work; Feasibility Study completed	34.6 F_{total} 6.74 TiO_2; 0.54 V_2O_5	Ore 4,641,000; Fe 160, 718; TiO_2 31,280; V_2O_5 2,506	Ore: 300,000,000 (entire deposit); 20, 000, 000 (Magnitny area)
Kruchininskoye	Apatite.titanium & magnetite ore	In reserve	22.5 F_{total} 8.55 TiO_2; 0.09 V_2O_5; 2.79-3.66 P_2O_5	Ore 617, 000 Fe 132, 000 $TiO_2$5, 000; P_2O_5 8, 600	P_2O_5 4, 000
Berezovskoye	Siderite (I) & limonite (II) ores	In reserve	I:36.6-38.9 F_{total}; II:46.9-50.6 F_{total}; 0.06-0.95 S	Ore 438, 000	
Sulumatskoye	Iron-bearing quartzite	In reserve	22.2 Fe_2O_3; 14.24 FeO	Ore 650, 000	Ore 2, 000, 000
Marurinskoye	Apatite-magnetite ore	Prospecting and appraisal work	20 Fe_2O_3; 0.07 V_2O_5; 2.2 P_2O_5		Ore 1, 300, 000; $P_2O_5$53, 000
		Manganese			
Gtomovskoye; "Priargunskoye PGHO"	Manganes ore	Under operation	18.2 Mn	Ore 330; Mn 60.4	Ore 136;Mn 2.4
		Copper, nickel and cobalt			
Udokan. Including the following areas:	Copper-bearing sandstones	First phase under development	1.45 Cu; 9.6 g/t Ag	Ore 1,375,227; Cu 19, 954.2	
Medny. Bluzhdayschy.		Feasibility study	1.45 Cu	Ore 41,702.3;	

Sekuschy		for construction of the mine		Cu 5700	
Chineyskoye(contact zone); "ZabaikalStalinvest". Including:	Copper sulfide ores	Detailed prospecting. the reserves have not been formally registered	0.6-0.8Cu; 0.1 Ni	Ore 1,000,000; Cu 4000	Cu 8,000
Rudny Area	Copper sulfide ores	Detailed prospecting. the reserves have not been formally registered	1.2$Cu_{conditional}$	Cu 1,170	14,800 of conventional copper
Kontaknovy Area	Copper sulfide ores	Detailed prospecting. the reserves have not been formally registered	0.68 Cu; 0.046 Ni; 0.012 Co		
Lugokanskoye deposit; "Gold Mining Company Lugokanskaya"	Gold-copper ores	Prospecting and appraisal work	1.7 Cu; 2.7 $Cu_{taking\ into\ account\ associated\ components}$; 0.5-7 g/t Au; 3-236 g/t Ag		Cu(2%) 1,700,000;
Bystrinskoye ore field "Gold Minig Company Lugokanskaya"	Gold-copper ores	Prospecting and appraisal work	1.58 Cu; 0.3 W_2O_3; 0.15 Mo		Cu 100,000 Au 150t (up to a depth of 200 m)
Novo-Shirokinskoye deposit "Novoshirokinsky Rudnik"	Gold-bearning polymetallic ore	Mine constructed to 80%	3.72 Pb; 1.77 Zn; 3.29 g/t Au; 86.54 g/t Ag; o.3 Cu; 86.27 g/t Cd	Ore 9,400; Pb 348.6; Zn 165.9; Au 30.8; Ag 811.1 t; Cu 27.7; Cd 808.3 t	Shirokinskoye ore field Pb 600-800; Au 40 t
Noyon-Tolgoiskoye deposit. "Nerchinskye rudniki"	Polymetallic ore	Reserve for extension of Klichinsky mine; prospecting and appraisal work	1.46 Pb; 1.55 Zn; 67.6 g/t Ag; 82 g/t Cd	Pb 205.4; Zn 217.4; Ag 948.9 kg	Pb(1.04%)714.6; Zn(1.22%)837.6; Ag3.061t(44.5 g/t)
Kamenskoye deposit	Polymetallic ore	Reserve for extension of Klichkinsky mine	1.7 Pb; 1.23 Zn; 23 g/t Ag; 0.11 Cd	Ore 2,600; Pb 45.2; Zn 32.9; Ag 55.4 t; Cd 259.3 t	
Vozdvizhenskoye deposit; "Nerchinskye Rudniki"	Polymetallic ore	Operation suspended	4.98 Pb; 4.63 Zn; 0.38 g/t Au; 100 g/t Ag; 0.039 Cd	Ore 1,500; Pb 41.8; Zn 46.1; Au 321 t; Ag 84 t; Cd 328.5 t	Ore 4,400; Pb 134.5; Zn 194.4; Au 1.7 t; Ag 457 t; Cd 1,760 t
Molybdenum					
Zhirekenskoye deposit; "Zhirekensky GOK"	Molybdenum-copper ore	Operation suspended	0.106 Mo; 0.08 Cu; 82 g/t Re; 97 g/t Se	Mo 80.6	Mo 600; Cu 1000 at Mo content of 0.07%, Cu 0.124%
Bugdanaiskoye deposit	Molubdenum ore	Prospecting and appraisal work	0.068 Mo	Ore about 900	
Tungsten					

Spokoyninskoye deposit; "Orlovsky GOK"	Tungsten ore	Operation suspended	0.27 W_20_3; 0.024 BeO; 18.1 muscovite	Ore 13,200; W_20_3 35.7; BeO 3.1; Muscovte 24000	
Bom-Gorkhon; TOO "Quatz"	Tungsten ore	Under operation W_20_3 - 1	Ore - 11300 12 W_20_3	W_20_3 10	
		Tin			
Sherlovogorskoye deposit (Eastern Field)>	Tin-bearning polymetallic ore	Detailed prospecting	0.5 Sn	Ore 22,400; Sn 11.3; Pb 185.3; Zn 149.2	
		Antimony			
Solonechenskoye deposit	Gold-antimony ore	Prospecting and appraisal work	8-10 Sb; 2-10 g/t Au		Sb 60
		Rare metals (titanium, tantalum, niobium, zirconium, germanium)			
Katuginskoye deposit; "Zabaikalsky GOK"	Cryolite and rare metals ore	Detailed prospecting	0.0193 Ta_2O_5; 0.297 Nb_2O_5; 1.09 ZrO_2; 2.056 cryolite	Ore 1,250,200 Ta_2O_3 241.3; $Nb_2O_5$3718.2; ZrO_2 13654.3; Cryolite 25711.6	Ore 742,441
Orlovskoye deposit; "Orlovsky GOK"	Tantalum ore	Operation suspended	0.0193 Ta_2O_5 0.26-0.0108 Li_2O 0.152 0.0046	Ta_2O_3 2.24 Li_2O 46.4 Nb_2O_5 2 RbO 28.1 CsO 0.85	
Zavitinskoye deposit; "Zabaikalsky GOK"	Lithium ore	Operation suspended	0.692 Li_2O 0.0139 Ta_2O_3 0.03 BeO	Extracted 70% of ore reservers	
Etykinskoye deposit; "Zabaikalsky GOK"	Rare metals ore	Mine under construction	0.11 Li; Ore contains: Ta. Nb_2O_5.Sn.Au.Ag W_2O_5.Rb. Mo. Cs	Ore 100,000	
Tarbogaiskoye deposit (Novy Area); "Tigninsky Ugolny Razrez"; "ChitaUgol"	Germanium-containing coal	Preparations for operation	74.75 g/t Ge		
		Uranium			
Stretsovsky Uranium District; "Priargunskoye PGHO"	Uranium and uranium-molybdenum ores	Under operation	0.2 U 0.01-0.1 Mo	Mineable reserves	U 0.26; U 75
		Gold			
Darasunskoye deposit; "ZabaikalZoloto" Gold ore	Gold ore	Under operation	14.6 g/t; 28.4 g/t	Ore 3,800; Au 59 t	Au 50 t
Alexandrovskoye deposit; "AmazarZoloto"	Gold ore	Under operation	8.3 g/t Au	Ore 649; Au 7.5 t	Au 7 t
Teremkinskoye deposit;	Gold ore	Under operation	11.4 g/t Au	Ore 457; Au 7.5 t	Au t

"ZabaikalZoloto"					
Taseyevskoye deposit; Joint Venture "Balgold Ltd." (Ores zones Nos. 1 and 2)	Gold ore	Detailed prospecting	2.6 g/t Au	Ore 67,000; Au 104.1 t (commercial reserves)	Feasibility study performed for ore reserves of 39,000
Itakinskoye deposit; "Ksenyevsky priisk" Including	Gold ore	Prospecting and appraisal work	3.3 g/t Au; 10.11 g/t Ag	Ore 18,900; Au 63.3 t; Ag 189 t	Ore 9,000; Au 37.6 t (4.15 g/t); Ag 189 t (8.13 g/t)
Makeyevsky area	Gold ore	Preliminary prospecting	3.7 g/t Au; 17.5 g/t Au	Ore 7,000; Au 26 t; Ag 123 t	
Klyuchevskoye deposit; "AmarZoloto"	Gold ore	Under operation	3.7 g/t Au (main orebody); 1.86-3.1 Au (other orebodies); 1.9 g/t Ag	Ore 24,500 Au 55.1 t	
Baleyskoye deposit; Joint Venture "Balgold Ltd."	Gold ore	Detailed prospecting	Au-2 g/t Au	Ore 19,400; Au 40.3 t Ag 19.9 t	Au 118 t
Ukoninskoye deposit; "Mining Company Itaka"	Gold ore	Detailed prospecting	6.8 g/t Au; 27.8 g/t Ag	Au max 30 t	
Bugdaninskoye deposit; (Experimental Area)	Gold-bearing ore	Detailed prospecting	6.6 g/t Au; 30 g/t Ag	Ore 4,000; Au 26.8 t; Ag 121.8 t	
Verkhne-Aliinskoye deposit; joint Venture "Balgold Ltd."	Gold ore	Detailed prospecting	11.7 g/t Au; 17 g/t Ag	Ore 1,600; Au 20.8 t	
Andryushinskoye deposit; Joint Venture "Balgold Ltd."	Gold ore	Detailed prospecting	7.8 g/t Au; 2.1 g/t Ag	Ore 1,000; Au 8 t; Ag 2.2 t	Ore 1,200; Au 10 t
Bogomolskoye deposit; "Priargunskoye PGHO"	Gold ore	Detailed prospecting	15.6 g/t Au; 120.3 g/t Ag	Ore 692; Au 10.8 t Ag 23.2 t	

METALLIFEROUS MINERALS

Iron, titanium and vanadium. The eastern regions of Russia face shortage of iron-containing raw materials (about 30 million tpy) which is covered by imports from the Kursk region, Karelia and Kazakhstan. The imported iron ores are of low quality and require additional upgrading.

The shortage of raw materials in Russia for production of ferrovanadium and technical-grade tungsten pentoxide is about 35-40%. It is predicted that in the future the demand for vanadium will increase by several times. The shortage of titanium-bearing raw materials is over 50%.

A radical solution would be development of the ore reserves of Siberia.

Iron ore production in the Eastern Trans-Baikal can be economically viable in case of integrated utilization of the ore components.

Chineyskoye is a major deposit of iron-titanium-vanadium and copper sulfide ores (free of sulfur and phosphorus). Of commercial significance are V, Ti, Fe, Cu and noble metals. The grades and reserves of the ore make this deposit unique. As to the vanadium reserves it is the world's largest deposit. With respect to its copper reserves it is the world's second largest deposit, second only to the Udokan deposit. About 75% of the reserves can be extracted by open-pit mining with an average stripping ratio of 3.8.

Within the Chineyskoye ore deposit there are 18 occurrences of magnetite-vanadium ore identified, which extend for up to 10 km along the strike and up to 8 km along the dip; the thickness varies from 2 m to 21 m.

Ore containing 80.2% Fe, 9.9% TiO_2 and 1.8% V_2O_5 was processed on a semi-commercial scale and the respective recoveries were 85%, 84% and 80%. A technology has been developed for smelting without coke to produce low-alloy steel and vanadium- and titanium-containing slag. The latter can be used for production of ferrovanadium, master alloys and titanium dioxide.

The concentrate produced was pelletized and roasted. The pellets contained 75% iron metal, 12.5% titanium dioxide and 1.7% vanadium pentoxide. The quality of the pellets was high.

The required capital investments for construction of a mine and an ore processing plant for a capacity of 10 million tpy of ore are estimated at about US $365 mullion, including the purchase cost of equipment of US $146 million.

The efficiency of the mine can be improved by parallel development of the Udokan deposit (this will reduce the capital cost requirement) and by conclusion of a product sharing agreement.

Kruchininskoy apatite-titaniferous magnetite ore deposit is located in an economically developed area and has very good prospects for development by open-pit mining method with a stripping ratio of 1.4 and a maximum pit depth of 300 m.

The ore is amenable to upgrading by magnetic separation and flotation to produce ilmenite (50.5% TiO_2), titaniferous magnetite (55% Fe and 9.5% TiO_2), apatite (39% P_2O_5) and sulfide platinum-containing concentrates.

With a mine capacity of 4.5 million tpy of ore it can produce 700,000 t of titaniferous magnetite concentrate, 300,000 t of ilmenite concentrate and 225,000 t of apatite concentrate.

The apatite concentrate production would completely meet the demand for short-in-supply mineral fertilizers in East Siberia and Russian Far East for 50 years.

Berezovskoye iron core deposit containing siderite ores has favorable conditions for development: up to 71% of ore reserves can be extracted by open-pit mining with an average stripping ratio of 0.37 m3/t of ore. About 90% of ore can be smelted without upgrading and the remaining part requires roasting and magnetic separation.

Sulumatskoye ore deposit contains iron-bearing quartzites. It can be develop primarily by open-pit mining method. Ores are amenable to upgrading using two- or three-stage magnetic separation. In the former case the ore concentrate contains 68.5% iron with a concentrate yield of 34-56%, and in the latter case 71.78% and 32.22%, respectively.

Mururinskoye apatite-magnetite ore deposit is located in the vicinity of the Baikal-Amur Railroad Line. The ore is amenable to upgrading to produce iron ore and phosphorus (40% P_2O_5) concentrates.

There are also a number of smaller magnetite deposits in the Chita region.

Manganese. The Trans-Baikal region has favorable prospects for discovery of manganese ore deposits. Taking into consideration the fact that Russia does not have any commercial manganese deposits it appears to be reasonable to carry out prospecting, appraisal and exploration work in this region to search for manganese occurrences.

Currently, the Gromovskoye manganese ore deposit is exploited for the purpose of hydrometallurgical processing or uranium ores. The use of this ore for production of ferromanganese is not viable due to high metal losses.

Copper, nickel and cobalt. The eastern part of the Trans-Baikal region has substantial non-ferrous ore reserves and first of all copper ores in the Udokan deposit of copper-bearing sandstones and the Chineyskoye deposit. There are 18 copper ore deposit and occurrences discovered in the Chita region.

Udokan copper deposit is one of the largest deposits in the world not being developed so far. This is the only deposit explored in detail within the central part of the Baikal-Amur Railroad Line. Its area is 30 km2 and the thickness of the copper bearing layer varies from 100 m to 350 m.

It is planned to develop by open-pit mining a top-priority area with 28.5% of the total ore reserves during the first phase. In general, about 80% of the reserves can be extracted by open-pit mining.

There are three types of ore in the deposit: sulfide ore (52%), complex ore (34%) and oxide ore (14%). The ore has virtually no deleterious impurities. It has been demonstrated that all types of ore are amenable to upgrading with copper recoveries varying from 72% to 90% to produce high-grade concentrates containing from 21% to 34% copper.

The annual capacity of the first phase has been calculated to be 7.5 million t of ore and 18 million m3 of material to be moved. The output will amount to 81,850 t of copper concentrate and 50.6 t of silver. It is assumed that part of concentrates (sulfide concentrate) will be processed at Russian copper smelters and the remaining amount will be exported to China. The required capital investments for the construction are estimated at US $381 million. The internal rate of return will be 11.8% with a discount rate of 10% provided that the mine will be operated on the basis of a product sharing agreement. In this case the payback period will be 10.3 years.

Currently, there is a railroad line under construction to provide access to the Chineyskoye deposit and it is planned to provide an access line to the Udokan deposit in 2001.

The **Chineyskoye** sulfide copper ore deposit has a bedded structure with dip angles varying from 3° to 35°. It can be developed by open-pit mining. The deposit extends for up to 6 km along the strike and up to 4.5 km along the dip and down to a depth of 700 m. The ore layer thickness varies from 1.2 m to 109.6 m. The ore reserves have been estimated for a cutoff grade of 0.6% Cu and a bed thickness of at least 5m.

The ore can be concentrated by means of flotation and magnetic separation. Copper and precious metals can be upgraded to produce complex copper concentrate; the tailings can be treated by wet magnetic separation to produce iron-titanium-vanadium concentrates. All ore varieties are amenable to upgrading.

The required capital expenditures for development and operation of the Chineyskoye deposit for a capacity of 1.5 million tpy of ore are estimated at US $120 million including US $95 million for construction of facilities for ore concentration and copper concentrate smelting.

Lugokanskoye gold-copper deposit can be developed by open-pit mining down to a depth of 150 m. Orebodies are located within three zones of an intrusion containing in total 25 orebodies. The ore is readily amenable to upgrading with production of sulfide bulk concentrate and recoveries of 90% Cu, 77% Au and 87% Ag.

Bystrinskoye gold-copper deposit can be exploited by open-pit mining down to a depth of 200 m at a capacity of 5 million tpy of ore to produce 71,000 t of copper concentrate, 1,875 kg of gold and 21,250 kg of silver.

Ores are amenable to upgrading to produce sulfide bulk concentrate with recoveries of 90% Cu, 75% Au and 85% Ag.

Lead and zinc. The Eastern Trans-Baikal region has the largest reserves of these metals in Russia. There are two main types of deposits: Nerchinsky and Novo-Shirokinsky types. The former type occurs in most of ore deposits and is represented by orebodies in carbonate rocks, while the Novo-Shirokinsky type occurs within silicate rocks.

Since 1995 all the Nerchinsky lead and zinc mines have suspended their operation.

Novo-Shirokinsoye gold-bearing polymetallic ore deposit has been developed by two shafts to a depth of 330 m (Fig.4). Appropriate development and construction work has been accomplished, a 110kV power transmission line constructed and construction of an ore processing plant almost completed.

Ore processing is performed by flotation and gravity concentration to produce commercial-grade lead, zinc and pyrite concentrates and a gold-containing gravity concentrate. With a mine capacity of 400,000 tpy of ore it will produce 13,000 of Zn, 1.1 t of Au, 30 t of Ag and 13,000 t of pyrite concentrate. The mine has been constructed to 80% and about US $12 million is required to complete the construction. The mine was not successful in finding investors, primarily due to the low profitability of the mine under the current taxation system.

A decision has been taken to conduct a feasibility study for development of the Novo-Shirokinskoye deposit on the basis of the Federal Law "On Product Sharing Agreement" in order to make the development of this deposit more attractive for investors.

Another major lead and zinc deposit is the Noyon-Tologoyskoye deposit containing ores that can be concentrated either by a combined gravity and flotation scheme or only by flotation to produce lead concentrate (52% Pb) and zinc concentrate (45% Zn) with recoveries of 81-91% Pb and 77-80% Zn. About 70% of gold and 97% of silver is recovered into lead and zinc concentrates. Estimates have indicated that in case of the development of the deposit by two open pits with capacities of 2 and 0.5 million tpy the profitability would be 11-17% with a payback period of 6 years.

Molybdenum. There are two stockwork molybdenum deposits in this region with similar mineral composition of ores. The Zhirekenskoye and Bugdainskoye deposits contain up to 95% of all molybdenum reserves. However, it should be pointed out that the ore grades are by several times lower than in similar deposits elsewhere in the world.

Zhirekenskoye copper-molybdenum deposit contains ore with the highest molybdenum contents in Russia. The deposit has been operated by the Zhirekensky GOK Company. During 1988-1994 the mine produced on average 2.4 million t of commercial-grade ore per year, which is lower than its design capacity by a factor of 1.5. The ore processing flowsheet includes wet autogenous grinding and ore flotation in 80 m3 flotation cells. It produces molybdenum concentrate with an average content of 47.2% Mo and a recovery of 50-80%, as well as copper concentrate (18-20% Cu and a recovery of 40-60%) and pyrite concentrate.

In the process of metallurgical processing of copper concentrate silver is recovered as by-product. No studies have been conducted to ensure recovery of Re, Se and Te. The rhenium content of the molybdenum concentrate is 54.2 g/t.

The molybdenum concentrate meets the specifications for manufacture of high-grade ferromolybdenum.

The mine has been shut down since the end of 1995 due to the low world market prices for molybdenum. At present the Siberian Aluminum Company has developed a program for re-commissioning of the mine.

MAIN ORE DEPOSITS OF CHITA OBLAST

Ore deposit; Mining or licensed company	Type of mineral	Degree of commercial development	Content of valuable mineral, %	Economic reserves, x 1000t	Prognosticated resources, x 1000t
		Fluorite			
Usuglinskoye; "Usugli Mine"	Fluorite ore	On care-and-maintenance basis	56.4	1,039/586	-
Uluntuiskoye;"Usugli Mine"	Fluorite ore	Under operation	67.8	557/378	-
Zhetkovskoye;"Kalanguisky PShK", "ZabaikalPlavik"	Fluorite ore	Operation shut down	37.6	978/370	150/57
Otsoluiskoye; "ZabaikalPlavik"	Fluorite ore	Under development	36.5	1,069/390	-
Solnechnoye; "ZabaikalPlavik"	Fluorite ore	Operation shut down	40.2	587/237	-
Briachanskoye; "ZabaikalPlavik"	Fluorite ore	Operation shut down	47.3	97.7/42.2	-
Abagatuiskoye; "ZabaikalPlavik"	Fluorite ore	Operation shut down	58.5	296/174	-
Buguturo-Abagatuiskoye Group (Novo-Buguturskoye, Shakhterskoye, Gorinskoye, Voldinskoye deposits)	Fluorite ore	Developed and licensed; in reserve for "ZabaikalPlavik"	34-40	5,839/2,077	-
Garsonuiskoye; TOO "Quarts"	Fluorite ore	4 out of 7 areas under development	39.8	9,290/3,663	-
		Potassium and aluminum minerals			
Sakunskoye (Golevskoye); "Synnyrite"	Alkaline syenite (synnyrite)	Detailed prospecting	17.9 K_2O; 20.8 Al_2O_3 0.2-1.5 Na_2O; 55.1 SiO_2	172,200	141,700
		Magnesite			
Larginskoye, Areas 1 and 2; "Eastern Mining and Geological Enterprise", including	Magnesite	Prospecting and appraisal work	17.9 Mg; 4.6 CaO; 4.0 SiO_2; 0.05-0.4 Fe_2O_3	C1+C2+P1-19,500	-
5% of reserves			Mg-46.7 Mg; 1.1 CaO; 0.6 SiO_2		
20 % of reserves			46.3 Mg; 2.0 CaO; 0.6 SiO_2		
Larginskoye deposit area (Bereinskoye, Timokhinskoye, Luchuiskoye)	Magnesite	Prospecting and appraisal work	MgO - 45-46; 3.5 CaO; 3.8 SiO_2	40,000	From 300,000 to 650,000
		Zeolite			
Shivertuiskoye; "Priargunskoye PGHO"	Zeolite	Under operation	60-90 Clinoptilolite	762,400	9,280,000
Kholinskoye;"Zeolitelnvest" ("Zabayakalsky GOK")	Zeolite	Under operation	62 Clinoptilolite	383,600	600,000

Bugdaninskoye molybdenum-containing polymetallic ore deposit is rated as unique and its molybdenum reserves exceed those in the Zhirekenskoye deposit, but the ore is less amenable to processing. About 90% of the ore reserves can be extracted by open-pit mining. Detailed prospecting of the deposit has been performed and ore evaluation tests completed on a semi-commercial scale. It is planned to use gravity concentration and flotation to produce 48% molybdenum concentrate and pyrite concentrate containing Au, Ag and Pb.

Tungsten. There are significant geological reserves of tungsten (both proven reserves and prognosticated resources) in the Eastern Trans-Baikal region.

Tungsten occurs in the form of independent deposits and in complex deposits where it is associated with Sn, Mo, Sb, Hg etc. The prognosticated WO3 resources have been estimated at 300,000 t. **Spokoininskoye** tungsten deposit was exploited until 1995 by open-pit mining with a capacity of 600,000 tpy of ore. The ore was treated by gravity concentration ensuring recoveries of 65-76%. The gravity concentration tailings can be used for production of beryllium flotation concentrate containing 5.6% BeO with a recovery of 34.7%.

Currently, work is in progress to resume production.

Tin. There are abundant reserves of tin in the Eastern Trans-Baikal region. Tin occurs both in tin deposits proper and in complex deposits containing W, Pb, Zn and other metals.

The main tin mine of the region exploited until 1992 is the **Sherlovogorskoye** deposit, but it was then shut down due to low tin recoveries (40-42%).

A technology has been developed for processing of complex tin-bearing polymetallic ores of the **Eastern Field of the Sherlovogorskoye deposit** to produce crude concentrates containing Sn, Zn and Ag with tin recoveries as high as 70%. A 500,000-tpy concentrator can produce annually 350 t of Sn, 4,000 t of Pb, 2,300 t of Zn and 20 t of Ag.

The overall prognosticated resources of primary tin in the southern part of the region are estimated at hundreds of thousands of tonnes. It is necessary to update the geological appraisal of the tin occurrences located in the economically developed districts of the region and they can serve as a source of tin to meet the demand of the Russian industry.

Antimony. This metal occurs extensively in the form of numerous ore and alluvial occurrences through out the entire region. Under favorable conditions the Chita Oblast can become one of the main supplier of antimony in Russia.

Rare metals (Li, Ta, Nb, Zr, Ge). At present the consumption of rare metals in Russia has significantly declined. At the same time, Russia takes the first place with respect to geological resources of rare metals in the world. They are concentrated primarily in the Chita Oblast with its Katuginskoye and Etykanskoye deposits.

Katuginskoye deposit contains large reserves of rare metal ores serving as a potential basis for a major mining and ore-processing complex. Its yttrium reserves account for about 40% of the world reserves. The ores are complex and contain up to ten valuable constituents.

It has been demonstrated that all these ores can be treated using a unified processing technology comprising gravity concentration, flotation, electromagnetic separation and hydrometallurgical treatment to produce tantalum-niobium, rare metals, cryolite, zirconium and quartz-feldspar concentrates.

In the feasibility study for geological appraisal of the Katuginskoye deposit it is assumed that it will be exploited by open-pit mining at a capacity of 3 million tpy of ore to produce 18,000 t of pyrochlore concentrate, 15,000 t of rare metals concentrate, 54,000 t of zirconium concentrate and 24,000 t of cryolite concentrate. The rate of return is assumed to be 18.9% with respect to the main assets and 52.55% with respect to mineable reserves. The required investments have been estimated at US $400 million with a payback period of 4.5 years. In case of favorable taxation schemes these figures will be 44.13% and 1.94 years, respectively.

With the development of the Katuginskoye deposit it will completely meet the demand of the Russian industry for tantalum, niobium, zirconium and rare-earth elements. A comparison of the estimated technical and economic performance values of this mine with other similar deposits indicates that the exploitation of the Katuginskoye deposit will provide significant advantages.

Orlovskoye tantalum deposit. The open pit mine was in operation during 1962-1992 and the ore was processed by gravity concentration, magnetic and electric separation and flotation to produce tantalum and lithium concentrates. The mine was shut down because it operated at a loss under the given conditions and due to the lack of demand for its products.

Zavitinskoye lithium deposit was exploited by open-pit mining, but currently its operation is suspended.

Etykinskoye rare metals deposit is one of the largest of its kind in Russia. The tantalum reserves are sufficient for 100 years of operation. The mine is currently under construction. The first phase of the ore processing plant was commissioned in 2000 and has a throughput rate of 750,000 tpy of ore. It produced tantalum-niobium concentrate.

A federal objective-oriented program has been adopted: "Mining production, extraction and application of lithium and beryllium. Development of production of tantalum, niobium and tin at the facilities of the RF Ministry for Atomic Energy". The plan is to produce annually 20,000 t of lithium and 30,000 t of beryllium in concentrates. It is assumed that the rate of return for production of beryllium product should be 13% with a payback period of 7.5 years.

The Eastern Trans-Baikal region is capable to meet the demand of Russia for rare metals and rare-earth elements during at least 100 years.

Tarbagaiskoye germanium-containing coal field. One of the main sources for production of germanium is coal. Some of the lignite deposits in the Chita Oblast have high germanium concentrations. In the past the Tarbagaiskoye coal mine had met the demand of the Russian industry for germanium, that was produced as by-product in the process of coal combustion. In 1992 the production of primary germanium was shut down.

Gold. The Trans-Baikal region has been since centuries a major producer of gold in Russia. There is a number of major ore and alluvial gold deposits. In addition, gold is also produced as a by-product of many metal mines of the region. At present, geological exploration has been almost completely terminated and the geological gold reserves do not increase

There are 305 **alluvial** gold occurrences with 20% of their reserves explored to an extent permitting dredging operations (gold concentrations of 0.2-0.4 g/m3), 77% are ready for open-pit mining (from 0.4 to 2.2 g/m3) and 3% for underground mining (2.5-3.7 g/m3).

The reserves available at individual alluvial gold operations vary from 1.5-2 years up to 25 years averaging 15-17 years.

Possibilities for expansion of the alluvial gold reserves within the traditional mining districts are rather limited. In this connection it is essential to carry out search and prospecting for new favorable areas in the north of the region.

Gold ore deposits have been exploited in the region since the early 19th century. The prevailing majority of deposits are of vein type. Commercial-grade orebodies have a length along the strike from tens of meters to 19 km and along the dip up to 300-400 m and in some deposits up to 1 km or more. The thickness of orebodies varies from 0.5-1.0 m to 40-126 m.

In general, the mineral reserves for the gold mining industry are represented by 29 gold ore deposits proper and 19 gold-bearing complex ore deposits (the latter account for about 60% of all proven gold reserves). The ore reserves developed for underground mining have a gold content from 6.5 to 20.5 g/t and for open-pit mining from 1.5 to 4.7 g/t. The gold average content of complex ores varies from 0.1-2 to 4.7 g/t. Ores in some deposits (about 25% of total reserves) are refractory and contain arsenic (arsenic content in concentrates varies from 0.8% to 4-6%).

At the current capacity of the gold mining operations the proven reserves of individual mines vary from 10 to 100 years. It should be pointed out that during the past 7 years the gold production from primary ore deposits has decreased by more than 8 times.

The prognosticated ore reserves for open-pit mining are located primarily in the economically developed districts of the region. The northern districts of the region might play a significant role in extension of the gold ore reserves.

Taseyevskoye deposit. Its exploitation was suspended in 1994 due to the unprofitable operation with the ore processing technology available at that time. It is possible to resume the operation only on the basis of a new technology for treatment of relatively low-grade ores and on the terms and conditions of a product sharing agreement.

At present all buildings and facilities of the mine are destroyed.

The deposit is currently being prepared for operation by a joint venture company - "Balgold Ltd." According to a feasibility study, to ensure an annual capacity of 1.75 million t of ore (to produce 5 t of gold per year), capital investments of US $184 million are required. During the operation of the future mine for 16 years the revenues to the governmental budget will reach US $144.5 million and about 3,000 new jobs will be created at the main production and auxiliary facilities.

It is planned to use flotation and sorption leaching for processing of the ore.

A federal law has been passed referring to the Taseyevskoye deposit: "On mineral resources that can be developed on the terms and conditions of a product sharing agreement".

Itakinskoye deposit. It consists of three ore areas. A feasibility study has been completed for ore and alluvial gold production from the Itaka-Mogochinskoye ore field. The Maleyevsky area can be exploited by open-pit mining during the initial phase with the use of gravity concentration and flotation with subsequent cyanidation and sorption of gold on carbon. The final product will be gold-silver alloy. The capacity of the complex will be about 3 t of gold per year. The profitability of the project with respect to production cost will be 20.6%.

Amazarkanskoye deposit. It is planned to run heap leaching tests as a possible route for processing the ore form this deposit at a capacity of 500,000 tpy.

Klyuchevskoye and Alexandrovskoye deposits. The ore is processed at the Klyuchevskaya and Davendinskaya concentrators producing concentrate with a minimum gold content of 30 g/t. Final gold extraction and refining is performed at the Uralelectromed plant and at the Prioksky refinery. It has been also contemplated to construct appropriate facilities in the town of Klyuchevskoy to produce 2 t of bullion gold per year.

Uranium. The Trans-Baikal region is one of the main uranium producing regions of Russia. There are six uranium ore districts of different sizes identified within the Chita Oblast. The largest ore district, not only in the Chita Oblast, but also in Russia, is the **Urulyunguyevsky (Steltsovsky) uranium ore district** consisting of 19 deposits of high-grade ores.

These deposits occur in magmatic and metamorphosed rocks and belong to vein-stockwork endogenous ore type with complex occurrence conditions. Taking into account the fact that there are different varieties of ores, it is required to carry out selective mining and separate the streams of different ore types starting from the face.

At present, about 40% of the total reserves have been already extracted. The mineable reserves in the Steltsovsky uranium ore district will be exhausted in about 25 years.

The proven ore reserves in this district can be increased by discovery of new orebodies at the flanks and at lower depths of the known deposits. There are good prospects for discovery of high-quality uranium ores well suited for in situ and heap leaching.

In 1991-2000 the Priargunskoye PGHO Company curtailed by half production of its main product - uranium oxide - and currently exports 100% of its main products because of the lack of demand in Russia.

At present, efforts are taken to introduce new mining and chemical technology, which is expected to increase the output of uranium oxide and reduce the production cost. This technology is based on an optimal combination of hydrometallurgical techniques, heap and in situ leaching of uranium ores. Depending on the uranium content of the ore it will be processed either by in situ leaching (uranium content of 0.105-0.160%), heap leaching (0.16-0.21%) or by hydrometallurgical methods (over 0.21%).

The use of the new technology will result in an increase of up to 50% in the proportion of uranium oxide produced by heap and in situ leaching and change over completely to these methods in the future.

There is a number of other, but rather small uranium occurrences in other ore districts of the Chita Oblast. There are favorable prospects for discovery of new uranium deposits in the north of the region.

Industrial Minerals

Fluorite (fluor spar). The Trans-Baikal region is a unique fluorite province on the Earth and holds the first place in Russia with respect to mining production, reserves and prognosticated resources of fluorite. The commercial reserves under exploitation account for only 15% of the total fluorite reserves in the region. Orebodies in the deposits are represented mainly by quartz-fluorite veins and mineralized zones.

Processing of these ores makes it possible to produce high-grade concentrates. A specific feature of the deposit is virtually complete absence of deleterious impurities (S, P, BaSO4, etc.) resulting in production of welding grades of fluorite.

In the past, five deposits were exploited by underground mining and one deposit by open-pit mining method and were the only producers of more than 10 grades of lump fluorite and fluorite flotation concentrate in Russia. Currently, the fluorite industry faces serious difficulties and is in financial and economic predicament. The main causes are the declining domestic demand and inability to compete with the imported products due to the relatively high production costs. In 1998-1999 virtually all fluorite mines were shut down. However, there is a program prepared with the purpose to surmount the crisis situation by reducing the production cost, exploiting deposits with high ore quality, using audit access to the orebodies and by increasing the output of lump fluorite. The program has been implemented since the end of 1999. In April 2000 the Usugli ore processing plant was put into operation for treatment of ore from the Uluntuiskoye deposit. The Kalanguiskaya ore processing plant is being prepared for commissioning.

Potassium and aluminum raw materials. **Synnyrite. Sakunskoye (Golevskoye) deposit** of raw materials for production of potassium and alumina can be exploited by open-pit mining with a stripping ratio of 1.48. The main products are chlorine-free potassium fertilizers (finely ground synnyrite, potassium nitrate or sulfate) and alumina. In addition, it is possible to produce such by-products as concentrate for ceramic production, an effective coagulant (aluminum oxychloride), white soot, potassium liquid glass and cement.

Magnesite. At present Russia is in a difficult situation as far as magnesite supply is concerned. In this connection the Larginskoye magnesite deposit with an extremely low iron content might be of commercial interest. The mining and geological conditions are favorable for open-pit mining with a stripping ratio of 0.7.

At a pit capacity of 500,000 tpy it is possible to produce 200,000 t of caustic magnesite with a magnesium content of 84%.

Zeolite. The Chita Oblast has leading positions in Russia with respect to the geological reserves of zeolite. The prognosticated resources of commercial grades of zeolite are estimated at 22.8 billion t. Zeolite is produced currently from two deposits. The ores from the **Shivertuiskoye deposit** have been subjected to a full cycle of medical investigations. They can be utilized in the agricultural sector, in industry, for construction purposes, for environmental technologies and for water treatment.

The region can satisfy the demand of the national economy for this mineral in any amounts.

Gemstones. The Trans-Baikal region has been an important center of production of gemstones and decorative stones in Russia since the middle of the 19th century. There are significant occurrences of pegmatites, colored tourmaline, beryl, topaz, mountain crystal, aquamarine, rubellite, smoky quartz, agate, chalcedony, onyx, carnelian, nephrite and charoite ("lilac stone"). The production of gemstones and decorative stones is rather limited. In addition to the above nonmetallic industrial minerals, some other minerals also occur in the Chita Oblast: feldspar, refractory clays, graphite, perlite, carbonate rocks, natural soda.

Prospects for development of mineral resources

The significant role of the Chita Oblast both in Russia and in the world in relation to its mineral resources and mining industry determines the long-term orientation of the economy of this region and necessitates active efforts aimed at the development of this sector of industry. The Chita Oblast is a major supplier of minerals and raw materials for the rest of the country.

A number of negative factors impose an adverse effect on the development of the mining and metallurgical industry of the Chita Oblast: extremely harsh climatic conditions, remote location far from industrial centers of the country, shortage of roads, inaccessibility of most parts of the region, lack of metallurgical and manufacturing plants, inefficient taxation policy, growing prices for transportation services, utilities, equipment and materials, large number of military facilities, etc.

Due to the above reasons, the rates of development of the mineral industries in the Eastern Trans-Baikal region are very slow. At present, many mines have been shut down due to the insolvency of consumers and for other reasons. Deposits ready for exploitations are not being developed and geological prospecting and exploration of favorable deposits has been suspended due to the lack of financing.

On the other hand, the mineral resources of the Chita Oblast are abundant and sufficient to satisfy the long-term demand of the Russian industries. Selection of deposits and mines for investing funds should take into account the following conditions:

- large commercial reserves of minerals or high grade of ores in case of regular or small reserves;
- use of open-pit mining method with a long service life of a mine or possibility to extract the available reserves within a short period of time in case of small deposits;
- application of advance technologies for ore and concentrate processing to ensure integrated recovery and utilization of valuable constituents;

- utilization of overburden rock and ore processing tailings;
- environmental safety of operations;
- forecast of the market development and demand on a long-term basis;
- application of terms and conditions specified in the law relating to the product sharing agreement.

The major deposits of its north-eastern part of the region have crucial significance from the viewpoint of the strategy of development of mineral resources in the Trans-Baikal region. There is a combination of very large deposits of various minerals within a range of 50-70 km in the vicinity of the Chara railroad station.

Construction of access railroad lines to the Chineyskoye and Udokan deposit and their development will provide highly favorable preconditions for accelerated development of the industry and facilitate exploitation of major deposits of rare metals ores (Katuginskoye), coal (Apsatskoye), synnyrite (Sakunskoye), etc. It will also provide unique opportunities for construction of a unified Chara complex of mining and metallurgical enterprises.

TRENDS IN RUSSIA IRON & NON-FERROUS METALS MINING

S. Solntsev, Mininstry of Industry, Science and Technology of the Russian Federation

In 2000 the production of iron and steel, as well as non-ferrous metals in Russia increased in terms of value (in comparable prices) by a factor of 1.7 and 1.5, respectively. These are one of the highest growth rates in the Russian economy. Will they be maintained during 2001? From this viewpoint, we offer a review of the results of the Russian mining industry in 2000.

Increase in metals production in 2000

Products	2000 level as percentage of 1999
Iron ore	105.9
Iron ore pellets	104.7
Bauxite	110.8
Alumina	107.5
Copper in concentrate	102.3
Lead in concentrate	103.3
Zinc in concentrate	100.8
Nickel	107.0
Cobalt	122.0
Molybdenum concentrate	101.8
Tungsten	90.2
Tin in concentrate	101.1
Gold mining production	114.5

Virtually all Russian mines operated in a stable mode and even exceeded the performance values of the previous year (except for a few mines in Siberia and in the Urals).

Production of commercial-grade iron ore increased by 5.2% and amounted to 87.1 million t as compared with 81.3 million t in 1999 and the production of iron ore pellets grew by 4.7% and reached 30.8 million t against 29.4 t in 1999.

The growth of the iron ore production was attributed to the increasing demand in the domestic market and growing export. The export increased primarily due to supplies to Ukraine and reached 7.4 million t (3.6 million t in 1999). At the same time a decline in the prices for iron ore supplied from the Sokolovsko-Sarbaisky mines resulted in an increase in the iron ore import from the Republic of Kazakhstan from 3.7 to 9.1 million t.

- Iron and steel industry in general;

- *- Mining production of iron ore*

At present the iron ore mines of Russia meet the demands of the domestic metallurgical works to the full extent. Part of production is exported ensuring revenues for governmental budgets, both federal and regional, and a stable financial position of the mining companies.

- Non-ferrous metals production in general;

- *- Aluminium industry;*
- *- Copper industry ;*
- *- Nickel and cobalt industry*

The existing tendencies suggest that the iron ore production (concentrate, sinter) will be maintained in 2001 at the level of 87.5 million t.

The production of copper concentrate increased in 2000 by 2.4%. The copper mines in the Republic of Bashkortostan (Uchaly, Bashkirsky, Buribayevsky) increased their production by 1.3%, the mines in the Orenburg region (Gaisky and Ormet) achieved an increase by 2.5%. The production of copper in concentrate in the Urupsky mine (Republic of Karachayevo-Cherkessia) increased its copper production by 15%.

The mines producing copper in concentrate as a by-product also increased their copper production: the Far East Mining Company by almost 2 times and the Primorsky mine (Maritime Province) by more than 2 times. However, these mines account for only 5% of the total production of copper in concentrate and their performance did not have any decisive effect on the overall copper output. Furthermore, they are located in remote areas, far from the copper smelters, and their products constitute sub-grade concentrates, which are exported.

It is expected that in 2001 the production of copper in concentrate will increase by 2–5% due to the fact that the Gaisky, Ormet, Safyanovskaya and Urupsky mines have increased their mining and processing capacities in 2000.

The production of zinc in concentrate was maintained in 2000 at the 1999 level despite the fact that some of the mines reported a significant increase (the mines in the Orenburg region by 1.7 times and the Salairsky mine by 1.5 times). This is explained by a decrease in production by the major zinc concentrate producers: the mines in Bashkortostan.

It is expected that in 2001 the overall production of zinc in concentrate will increase by 3–5% due to more stable operation of the Uchaly and Bashkirsky mines.

The production of lead in concentrate grew by 7% in 2000 due to its growth in the Salairsky (by 1.5 times) and Dalpolymetall mines (by 10%). It is predicted that this production level will be maintained during 2001.

The output of tin in concentrate increased by 6%. A major contribution to this growth made the Far East Mining Company due to an increase in production by 22% reached due to commissioning of the facilities at the 450m level with a capacity of 300,000 tpy to make up for the decommissioned capacities of the Molodyozhny mine. The production of tin in concentrate at the Deputatskolovo mine grew by 1.6%. Tin concentrate production was resumed at the Khinganskoye Olovo mine, that had been shut down for two years.

It is predicted that in 2001 the output of tin in concentrate will slightly increase (2–3%) as a result of an increase in the mining production at the Khinganskoye Olovo mine.

Currently, the domestic demand for copper, zinc, lead and tin is completely met by supplies of concentrates produced by Russian mines. This is possible even despite the fact that due to high railroad tariffs and remote locations, the major mines of the Russian Far East and the Kemerovo region have to export most of their zinc and lead concentrates.

ORE LEACHING SYSTEMS

A.E. Vorobyev, *Doctor of Technical Sciences, Professor (Moscow State Mining University)*
K.G. Kargintsev, *Cand. Techn. Sc. (Government of Republic of North Osetia-Alania)*
E.S. Odintsova, *(Moscow State Mining University)*

The economic performance of a leaching mining operation is dependent to a high degree on the cost of reagents. For this reason it is essential to reduce the reagent requirement in order to improve the performance of a mine. This can be achieved by selection of appropriate leach solution spraying and permeation systems.

Spraying systems

The following methods for leach solution feeding are applied for treating hard-rock deposits:
Hydrostatic method implies filling of the entire volume of the porous material with leach solution, keeping it for a certain time and collection of pregnant solution. A required condition for the hydrostatic leaching method is sufficient impermeability of the lateral host rock. For this reason the leaching zone should be adequately sealed by means of sealing liners, the operation and reliability of which is associated with certain technical difficulties. Filtration method is based on continuous movement of leach solution throughout the lump material under the condition that it is completely filled with leach solution. The requirements relating to the impermeability of the host rock are similar or even stricter than for the hydrostatic method.

Infiltration method is most commonly used in the mining practice. It is based on seepage of leach solution throughout the lump material, but it does not require complete filling of the latter with solution. Sufficient time should be ensured for the contact of solution with the ore surface in the presence of air oxygen; in this case the mass exchange processes occur under most favorable physical and chemical conditions. Leach solution is fed from the surface of the material by spraying, sprinkling or flooding through perforated spraying tubes. The hydrostatic method is applied in stable and consistent rocks in single-bed ore bodies having relatively small thickness and steep dip angle. The filtration method can be used for multi-level deposits under various geological conditions. The infiltration method is especially efficient when applied for heap leaching, because it ensures the most efficient use of leach solutions from the viewpoint of the physical and chemical hydrodynamics of mass transfer.

The process of wetting of an ore lump by leach solution begins when the solution reaches its surface. A most uniform distribution of solution over the lump surface is ensured when the entire lump is enclosed by solution. In case of heat leaching this is realistic for small ore particles. Larger ore lumps can contact with solution moving upward or downward in the form of streams and drops. In most cases the leach solution contacts an air dry or moist ore lump after it has already wetted the neighboring ore lumps.

Depending on the treatment system, leach solution can be applied by means of sprinkling, pulverization, flooding or distributed by means of blasting.

Sprinkling is performed with the aid of pressurized distribution hoses, vertical perforated tubes, rotating sprinklers, emitters, lawn-sprinkling devices, and plastic jet-type spraying systems of Segner's wheel type.

Pressurized distribution hoses are laid on the surface of an ore bed. Hoses are perforated with a predetermined number and a certain pitch of openings. Leach solution is fed to the hose network by slurry pumps with open turbine wheels.

Vertical perforated tubes are inserted into an ore bed at uniform intervals (5 m to 10 m). This facilitates supply of solution and air into the interior of an ore bed and intensify the leaching process. Such a system eliminates the problem of solution loss due to evaporation, which is especially important in arid regions, and the problem of solution freezing on the bed surface at freezing temperatures in winter time.

Rotating sprinklers can be of two types. The first type is wigglers constituting soft flexible hoses inserted into openings in solution supply tubes. They ensure uniform distribution of leach solution over the ore bed surface due to irregular wiggling of flexible hoses. Another type is wobblers constituting eccentric rotating sprinklers. They are normally installed on steel supports more than 1.2 m high. Due to eccentric rotation they ensure spraying of the ore bed with large drops of solution reducing thereby the evaporation rate. The number of wobblers to be installed is determined by the density of spraying under a given pressure. The required spraying density is achieved by selection of appropriate sprinkler type, the optimum distribution of sprinklers and sufficient solution pressure (Fig. 1).

Sprinklers are selected to ensure uniform spraying intensity within the radius of their action. First, the sprinklers are installed at the corners of an ore bed and then along the bed perimeter at a certain distance from the bed edge to avoid spraying outside the bed limits. They are installed at certain intervals so that their action ranges overlap each other. Then sprinklers are installed over the remaining part of the ore bed.

Emitters ensure spraying in a manner similar to the spraying systems used in agriculture. They use the principle of turbulent stream and are connected in a line to ensure uniform distribution of leach solution over the ore bed surface. Emitted solution drops pass through meandering channels losing the pressure and slowly flow out of the channels. The emitters commonly used for this purpose operate under a relatively low pressure (from 15–20 kPa to 100–140 kPa). Emitters are often submersed into an ore bed down to a depth of 20–25 cm below the surface or in some cases installed on the surface. The most essential factor determining the need for submersing the emitters is the climatic conditions. In areas with cold weather it is recommended during winter months to submerse the emitters directly into the ore bed. The distribution and the required number of emitters is calculated to ensure sufficient intensity of spraying, i.e., approximately 0.003 l/sec(m2 or 11 l/hr(m2. The main advantage of emitters is continuous dripping of leach solution with a minimum impact force. They also have the following advantages:

- possibility for use in winter time;
- lower leach solution loss due to water evaporation;
- less destruction of the bed surface.

The above advantages are significant if these factors are considered for estimate of gross costs. The main disadvantage of emitters is possible formation of calcium carbonate scale in small emitter channels. For this reason, the ponds used for collection of mother solution after recovery of valuable constituents from pregnant solution should ensure adequate treatment of solution to be recycled to heap leaching sites.

Sprinklers of Segner's wheel type constitute a device connected to outlets of a feeding pipe in the form of flexible plastic hoses about 0.5 m long. Under the effect of pressure they rotate like a Segner's wheel and ensure efficient spraying of leach solution (Fig. 2).

Flooding can be performed by means of trenches made at equal intervals across the entire width of a site. Perforated tubes of 100 mm diameter are laid in the trenches and backfilled with gravel; an ore bed about 6 m to 9 m high with a lump size of about 25 mm is laid over the site. The ends of the tubes are connected by two parallel PVC pipes of 150 mm diameter, through which pregnant solution is sent to collecting tanks.

Such leaching systems are efficient in areas with arid climate where sprinkling or spraying results in substantial loss of leach solution due to evaporation. They can be also used in case of low permeability of the ore bed posing limitations to the solution seepage. It is not recommended to apply the flooding method for materials with high seepage rates (over 30 m/day). Otherwise, the solution level inside the bed might rise too high and results in instability of the bed.

In some cases, cascades of special ponds are provided on the ore bed surface separated from each other with small dams. Solution is fed to flood individual limited areas of the bed. This method is simpler from the technical viewpoint as compared with the other methods. Flooding of an ore bed makes it possible to cover it with leach solution with a layer up to 10 cm or more above the bed surface. Solution infiltrates into cracks and pores over the entire bed area and the air is pressed out of the pores downward under the effect of the solution column. Since the total pore volume normally accounts for 15% to 40% of the entire ore volume, the continuous solution layer increases along with the penetration of solution into the interior of the bed. Along with the solution movement downward, the solution flows down the surface of crushed material at a higher rate than the rate of wetting due to the difference in the energy of wetting by liquid and gas. The air flows downward at a lower rate, air bubbles are held in cracks by the capillary pressure forces and are forced into the bed at a rate by 3 to 5 times lower than the rate of solution flow. For this reason the solution flowing downward is continuously enriched with air. During a period of 6 to 24 hours between solution supply, a new air-filled porous space is formed in a bed up to 3–4 m thick. During such a period leaching proceeds in an infiltration mode with pores filled with solution by about 50% and there is an amount of oxygen at least 10 times larger than required for gold leaching. In this case, the bed surface is covered with solution during not more than 2 to 4 hours per day and during the rest of the time clean atmospheric air is sucked into the ore bed. While in the case of leach solution spraying there is emission of cyanides and hydrocyanic acid observed during the entire leaching period, in the case of flooding, emission of deleterious substances occurs primarily in the process of solution feeding to the bed surface and the overall amount of cyanides emitted to the atmosphere is reduced.

The system for leach solution distribution comprises pipes for supply of solution; pressure-less distribution mechanism including a feeding outlet pipe installed in a manner permitting its rotation; and a stationary disc with distribution pipe outlets connected to the solution feeding pipes. This system permits alternating flooding of heap sections on the heap surface. Due to continuous flow of solution through the distribution system and pipes on the heap surface, the live cross-section of which virtually does not undergo any changes during their entire life and due to the relatively high leach solution requirement (150-250 m3), there is no crystallization of calcium compounds on the movable and stationary pipe outlets of the system and on the internal tube walls. In addition, the pressure loss due to the hydraulic resistance of the solution supply system is reduced. The number of distribution pipe outlets is equal to the number of heap surface sections to be flooded. The time required for flooding one section is 30 to 60 minutes and is dependent on the capacity of the circulation pump. Each section is flooded once or several times (up to 4 times) per day depending on the permeability of the crushed material and the process specifications for heap leaching.

The leaching agents used include acids, alkalis, organic compounds and bacteria.

Leaching can be performed with or without intensification of the process. The process can be enhanced by using the following methods: heating of leach solution, saturation of the material to be leached with oxygen (by providing an aeration pipe network in the bed) and preliminary activation of ore.

Spraying can be implemented under high pressure or under atmospheric pressure.

In order to ensure higher recoveries of valuable constituents it is also necessary to take into consideration the content of leaching reagents in the leach solution, solution addition rate and frequency of spraying. These factors are determined at the stage of laboratory studies. If a given ore does not pose any difficulties with respect to solution seepage, then the spraying density can be maintained within a range from 3.6 to 21.6 l/hr(m2. Typical spraying rates vary within a narrower range from 7.2 to 10.8 l/hr x m2.

Systems for collection of pregnant solution

The technology used for in-situ and heap leaching should guarantee prevention of migration of leach and pregnant solutions to underground aquifers. In many cases, in order to avoid leakage of solutions into the underlying rock, a sealing liner is provided at the base of the blocks planned for in-situ leaching or the site for heap leaching.

In case of in-situ leaching, in order to provide sealing of the block base, it is necessary to provide undercutting workings about 2.5–3 m high using short-hole drilling method. Then a layer of sand is laid on the working bottom and covered with polyethylene film, which is in turn covered by a layer of finely crushed rock about 0.4–0.6 m thick. Pregnant solution is collected in a drainage working located above the chamber floor; the walls and the bottom of the chamber are covered with a hydroinsulation layer. Pregnant solution is pumped from the drainage working or transported via ore passes to the central solution collector tank. The experience available indicates that in most cases the rock is consistent enough and does not require any sealing in case of solution seepage mode. It suffices to drill in the chamber bottom discharge holes from the roof of the drainage working.

If the hydrogeological setting of the deposit permits pumping of pregnant solution from the underground water level without contaminating the underground water, it is possible to run the operation without sealing.

Collection system using pressure-less underlying crushed ore bed

In case of heap leaching the pregnant solution can be collected by means of a containment wall built around the heap in order to maintain a certain level of leach solution in the heap. The pregnant solution overflows the wall into a collecting trench. A pipe is laid in the trench to remove the solution into a pump sump; then the solution is pumped to the pregnant solution pond. The rate of pregnant solution removal from the ore bed increases with a steeper slope angle of the heap base. It is very advantageous to construct a heap on gentle slopes. The orientation and configuration of a site can be modified in order to facilitate easier collection of pregnant solution by gravity flow toward the lowest point for subsequent pumping to the pregnant solution pond.

If the site is too steep or too flat in order to achieve a required slope, excavation and earth moving might be necessary. There are also less expensive alternatives available than earth moving. For example, construction of a site with variable bottom slope, i.e., the site bottom is flatter than its top. Furthermore, for sites with variable slope it is preferable to select valley-type or stepped bottoms.

Spraying of an ore bed can be also performed by means of pulverizing the leach solution if the particle size of leached ore is minimal. For this purpose appropriate nozzles should be installed on spraying devices. Depending on the principle of operation, jet configuration and pulverization method, nozzle types are classified as centrifugal, centrifugal-jet, impact-jet and combined nozzles.

Distribution of leach solution by blasting can be applied by drilling drill-holes in the block and charging into them, along with blasting agent, containers with leach solution, which is distributed then in the fragmented ore.

Leach solution feeding devices can be located either on the surface or inside the ore bed. In the former case, perforated tubes and hoses are uniformly laid over the ore bed surface. Since the leaching process slows down at low temperatures, it is advisable for regions with cold winters to use special technologies incorporating preliminary leveling of the site (1) and provide a sealing liner (2). Then a perforated pipeline network (3) is provided. During summer time, an ore bed is prepared with a bowl-like surface. In winter leach solution is fed to the pipeline. When solution is fed in the absence of large volumes of water, the reagent in the form of a film migrates into the upper layers of the bed (4) leaching out the contained gold. The gold-bearing solution moves to the surface of the bed and forms an ice lens (5); ice is periodically removed with the aid of a telpher. During warm season, the reagent is fed to the bed surface and the pipeline serves for solution collection (Fig. 3).

The internal solution supply systems include vertical injection drill-holes.

The spraying systems are also classified depending on the direction of solution feeding to the ore mass. The most common way is movement of solution downward by gravity. But in case of a hydraulic lock, it is possible to reverse the solution migration direction.

Reversing of the leach solution migration direction can be also achieved by other methods, e.g., with lower metal concentrations in pregnant solutions, calmatation is performed in the area where the reagent stream is formed within the intensive leaching zone. This is done with the aid of spraying drill-holes drilled in the ore bed and provided with perforated polyethylene casings.

In case of filtration leaching, a much higher solution flow rate is achieved directly above the solution feeding points and it decreases with a longer distance from the feeding points. As a result, a so called "intensive leaching zone" is formed where the valuable constituent is recovered into solution much faster than in the peripheral part of the infiltration stream. In order to eliminate this drawback, the intensive leaching zone is subjected to partial calmatation, facilitating thereby supply of leach solution to the peripheral area and its active treatment.

Depending on the method used for distribution of leach solutions, there are systems with conventional distribution and with stream dissipation. In the latter case, at least one additional layer is provided: 50 to 120 mm thick and composed of fine-grained material. This ensures distribution of the hydrodynamic stream throughout the entire cross-section of the ore bed.

Swelling of the material subjected to leaching significantly affects the leach solution migration pattern. For this reason, in case of heap leaching of ores with a high content of clayey material it should be taken into consideration that clay swelling is of osmotic character and it may be caused by a difference in the salt concentrations in the solutions contained inside the pores and encompassing the rock. If the concentration of the external solution is lower than that of the pore solution, the material begins to swell. To prevent swelling of clayey ores and improve their permeability it is advisable to feed leach solutions already containing some metals to be leached, rather than "pure" leach solutions.

Bottom tube drainage for collection of pregnant solution

Perforated tubes are laid inside the drainage layer to facilitate collection of pregnant solutions. In addition, they prevent formation of free water pressure imposed on the site base in flow-sheets using gravity drainage and reduce losses of pregnant solution due to leakage.

Drainage tubes can be directly connected to the system of tubes leading to the pregnant solution collection ponds or can be laid in a bypass collection trench or a collection tank.

A collecting drainage system should be designed to keep the saturation zone as low as possible, but at the same time, it should ensure a constant and minimum gradient of the solution stream in the bed.

A collection system should act as a filter for ore: fine particles should not be entrained by the solution stream and leave the bed via the collection pipes and trenches.

Similar to the liner, the pregnant solution collection system must be chemically resistant against leach solution. Appropriate opening sizes should be selected or filtering devices installed at the tube openings and the drainage material destruction by solutions should be minimized.

GOLD MINING INDUSTRY AND MARKET DEVELOPMENTS

FIRST RUSSIAN GOLD EXPORT FINANCING ARRANGED BY EBRD AND STANDARD BANK LONDON

Russia's alluvial gold mining industry shone brighter today, after the European Bank for Reconstruction and Development (EBRD) and Standard Bank London Limited (SBL) announced a jointly arranged programme to finance Russian gold exports, the first internationally led pre-production alluvial gold export financing facility for Russia. EBRD and SBL have disbursed funds to selected Russian mining customers of Bank Zenit, the first Russian bank to join the programme.

The three - year programme provides each company with an initial 360 day pre-production gold purchase facility, to finance up to 12 tons of gold. As export levels increase, hard currency reserves are expected to rise.

"This transaction will mobilise new financing for the gold sector," said Riccardo Puliti , Senior Banker of the EBRD. "In addition, the facility will also foster co-operation between Russian and international bullion banks." The facility aims to increase the trust and confidence among international and Russian bullion banks and to improve information among Western banks to create the conditions for the development of a capital market for short-term and long-term syndicated loans to the Russian gold industry.

Pre-payments for 2000 gold deliveries are now complete, and have enabled the mining companies to purchase the equipment and supplies required for the Russian alluvial gold mining season this year. The mining companies have all been reviewed by an independent technical mining agent appointed by the EBRD, in order to verify gold production capacity. Russia produced approximately 100 tons of gold in 1999 and the alluvial gold mining sector was responsible for the majority of this production.

Bank Zenit has joined the financing as a co-arranger, making the first disbursements under the financing in December 1999 prior to the start of EBRD and SBL disbursements, and the bank hopes to introduce additional customers into the financing in the coming years. The statement of the Chairman of Bank Zenit reflects this, "This year's financing is only the first step and we consider the work done as an investment necessary for the development of cooperation on a much larger scale."

All the parties in the financing emphasize the importance of continued cooperation of financiers in the Russian gold industry. "We are particularly attracted to the manner in which this financing combines international and Russian financing resources, in the continuing development of the Russian gold mining industry," said Martin Botha, a Director at SBL. "It will be the first time that small and medium-sized Russian alluvial gold producers will have been exposed to Western credit criteria, international environmental standards and best practice due diligence."

This transaction was facilitated by an EBRD-sponsored technical cooperation study, the purpose of which was to provide the international investors with a comprehensive overview of the Russian alluvial gold industry. The assignment was tendered internationally, carried out in the third and fourth quarters of 1999, and was funded by the Canadian Government.

SBL, is the international merchant banking operation of the South African Standard Bank Group, and is a leading private sector provider of international mining finance. SBL is one of the larger international physical gold traders actively involved in purchasing Russian gold. All of the gold exported from Russia under this EBRD facility will be bought by SBL.

HARMONY GOLD'S INVESTMENT IN RUSSIAN GOLD MINING SHOULD SEND STRONG MESSAGE TO SOUTH AFRICAN GOVERNMENT.

If the dividend payment can be taken as a sign of confidence in the future there is no doubt that Bernard Swanepoel and his team at Harmony Gold reckon that the outlook for the current year bids fair to be another success. It is an ideal moment for him to be presenting at our 7th Minesite Mining Forum which is due to take place in London on Tuesday September 10th , but this means that the audience will be even bigger than usual so early booking is advised.

The company has just announced improved operational profits for the fifth quarter in a row and earnings per share, after write-downs for the past financial year, totalled 1, 094 cents, an increase of 882 per cent on the 111.5 cents reported for the previous financial year. Small wonder that Harmony has rewarded its shareholders so generously with a total payment of 500 cents which is more than three times that of the previous year as there have been one or two slight hiccups along the way such as strikes and mine accidents caused by seismic problems.

Production actually increased to 2.7 million ounces which is an increase of 25 per cent on the year to end June 2001 and Harmony expects a further increase of 16 per cent this year to 3.1 million ozs. This rate of production is well supported by resources and reserves as the company has just announced that as at the end of June resources were in excess of 295 million ounces and 49 million of these were in the reserve category. These ore reserves were calculated at a gold price of US$295/oz so they are on the conservative side, but that has always been Harmony's policy. It reflects the anti-hedging stance of the company which gives shareholders full exposure to increases in the gold price as and when they occur.

The 17 per cent increase in production in the June quarter to 780,480 ozs was mainly due to improved operational performance by the Free State, Elandskraal and Free Gold operations and the inclusion of Hill 50 in Australia. In fact the company used the past three months to integrate its two acquisitions which were 50% of Free Gold in South Africa and 100 per cent of Hill 50 . Overall cash costs of production increased marginally from US$176/oz to US$178/oz due to a slight strengthening in the Rand/US$ exchange rate, but this still left a healthy gross margin US$130/oz at the present gold price.

The Free State operations performed well with a 47 per cent hike in cash operating profits in the June quarter, but Evander was faced by lower tonnage and recovery grade which inevitably lifted working costs to the detriment of profitability. Randfontein's results were hit by a strike, but the impact on cash operating profits was limited and Elandskraal had a cracking quarter with profits 51 per cent up on the previous period as the benefits of the development programme start to show through on recovery grades. But it is the performance of Freegold, the joint venture between Harmony and the black empowerment company ARM (African Rainbow Gold) in which the London audience will be interested.

Its production rose by 19 per cent in the June quarter and operating costs fell by 23 per cent so its profit margin is US$177/oz at the present gold price of US$307/oz, but it is Bernard Swanepoel's views on black empowerment partnerships and the pressures being put on South African gold producers by the Minerals Bills which are eagerly awaited. Pierre Lassonde took a big swing at it during the Diggers 'n' Dealers conference in Australia saying that sovereign risk has now reared its head in South Africa with the real possibility of gold mines being nationalised. Bernard Swanepoel preferred deeds to words and went out and bought a 32.5 per cent interest in a private Russian mine producing 150,000 ounces of gold a year.

He then went on to say that there was plenty of scope to boost the operation to an annual 200,000 ounces and that the ounces will be as cheap as those Harmony had been buying in South Africa. In fact there is reason to believe that they could be a whole lot cheaper and another deal may be envisaged as very little detail has been given on the Russian deal as to partners or whereabouts. The message will certainly get back to the South African Government that the big producers are not going to sit around and wait to see what happens and this is just the sort of pressure that is required. Some analysts in South Africa and North America tend to be a bit nervous of Russia, but moves such as this will set them thinking.

"SOUTHERN-URAL GOLDEN MINING COMPANY" SOLD IN MAY OF THIS YEAR TO MNPO "POLIMETALL" IS EXPERIENCING DIFFICULTIES.

Even the management of the company doesn't know plans of the new owner - overseas investor, whose name has not been advertised yet. Recently, the company has lost the competition for gold ore object, located within a few kilometers from the company's work site. The company also refused to participate in a competition for another object. Observers say, that the question is not about the fight for the objects (which total value and predicted gold resources don't exceed 10 tons), but for the presence in the region itself. The thing is, that the main competitor of "Polimetall" (now, also of the new foreign company) in Orenburg region is Ural Mine-metallurgical company, which now to all appearances have won the competition. At this moment, "Southern-Ural gold mining company" practically doesn't have the raw material base. In particular, the main gold deposit of the mine, which the company has the license for, is completely exhausted. The work is performed only to the piles of already extracted ore. Now, the company is trying to use the remaining resources, specifically, the company is looking into possibilities of exploitation of the ore, which previously was not taken into consideration due to it's low indices. The total announced volume of extraction this year was only 60 kg (as a reminder, the company was extracting up to 370 kg per year during better times).

IN THE BEGINNING OF OCTOBER THE PRICE FOR PALLADIUM FELL LOWER THAN THE PRICE FOR GOLD.

The reduction of price for palladium may influence the decrease in profit of "Norilsk Nikel", the largest Russian palladium manufacturer. Because palladium demand today is greater than it's supply, "Norilsk Nickel" is not concerned with the price reduction. Analysts think, that the further behavior of price for palladium depends on condition of the world economy in general.

NAVOINSKY INTEGRATED MINING-METALLURGICAL PLANT CONDUCTS EXPERIMENTAL WORK ON MINING OF DEEP STRIPPING ROCKS WITH AN AVERAGE GOLD CONTENT OF 1.0 G/T.

The experimental industrial unit developed for this purpose allows the extraction of about 20% of rock mass with the gold content of 2.2 g/t from stripping rocks.

THE OPENING UP OF PARNOKSK FERRO-MANGANESE DEPOSIT BEGAN ON OAO "MANGANESE KOMI".

Holding "Euromet" ("Manganese Komi" is a part of "Euromet") invested in purchase of equipment for the separation plant and also in explosive-drilling work, specifically: it has purchased drilling unit SBU-100G;built laboratory and shipment terminal; conducted test drilling on the spot "Magnitnyi-2. Right now the State Gold Committee is confirming the supply, the extraction will start in 2003. Geological prospecting work was moved to another spot, where the supply may increase. The detailed experimental analysis of company's work has been conducted. Significant restrain on the project development is the orientation of metallurgical plants, main consumers of manganese production, - to buy raw material from Kazakhstan and Ukraine.

However, the leaders of group of companies "Manganese" still hope that the government will support the development of the Russian raw material base, because this is not only the manganese problem. The head of Komi, Vladimir Torlopov visited Parnok, during the Mining Conference. He highly evaluated the conducted work and promised support. The question, also discussed at the Conference, was that despite of the understanding of a problem on the governmental level, we still experience difficulties in sale, because some forces inside Russia lobby the interests of Kazakhstan and Ukraine, investing Russian money into economy of these countries. Vladimir Torpolov said, that Komi was not welcome on manganese market, but we can't let this question slide, it deserves the discussion on the federal legislative level. In the mean time everything possible is being done in the republic with significant governmental support. The ore shipment to Ural plants has restarted. The work on the mine continues.

ZHOKVES ROSENBERG, GENERAL DIRECTOR DEPUTY OF "MINING COMMITTEE "NORILSK NICKEL" WAS APPOINTED "MINING COMMITTEE "NORILSK NICKEL" BOARD VICE CHAIRMAN.

He will supervise the main direction of scientific technical progress of the company; development of perspective technologies and technological processes, with consideration of world tendencies; increase in technical level of manufacture and output; development of ecological politics. Zhokves Rosenberg was born in 1943 in Tomsk region. He graduated from Dnepropetrovsk Mining Institute in 1967. From 1959 to 1981 he worked in the mining chemical business. Since 1981 he had worked at Norilsk mining-metallurgical integrated plant, from head technologist of sulphur manufacturing to finance and trade director. From 1997 to 2000 he worked as a director of finance, general director deputy at "Norilsk Nickel". Since 2001 - he has been a general director deputy at "Mining Committee "Norilsk Nickel"

LAST WEEK SECOND MEETING - SEMINAR OF TOP CEOS OF URAL MINING-METALLURGICAL COMPANY SUMMARIZED THE RESULTS.

The topic of the seminar was "The increase in mining business efficiency"
The main purpose of the meeting - to increase manufacturing efficiency by trading experience between businesses and subsequently introduce new knowledge within the holding, was achieved.

First of all, the participants of the seminar learned about the project "Perspective program development of the raw material base for Ural Mining Committee Holding, which implies further functioning of holding businesses at the current output level, with increased level for some businesses. For example, the Gaisk GOK plans to increase mining up to 7.7 millions tones of ore per year by means of the reconstruction of an underground mine and separation factory, and also by means of exploitation the deposit "Osennyi" ("Autumn"). The reconstruction of production at Volkov quarry is expected to bring the mine efficiency up to 2.5 mln. tons per year. The holding had placed special hopes on the perspective mining of Udokan Deposit; it is expected to bring additional 15 mln. tons of ore per year (up to 150 thousands tons of copper).

THE MAIN CANDIDATES FOR MINING OF UDOKAN DEPOSIT ARE URAL MINING COMMITTEE AND "NORNICKEL".

The Ministry of Property Relations of Russian Federation submitted tender's terms of rights to mine Udokan Deposit to Chita regional administration. However, tender's terms didn't suit the administration of Chita. Chitinians think, that only the contest with limited number of participants should determine the deposit's future. The regional administration supports proposition of the governor - Eduard Rossel, to accept only domestic investors into the contest. Ural Mining Committee and the company "Norilsk Nickel" are among major candidates. Companies "Sibal", "Kazakhmed", "New resources" are also interested in the mining.

LEGALIZATION OF RUSSIAN SILVER EXPORT.

Yesterday, the Department of Governmental Information stated that the government chairman of Russian Federation, Mikhail Kasianov, signed the resolution for repeal of 6.5% export duty for silver. Silver's manufacturers will be the primary beneficiaries of this action; respectively it could lead to the increase in Russian silver production.

INTERREGIONAL SCIENTIFIC MANUFACTURING ASSOCIATION "POLIMETALL" HAS LAUNCHED THE MINING METALLURGICAL COMPLEX AT THE PROJECT OUTPUT LEVEL ON THE ONE OF THE LARGEST RUSSIAN GOLD - SILVER DEPOSITS "LUNNOE".

The start up will bring additional 120 tons of silver per year.
This will increase the annual silver extraction in Russia by 30%
Gold - silver deposit "Lunnoe", one of the largest in the country, is located in the North-Eastern Russia, 680 km to the North of Magadan. "Lunnoe's" industrial supply is 3 000 tons of silver and over 14 000 tons of gold.The exploitation of the deposit "Lunnoe" conducts "Silver of the Territory" ("Serebro Teritorii"), the branch company of MNPO "Polimetall". The company also conducts independent geological prospecting and deposit search work.

MNPO "Polimetall" implemented the project in the end of 1999.
The company was doing mining metallurgical complex construction on it's own and with the help of specialized contractors.The total investment volume of the project was $ 40 millions. As a result the enterprise, built at the deposit "Lunnoe" is capable to carry out the complete range of work: extraction and treatment of the ore, leaching in the cascade of reactors, deposition of silver and gold on the Merrill Crow unit, Zinc cementite production with noble metal content up to 60%. Besides, "Silver Territory" continues search work to increase the supply of deposit "Lunnoe". Starting 2003, the annual silver extraction at "Lunnoe" will be about 120 tons. As a result, the annual extraction of Russian silver will increase by 30%.

After the start up of the mining metallurgical complex in September of 2002, the volume of silver extracted from deposit "Dukat" by MNPO "Polimetall" will go over 600 tons per year, which will make up more than 60% of the total annual silver extraction volume for Russia.

Due to this fact, MNPO "Polimetall" will join the rank of world leading silver mining companies. MNPO "Polimetall" is number one company in silver mining in Russia and belongs to top ten companies in volume of gold extraction. "Polimetall", the highest technological mining company of the Russian Federation, is a part of the structure of group of companies "East". The group also includes companies like "Baltic Plant", "Tihvinskyi transport machinery construction plant "Titran" and other large enterprises.

"POLIMETALL" HAS BUILT THE FACTORY IN BURYATIA.

Yesterday, the management of Petersburg holding "Polimetall" announced the end of construction work. The factory is located on the territory of the gold deposit Barun-Holba (Buryat Republic). Holding invested about $30 millions in the project.

The official start up of the factory, with extraction volume 2 tons of gold per year, will happen in two months. Petersburg holding "Polimetall" belongs to the group of companies "East"; it owns capital shares of 13 mining companies. In 1999 the holding has purchased the capital share of "Zun Hada", the owner of the exploitation license for the gold deposit Barun-Holba in Buryatia, located 120 km from the regional center of Orlik Okinskiy region.

The industrial supply of Barun-Holba deposit is 8.9 tons of gold. However, holding specialists counting on their own account (through finance of the search and geological prospecting work) hope to justify that resources of the deposit are 63 tons. If they are lucky to confirm it, the factory's output will be covered for more than 30 years.

PETERSBURG HOLDING "POLIMETALL" STARTED A NEW PROJECT: THE CONSTRUCTION OF HADZHINSK MINING METALLURGICAL COMPLEX IN OHOTSK AREA OF KHABAROVSK REGION.

The project was positively evaluated by a non-departmental expertise. Supposedly, the complex, with the output of 500 thousands tons of ore per year will start up in 2003. In 2003 Ohotsk mining geological company, which capital share holds "Polimetall", plans to start extraction on Hadzhinskyi deposit, with the total gold volume of 4 tons and silver 80-85 tons per year. "Polimetall" specialists have developed the construction of the complex, extraction technology and ore treatment processes. Up until present moment, Ohotsk company has built 46 out of 90 km of the road from Ohotsk to Hakandzhinxk deposit. Next year Petersburg holding plans to invest not less than $12 millions into the project. The total cost of it is evaluated at $50 millions.

KOLSKYI MINING METALLURGICAL COMPANY HAS WON THE CONTEST FOR THE EXPLOITATION OF TITANIUM-MAGNETITE-ILMENITE DEPOSIT "GREMIAHA-VYRMES" (MURMANSK REGION).

The ore supply there is evaluated at 87 mln. tons. The opening up of the deposit requires $ 300-350 mln.

"Gremiaha-Vyrmes" located in the central part of Murmansk region, is one of the largest Russian deposits of titanium-magnetite-ilmenite ore. In 1995-1996 six ore bodies with perspective supply of about 87 mln ore tons were discovered on the location. The most valuable is the ilmenite supply (it is used in production of titanium and it's derivatives). It may completely cover the demand of Russian industry in this ore.

Right now Russia is experiencing the deficit in this raw material; domestic businesses have to purchase from overseas (mostly from Ukraine) about 300 thousands tons of ilmenite concentrate.

The contest for exploitation of "Germiaha-Vyrmes" deposit was announced in July of last year.To participate in the contests, prospects had to offer optimal technical solutions for deposit exploitation, plans for mineral and environmental protection, and also satisfy some social requirements, such as involve local geological prospecting companies and provide new vacancies for population.

The lost party wasn't offended either. Before the announcement of the final contest results, Kolskyi Mining Metallurgical Committee and "Apatit" signed the general agreement and protocol to conduct joint search and exploitation of the deposit, in case if Mining Metallurgical Committee receives the exploitation license. Kolskyi Mining Metallurgical Committee went for it, just because the exploitation work requires major investments, not easily found even by such a giant. In preliminary estimation, the exploitation of the contest lot and construction of mining complex with 1mln tons outcome of ore per year requires $300-350 mln.

Specialists estimated, that ore supply of "Germiaha-Vyrmes" deposit should last 20-30 years. The search and drilling stage will take about 3 years. Mining business should start the work in five years after receiving the license.

KOMATSU IS STRENGTHENING IN KAZAKHSTAN

Office of service-dealer Komatsu has been opened in SSGPO company. It will service and maintain mining machinery. The company is represented by Adani on Kazakhstan market. Joint venture has been working in republic for two years. As was informed earlier, SSGPO bought a lot of dump trucks HD-785. Five trucks have already been assembled and start working at Sokolovsky open pit mine. Engine output is 1050 hp, payload – 91 ton, body volume is 60 cu m. There is no rivalry to HD-785 in CIS. SSGPO has had experience of operation of such machinery – earlier the company bought Komatsu dozers and machines had never let down the company during complicated industrial process. Now the company is operating 11 dozers in total. Thus, there are two service-centers. Since 2000 representatives of Caterpillar has been working in the company who are making technical maintenance of CAT-777D dump trucks. Then the company bought a lot of 10 trucks. Soon another lot of American dump trucks will be bought. Servicing, in this case of Japanese dozers and dump trucks Komatsu as well as CAT 777-D, is very profitable for the company. Spare parts and accessories are delivered directly from manufacturer and servicing is made by specialists of these companies. Among customers of Komatsu are such mining and metallurgical companies as Poltava GOK, Sev GOK, Lebedinsky and Mikhailovsky GOKs. As representatives of Almaata branch of Komatsu Ltd. informed, Donsky GOK (Khromtau) subordinated with SSGPO to Euroasian Industrial Association also is going to buy Japanese mining machiner

BLACK GRANITE

The first in the region experimental-industrial open pit mine for extraction of black granite was opened in Pechenga district of Murmansk reg., the site contains more than 4 million cu m of stone. Therefore even at its annual extraction of 1,5-3000 cu m, local reserves will be extracted during 400 years. Stone is extracted by state enterprise Arktikvoenreserve, which obtained the license for subsoil use. At the first stage 50 jobs will be created, providing for annual output up to 3200 cu m of decorative stone and profit of 25 m rub. In near future deposits with white and pink granite can be developed.

RUSSIAN ENGINES FOR BYELORUSSIA

Union state of Byelorussia and Russia is making its first steps. Recently its parliamentary assembly took the decision to allocate $16 million this year to Yaroslovaky plant Avtodiesel and to other enterprises taking part in Russian-Byelorussian programme Development of Diesel Motor Building. The funds will be spent for preparation of commercial production of engine 7511 rated up to 800 hp. They will comply with Euro-2 standard. BelAZ and MAZ dump trucks will be equipped by such engines. New programme has united four Byelorussian and Russian companies.

NEW SHOVEL

The fleet of Russian shovels has been updated. Plant Tas-Spetsmash, a branch of Tekhagroservice, has launched production of shovel-grader on KamAZ chassis. This multifunctional machine has telescopic attachment. It is intended for earth moving at grounds of 1-4 classes, grading and loading. Its dumping height is 5,1 m, max. radius of digging – 8,7 m, digging depth up to 4.9 m. Boom is 3,1 m. Full rotation of bucket allows to operate it both as backhoe and shovel. By request, machine is completed with different kinds of changeable attachments

NORILSK NICKEL WITHDREW

Board of Norilsk Nickel took the decision to abandon its only international project. As specialists say, it does not provide for repayment of investments and does not facilitate growth of investor's capitalization. It was planned to extract 50000 ton of nickel and 3500 ton of cobalt per year at the deposit. Three-lateral agreement with Canadian Argosy Minerals Inc. and New Caledonia's Societe Miniere de la Tontouta laid the basis for the project for nickel extraction at Neketi-Bogota deposit. Since the very start the project seemed to be capital-intensive. At least $800 million should be invested in the project. Since autumn 2001, when works started, the Russian company has already invested $7,5 million. Chairman of Board said that transformation into international company was not the goal of Norilsk Nickel. The company is ready to take part in new projects in Russia and abroad but only if they are large-scale and profitable.

CIVILIZED MINING

It is planned to transform from administrative to agreement relations in mining in Russia. Such is the concept of draft bill introduced by President's administration for consideration of government. The proposal was placed by commission for differentiation of powers between federal authorities and subjects of federation. Its head Dmitry Kozak explained that existing licenses for deposits would become null and void and instead of them contract and concession will regulate relations between state and subsoil user. Then, as it is considered, civil-legal regulation of sufficiently complicated ties between state and private users will be achieved in sphere of mineral sources of the country. Thus, it is planned to create favourable conditions for investments and provide more guarantees to both parties for the foreseeable future.

The scheme of future relations is simple. "After sale of minerals extracting company is reimbursed for its normative and stipulated by technology costs as well as normal profit which amount is set in concession agreement", the note to bill explains. The bill does not introduce anything new. It is known that in Arabic countries successfully developing hydrocarbonate raw material oil companies are only concessionaires. State is owner of extracted raw material here and disposes of it at its own discretion.

KUDRIN - HEAD OF ALROSA SUPERVISORY COUNCIL

Vice-Prime Minister of Government Alexey Kudrin was elected Chairman of Supervisory Council of ALROSA. Vyacheslav Shtirov, President of Sakha republic was elected the first Deputy Chairman, Deputy Chairman - Andrey Kirillin, President of ALROSA in 1994-1995. Earlier Supervisory Council had two co-chairmen representing interests of the largest shareholders - Government of Russia and Government of Yakutia.

GOK CONSTRUCTION

Construction of mining and ore dressing works at Udokan deposit can begin in 2003. Such dates were announced by Governor of Chita region R. Geniatulin at press-conference. Practically all obstacles to hold tender for deposit development are eliminated. The tender can be held this year. Today many companies express interest in Udokan deposit, with majority being Russian one. The predicted amount of investment in development of one of the largest copper deposit - Udokan and construction of infrastructure and processing complex is $250, General director of Ural mining and metallurgical company A. Kozitsin informed. He emphasized that these are preliminary estimate. The period of recoupment at the planned extraction of 10-12 m ton of copper ore is 6-7 years.

NET PROFIT OF MINING AND METALLURGICAL COMPANY NORILSK NICKEL

Net profit of Mining and Metallurgical Company Norilsk Nickel in the first quarter of 2002 according to Russian standards of book-keeping made up 3740800 th. Rub. According quarterly report of the company, for the same period of 2001 Nornickel received 14776559 th. Of net profit. Thus, there is 4-fold drop in terms of that figure, because this year activity of subsidiaries of GMK Norilsk Nickel were not taken into account. According to report, in 1 quarter of 2002 share of precious metals in total sales of metals of Nornickel accounted for 20,9% (55,1% in 2001), nickel - 49,8% (23,9%), copper - 24,6% (18,8%). Ore extraction accounted for 100,1%, including: high-grade - 101,6%, ingrained ores - 98,5% and copper ore - 98,2%. As a whole, all mining enterprises, concentration and agglomeration plant worked according to plans..

RUSAL - TRANSNATIONAL CORPORATION?

Russian Aluminium plans to make a deal for the astronomic in Russian practice amount in $4 bn. Executive director of the company A. Buligin informed that merger with the largest British companies Rio Tinto and BHP Billityon are considered. Besides, Rusal considered bankrupt American company Kaiser Aluminum and Indian Nalco, which ranks second in terms of output in the country. Rusal is going in such a way to expand its niche in extraction of bauxite - basic raw material for aluminum production. It is still undecided if it is joint venture or Rusal will buy out assets, however, foreign partners will be able to buy part of shares of the Russian company. Foreign companies comment that information cautiously.

LOBBYISTS UNION

Three largest producers of chemical fertilizers of Russia - agrochemical corporation Azot, association Fosagro and mineral-chemical company Evrochim has announced creation of Fund of Industry of chemical fertilizers to lobby its interest in the government. In the future the fund plans to create single structure to buy gas and electric power for all its founders. The creation of fund was announced by its President, head of Azot, Boris Titov. No integration of the enterprises is planned at the first stage. Its basic goals are struggle to abolish export duties for Russian fertilizers, quota and duties of EU and USA for import of fertilizers as well as prevention of introduction of new antidumping duties. According to Eurochim President (branch of MDM group) N. Levitsky, fund will also try to achieve preferences for excise or introduce reduction of ratios while buying gas from Gazprom, improvement of the situation with VAT return to exporters of fertilizers. In the future Fosagro, Evrochim, Azot are planning to create on the basis of fund single company for buying electric power from federal power market and administrator of trading system at UES of Russia. Within fund three holdings do not agree neither markets distribution, neither prices as it contradicts antitrust legislature. Apatite, Murmansk will delegate authorities of single executive body to managing organization FosAgro AG. Such decision was voted by shareholders of Apatite at its extraordinary general meeting. Now Board of directors must sign on behalf of company agreement on management with managing organization FosAgro Ag. Soon results of voting held at three chemical fertilizers enterprises to be transferred under its direct management in Voskresensk, Balakovo and Meleuzovsk will be announced.

ZINC DEMAND IS ON THE RISE

The main zinc supplier of the Russian market - Cheliabinsk plant started to step up production after some drop. It satisfies 95% of consumption of domestic market. Zinc production have rised up to 200 ths. Ton this year against 145 ths. ton - last year.

Domestic demand for zinc is estimated at 125 th. Ton in 2002 in Russia. Share of Cheliabinsk zinc plant is app. 95% of the market. That was a result of modernization of the plant, into which $215-220 m was invested.

For 4 months of 2002 the plant produced 52,65 th. ton of zinc, by 2,7% more than planned (51,26 th. Ton.). For 4 months 32,64 ths. Ton of zinc was sold on the local market or 67,8% of all sales, 11,48 th. Ton or 23,8% of sales was exported.
Part of products was produced under tolling schemes. Sales on the domestic market made up 8,66 th. Ton or 67,6% of all sold products, 4,14 th. Ton or 32,4% - exported. The average selling price of zinc at domestic market for 4 months of 2002 made up $832 per ton, while the average export price of ton of zinc made up for that period $721 (in April $855 and $772 accordingly).

THE RUSSIANS AND ARMENIANS: COMMON ALUMINUM

Russian Aluminum has invested in Russian-Armenian JV Armenal app. $20 m as capital and fixed assets. For the last 2 years some works aimed at upgrading of quality were carried out that allowed to make its products competitive on foreign markets.
In January-April 2002 output increased 1.9-fold vs. the same period of 2001. According to the Ministry of Trade and Economic Development of Armenia, Armenal in January-April 2002 produced products to the amount of 1,25 bn drums ($1=581 drum) that is by 132% more year-on-year.

THE WEALTH OF THE RUSSIAN SOIL

Rapid soaring of the world prices for PGM entails revision by Russia a number of gold deposits to reveal PGM there. It was found out that at the largest gold deposit Sukhoy Log in some intersections for example up to 102,3 m PGM content is 1,45 g/ton (including in the interval 40.5 m - 2,42 g/ton). Platinum dominates over palladium. Among PGM minerals hard solutions of platinum-iron-copper content are widely revealed, $PtAs_2$ and tellurium-bismutite of palladium and silver. Grain of platinum are 1 mkm in diameter and are encapsulated in pyrite. Gold reserves at the deposits are registered officially as 1089 ton with gold content of 2.7 g/ton. Investigation demonstrated that PGM is available in ores of some other large gold deposits - Natalka, Nezhdaninsky, Olympiada, Zun-Kholba. PMG is found in ore of Muruntau deposit (South Uzbekistan). Besides Norilsk mining and industrial region, among the most important potential projects in Russia there are sulfide copper-nickel deposit Kingash in Krasnoyarsk region, and Chineysky deposits of titanium-iron-chrome ores with PGM in Chita region. In Karelia deposit of Bushveld type has been found - Burakovo chromite with PGM, at Kola peninsula - platinoid Fedorovo-Pansky with predicted resources of Pd+Pt+Au of app. 400 ton. The deposit is localized within metallogenic province including well-known Finnish Pennikat-Portimo. The alluvial deposits of Russia allow to extract up to 7-8 ton of metal annually. The geologists came to the conclusion that exploration of occurrences of metal of that group should be made in black slate widths as well as in copper sandstones.

EXPORT OF PHOSPHOROUS FERTILIZERS FROM RUSSIA IN SEPTEMBER-OCTOBER 2001

The basic selling market for the Russian fertilizers remained to be Latin America and China. The Russian diammonium phosphate fertilizer was sold at the price of $134-136 per ton (in ports of Russia) and ammonium phosphate fertilizer - at the price of $140-145 per ton. While the market is saturating, demand for phosphate fertilizers start falling on the market of Brasilia and Argentine, that exerts pressure on the prices. The first signs of the Brazilian market saturation appeared already in September.

The ammonium phosphate fertilizer offered at the price $165-167 (in ports of Brasilia) from USA and Russia was sold at the price of $161-163 per ton. The shipments from St. Petersburg to Argentine were carried out at the price of $158 per ton (in Argentine ports). In the first half of 2001 Brasilia bought 378,2 th. Ton of ammonium phosphate fertilizers, including 160 th. Ton was delivered from Russia. At the end of September Russian ammonium phosphate fertilizer was delivered to Brasilia at the price of $140 per ton in ports of Russia, in Europe ammonium phosphate was delivered at the price of $145-150 per ton in ports of Russia. As a whole, export of the Russian phosphorous fertilizers dropped in the first half of 2001 year-on-year and made up: diammonium phosphate fertilizer - 570 th. Ton against 630 th. Ton, ammonium phosphate fertilizer - 800 th. Ton against 930 th. Ton.

Russian compound fertilizers (NPK 16:16:16) were continued to be delivered to China. From January till July 2001 675,6 th. Ton was delivered to China recalculated for nutriment against 630,4 th. Ton for the same period last year. The largest lots of goods were contracted for Mexico. In September the last sale of compound fertilizer was registered at the price of $128 per ton in ports of Russia. The goods was sold till the end of the year.

Drop of export of apatite concentrate of the Russian origin is registered, which made up only 1,46 m ton in first half of 2001 against 1,67 m ton delivered in first half of 2000. Drop of export took place due to sharp drop of deliveries to Ukraine and Lithuania. The deliveries to Ukraine were stopped even in 2000 due to increase in value of production of apatite concentrate and growth of transport expenditures for its delivery to Ukraine as well as the fact that production of phosphorous fertilizers at Ukranian plants under tolling agreements practiced during that period under slump of demand for world markets for phosphrous fertilizers and price drop has become unjustified. Ukraine started to buy phosphorous concentrate from North Africa to provide the internal market and continued to import simple phosphorous fertilizers from Russia. Sharp drop of concentrate to Lithuania is explained by large delays in payments for delivered goods.
The price of apatite concentrate continued to remain at the price $43-45 per ton in ports of Russia, Murmansk.

DYNAMIT NOBEL PUTS INTO OPERATION A PLANT TO PRODUCE EMULSION EXPLOSIVES IN UZBEKISTAN

German Dynamit Nobel in the middle of 2002 is going to put into operation plant to produce emulsion explosives worth $10 m.
The capacity of the plant to be built in Muruntau open pit mine in Central Kizilkumi (basic gold ore basis of Navou Mining and Metallurgical Works) will make up 45000 ton of explosives per year.
The largest world producer of gold Newmont Mining Corporation USA, the largest investor in Uzbekistan, is going to invest another $5 m into prospecting of gold reserves of Uzbekistan during 5 years.

On June 12 memorandum on mutual understanding between Uzbekistan and Newmont Mining Corporation for prospecting and preparation for exploitation of gold reserves in Karakalpakstan (the north-west of Uzbekistan) was signed in Goskomgeo.

SAMARKANDMRAMOR SEEKS INVESTORS

Samarkandmramor of JSC Uzstroymaterials produces marble and granite blocks, marble plates, decorative road metal, bentonite clay. Its annual output is 9,2 th. Sq m of marble plates, 12 000 cu m of marble blocks, 325,1 cu m of granite blocks.

SUAL-HOLDING SET UP WORKING GROUP FOR CONSTRUCTION PROJECT OF BAUXITE COMPLEX ON THE BASIS OF SREDNE-TIMAN ALUMINA DEPOSIT IN KOMI REPUBLIC

The construction is planned to begin in near future, so that start producing one million ton of ore per year at Timan deposit. SUAL will cut development of bauxites at North-Ural bauxite mine simultaneously. On the basis of deposit in Komi the company plans to construct aluminum complex to produce one million ton of alumina and more than 500 000 th. Ton of aluminum per year. Investments of $1,75 bn must be raised for the project. Now SUAL is conducting talks with potential investors. SUAL-holding is the second largest company producing aluminum in Russia and 5th in the world for production of alumina. In 2001 SUAL enterprises produced 602 000 ton of aluminum, by 1,2% more than in 2000 and 1,7 m ton of alumina (by 3,18% more). Today 22% of products is delivered to the Russian market, 48% - to Europe, 16% is exported to Asia, 14% - to USA.

GMK NORILSKY NICKEL AND OUTOKUMPU SIGNED CONTRACT FOR DESIGNING OF NEW ORE DRESSING PLANT IN NORILSK AT THE END OF LAST WEEK

Under the contract, maximum duration of technical project performance is 295 days. Designing will take 130 days, another 150 days will be spent for study and analysis of documentation by customer with Russian state expertise. After thorough study and analysis of project the company will take decision on start up of plant construction. New ore dressing plant at Norilsk-1 deposit will replace operating plant built in 1948. At present the plant has high current cost. It processes both high grade (sulphide) ore of deposits of Norilsk industrial region and disseminated ores with low content of non-ferrous metal but rich in PGM. The plant is assumed to be built in proximity from Zapolyarny and Medvezhy Ruchey mines, where the most of disseminated PGM ores of Zapolyarny branch of GMK Norilsk Nickle is extracted. In early September 2001 in Helsinki GMK Norilsk Nickel signed with Outokumpu agreement for construction of ore dressing plant in Norilsk and raising capacity of operating ore dressing plant in Talnakh. Total value of construction is evaluated by Outokumpu in $220-250 m. The parties agreed to construct new ore dressing plant on turn-key basis. The Finnish company will design plant and equip it by all necessary equipment and materials, will make assembly and supervision of erection during guarantee operation. The construction of Norilsk ore dressing plant and modernization of Talnakhsky ore dressing plant are envisioned by programme of development of Norilsk Nickel enterprises for the period of 2010, according to which investments in modernization will make up app. $3,5 bn. Investments in construction of ore dressing plant are expected to be paid off during 3-4 years.

COAL OUTPUT IN RUSSIA

As of July 15, 5502,9 kg of gold was extracted in Irkutsk region. In Bodaibo region - 5361,6 kg. Lenzoloto extracted 227,1 kg of gold. Branches of Lenzoloto has extracted: Nadezhdinsky - 486,2 kg, Svetloye - 528,2 kg, Marakan - 271,1 kg, Dalnyaa Taiga - 165,3 kg, Lensib - 722,1 kg, Sevzoloto - 373,3 kg, Chara - 155,9 kg, Lensky Mining Company - 30,7 kg, Bodaybo Nedra - 198,3 kg. More than 170 kg of Ore gold was extracted by: Pervenets - 110,3 kg and Visochayshy- 61,3 kg. Lena prospector's company extracted 397 kg, Vitim - 860 kg, Redkon - 167,4 kg, Tayga - 163,6 kg.

RUSSIA-ARMENIA AGREEMENT ON DELIVERIES OF RAW DIAMONDS IN THE PERIOD OF 2002-2006

Council of RF Federation has ratified agreement between Russia and Armenia for 2002-2006. Russia will deliver to Armenia 400 ths. karat of jewelry diamonds annually in 2002-2004; in 2005-06 that volume will rise to 450 ths. karat. In 2002 400 ths. karat of technical diamonds will be delivered to Armenia, and that volume will rise annually by 100 ths. karat annually, till 2006. Armenia is not entitled to re-export diamonds received within that agreement.

ALROSA PUT INTO OPERATION THE FIRST DIAMOND UNDERGROUND MINE

On July 19 ALROSA's first underground diamond mine International reached design capacity equal to number of diamonds worth app. $300 m/year. They will be extracted from nearly 500000 ton of kimberlite; most of them are of jewelry grades. Capital investments made up nearly $250 m, life of mine is estimated to be 25-27 years. At present ALROSA smoothly transfers from surface mining of diamonds to underground mining. In 2001 the company extracted diamonds to the amount of $1680 m, by 2,6% more than in 2000.

AMANTAYTAU GOLDFIELDS HAS OBTAINED CREDIT OF $31 M FOR GOLD EXTRACTION

Uzbek-British JV Amantaytau Goldfields has obtained credit of $31 m for gold extraction in Uzbekistan.The credit was granted by international bank syndicate of Societe Generale, Hypovereinsbank and National bank for foreign economic activity of Uzbekistan. Thee open financing of project in Kizilkum desert organized on a par with British Oxus Mining Plc and Uzbek government in JV Amantaytau Goldfields.
It is the first time when the financing of gold extraction project in Uzbekistan is carried out without government guarantees.

UZBEKISTAN SEARCHES FOR INVESTORS

Large uranium reserves are found only 50 countries of the world, with 25 countries producing it. Among the world leaders are the following countries: Canada (8500 ton annually), Australia (6500), Namibia and Niger (up to 2900). Russia is the 5th (2600), then - Uzbekistan (2300), Kazakhstan (2000), USA (1800). The highest price is $130 per one kg. World output has been dropping by 5-8% annually of late. In the future stepping up of extraction in Canada and Australia is expected, they possess the richest resources of uranium. The proven world reserves are estimated to amount to 4 million ton. There are theoretical uranium reserves which raise total volume up to 10 million ton.

SIX NEW LONGWALLS ARE PUT INTO OPERATION AT KUZBASSUGOL ENTERPRISES IN JULY

They are mines Polisaevsky, Komsomolets, mine department Siberian, Fizkulturnik. The most important event was coming on stream of the widest longwall at Berezovsky mine. Reserves of coking coal of that longwall (layer XXI) total more than million tons. A. Zhuravlev's team (head of site S. Kochergin) has already started to extract coal with the help of complex Glinnik and miner KGS-245. Daily app. 2000 ton of hard fuel is mined in new longwall. In August another three longwalls are planned to become operational, one of them at Pervomaysky mine. Here equipment from longwall 3171 will be transferred to longwall 3173 during 40 days. Such short period is explained by intention to reduce to min. disruption in stoping. Coal reserve in new longwall is app. One million ton.

KRASNOGORSKY COAL DRESSING PLANT IS PUT INTO OPERATION

On Feb. 19, 2002 Krasnogorsky coal dressing plant was put into operation at Krasnogorsky Open Pit mine (Mezhdurechensk).The opening of plant with planned annual processing volume of 2500000 ton was attended by representatives of Kemerovo reg. And city administration and Yuzny Kuzbass coal company.
Technology and technological project were developed by CETCO, USA. Completing and delivery of equipment of the leading manufacturers is made by Konares Trading AG, Switzerland and Altair Technologies Ltd. Cyprus.

The plant was built according to individual project taking into account gradual processing of four layers of different types of coal. The most efficient technologies of coal concentration are applied. The latest high-precision equipment of the leading world producers is installed. The technological process is easily regulated and allow to produce commercial product proceeding from individual requirement of dozens of coal consumers. The running cost is low. Operation and servicing of plant is simple. The closed loop water supply system protect the environment. Plant control is made via automated dispatcher system on the basis of PLC providing for optimal technological parameters and safe operation of equipment.

SEVERSTAL IS MASTERING NEW PRODUCTS

Severstal has mastered 45 new kinds of products during the first half of 2002. More than 70000 ton of new kinds of metal rolling stock to the amount of 596,5 m rub. Was shipped to domestic and foreign markets. Realization of program of introduction of new technologies and expansion of product line is carried out for three key directions: motor industry, shipbuilding, fuel and energy, grade and hardware. To expand niche in motor industry and to squeeze imported products, production of automobile sheet steel was launched, including with aluminum silicate covering on the basis of IF-steel produced with the help of vacuum evaporation of steel. The first deliveries of new products of 400 ton were made to VAZ and UAZ motor works.

NEW EQUIPMENT AT SEVURALBAUXITRUDA

New equipment is installed at Valentorsky deposit of Sevuralbauxitruda (SUBR). In particular, hydraulic hammer was purchased helping to process oversized materials at copper deposit. Purification works at the deposit have been constructed according to new technology - electrical chemical. Currently adjustment is under way. Waste waters discharge by its quality rates will be within the standards.

RECONSTRUCTION OF COPPER SMELTING PLANTS OF URAL MINING AND METALLURGICAL COMPANY

Outokumpu specialists paid a visit to Sredneuralsky Copper Smelting plant. In the course of joint work the optimal concept for reconstruction of copper smelting plants of Ural Mining and Metallurgical Company will be selected on the basis of Finnish technologies. At present, as a result of serious and long-term joint work the concept of reconstruction of four copper smelting plants has been prepared in five versions. They are Sredneural copper smelting plant, Mednogorsky copper-sulfur works, Svyatogor, Production of Polymetals in Kirovograd. At the final joint meeting held on July 25 in Revda the optimal variant is chosen, which, in its turn, will be submitted to consideration of UGMK administration

CHANGE OF TECHNOLOGY OF GOLD EXTRACTION AT POKROVSKY MINE

British delegation visited Pokrovsky Mine (Amur reg.), one of 5 largest gold mining companies of Russia. Assets of Peter Hambo Bank, the main investor of the project helped to revive that company. So far Pokrovsky Mine extracted gold by heap leaching. Now the company has constructed the ore dressing plant which allows to extract more gold from ore. Chairman of Board of Peter Hambo Bank decided to attend mine personally to check, if funds are spent rationally and investing should be continued.

GEOLOGICAL PROSPECTING OF NATURAL STONE IN KARELIA

The competition is announced by republic ministry of economic development for state order for geological prospecting of natural stone as raw material for production of road metal. State enterprise North Prospecting Expedition and Karelprirodresurs filed request for open competition for state order for geological prospecting and evaluation of occurrences of natural stone as raw material for production of road metal in central and south Karelia. 390 ths. Rub. Will be allocated from the budget for study of deposits, the funds are sufficient to finance only one company. By the end of July a winner will be announced who will explore deposits during 2002.

DELIVERIES OF O& K MACHINERY TO KARELIA

Russian Kamen extracting granite at Ukkomyaki gneiss-granite deposit in Pitkyaranta district of Karelia is going to purchase loader of Orenschtain Und Koppel AG of 21 ton payload at the expense of own funds in August 2002, which will allow to raise extraction of granite up to 100 cu m per month. At present the loader of the same company of 11 ton payload is being operated. Extraction of granite began last September. In 1 quarter of 2002 40-50 cu m per month was extracted, in June the same volume was extracted. By the end of summer 2002 the company is going to extract up to 100 cu m per month. In 2002 the company plans to mine 1000 cu m of stone. The stone blocks are of pink, red, gray, black and blended colors. Products are delivered to St. Petersburg, Lithuania, Bashkiria, Saratov, Kondopoga. In October 2002 shop for stone processing was built where stone is cut.

RESULTS OF IRON ORE EXTRACTION IN RUSSIA

In first half of 2002 41 m ton of iron ore was produced in Russia, by 0,4% less year-on-year. In June 2002 iron ore production dropped by 2,6% vs. June 2002 and by 1,5% vs. May. 23,8 m ton of finished rolling stock was produced in 1 half of 2002 or 102,3% compared with 1 half of 2001. In June production of finished ferrous rolling stock rose by 2,9% compared with June 2001 and by 0,7% more than in May 2002. Steel pipe production totaled 2,4m ton in 1 half year or 88,7% vs. the same period of 2001.

EXPANSION OF VORKUTAUGOL MARKETS

Vorkutaugol plans to expand foreign markets. Now company has got an opportunity to export coal to USA and Brasilia. All in all, Vorkutaugol plans to export one million ton of coal in 2002. Vorkutaugol exports coal to Finland, Sweden and Ukraine. The company had to refocus its export, when in February 2002 Severstal in violation of signed contract cut volume of purchases of Vorkuta coal by half. That entailed drop of hard coal extraction. Therefore in 2002 Vorkutaugol plants to cut extraction of coking coal by one million ton - to 8 million ton or 11% vs. 2001.

COAL EXTRACTION IN RUSSIA IN FIRST HALF OF 2002

During January-June 2002 coal extraction as a whole in Russia dropped by 15,9 m ton. For that period coal extraction total 119,3 m ton and dropped vs. the same period of last year by 15,9 m ton. The companies subordinated to Power Ministry extracted 111,4 m ton of coal (-17,1 m ton). Basically, reduction of fuel coal extraction took place - by 15,6 m ton vs. 1 quarter of 2001, coking coal extraction dropped by 0,3 m ton. Remains of power coal at warehouses of mines and open pit mines for June 2002 rose by 200 ths. Ton and made up 8,65 m ton as of July 1. However, starting from 2nd quarter change of dynamics at coal market is observed. Independent producers started to reduce selling prices that accompanied by growth of prices for gas by 15% since July 1 change parity of prices for coal products for the better. According to new energy strategy of Russia, coal share in total production of fuel should double. At present coal in fuel and energy balance of USA accounts for 56%, Germany -55%, China - 70% and Russia - only 19%.

EXTRACTION OF DIAMONDS AT THE LARGEST EUROPEAN DEPOSIT

Developers started the first stage of mining stripping works at the largest in Europe diamonds deposit named after Lomonosov, which, according to specialists estimates, contains up to quarter of all reserves of Russian diamonds. It was found in 1980. However, due to some reasons industrial development has not started yet. De Beers studied the situation for a long time and even bought large shareholding of Severalmaz, which posses the right for development of the deposit. After strategic investor - ALROSA came, for two last years Severalmaz with support of main shareholders - ALROSA and Arkhangelsk reg. administration - have successfully defended new conditions for diamond deposits, finished preparation of project of GOK and made the first step for industrial mining of Pomorsky diamonds.

Lomonosov deposit has a number of peculiarities with large number of water inflows and low bearing capacity of grounds. Therefore to limit negative impact of these factors hydromechanisation was selected for capital mining operations for extraction of less hard rocks. It's a novelty idea - such method has never been used before for development of primary deposits of diamonds - it was approved by Supervisory Council in April. Currently the main goal of Severalmaz is to drive 30 m of water and ground that cover kymberlite body containing diamonds.

Now suction dredge of Sevhydromechanization began pumping out of water. It capacity is 200 cu m/hr. In autumn earth moving machinery, shovels and dump trucks will be delivered to the open pit mine. Since next year, when water level drops, two methods - hydromechnisation and traditional earth moving - will be applied simultaneously. According to specialists of Severalmaz, ore body is to be uncovered already in 2004. The first industrial diamonds will be mined in 2005.

CONSTRUCTION OF PLANT PRODUCING EXPLOSIVES AT KORSHUNOV GOK

Korshunov GOK will construct the plant for production of explosives that will allow to save 30 m rub. Per year. Now nearly three million dollars are spent for purchase of explosives. The construction will cost two million dollars and will be paid off for one year and a half or two years. Agreement for construction has already been concluded with subcontractor. Financing of construction is still unresolved.

SEARCH OF DEVELOPERS AND INVESTORS INTO CLAY DEPOSITS OF BURYATYA

Reserves of clay deposits of Ust-Ordinsky Buryatia autonomous district have not been in demand yet. Administration announced several times competitions for development of clay deposit but potential soil users were not found. It was planned to mine 150 ths. Cu m of clay in 2001. In fact, extracting enterprises mined nearly 50 ths. Cu m. The local demand in clay totaled 50 ths. Cu m for 2002. Clay is mainly used in sand and gravel mixture for repair of road bed. Clay is mainly extracted from two deposits- Kamenksky deposit that contains nearly 233 m ton, Rodninsky - 852 ths. Ton. License for development of Kamenksky deposit belongs to Angarsky ceramic plant, Rodninsky - Olonsky brick plant. Reserves of Milzansky deposit total more than two million ton of clay, but prospecting was stopped there.

PLANT FOR PROCESSING BARITES IS PUT INTO OPERATION IN KOMI REPUBLIC

After adjustment of equipment dressing plant for processing of barites near Vorkuta was put into operation. Adjustment of equipment and storing of raw material is made by Hoylinsky GOK. In mid-June the trial start-up of equipment took place. The test-run of first stage of equipment to process 60 ths. Ton of ore per year was performed. Good results were registered. The next start-up is not defined, but it will take place after elimination of defects and adjustment of equipment. Complete start-up will allow to produce high grade barite concentrate applied mainly for prospecting of oil and gas deposits. It is planned to raise output up to 120 ths. Ton per year by 2003.

RUSSIAN MINING AND GOLD MINING INDUSTRY: ALPHABETICAL LISTING

1 ABAKAN ORE EXTRACTION ENTERPRISE

Number of Employees: *2,569.00*
CEO: ***Nikolai I.Baibarodov***
Address: 662750, Khakass Republic, Tashtyp Dist., Abaza, Lenina St., 35-a
Phone: **2-93-51**
Fax: **N/A*)**
Products: **iron ore 1,313 ths tons**

2 ALTAI FIELD

Number of Employees: *506.00*
CEO: ***Gennady P.Lebskikh***
Address: 652980, Russia, Kemerovo Reg., Tashtagol, pos. Spassk, Klubnaya St., 5
Phone: **5-00, 5-12**
Fax: **N/A*)**
Products: **precious metals**

3 ARTEMOVSK MINE

Number of Employees: *903.00*
CEO: ***Mikhail A.Itygin***
Address: 662951, Russia, Krasnoyarsk Terr., Kuragino Dist., Artemovsk, Olkhovskaya St., 126
Phone: **2-12-90**
Fax: **N/A*)**
Products: **precious metals**

4 BAKAL ORE EXTRACTION ENTERPRISE

Number of Employees: *3,857.00*
CEO: ***Valentin A.Krasnoborov***
Address: 456900, Russia, Chelyabinsk Reg., Satka Dist., Bakal, Lenina St., 13
Phone: **35-95**
Fax: **N/A*)**
Products: **iron ore 59,193 tons**
agglomerate 1,699,268 tons
quartzite

5 BERELEKHSKY ORE CONCENTRATING MILL

Number of Employees: *628.00*
CEO: ***V. P.Myasnikov***
Address: 686310, Russia, Magadan Reg., Susuman Dist., pos. Shiroky
Phone: **2-73, 5-23, 2-81**
Fax: **N/A*)**
Products: **precious metals**

6 BEREZOVSKY MINE

Number of Employees: *2,305.00*
CEO: ***Boris A.Letyagin***
Address: 624070, Russia, Sverdlovsk Reg., Berezovsky, Lenina St., 73
Phone: **(34369) 2-30-05**
Fax: **N/A*)**
Products: **gold 134,600 grammes**
silver 211,900 grammes
crushed stone

7 BILIBINO ORE CONCENTRATING MILL

Number of Employees: *2,710.00*
CEO: ***Boleslav I.Vasilyauskas***
Address: 6866510, Russia, Magadan Reg., Chukotka Autonomous District, pos. Bilibino, Lenina Sq., 6
Phone: **2-50-33**
Fax: **N/A*)**
Products: **precious metals**

8 BOGOSLOVSKOYE ORE EXTRACTION ENTERPRISE

Number of Employees: *3,032.00*
CEO: ***Ivan P.Prutyan***
Address: 624460, Russia, Sverdlovsk Reg., Krasnoturyinsk, Oktyabrskaya St., 28
Phone: **(34314) 2-34-20**
Fax: **N/A*)**
Products: **ore 2,016 ths tons**

9 BURIBAY ORE EXTRACTION ENTERPRISE

Number of Employees: *886.00*

10 CLOSED JOINT-STOCK COMPANY "NEZHDANINSKOYE"

CEO: *Iskandar M.Zainagabdinov*
Address: 453801, Bashkortostan Republic, pos.Ak'yar, Lenina St., 50
Phone: N/A

Fax: N/A*)
Products: **wood sawn lengthwise 1 ths cu m**
crushed stone 45 ths cu m
copper ore 134 ths tons

Number of Employees:
CEO: *Vasily I.Lazarev*
Address: 678722, Republic Sakha (Yakutia), Tomponsky Dist., s. Nezhdaninskoye

Phone: **2-35, 5-11, 6-49**
Fax: N/A*)
Products: **gold**

11 COMPANY "BARIT"

Number of Employees: *160.00*
CEO: *Vasily V.Kazantsev*
Address: 652684, Russia, Kemerovo Reg., Guryevsk, pos. Ursk, Shosseiny Per., 5-a
Phone: **3-35-99**
Fax: N/A*)
Products: **precious metals**

12 COMPANY "ZOLOTO-DZHUG-DZHURA"

Number of Employees:
CEO: *Igor N.Sharkov*
Address: 678626, Republic Sakha (Yakutia), Ust-Maisky Dist., pos. Solnechnyi

Phone: **2-11-01, 2-12-08**
Fax: N/A*)
Products: **gold**

13 DEGTYARSK ORE EXTRACTION ENTERPRISE

Number of Employees: *2,471.00*
CEO: *Vladimir G.Turovsky*
Address: 623273, Russia, Sverdlovsk Reg., Degtyarsk, Kalinina St., 10
Phone: **32-16**
Fax: N/A*)
Products: **copper ore 539 ths tons**
lime 135 ths tons
crushed stone

14 DZHIDOKOMBINAT

Number of Employees: *3,035.00*
CEO: *Vladimir V.Perelyaev*
Address: 671930, Buryat Republic, Zakamensk, Lenina St., 23
Phone: **(301371) 21-92**
Fax: N/A*)
Products: **tungsten concentrate**

15 ENTERPRISE "KHINGANOLOVO"

Number of Employees: *856.00*
CEO: *Yury A.Nedorezov*
Address: 682001, Russia, Yevteyskaya Autonomous Oblast, Obluchye Dist., pos. Khingansk, Shkolnyi Ave., 1

Phone: **1-28, 2-97**
Fax: N/A*)
Products: **tin concentrate**

16 ENTERPRISE "KMARUDA"

Number of Employees: *1,885.00*
CEO: *Vladimir A.Artemenko*
Address: 309510, Russia, Belgorod Reg., Gubkin, Artema St., 2
Phone: **(07241)2-25-77**

Fax: N/A*)
Products: **iron ore 3,107,696 tons**
iron concentrate 1,336,356 tons
agglomerated iron ore

17 FAR EASTERN MINING and METALLURGICAL PRODUCTION COMPANY "DALPOLIMETALL"

Number of Employees: *4,648.00*
CEO: *Boris F.Zuban*
Address: 692430, Russia, Primorskiy Terr., Dalnegorsk, 50 let Oktyabrya Ave., 93

Phone: **(42373) 9-13-90**

18 GAI ORE CONCENTRATING MILL

Number of Employees: *5,573.00*
CEO: *Nikolai F.Ivanov*
Address: 462630, Russia, Orenburg Reg., Gai, Promyshlennaya St., 1
Phone: **2-24-22**

Fax: N/A*)
Products: **copper ore 2,913 ths tons**

flotation iron pyrite 721,984 tons

Fax: **N/A*)**

Products: **bismuth 11.145 tons**
concentrates

crushed stone 353,880 cu m

19 **GOLD MINING ENTERPRISE "TUVAZOLOTO"**

Number of Employees: *32.00*
CEO: ***Dadar S. Mokgush***
Address: 667003, Tyva Republic, Kyzyl, Gornaya St., 7/1
Phone: **(39422) 3-03-22**
Fax: **N/A*)**
Products: **gold 131 kg**
silver

20 **GOREVSKY ORE CONCENTRATING MILL**

Number of Employees: *380.00*
CEO: ***Alexander V.Salmanov***
Address: 663412, Russia, Krasnoyarsk Terr., Motygino Dist., pos. Novoangarsk, Naberezhnaya St., 5

Phone: **3-40**
Fax: **N/A*)**
Products: **lead and zinc ore 99 ths tons**

21 **IRBA ORE EXTRACTION ENTERPRISE**

Number of Employees: *1,051.00*
CEO: ***Anatoly P.Pristavka***
Address: 663943, Russia, Krasnoyarsk Terr., Kuragino Dist., pos. Bolshaya Irba
Phone: **54-00**
Fax: **N/A*)**
Products: **iron ore 1,599 ths tons**
metal articles
oxygen

22 **JOINT-STOCK COMPANY "ALDANSLYUDA"**

Number of Employees:
CEO: ***Alexander V.Zykov***
Address: 678953, Republic Sakha (Yakutia), Aldan Dist., Tommot-1
Phone: **4-14-77, 4-15-88**
Fax: **N/A*)**
Products: **ceramic raw materials**

23 **JOINT-STOCK COMPANY "APATIT"**

Number of Employees: *17,863.00*
CEO: ***Anatoly V.Pozdnyakov***
Address: 184230, Russia, Murmansk Reg., Kirovsk, Leningradskaya St., 1
Phone: **2-15-90, 2-14-76**

Fax: **N/A*)**
Products: **apatite concentrate 9,900 ths tons**

nepheline concentrate 1,600 ths tons

24 **JOINT-STOCK COMPANY "DEPUTATSKOLOVO"**

Number of Employees:
CEO: ***Vladimir A.Dyakonov***
Address: 678540, Republic Sakha (Yakutia), Ust-Yansky Dist., pos. Deputatsky, Energeticheskaya St., 1

Phone: **2-18-61, 2-78-89, 2-12-34**

Fax: **N/A*)**
Products: **gold, unwrought tin**

25 **JOINT-STOCK COMPANY "ENISEIZOLOTO"**

Number of Employees: *114.00*
CEO: ***Vladislav V.Smirnov***
Address: 660049, Russia, Krasnoyarsk, Krasnoi gvardii St., 24
Phone: **(3912) 21-22-38**
Fax: **(3912) 21-80-53**
Products: **precious metals**
periclase

26 **JOINT-STOCK COMPANY "INDIGIRZOLOTO"**

Number of Employees:
CEO: ***Konstantin K.Chokuibayev***
Address: 678730, Republic Sakha (Yakutia), Oimyakon Dist., pos. Ust-Nera

Phone: **3-02, 2-01-22**
Fax: **N/A*)**
Products: **gold**

27 **JOINT-STOCK COMPANY "KARELSKY OKATYSH"**

28 **JOINT-STOCK COMPANY "KULARZOLOTO"**

Number of Employees:

Number of Employees: *8,536.00*
CEO: *Nikolai P.Ershov*
Address: 186989, Republic Karelia, Kostomuksha, Zvezdnaya St., 29
Phone: 2-25-11, 2-13-69
Fax: N/A*)
Products: iron ore 8,099.7 ths pcs
iron ore pellets 7,755.2 ths tons
pre-cast ferroconcrete structures

CEO: *Vyacheslav P.Volkov*
Address: 678573, Republic Sakha (Yakutia), Ust-Yansky Dist., pos. Severnyi
Phone: 2-10, 2-04, 5-30
Fax: N/A*)
Products: gold

29 **JOINT-STOCK COMPANY "MOLIBDEN"**

Number of Employees: *3,536.00*
CEO: *Vasily M.Maslov*
Address: 662511, Khakass Republic, Ust-Abakan Dist., Sorsk
Phone: 74-41
Fax: N/A*)
Products: molybdenum concentrate 7,217 tons
copper concentrate 2,537 tons

30 **JOINT-STOCK COMPANY "ZOLOTO YAKUTII"**

Number of Employees:
CEO: *Taras G.Desyatkin*
Address: 677892, Republic Sakha (Yakutia), Yakutsk, Lenina Ave., 28
Phone: (41122) 4-05-59, 4-13-37, 2-95-32
Fax: N/A*)
Products: products of non-ferrous metallurgy

31 **KACHKANAR ORE CONCENTRATING MILL**

Number of Employees: *10,094.00*
CEO: *Nikolai Ya.Yeremin*
Address: 624356, Russia, Sverdlovsk Reg., Kachkanar, Sverdlova St., 2
Phone: (34341) 2-15-31
Fax: N/A*)
Products: iron ore 286,817 tons
agglomerated ore 2,964,810 tons
pellets

32 **KARAMKEN ORE CONCENTRATING MILL**

Number of Employees: *637.00*
CEO: *Nikolai M.Silyutin*
Address: 686112, Russia, Magadan Reg., Khasynsky Dist., pos. Karamken
Phone: 9-04-81, 9-04-77
Fax: N/A*)
Products: precious metals

33 **KAZ ORE EXTRACTION ENTERPRISE**

Number of Employees: *1,410.00*
CEO: *Gennady V.Goltsov*
Address: 652930, Russia, Kemerovo Reg., Tashtagol, pos. Kaz, Lenina St., 16
Phone: 3-00, 5-00
Fax: N/A*)
Products: iron concentrate 767.9 ths tons
ore waste 527.6 ths tons

34 **KHABAROVSK GOLD-MINING PRODUCTION COMPANY "PRIMORZOLOTO"**

Number of Employees: *3,611.00*
CEO: *Valery I.Chekhovich*
Address: 680007, Russia, Khabarovsk, Shevchuka St., 28-a
Phone: (4210) 36-15-39
Fax: N/A*)
Products: precious metals

35 **KHOLUI STITCH EMBROIDERY FACTORY**

Number of Employees: *118.00*
CEO: *Mikhail V.Korolkov*
Address: 155633, Russia, Ivanovo Reg., Yuzha Dist., pos. Kholui, Krasnoarmeiskaya St., 8
Phone: 2-91-32
Fax: N/A*)
Products: stitch embroidery articles

36 **KHRUSTALNENSKY ORE CONCENTRATING MILL**

Number of Employees: *3,902.00*
CEO: *Valery V.Lomovtsev*
Address: 692420, Russia, Primorskiy Terr., pos. Kavalerovo, Arsenyeva St., 96
Phone: 9-17-67
Fax: N/A*)
Products: tin concentrate
tin ore

consumer goods

37 **KOMSOMOLSKY ORE CONCENTRATING MILL**

Number of Employees: ***2,165.00***
CEO: ***Anton N.Prudnikov***
Address: 686610, Russia, Magadan Reg., Chukotka Autonomous District, Chaunsky Dist., pos. Komsomolsky
Phone: **5-13**
Fax: **N/A*)**
Products: **precious metals**

38 **KORSHUNOVSKY ORE CONCENTRATING MILL**

Number of Employees: ***6,730.00***
CEO: ***Vladimir N.Khokhlov***
Address: 665680, Russia, Irkutsk Reg., Nizhneilimsky Dist., Zheleznogorsk-Ilimsky
Phone: **58-27**
Fax: **N/A*)**
Products: **iron ore 13,122 ths tons**

39 **KOVDOR ORE CONCENTRATING MILL COMPANY**

Number of Employees: ***5,700.00***
CEO: ***Vyacheslav P.Lyakhov***
Address: 184140, Russia, Murmansk Reg., Kovdor, Parkovaya St., 5
Phone: **7-20-20, 7-27-53**
Fax: **7-27-34, 7-27-53**
Products: **iron ore concentrate 4,500 ths tons**
apatite concentrate 506 ths tons
ground baddeleyite 3.4 ths tons

40 **KRASNODAR MINE**

Number of Employees: ***140.00***
CEO: ***Victor I.Shevchuk***
Address: 353302, Russia, Krasnodar Terr., Abinsk Dist., pos. Kholmsky, Rudnichnaya St., 5
Phone: **9-21-16**
Fax: **N/A*)**
Products: **ore and ore concentration**

41 **KRASNOKAMSNSK ORE EXTRACTION ENTERPRISE**

Number of Employees: ***1,295.00***
CEO: ***Grigory V.Zakharyuta***
Address: 662955, Russia, Krasnoyarsk Terr., Kuragino Dist., pos. Krasnokamensk
Phone: **4-00**
Fax: **N/A*)**
Products: **iron ore 823.9 ths tons**

42 **LYUBERTSY ORE CONCENTRATING MILL COMPANY**

Number of Employees: ***106.00***
CEO: ***Vyacheslav M.Furman***
Address: 140053, Russia, Moscow Reg., Lyubertsy Dist., pos. Kotelniki, Karyernaya St., 13
Phone: **(095) 559-36-36, 559-36-77**
Fax: **N/A*)**
Products: **moulding sand**

43 **MALYSHEVA ORE EXTRACTION ENTERPRISE**

Number of Employees:
CEO: ***Mikhail T.Kochnev***
Address: 624066, Russia, Sverdlovsk Reg., Asbest, pos. Malysheva
Phone: **(34365) 5-15-53**
Fax: **N/A*)**
Products: **consumer goods**

44 **MARITIME GOLD FIELD**

Number of Employees: ***251.00***
CEO: ***Fedor T.Zabolotnyi***
Address: 692131, Russia, Primorskiy Terr., Krasnoarmeisky Dist., pos. Vostretsovo
Phone: **9-24-42, 9-24-34**
Fax: **N/A*)**
Products: **gold**

45 **MARITIME ORE CONCENTRATING MILL**

Number of Employees: ***940.00***
CEO: ***Ivan S.Shepeta***
Address: 692133, Russia, Primorskiy Terr., Krasnoarmeisky Dist., pos. Vostok

Phone: **9-71-45**

46 **METALLURGICAL PLANT "SEVERONIKEL"**

Number of Employees:
CEO: ***Vasily M.Khudyakov***
Address: 184280, Russia, Murmansk Reg., Monchegorsk
Phone: **3-50-98, 3-54-89**
Fax: **N/A*)**

Fax: N/A*)
Products: **copper concentrate 1,140 ths tons**
tungsten ore 410 tons
tungsten concentrate 3,823 tons

Products: **cobalt**
cobalt metal
cobalt concentrate

47 MIKHAILOVSKY ORE CONCENTRATING MILL

Number of Employees: ***11,721.00***
CEO: ***Alexei I.Dremin***
Address: 307130, Russia, Kursk Reg., Zheleznogorsk, Lenina St., 21
Phone: 2-38-71
Fax: N/A*)
Products: iron ore 11,715.5 tons
non-alloy steel 14,685 tons
consumer goods

48 MINDYAK MINE

Number of Employees: ***664.00***
CEO: ***Shafkat A.Mannarov***
Address: 453744, Bashkortostan Republic, Uchaly Dist., pos.Mindyak, Pochtovaya St., 1
Phone: 4-51-11
Fax: N/A*)
Products: removal of wood 4,208 cu m
wood sawn lengthwise 581 cu m
crushed stone 5,777 cu m

49 MINE "BERIKULSKAYA"

Number of Employees: ***587.00***
CEO: ***Mikhail P.Rudko***
Address: 652232, Russia, Kemerovo Reg., Tisul Dist., pos. Stary Berikul, Gornyaka St., 1
Phone: 2-12-80
Fax: N/A*)
Products: precious metals 304 kg

50 MINE "KOMSOMOLSKAYA"

Number of Employees: ***505.00***
CEO: ***Yevgeny D.Sheroshenko***
Address: 652231, Russia, Kemerovo Reg., Tisul Dist., pos. Komsomolsk
Phone: 2-34-56
Fax: N/A*)
Products: precious metals

51 MINE "RUDNAYA"

Number of Employees: ***520.00***
CEO: ***Valery I.Ivanov***
Address: 618850, Russia, Perm Reg., Gornozavodsk Dist., pos. Sarany
Phone: N/A
Fax: N/A*)
Products: chromite ore 122,185 tons

52 MINE "TSENTRALNY"

Number of Employees: ***438.00***
CEO: ***Alexander I.Sergomanov***
Address: 652226, Russia, Kemerovo Reg., Tisul Dist., pos. Tsentralny, Lenina St., 6
Phone: N/A
Fax: N/A*)
Products: precious metals

53 MINE "VESELYI"

Number of Employees: ***431.00***
CEO: ***Nikolai P.Starodubtsev***
Address: 659711, Altay Republic, Choisky Dist., s. Seika
Phone: 2-21-50
Fax: N/A*)
Products: gold 268.2 kg
silver 76.6 kg
copper

54 MINE NAMED AFTER MATROSOV

Number of Employees: ***1,162.00***
CEO: ***V. P.Galchenko***
Address: 686050, Russia, Magadan Reg., Tenkinsky Dist., pos. Matrosov
Phone: 5-02
Fax: N/A*)
Products: precious metals

55 MINING COMPAMY

Number of Employees: ***997.00***
CEO: ***Nikolai I.Belyakov***
Address: 624358, Russia, Sverdlovsk Reg., Nizhnyaya Tura, pos. Is, Artema St., 36
Phone: (3434222) 3-63

56 MINING ENTERPRISE "URGALSKOYE"

Number of Employees: ***3,339.00***
CEO: ***Valery M.Pavlyuchenko***
Address: 682080, Russia, Khabarovsk Terr., Verkhnebureinsky Dist., pos. Chegdomyn
Phone: 9-43-00, switch 9-41-30

Fax: N/A*)
Products: **gold 0.12 tons**
platinum 0.10 tons
cast articles of steel 402 tons

Fax: N/A*)
Products: **coal 1,812 ths tons**

57 **MINING PRODUCTION COMPANY "URALRUDA"**

Number of Employees: *3,875.00*
CEO: *Vladimir M.Zakharov*
Address: 620011, Russia, Yekaterinburg, Mamina-Sibiryaka St., 58
Phone: (3432) 55-47-71
Fax: (3432) 55-50-28
Products: **iron ore 1,818,254 tons**
non-alloy steel 22,436 tons
dolomite

58 **MUNDYBASH CONCENTRATING and AGGLOMERATING MILL COMPANY**

Number of Employees: *1,416.00*
CEO: *Vladimir F.Voronkov*
Address: 652900, Russia, Kemerovo Reg., Tashtagol, pos. Mundybash, Sovetskaya St., 22
Phone: 3-00, 5-00, 3-11
Fax: N/A*)
Products: **agglomerated ore 1,730.9 ths tons**

59 **NEVYANSK FIELD**

Number of Employees: *788.00*
CEO: *Anany S.Sakantsev*
Address: 624170, Russia, Sverdlovsk Reg., Nevyansk, Kirova St., 18
Phone: (34356) 2-16-50
Fax: N/A*)
Products: **gold 348,820 grammes**
silver
platinoids

60 **OLENEGORSK ORE CONCENTRATING MILL (JOINT-STOCK COMPANY "OLKON")**

Number of Employees: *5,615.00*
CEO: *Victor V.Vasin*
Address: 184284, Russia, Murmansk Reg., Olenegorsk, Leningradsky Ave., 2
Phone: 2-30-02, 2-25-50, 2-47-61
Fax: (095) 979-10-77
Products: **iron concentrate 4,312 ths tons**
crushed stone

61 **OPEN JOINT-STOCK COMPANY "SIBRUDA"**

Number of Employees: *17,620.00*
CEO: *Victor A.Kovalenko*
Address: 654080, Russia, Kemerovo Reg., Novokuznetsk, Kommunalnaya St., 21
Phone: (3843) 48-71-12, 48-74-21, 48-71-24

Fax: (3843) 48-72-25
Products: **iron ore 8,957 ths tons**
limestone
quartzite

62 **OPENCAST COLLIERY (STRIPPING) "NAZAROVSKY"**

Number of Employees: *2,329.00*
CEO: *Valentin A.Russky*
Address: 662200, Russia, Krasnoyarsk Terr., Nazarovo
Phone: (39155) 2-26-00
Fax: N/A*)
Products: **coal 10 mln tons**

63 **ORE EXTRACTION ENTERPRISE "LERMONTOVSKOYE"**

Number of Employees: *700.00*
CEO: *Victor A.Maiorov*
Address: 692028, Russia, Primorskiy Terr., Pozharskoye Dist., pos. Svetlogorye

Phone: (42357) 3-53-35
Fax: (42357) 2-17-01
Products: **tungsten concentrate 2,600 tons**

64 **ORLOVSKY ORE CONCENTRATING MILL**

Number of Employees: *844.00*
CEO: *Nikolai S.Bylkov*
Address: 674470, Russia, Chita Reg., Aginskoye Dist., pos. Novoorlovsk
Phone: 3-13-77

Fax: N/A*)
Products: **tungsten concentrate 1,523 tons**

65 **OROTUKAN ORE CONCENTRATING MILL**

66 **PIKALEVO PRODUCTION ENTERPRISE "GLINOZEM"**

Number of Employees: *903.00*
CEO: *B. N.Potvorov*
Address: 686210, Russia, Magadan Reg., Yagodnoye Dist., pos. Orotukan
Phone: 4-13-05

Fax: N/A*)
Products: precious metals

Number of Employees: *5,877.00*
CEO: *Khoren A.Badalyants*
Address: 187600, Russia, Leningrad Reg., Boksitogorsk Dist., Pikalevo, Spryamlennoye Shosse

Phone: 4-21-33, 4-75-00
Fax: 4-35-05
Products: alumina

67 POLYARNYI ORE CONCENTRATING MILL

Number of Employees: *2,327.00*
CEO: *Yury N.Peretyatko*
Address: 686860, Russia, Magadan Reg., Chukotka Autonomous District, Shmidtovsky Dist., pos. Polyarnyi
Phone: 3-32, 3-07, 2-72
Fax: N/A*)
Products: precious metals

68 PRODUCTION COMPANY "KOVDORSLYUDA" COMPANY

Number of Employees: *2,592.00*
CEO: *Peter I.Vasev*
Address: 184140, Russia, Murmansk Reg., Kovdor, Konovalova St., 7
Phone: 7-13-75, 7-19-01
Fax: N/A*)
Products: vermiculite mica
inflated vermiculite
concentrated pegmatite

69 PRODUCTION COMPANY "SEVEROVOSTOKZOLOTO"

Number of Employees:
CEO: *Valery N.Braiko*
Address: 685000, Russia, Magadan, Proletarskaya St., 12
Phone: (41300) 2-44-03
Fax: N/A*)
Products: precious metals

70 PRODUCTION COMPANY "SEVURALBOKSITRUDA"

Number of Employees: *9,606.00*
CEO: *Vitaly A.Potylitsyn*
Address: 624470, Russia, Sverdlovsk Reg., Severouralsk, Vatutina St., 5

Phone: (34310) 2-44-52
Fax: N/A*)
Products: limestone 345,395 tons
cast articles of pig iron 10 tons
cast articles of steel 565 tons

71 PRODUCTION COMPANY "YUZHURALZOLOTO"

Number of Employees:
CEO: *Yury I.Nosyrev*
Address: 457020, Russia, Chelyabinsk Reg., Plast, Oktyabrskaya St., 24
Phone: (35160) 9-11-63
Fax: N/A*)
Products: precious metals

72 PRODUCTION COMPANY "ZABAIKALREDMET"

Number of Employees: *6,154.00*
CEO: *Igor N.Kozyrenko*
Address: 673383, Russia, Chita Reg., Shilka Dist., pos. Pervomaisky
Phone: 4-15-93
Fax: N/A*)
Products: rare metals

73 PROSPECTING ARTEL "KAMCHATKA" COMPANY

Number of Employees:
CEO: *Orest M.Sychinsky*
Address: 683017, Russia, Kamchatka Reg., Petropavlovsk-Kamchatsky, Tsiolkovskogo St., 8
Phone: (41500) 6-93-03
Fax: (41500) 6-93-03
Products: precious metals

74 RESEARCH and PRODUCTION COMPANY "YAKUTALMAZ"

Number of Employees:
CEO: *Lev A.Safonov*
Address: 678170, Republic Sakha (Yakutia), Mirnyi, Lenina St., 6
Phone: (41136) 2-27-71
Fax: (41136) 2-44-51
Products: diamonds

75 SALAIR ORE CONCENTRATION MILL

Number of Employees: *2,109.00*
CEO: ***Gennady I.Fedorov***
Address: 652681, Russia, Kemerovo Reg., Salair, Gagarina St., 7
Phone: **42-11, 43-51**
Fax: **2-21-64**
Products: **lead concentrate 1,647 tons**
zinc concentrate 8,409 tons
baryta concentrate 116 ths tons

76 SARALA MINE

Number of Employees: *603.00*
CEO: ***Vladimir A.Barsukov***
Address: 662266, Khakass Republic, Ordzhonikidzevsky Dist., pos. Priiskovyi, Sovetskaya St., 57
Phone: **2-32**
Fax: **N/A*)**
Products: **gold 238 tons**
silver 230 tons
wood sawn lengthwise 557 cu m

77 SEVERO-YENISEISKY ORE CONCENTRATING MILL

Number of Employees: *2,411.00*
CEO: ***Gennady P.Shevyakhor***
Address: 663280, Russia, Krasnoyarsk Terr., Sovetskaya St., 2
Phone: **2-73**
Fax: **N/A*)**
Products: **precious metals**
removal of wood 19.6 ths cu m
concrete 173 ths cu m

78 SEVEROONEZHSK BAUXITE MINE

Number of Employees: *566.00*
CEO: ***Vladimir V.Chernov***
Address: 164268, Russia, Arkhangelsk Reg., Plesetsk Dist., pos. Severoonezhsk
Phone: **6-48-60, 6-63-30**
Fax: **N/A*)**
Products: **bauxites 330 ths tons**

79 SHEREGESH ORE EXTRACTION ENTERPRISE

Number of Employees: *2,470.00*
CEO: ***Anatoly A.Gerter***
Address: 652971, Russia, Kemerovo Reg., Tashtagol, pos. Sheregesh, Sovetskaya St., 1-a
Phone: **22-83, 21-51**
Fax: **N/A*)**
Products: **iron ore concentrate 1,527 ths tons**
wood sawn lengthwise 1,871 cu m
electrodes

80 SHERLOVAYA GORA ORE CONCENTRATING MILL

Number of Employees: *677.00*
CEO: ***Valery N.Kononov***
Address: 674612, Russia, Chita Reg., Borzya Dist., pos. Sherlovaya Gora, Oktyabrskaya St., 12
Phone: **11-04**
Fax: **N/A*)**
Products: **tin concentrate**

81 SOLNECHNYI ORE CONCENTRATING MILL

Number of Employees: *4,205.00*
CEO: ***Nikolai A.Kovalchuk***
Address: 681901, Russia, Khabarovsk Terr., pos. Solnechnyi, Lenina St., 27
Phone: **9-12-92**
Fax: **91-26-02**
Products: **copper concentrate 10,706 tons**
tungsten 237 tons
lead concentrate

82 SOUTH EASTERN GEOLOGICAL PROSPECTING PARTY

Number of Employees: *800.00*
CEO: ***Victor V.Korablinov***
Address: 453640, Bashkortostan Republic, Sibai-2
Phone: **(34775) 3-35-22, 3-32-69, 3-21-88**
Fax: **N/A*)**
Products: **copper, gold, manganese, building materials**
road engineering
folk handicraft articles of semi-precious stones

83 SOUTH URALS BAUXITE MINE

Number of Employees: *890.00*
CEO: ***Nikolai A.Yegorov***
Address: 456155, Russia, Chelyabinsk

84 SREDNEKAN ORE CONCENTRATING MILL

Number of Employees: *406.00*
CEO: ***Yu. F.Sivokon***
Address: 686160, Russia, Magadan Reg.,

Reg., Satka Dist., pos.Mezhevoi, K.Marksa St., 5-a

Phone: **3-69**
Fax: **N/A*)**
Products: **bauxites 453 ths tons**

Srednekan Dist., pos. Ust-Srednekan

Phone: **2-83**
Fax: **N/A*)**
Products: **precious metals**

85 **STOILENSKY ORE CONCENTRATING MILL**

Number of Employees: ***6,340.00***
CEO: ***Fedor I.Klioka***
Address: 309530, Russia, Belgorod Reg., Staryi Oskol
Phone: **(0725)24-43-09**
Fax: **N/A*)**
Products: **iron ore 13,750,000 tons**

86 **SUSUMAN ORE CONCENTRATING MILL**

Number of Employees: ***1,644.00***
CEO: ***Vladimir K.Khristov***
Address: 686310, Russia, Magadan Reg., Susuman, Zavodskaya St., 1
Phone: **2-21-16**
Fax: **N/A*)**
Products: **precious metals**

87 **SYCHEVO ORE CONCENTRATING MILL**

Number of Employees: ***757.00***
CEO: ***Alexander A.Rusakov***
Address: 143611, Russia, Moscow Reg., Volokolamsk Dist., pos. Sychevo
Phone: **7-42-22**
Fax: **N/A*)**
Products: **crushed stone 764 ths cu m**
gravel 264 ths cu m
natural sands

88 **TASHTAGOL ORE EXTRACTION ENTERPRISE**

Number of Employees: ***2,676.00***
CEO: ***Alexander S.Mordvintsev***
Address: 652970, Russia, Kemerovo Reg., Tashtagol, Lenina St., 21
Phone: **(38473) 2-16-72, 2-33-00, 2-35-00**
Fax: **N/A*)**
Products: **blast-furnace concentrate 857.5 ths tons**
primary concentrate 988.9 ths tons
ore waste 312 ths cu m

89 **TEMIRTAU ORE EXTRACTION ENTERPRISE**

Number of Employees: ***983.00***
CEO: ***Alexander I.Sazhin***
Address: 652920, Russia, Kemerovo Reg., Tashtagol, pos. Temirtau, Tsentralnaya St., 12
Phone: **1-13-00, 1-15-00**
Fax: **N/A*)**
Products: **iron concentrate 226.2 ths tons**
dolomite 116.3 ths tons
crushed iron ore rock

90 **TENKINSKY ORE CONCENTRATING MILL**

Number of Employees: ***1,454.00***
CEO: ***Stepan K.Evseyev***
Address: 686050, Russia, Magadan Reg., Tenkinsky Dist., pos. Ust-Omchug, Komsomolskaya St., 35
Phone: **26-50**
Fax: **N/A*)**
Products: **precious metals**
parts of mining machinery 13 mln rbls

91 **TSIPIKANSKY FIELD**

Number of Employees: ***470.00***
CEO: ***Valery A.Maksimov***
Address: 671511, Buryat Republic, Bauntovsky Dist., pos. Malovsk
Phone: **5-52-32**
Fax: **N/A*)**
Products: **gold**

92 **TURGOYAK ORE EXTRACTION ENTERPRISE**

Number of Employees: ***648.00***
CEO: ***Valery G.Barannikov***
Address: 456305, Russia, Chelyabinsk Reg., Miass
Phone: **(35135) 3-32-20, 3-10-10**
Fax: **N/A*)**
Products: **limestone 3,451,682 tons**

93 **TYRNYAUZ TUNGSTEN and MOLYBDENUM PLANT**

Number of Employees: ***4,369.00***

94 **UCHALY ORE CONCENTRATING MILL COMPANY**

Number of Employees: ***4,027.00***

CEO: *Boris Kh.Blaev*
Address: 361600, Kabardino-Balkar Republic, Tyrnyauz, Stroitelei Ave., 19
Phone: 2-25-45
Fax: N/A*)
Products: concentrate

CEO: *Anatoly P.Khmelev*
Address: 453730, Bashkortostan Republic, Uchaly, Promploshchadka
Phone: 3-05-46
Fax: N/A*)
Products: flotation iron pyrite 45% 1,325 ths tons
non-metalliferous building materials 880 ths cu m
rubble stone 2 ths cu m

95 URUP ORE CONCENTRATING MILL

Number of Employees: *1,052.00*
CEO: *Sergei S.Kondratyeyev*
Address: 357160, Karachai-Cherkess Republic, Urup Dist., pos. Mednogorsky
Phone: 3-53-96
Fax: N/A*)
Products: copper ore 430 ths tons
copper concentrate 6,435 ths tons
iron pyrite 59,607 ths tons

96 VISHNEVOGORSK ORE CONCENTRATING MILL

Number of Employees: *648.00*
CEO: *Ivan I.Mostinets*
Address: 456831, Russia, Chelyabinsk Reg., Kasli Dist., pos.Vishnevogorsk, Lenina St., 61
Phone: 9-42-90, 9-41-22
Fax: N/A*)
Products: niobium concentrate
felspar 159,091 tons

97 VYSOKOGORSKY ORE CONCENTRATING MILL

Number of Employees: *7,189.00*
CEO: *Sergei L.Ustyuzhanin*
Address: 622002, Russia, Sverdlovsk Reg., Nizhny Tagil, Frunze St., 17
Phone: (3435) 24-48-66
Fax: N/A*)
Products: iron ore 1,314,450 tons
agglomerated ore 3,429,239 tons
limestone

98 WORKS "YUZHURALNIKEL"

Number of Employees: *11,859.00*
CEO: *Alexander A.Pashkovsky*
Address: 462424, Russia, Orenburg Reg., Orsk
Phone: 57-27-54, 57-21-30
Fax: N/A*)
Products: nickel ore 4,116 ths tons
nickel 22,747 tons
cobalt, metal products of cobalt metallurgy 583 tons

99 YAGODNOYE ORE CONCENTRATING MILL

Number of Employees: *2,011.00*
CEO: *G.I.Antoshchuk*
Address: 686230, Russia, Magadan Reg., pos. Yagodnoye, Lenina St., 60
Phone: 23-32
Fax: N/A*)
Products: precious metals

100 YEGORYEVKA COMPANY

Number of Employees: *201.00*
CEO: *Valery N.Novgorodsky*
Address: 633570, Russia, Novosibirsk Reg., Maslyanino Dist., s. Yegoryevka
Phone: 3-32-16, 3-32-32
Fax: N/A*)
Products: gold, diamonds

101 ZHIREKEN ORE CONCENTRATING MILL

Number of Employees: *1,541.00*
CEO: *Victor M.Stolyarov*
Address: 673710, Russia, Chita Reg., Chernyshevsk Dist., pos. Zhireken
Phone: 1-15
Fax: N/A*)
Products: molybdenum concentrate

102 ZLATOUST ORE EXTRACTION ENTERPRISE

Number of Employees: *1,398.00*
CEO: *Nikolai G.Ageyenkov*
Address: 456933, Russia, Chelyabinsk Reg., Kusa Dist., pos.Magnitka, Spartaka St., 6
Phone: 33-11, 39-60, 33-41
Fax: N/A*)
Products: agglomerate 400 ths tons

agglomerated siderite ore 300 ths tons

crushed stone

MINING AND GOLD MINING: BY EMPLOYEES

1	JOINT-STOCK COMPANY "APATIT"	17863	*Murmansk Oblast*	joint-stock	25
2	OPEN JOINT-STOCK COMPANY "SIBRUDA"	17620	*Kemerovo Oblast*	joint-stock	61
3	WORKS "YUZHURALNIKEL"	11859	*Orenburg Oblast*	state	21
4	MIKHAILOVSKY ORE CONCENTRATING MILL	11721	*Kursk Oblast*	state	48
5	KACHKANAR ORE CONCENTRATING MILL	10094	*Sverdlovsk Oblast*	joint-stock	33
6	PRODUCTION COMPANY "SEVURALBOKSITRUDA"	9606	*Sverdlovsk Oblast*	state	70
7	JOINT-STOCK COMPANY "KARELSKY OKATYSH"	8536	*Krelia Republic*	joint-stock	29
8	VYSOKOGORSKY ORE CONCENTRATING MILL	7189	*Sverdlovsk Oblast*	state	98
9	KORSHUNOVSKY ORE CONCENTRATING MILL	6730	*Irkutsk Oblast*	state	40
10	STOILENSKY ORE CONCENTRATING MILL	6340	*Belgorod Oblast*	joint-stock	86
11	PRODUCTION COMPANY "ZABAIKALREDMET"	6154	*Chita Oblast*	state	72
12	PIKALEVO PRODUCTION ENTERPRISE "GLINOZEM"	5877	*Leningrad Oblast*	state	66
13	KOVDOR ORE CONCENTRATING MILL COMPANY	5700	*Murmansk Oblast*	joint-stock	41
14	OLENEGORSK ORE CONCENTRATING MILL (JOINT-STOCK COMPANY	5615	*Murmansk Oblast*	joint-stock	60
15	GAI ORE CONCENTRATING MILL	5573	*Orenburg Oblast*	state	15
16	FAR EASTERN MINING and METALLURGICAL PRODUCTION COMPANY "DALPOLIMETALL"	4648	*Primorskiy Kray*	state	14
17	TYRNYAUZ TUNGSTEN and MOLYBDENUM PLANT	4369	*Bashkortostan Republic*	state	94
18	SOLNECHNYI ORE CONCENTRATING MILL	4205	*Khabarovsk Kray*	state	82
19	UCHALY ORE CONCENTRATING MILL COMPANY	4027	*Bashkortostan Republic*	joint-stock	95
20	KHRUSTALNENSKY ORE CONCENTRATING MILL	3902	*Primorskiy Kray*	state	38

21	MINING PRODUCTION COMPANY "URALRUDA"	3875	*Sverdlovsk Oblast*	state	57
22	BAKAL ORE EXTRACTION ENTERPRISE	3857	*Chelyabinsk Oblast*	state	4
23	KHABAROVSK GOLD-MINING PRODUCTION COMPANY "PRIMORZOLOTO"	3611	*Khabarovsk Kray*	state	36
24	JOINT-STOCK COMPANY "MOLIBDEN"	3536	*Khakass Republic*	joint-stock	31
25	MINING ENTERPRISE "URGALSKOYE"	3339	*Khabarovsk Kray*	state	56
26	DZHIDOKOMBINAT	3035	*Buryat Republic*	state	13
27	BOGOSLOVSKOYE ORE EXTRACTION ENTERPRISE	3032	*Sverdlovsk Oblast*	state	8
28	BILIBINO ORE CONCENTRATING MILL	2710	*Magadan Oblast*	state	7
29	TASHTAGOL ORE EXTRACTION ENTERPRISE	2676	*Kemerovo Oblast*	state	89
30	PRODUCTION COMPANY "KOVDORSLYUDA" COMPANY	2592	*Murmansk Oblast*	joint-stock	68
31	ABAKAN ORE EXTRACTION ENTERPRISE	2569	*Khakass Republic*	state	1
32	DEGTYARSK ORE EXTRACTION ENTERPRISE	2471	*Sverdlovsk Oblast*	state	12
33	SHEREGESH ORE EXTRACTION ENTERPRISE	2470	*Kemerovo Oblast*	state	80
34	SEVERO-YENISEISKY ORE CONCENTRATING MILL	2411	*Krasnoyarsk Kray*	state	78
35	OPENCAST COLLIERY (STRIPPING) "NAZAROVSKY"	2329	*Krasnoyarsk Kray*	state	62
36	POLYARNYI ORE CONCENTRATING MILL	2327	*Magadan Oblast*	state	67
37	BEREZOVSKY MINE	2305	*Sverdlovsk Oblast*	state	6
38	KOMSOMOLSKY ORE CONCENTRATING MILL	2165	*Magadan Oblast*	state	39
39	SALAIR ORE CONCENTRATION MILL	2109	*Kemerovo Oblast*	state	76
40	YAGODNOYE ORE CONCENTRATING MILL	2011	*Magadan Oblast*	state	99
41	ENTERPRISE "KMARUDA"	1885	*Belgorod Oblast*	state	19
42	SUSUMAN ORE CONCENTRATING MILL	1644	*Magadan Oblast*	state	87

43	ZHIREKEN ORE CONCENTRATING MILL	1541	*Chita Oblast*	state	101
44	TENKINSKY ORE CONCENTRATING MILL	1454	*Magadan Oblast*	state	91
45	MUNDYBASH CONCENTRATING and AGGLOMERATING MILL COMPANY	1416	*Kemerovo Oblast*	joint-stock	58
46	KAZ ORE EXTRACTION ENTERPRISE	1410	*Kemerovo Oblast*	state	35
47	ZLATOUST ORE EXTRACTION ENTERPRISE	1398	*Chelyabinsk Oblast*	joint-stock	102
48	KRASNOKAMSNSK ORE EXTRACTION ENTERPRISE	1295	*Krasnoyarsk Kray*	state	43
49	MINE NAMED AFTER MATROSOV	1162	*Magadan Oblast*	state	55
50	URUP ORE CONCENTRATING MILL	1052	*Kabardino-Balkar Republic*	state	96
51	IRBA ORE EXTRACTION ENTERPRISE	1051	*Krasnoyarsk Kray*	state	22
52	MINING COMPAMY	997	*Sverdlovsk Oblast*	state	23
53	TEMIRTAU ORE EXTRACTION ENTERPRISE	983	*Kemerovo Oblast*	state	90
54	MARITIME ORE CONCENTRATING MILL	940	*Primorskiy Kray*	state	47
55	OROTUKAN ORE CONCENTRATING MILL	903	*Magadan Oblast*	state	65
56	ARTEMOVSK MINE	903	*Krasnoyarsk Kray*	state	3
57	SOUTH URALS BAUXITE MINE	890	*Chelyabinsk Oblast*	state	84
58	BURIBAY ORE EXTRACTION ENTERPRISE	886	*Bashkortostan Republic*	joint-stock	9
59	ENTERPRISE "KHINGANOLOVO"	856	*Yevteyskaya Autonomous Oblast*	state	18
60	ORLOVSKY ORE CONCENTRATING MILL	844	*Chita Oblast*	state	64
61	SOUTH EASTERN GEOLOGICAL PROSPECTING PARTY	800	*Bashkortostan Republic*	state	83
62	NEVYANSK FIELD	788	*Sverdlovsk Oblast*	state	59
63	SYCHEVO ORE CONCENTRATING MILL	757	*Moscow Oblast*	joint-stock	88
64	ORE EXTRACTION ENTERPRISE "LERMONTOVSKOYE"	700	*Primorskiy Kray*	state	63

65	SHERLOVAYA GORA ORE CONCENTRATING MILL	677	*Chita Oblast*	state	81
66	MINDYAK MINE	664	*Bashkortostan Republic*	joint-stock	49
67	TURGOYAK ORE EXTRACTION ENTERPRISE	648	*Chelyabinsk Oblast*	state	93
68	VISHNEVOGORSK ORE CONCENTRATING MILL	648	*Chelyabinsk Oblast*	joint-stock	97
69	KARAMKEN ORE CONCENTRATING MILL	637	*Magadan Oblast*	state	34
70	BERELEKHSKY ORE CONCENTRATING MILL	628	*Magadan Oblast*	state	5
71	SARALA MINE	603	*Khakass Republic*	state	77
72	MINE "BERIKULSKAYA"	587	*Kemerovo Oblast*	state	50
73	SEVEROONEZHSK BAUXITE MINE	566	*Arkhangelsk Oblast*	joint-stock	79
74	MINE "RUDNAYA"	520	*Perm Oblast*	state	52
75	ALTAI FIELD	506	*Kemerovo Oblast*	state	2
76	MINE "KOMSOMOLSKAYA"	505	*Kemerovo Oblast*	state	51
77	TSIPIKANSKY FIELD	470	*Buryat Republic*	state	92
78	MINE "TSENTRALNY"	438	*Kemerovo Oblast*	state	53
79	MINE "VESELYI"	431	*Altay Republic*	state	54
80	SREDNEKAN ORE CONCENTRATING MILL	406	*Magadan Oblast*	state	85
81	GOREVSKY ORE CONCENTRATING MILL	380	*Krasnoyarsk Kray*	state	17
82	MARITIME GOLD FIELD	251	*Primorskiy Kray*	state	46
83	YEGORYEVKA COMPANY	201	*Novosibirsk Oblast*	joint-stock	100
84	COMPANY "BARIT"	160	*Kemerovo Oblast*	state	74
85	KRASNODAR MINE	140	*Krasnodar Kray*	joint-stock	42
86	KHOLUI STITCH EMBROIDERY FACTORY	118	*Ivanovo Oblast*	state	37
87	JOINT-STOCK COMPANY "ENISEIZOLOTO"	114	*Krasnoyarsk Kray*	joint-stock	27
88	LYUBERTSY ORE CONCENTRATING MILL COMPANY	106	*Moscow Oblast*	joint-stock	44
89	GOLD MINING ENTERPRISE "TUVAZOLOTO"	32	*Tyva Republic*	state	16
90	JOINT-STOCK COMPANY		*Sakha (Yakut)*	joint-stock	28

	"INDIGIRZOLOTO"	*Republic*		
91	RESEARCH and PRODUCTION COMPANY "YAKUTALMAZ"	*Sakha (Yakut) Republic*	state	75
92	PROSPECTING ARTEL "KAMCHATKA" COMPANY	*Khabarovsk Kray*	joint-stock	73
93	PRODUCTION COMPANY "YUZHURALZOLOTO"	*Chelyabinsk Oblast*	state	71
94	PRODUCTION COMPANY "SEVEROVOSTOKZOLOTO"	*Magadan Oblast*	state	69
95	METALLURGICAL PLANT "SEVERONIKEL"	*Murmansk Oblast*	state	20
96	CLOSED JOINT-STOCK COMPANY "NEZHDANINSKOYE"	*Sakha (Yakut) Republic*	joint-stock	10
97	COMPANY "ZOLOTO-DZHUG-DZHURA"	*Sakha (Yakut) Republic*	joint-stock	11
98	JOINT-STOCK COMPANY "ZOLOTO YAKUTII"	*Sakha (Yakut) Republic*	joint-stock	32
99	JOINT-STOCK COMPANY "ALDANSLYUDA"	*Sakha (Yakut) Republic*	joint-stock	24
100	JOINT-STOCK COMPANY "KULARZOLOTO"	*Sakha (Yakut) Republic*	joint-stock	30
101	MALYSHEVA ORE EXTRACTION ENTERPRISE	*Sverdlovsk Oblast*	state	45
102	JOINT-STOCK COMPANY "DEPUTATSKOLOVO"	*Sakha (Yakut) Republic*	joint-stock	26

MINING AND GOLD MINING BY PRODUCTS

PRODUCTS	COMPANY	Number in Alphabetical Section
1 ceramic raw materials	JOINT-STOCK COMPANY "ALDANSLYUDA	
2 cobalt cobalt metal cobalt concentrate	METALLURGICAL PLANT "SEVERONIKEL"	20
3 consumer goods	MALYSHEVA ORE EXTRACTION ENTERPRISE	45
4 diamonds	RESEARCH and PRODUCTION COMPANY "YAKUTALMAZ"	75
5 gold	JOINT-STOCK COMPANY "KULARZOLOTO"	30
6 gold	CLOSED JOINT-STOCK COMPANY "NEZHDANINSKOYE"	10
7 gold	COMPANY "ZOLOTO-DZHUG-DZHURA"	11
8 gold	JOINT-STOCK COMPANY "INDIGIRZOLOTO"	28
9 gold, unwrought tin	JOINT-STOCK COMPANY "DEPUTATSKOLOVO"	26
10 precious metals	PROSPECTING ARTEL "KAMCHATKA" COMPANY	73
11 precious metals	PRODUCTION COMPANY "YUZHURALZOLOTO"	71
12 precious metals	PRODUCTION COMPANY "SEVEROVOSTOKZOLOTO"	69
13 products of non-ferrous metallurgy	JOINT-STOCK COMPANY "ZOLOTO YAKUTII"	32
14 gold 131 kg silver	GOLD MINING ENTERPRISE	16

15 moulding sand	LYUBERTSY ORE CONCENTRATING MILL COMPANY	44
16 precious metals periclase	JOINT-STOCK COMPANY "ENISEIZOLOTO"	27
17 stitch embroidery articles	KHOLUI STITCH EMBROIDERY FACTORY	37
18 ore and ore concentration	KRASNODAR MINE	42
19 precious metals	COMPANY "BARIT"	74
20 gold, diamonds	YEGORYEVKA COMPANY	100
21 gold	MARITIME GOLD FIELD	46
22 lead and zinc ore 99 ths tons	GOREVSKY ORE CONCENTRATING MILL	17
23 precious metals	SREDNEKAN ORE CONCENTRATING MILL	85
24 gold 268.2 kg silver 76.6 kg copper	MINE "VESELYI"	54
25 precious metals	MINE "TSENTRALNY"	53
26 gold	TSIPIKANSKY FIELD	92
27 precious metals	MINE "KOMSOMOLSKAYA"	51
28 precious metals	ALTAI FIELD	2
29 chromite ore 122,185 tons	MINE "RUDNAYA"	52
30 bauxites 330 ths tons	SEVEROONEZHSK BAUXITE MINE	79
31 precious metals 304 kg	MINE "BERIKULSKAYA"	50

32 **gold 238 tons** silver 230 tons wood sawn lengthwise 557 cu m	**SARALA MINE**	**77**
33 **precious metals**	**BERELEKHSKY ORE CONCENTRATING MILL**	**5**
34 **precious metals**	**KARAMKEN ORE CONCENTRATING MILL**	**34**
35 **limestone 3,451,682 tons**	**TURGOYAK ORE EXTRACTION ENTERPRISE**	**93**
36 **niobium concentrate** felspar 159,091 tons	**VISHNEVOGORSK ORE CONCENTRATING MILL**	**97**
37 **removal of wood 4,208 cu m** wood sawn lengthwise 581 cu m crushed stone 5,777 cu m	**MINDYAK MINE**	**49**
38 **tin concentrate**	**SHERLOVAYA GORA ORE CONCENTRATING MILL**	**81**
39 **tungsten concentrate 2,600 tons**	**ORE EXTRACTION ENTERPRISE "LERMONTOVSKOYE"**	**63**
40 **crushed stone 764 ths cu m** gravel 264 ths cu m natural sands	**SYCHEVO ORE CONCENTRATING MILL**	**88**
41 **gold 348,820 grammes** silver platinoids	**NEVYANSK FIELD**	**59**
42 **copper, gold, manganese, building materials** road engineering folk handicraft articles of semi-precious stones	**SOUTH EASTERN GEOLOGICAL PROSPECTING PARTY**	**83**
43 **tungsten concentrate 1,523 tons**	**ORLOVSKY ORE CONCENTRATING MILL**	**64**
44 **tin concentrate**	**ENTERPRISE "KHINGANOLOVO"**	**18**
45 **wood sawn lengthwise 1 ths cu m** crushed stone 45 ths cu m copper ore 134 ths tons	**BURIBAY ORE EXTRACTION ENTERPRISE**	**9**
46 **bauxites 453 ths tons**	**SOUTH URALS BAUXITE MINE**	**84**
47 **precious metals**	**ARTEMOVSK MINE**	**3**

48 **precious metals**	**OROTUKAN ORE CONCENTRATING MILL**	**65**
49 **copper concentrate 1,140 ths tons** tungsten ore 410 tons tungsten concentrate 3,823 tons	**MARITIME ORE CONCENTRATING MILL**	**47**
50 **iron concentrate 226.2 ths tons** dolomite 116.3 ths tons crushed iron ore rock	**TEMIRTAU ORE EXTRACTION ENTERPRISE**	**90**
51 **gold 0.12 tons** platinum 0.10 tons cast articles of steel 402 tons	**MINING COMPAMY**	**23**
52 **iron ore 1,599 ths tons** metal articles oxygen	**IRBA ORE EXTRACTION ENTERPRISE**	**22**
53 **copper ore 430 ths tons** copper concentrate 6,435 ths tons iron pyrite 59,607 ths tons	**URUP ORE CONCENTRATING MILL**	**96**
54 **precious metals**	**MINE NAMED AFTER MATROSOV**	**55**
55 **iron ore 823.9 ths tons**	**KRASNOKAMSNSK ORE EXTRACTION ENTERPRISE**	**43**
56 **agglomerate 400 ths tons** agglomerated siderite ore 300 ths tons crushed stone	**ZLATOUST ORE EXTRACTION ENTERPRISE**	**102**
57 **iron concentrate 767.9 ths tons** ore waste 527.6 ths tons	**KAZ ORE EXTRACTION ENTERPRISE**	**35**
58 **agglomerated ore 1,730.9 ths tons**	**MUNDYBASH CONCENTRATING and AGGLOMERATING MILL COMPANY**	**58**
59 **precious metals** parts of mining machinery 13 mln rbls	**TENKINSKY ORE CONCENTRATING MILL**	**91**
60 **molybdenum concentrate**	**ZHIREKEN ORE CONCENTRATING MILL**	**101**
61 **precious metals**	**SUSUMAN ORE CONCENTRATING MILL**	**87**
62 **iron ore 3,107,696 tons** iron concentrate 1,336,356 tons agglomerated iron ore	**ENTERPRISE "KMARUDA"**	**19**
63 **precious metals**	**YAGODNOYE ORE CONCENTRATING MILL**	**99**

Products	Enterprise	
64 lead concentrate 1,647 tons zinc concentrate 8,409 tons baryta concentrate 116 ths tons	**SALAIR ORE CONCENTRATION MILL**	**76**
65 precious metals	**KOMSOMOLSKY ORE CONCENTRATING MILL**	**39**
66 gold 134,600 grammes silver 211,900 grammes crushed stone	**BEREZOVSKY MINE**	**6**
67 precious metals	**POLYARNYI ORE CONCENTRATING MILL**	**67**
68 coal 10 mln tons	**OPENCAST COLLIERY (STRIPPING) "NAZAROVSKY"**	**62**
69 precious metals removal of wood 19.6 ths cu m concrete 173 ths cu m	**SEVERO-YENISEISKY ORE CONCENTRATING MILL**	**78**
70 iron ore concentrate 1,527 ths tons wood sawn lengthwise 1,871 cu m electrodes	**SHEREGESH ORE EXTRACTION ENTERPRISE**	**80**
71 copper ore 539 ths tons lime 135 ths tons crushed stone	**DEGTYARSK ORE EXTRACTION ENTERPRISE**	**12**
72 iron ore 1,313 ths tons	**ABAKAN ORE EXTRACTION ENTERPRISE**	**1**
73 vermiculite mica inflated vermiculite concentrated pegmatite	**PRODUCTION COMPANY "KOVDORSLYUDA" COMPANY**	**68**
74 blast-furnace concentrate 857.5 ths tons primary concentrate 988.9 ths tons ore waste 312 ths cu m	**TASHTAGOL ORE EXTRACTION ENTERPRISE**	**89**
75 precious metals	**BILIBINO ORE CONCENTRATING MILL**	**7**
76 ore 2,016 ths tons	**BOGOSLOVSKOYE ORE EXTRACTION ENTERPRISE**	**8**
77 tungsten concentrate	**DZHIDOKOMBINAT**	**13**
78 coal 1,812 ths tons	**MINING ENTERPRISE "URGALSKOYE"**	**56**

Product	Company	
79 **molybdenum concentrate 7,217 tons** copper concentrate 2,537 tons	**JOINT-STOCK COMPANY "MOLIBDEN"**	**31**
80 **precious metals**	**KHABAROVSK GOLD-MINING PRODUCTION COMPANY "PRIMORZOLOTO"**	**36**
81 **iron ore 59,193 tons** agglomerate 1,699,268 tons quartzite	**BAKAL ORE EXTRACTION ENTERPRISE**	**4**
82 **iron ore 1,818,254 tons** non-alloy steel 22,436 tons dolomite	**MINING PRODUCTION COMPANY "URALRUDA"**	**57**
83 **tin concentrate** tin ore consumer goods	**KHRUSTALNENSKY ORE CONCENTRATING MILL**	**38**
84 **flotation iron pyrite 45% 1,325 ths tons** non-metalliferous building materials 880 ths cu m rubble stone 2 ths cu m	**UCHALY ORE CONCENTRATING MILL COMPANY**	**95**
85 **copper concentrate 10,706 tons** tungsten 237 tons lead concentrate	**SOLNECHNYI ORE CONCENTRATING MILL**	**82**
86 **concentrate**	**TYRNYAUZ TUNGSTEN and MOLYBDENUM PLANT**	**94**
87 **bismuth 11.145 tons** concentrates	**FAR EASTERN MINING and METALLURGICAL PRODUCTION COMPANY "DALPOLIMETALL"**	**14**
88 **copper ore 2,913 ths tons** flotation iron pyrite 721,984 tons crushed stone 353,880 cu m	**GAI ORE CONCENTRATING MILL**	**15**
89 **iron concentrate 4,312 ths tons** crushed stone	**OLENEGORSK ORE CONCENTRATING MILL (JOINT-STOCK COMPANY "OLKON")**	**60**
90 **iron ore concentrate 4,500 ths tons** apatite concentrate 506 ths tons ground baddeleyite 3.4 ths tons	**KOVDOR ORE CONCENTRATING MILL COMPANY**	**41**
91 **alumina**	**PIKALEVO PRODUCTION ENTERPRISE "GLINOZEM"**	**66**
92 **rare metals**	**PRODUCTION COMPANY "ZABAIKALREDMET"**	**72**
93 **iron ore 13,750,000 tons**	**STOILENSKY ORE CONCENTRATING MILL**	**86**

94 **iron ore 13,122 ths tons**	**KORSHUNOVSKY ORE CONCENTRATING MILL**	**40**
95 **iron ore 1,314,450 tons** agglomerated ore 3,429,239 tons limestone	**VYSOKOGORSKY ORE CONCENTRATING MILL**	**98**
96 **iron ore 8,099.7 ths pcs** iron ore pellets 7,755.2 ths tons pre-cast ferroconcrete structures	**JOINT-STOCK COMPANY "KARELSKY OKATYSH"**	**29**
97 **limestone 345,395 tons** cast articles of pig iron 10 tons cast articles of steel 565 tons	**PRODUCTION COMPANY "SEVURALBOKSITRUDA"**	**70**
98 **iron ore 286,817 tons** agglomerated ore 2,964,810 tons pellets	**KACHKANAR ORE CONCENTRATING MILL**	**33**
99 **iron ore 11,715.5 tons** non-alloy steel 14,685 tons consumer goods	**MIKHAILOVSKY ORE CONCENTRATING MILL**	**48**
100 **nickel ore 4,116 ths tons** nickel 22,747 tons cobalt, metal products of cobalt metallurgy 583 tons	**WORKS "YUZHURALNIKEL"**	**21**
101 **iron ore 8,957 ths tons** limestone quartzite	**OPEN JOINT-STOCK COMPANY "SIBRUDA"**	**61**
102 **apatite concentrate 9,900 ths tons** nepheline concentrate 1,600 ths tons	**JOINT-STOCK COMPANY "APATIT"**	**25**

RUSSIAN INDUSTRY: MINING AND GOLD MINING

1	Altay Republic	*MINE "VESELYI"*	*state*	54
2	Arkhangelsk Oblast	*SEVEROONEZHSK BAUXITE MINE*	*joint-stock*	79
3	Bashkortostan Republic	*TYRNYAUZ TUNGSTEN and MOLYBDENUM PLANT*	*state*	94
4	Bashkortostan Republic	*MINDYAK MINE*	*joint-stock*	49
5	Bashkortostan Republic	*BURIBAY ORE EXTRACTION ENTERPRISE*	*joint-stock*	9
6	Bashkortostan Republic	*SOUTH EASTERN GEOLOGICAL PROSPECTING PARTY*	*state*	83
7	Bashkortostan Republic	*UCHALY ORE CONCENTRATING MILL COMPANY*	*joint-stock*	95
8	Belgorod Oblast	*ENTERPRISE "KMARUDA"*	*state*	19
9	Belgorod Oblast	*STOILENSKY ORE CONCENTRATING MILL*	*joint-stock*	86
10	Buryat Republic	*DZHIDOKOMBINAT*	*state*	13
11	Buryat Republic	*TSIPIKANSKY FIELD*	*state*	92
12	Chelyabinsk Oblast	*VISHNEVOGORSK ORE CONCENTRATING MILL*	*joint-stock*	97
13	Chelyabinsk Oblast	*BAKAL ORE EXTRACTION ENTERPRISE*	*state*	4
14	Chelyabinsk Oblast	*ZLATOUST ORE EXTRACTION ENTERPRISE*	*joint-stock*	102
15	Chelyabinsk Oblast	*PRODUCTION COMPANY "YUZHURALZOLOTO"*	*state*	71
16	Chelyabinsk Oblast	*SOUTH URALS BAUXITE MINE*	*state*	84
17	Chelyabinsk Oblast	*TURGOYAK ORE EXTRACTION ENTERPRISE*	*state*	93
18	Chita Oblast	*ORLOVSKY ORE CONCENTRATING MILL*	*state*	64
19	Chita Oblast	*PRODUCTION COMPANY "ZABAIKALREDMET"*	*state*	72
20	Chita Oblast	*SHERLOVAYA GORA ORE CONCENTRATING MILL*	*state*	81

21	Chita Oblast	*ZHIREKEN ORE CONCENTRATING MILL*	*state*	101
22	Irkutsk Oblast	*KORSHUNOVSKY ORE CONCENTRATING MILL*	*state*	40
23	Ivanovo Oblast	*KHOLUI STITCH EMBROIDERY FACTORY*	*state*	37
24	Kabardino-Balkar Republic	*URUP ORE CONCENTRATING MILL*	*state*	96
25	Kemerovo Oblast	*MINE "BERIKULSKAYA"*	*state*	50
26	Kemerovo Oblast	*MINE "KOMSOMOLSKAYA"*	*state*	51
27	Kemerovo Oblast	*MINE "TSENTRALNY"*	*state*	53
28	Kemerovo Oblast	*KAZ ORE EXTRACTION ENTERPRISE*	*state*	35
29	Kemerovo Oblast	*MUNDYBASH CONCENTRATING and AGGLOMERATING MILL COMPANY*	*joint-stock*	58
30	Kemerovo Oblast	*OPEN JOINT-STOCK COMPANY "SIBRUDA"*	*joint-stock*	61
31	Kemerovo Oblast	*COMPANY "BARIT"*	*state*	74
32	Kemerovo Oblast	*ALTAI FIELD*	*state*	2
33	Kemerovo Oblast	*TASHTAGOL ORE EXTRACTION ENTERPRISE*	*state*	89
34	Kemerovo Oblast	*TEMIRTAU ORE EXTRACTION ENTERPRISE*	*state*	90
35	Kemerovo Oblast	*SALAIR ORE CONCENTRATION MILL*	*state*	76
36	Kemerovo Oblast	*SHEREGESH ORE EXTRACTION ENTERPRISE*	*state*	80
37	Khabarovsk Kray	*SOLNECHNYI ORE CONCENTRATING MILL*	*state*	82
38	Khabarovsk Kray	*MINING ENTERPRISE "URGALSKOYE"*	*state*	56
39	Khabarovsk Kray	*PROSPECTING ARTEL "KAMCHATKA" COMPANY*	*joint-stock*	73
40	Khabarovsk Kray	*KHABAROVSK GOLD-MINING PRODUCTION COMPANY "PRIMORZOLOTO"*	*state*	36
41	Khakass Republic	*ABAKAN ORE EXTRACTION ENTERPRISE*	*state*	1

42	Khakass Republic	*SARALA MINE*	*state*	77
43	Khakass Republic	*JOINT-STOCK COMPANY "MOLIBDEN"*	*joint-stock*	31
44	Krasnodar Kray	*KRASNODAR MINE*	*joint-stock*	42
45	Krasnoyarsk Kray	*JOINT-STOCK COMPANY "ENISEIZOLOTO"*	*joint-stock*	27
46	Krasnoyarsk Kray	*SEVERO-YENISEISKY ORE CONCENTRATING MILL*	*state*	78
47	Krasnoyarsk Kray	*KRASNOKAMSNSK ORE EXTRACTION ENTERPRISE*	*state*	43
48	Krasnoyarsk Kray	*IRBA ORE EXTRACTION ENTERPRISE*	*state*	22
49	Krasnoyarsk Kray	*ARTEMOVSK MINE*	*state*	3
50	Krasnoyarsk Kray	*OPENCAST COLLIERY (STRIPPING) "NAZAROVSKY"*	*state*	62
51	Krasnoyarsk Kray	*GOREVSKY ORE CONCENTRATING MILL*	*state*	17
52	Krelia Republic	*JOINT-STOCK COMPANY "KARELSKY OKATYSH"*	*joint-stock*	29
53	Kursk Oblast	*MIKHAILOVSKY ORE CONCENTRATING MILL*	*state*	48
54	Leningrad Oblast	*PIKALEVO PRODUCTION ENTERPRISE "GLINOZEM"*	*state*	66
55	Magadan Oblast	*KOMSOMOLSKY ORE CONCENTRATING MILL*	*state*	39
56	Magadan Oblast	*SUSUMAN ORE CONCENTRATING MILL*	*state*	87
57	Magadan Oblast	*PRODUCTION COMPANY "SEVEROVOSTOKZOLOTO"*	*state*	69
58	Magadan Oblast	*POLYARNYI ORE CONCENTRATING MILL*	*state*	67
59	Magadan Oblast	*KARAMKEN ORE CONCENTRATING MILL*	*state*	34
60	Magadan Oblast	*MINE NAMED AFTER MATROSOV*	*state*	55
61	Magadan Oblast	*YAGODNOYE ORE CONCENTRATING MILL*	*state*	99
62	Magadan Oblast	*SREDNEKAN ORE CONCENTRATING*	*state*	85

		MILL		
63	Magadan Oblast	*BERELEKHSKY ORE CONCENTRATING MILL*	*state*	5
64	Magadan Oblast	*BILIBINO ORE CONCENTRATING MILL*	*state*	7
65	Magadan Oblast	*TENKINSKY ORE CONCENTRATING MILL*	*state*	91
66	Magadan Oblast	*OROTUKAN ORE CONCENTRATING MILL*	*state*	65
67	Moscow Oblast	*SYCHEVO ORE CONCENTRATING MILL*	*joint-stock*	88
68	Moscow Oblast	*LYUBERTSY ORE CONCENTRATING MILL COMPANY*	*joint-stock*	44
69	Murmansk Oblast	*KOVDOR ORE CONCENTRATING MILL COMPANY*	*joint-stock*	41
70	Murmansk Oblast	*PRODUCTION COMPANY "KOVDORSLYUDA" COMPANY*	*joint-stock*	68
71	Murmansk Oblast	*OLENEGORSK ORE CONCENTRATING MILL (JOINT-STOCK COMPANY "OLKON")*	*joint-stock*	60
72	Murmansk Oblast	*METALLURGICAL PLANT "SEVERONIKEL"*	*state*	20
73	Murmansk Oblast	*JOINT-STOCK COMPANY "APATIT"*	*joint-stock*	25
74	Novosibirsk Oblast	*YEGORYEVKA COMPANY*	*joint-stock*	100
75	Orenburg Oblast	*GAI ORE CONCENTRATING MILL*	*state*	15
76	Orenburg Oblast	*WORKS "YUZHURALNIKEL"*	*state*	21
77	Perm Oblast	*MINE "RUDNAYA"*	*state*	52
78	Primorskiy Kray	*ORE EXTRACTION ENTERPRISE "LERMONTOVSKOYE"*	*state*	63
79	Primorskiy Kray	*KHRUSTALNENSKY ORE CONCENTRATING MILL*	*state*	38
80	Primorskiy Kray	*FAR EASTERN MINING and METALLURGICAL PRODUCTION COMPANY "DALPOLIMETALL"*	*state*	14
81	Primorskiy Kray	*MARITIME ORE CONCENTRATING MILL*	*state*	47
82	Primorskiy Kray	*MARITIME GOLD FIELD*	*state*	46

83	Sakha (Yakut) Republic	*COMPANY "ZOLOTO-DZHUG-DZHURA"*	*joint-stock*	11
84	Sakha (Yakut) Republic	*JOINT-STOCK COMPANY "ZOLOTO YAKUTII"*	*joint-stock*	32
85	Sakha (Yakut) Republic	*RESEARCH and PRODUCTION COMPANY "YAKUTALMAZ"*	*state*	75
86	Sakha (Yakut) Republic	*JOINT-STOCK COMPANY "KULARZOLOTO"*	*joint-stock*	30
87	Sakha (Yakut) Republic	*CLOSED JOINT-STOCK COMPANY "NEZHDANINSKOYE"*	*joint-stock*	10
88	Sakha (Yakut) Republic	*JOINT-STOCK COMPANY "ALDANSLYUDA"*	*joint-stock*	24
89	Sakha (Yakut) Republic	*JOINT-STOCK COMPANY "INDIGIRZOLOTO"*	*joint-stock*	28
90	Sakha (Yakut) Republic	*JOINT-STOCK COMPANY "DEPUTATSKOLOVO"*	*joint-stock*	26
91	Sverdlovsk Oblast	*NEVYANSK FIELD*	*state*	59
92	Sverdlovsk Oblast	*DEGTYARSK ORE EXTRACTION ENTERPRISE*	*state*	12
93	Sverdlovsk Oblast	*MINING PRODUCTION COMPANY "URALRUDA"*	*state*	57
94	Sverdlovsk Oblast	*BOGOSLOVSKOYE ORE EXTRACTION ENTERPRISE*	*state*	8
95	Sverdlovsk Oblast	*PRODUCTION COMPANY "SEVURALBOKSITRUDA"*	*state*	70
96	Sverdlovsk Oblast	*BEREZOVSKY MINE*	*state*	6
97	Sverdlovsk Oblast	*MINING COMPAMY*	*state*	23
98	Sverdlovsk Oblast	*MALYSHEVA ORE EXTRACTION ENTERPRISE*	*state*	45
99	Sverdlovsk Oblast	*KACHKANAR ORE CONCENTRATING MILL*	*joint-stock*	33
100	Sverdlovsk Oblast	*VYSOKOGORSKY ORE CONCENTRATING MILL*	*state*	98
101	Tyva Republic	*GOLD MINING ENTERPRISE "TUVAZOLOTO"*	*state*	16
102	Yevteyskaya Autonomous	*ENTERPRISE "KHINGANOLOVO"*	*state*	18

SUPPLEMENTS

LARGEST GOLD MINING COMPANIES IN RUSSIS

Mining of gold, tons

	Company	Owner	Revenue, $ million	Profit, $ mln	Regions of Russia	2010	2011	2012
1	Polyus Gold	Kerimov (40.22%), Z. Mutsoev (18.5%), G. Yushvaev (19.28)	2340	558	Krasnoyarsk Territory, the Irkutsk, Magadan, Amur regions and the Republic of Sakha-Yakutia	39.67	42.85	48.8
2	"Petropavlovsk"	Fund BlackRock Inc. (10.96%), P. Maslowski (8.98%), P. Hambro (4,62%), Vanguard Precious Metals and Mining Fund (4,13%)	1262.5	240.5	Amur Oblast, Amur region	13.92	21.25	22.1
3	"Polymetal"	ICT Group A. Nesis (17,9%), PPF Group P. Kellner (20.86%), A. Mamut (10.12%)	1326	409	Magadan, Sverdlovsk Region, Khabarovsk, Chukotka	11.07	10.97	18.3
4	Chukotka Hydropower	Kinross Gold (Canada)	977.5	220.7	Chukotka	19.91	16.06	14.5
5	Nordgold NV	A. Mordashov	1,182	252	The Republic of Buryatia, the Republic of Sakha-Yakutia, Amur region, the Amur region	9.3	10.6	10.18
6	Highland Gold Mining	Roman Abramovich	300	103.8	Khabarovsk, Amur Region	6.23	5.74	6.74

					Chukotka			
7	"Uzhuralzoloto"	K. Strukov	140	0,041	Chelyabinsk region, Trans-Baikal and Krasnoyarsk Krai, the Republic of Khakassia	4.8	5.14	6.5
8	"Very High"	S. Dokuchaev, N. Opaleva, Tikhonov, fund BlackRock Inc.	230	87	Irkutsk Oblast, the Republic of Sakha-Yakutia	3.76	4.44	5.23
9	"Sovrudnik"	R. and B. Gainutdinova (51%)	52.3	7.4	Krasnoyarsk Territory	3.45	3.46	3.9
10	"Sysymanzoloto"	V. Hristov, LA Gerasimova	154.5	20	Magadan region	3.55	3.26	3.7
11	"Seligdar"	Management, IG "Russian Funds"	168,96	15	Orenburg region, the Altai Territory, the Republic of Buryatia, the Republic of Sakha-Yakutia	3.15	3.03	2.95

SOURCE:
"Expert" on the basis of these companies and the Russian Union of Gold

THE LEADING GOLD MINING COMPANIES

1. "Polyus Gold", JSC http://www.polyusgold.ru/
2. "GC" Petropavlovsk ", JSC http://www.petropavlovsk.net/
3. "Chukotka Hydropower", JSC http://www.kinross.com/
4. "Polymetal", JSC http://www.polymetal.ru/
5. "Nordgold NV" http://www.nordgold.com
6. "Highland Gold Mining" http://www.highlandgold.com/
7. "Uzhuralzoloto CC", JSC http://www.ugold.ru/
8. "Very High", JSC http://www.gvgold.ru
9. "Sovrudnik", LLC http://www.sovrudnik.ru/
10. "Sysymanzoloto", JSC
11. "Seligdar" a / c, of http://www.seligdar.ru/
12. "Mine Soloviev", JSC http://www.solov.ru/
13. "Vitim", a / c
14. "Western", a / c
15. "Search", LLC http://talinja.ru/
16. "Kamchatka Gold", JSC http://www.zolotokamchatki.ru/

17. Cupid Gold "LLC
18. "Mine Karalveem", JSC
19. "Far Eastern resources" of http://dvres.ru/
20. "Friends", LLC
21. "Omsukchanskaya Hydropower", JSC

22. "Ojna", a / c
23. "Chukotka", a / c, LLC
24. "Concern" Arbat ", JSC
25. "Status", LLC
26. "Vasilevsky Rudnik", JSC http://www.vrgm.ru/

ALTAY

Altai-2 CAH, a / c, LLC
Altai Mining and Geological Party, LLC
Miner, a / c DCP, LLC
Road, c / a Company
Gold Kuryi, Ltd.
Search, a / c, LLC
Togul DCP-1, a / c, LLC

ALTAI REPUBLIC

Altaygeoresurs, Ltd.
Aurum RA, Ltd.
Hilarious of mine
Hope, Inc.
Cyanosis, a / c, LLC

AMUR REGION

Alexander, a / c
Amur-Dore, FOR
Amur Mountain Center, Inc.
Argali, a / s Company
Aurum DCP, LLC
Berezitoviy mine, Ltd.
Wang, Ltd.
East-1, a / c
East, a / c, LLC
Goldregion, Ltd.
Mining Company, Ltd.
Dagmara, Ltd.
Distant, Inc.
Dambuki mine, Inc.
Dzheltula, DCP, LLC
Dawn-1 / A, Inc.
Zeisky lesoperevalochnye Plant
Zeya-Aurum, Ltd.
Zeyazoloto, Ltd.
Zeyazoloto, MUP
Zimovichi, DCP, LLC
The index DCP, LLC
Zolotorazvedka, Ltd.
Karakkansky Mine, LLC

Cascade, LLC
Koboldo, of CAH
Crystal, PKF Ltd.
The May, Inc.
Malomyrsky mine, Ltd.
Marist, Ltd.
Bear St. Petersburg, LLC
Nagima, Ltd.
Nekla, Ltd.
New Century, a / c, LLC
Grain, a / c, LLC
Odolgo, GAD, LLC
Oroldyan, Ltd.
Parity TPK, Ltd.
Pyrite, Ltd.
Pokrovsky Rudnik, Inc.
Dawn, c / a of
Rosszoloto, Ltd.
Placers, Ltd.
North, Inc.
North, a / c, LLC
Siberia, Ltd.
Sogzhoy, Ltd.
Soloviev mine, Inc.
Union, a / c, LLC
Satellite, LLC
Stanovik, Inc.
Tokursky mine, Ltd.
Tukuringra, of CAH
Hergu, Inc.
Elga, Ltd.
Clearly, Ltd.

THE REPUBLIC OF BASHKORTOSTAN

Bashkir FCA NPF
Bashkir silos, Inc.
Bashkirgeologiya, Inc.
Vatan, Ltd.
Geotechnology, Ltd.
Golden Valley a / c, LLC
Uchalinsky Mining, Inc.

THE REPUBLIC OF BURYATIA

Bagdarinskaya Hydropower JSC
Bagdarinskaya GRE, Inc.
Bamaz, Ltd.
BuryatZoloto, Inc.
Vitimgeoprom, Inc.
Sunrise, LLC
Dylacha, SREO
Eleninskaya, a / c, LLC
Zakamensk, Ltd.
West, a / c, LLC

Golden East Siberia, Ltd.
Gold Ranks, Ltd.
Ivanovo, Inc.
The Cardinal, LLC
Courbet, c / a, LLC
Auri HDV mode, Ltd.
North, a / c, LLC
Sininda-1, a / c, LLC
SINTEK, Inc.
Prospectors Karalon, Ltd.
Terra, LLC
Tula, Ltd.
Harasun, Ltd.
Tsipikansky mine, Ltd.
Chinakal, Ltd.
Yucatan, Ltd.
Yanguda, Ltd.

JEWISH AUTONOMOUS REGION

Bogdar, Ltd.
Eastern Mining Co., Ltd.
Trans-Baikal Territory
Agin-ferrous metals, of
Aginsk Plant, LLC
Amazarkan SC, Inc.
Balci, a / c, LLC
Burabai, Ltd.
Gazimur, Ltd.
Geoldobycha, FGUDP
Goremnak, Ltd.
Granite, LLC
GRE number 324, OOO
Davenda, Ltd.
Darasunsky mine, Ltd.
Dauriya a / c, PC
Gums, Ltd.
Dzhergun, Ltd.
Iron Ridge, LLC
Zheltuga-dredging, Ltd.
Zhireken Mining, Inc.
Zhireken FMZ, Ltd.
Zabtrans, Ltd.
Gold of Siberia, Inc.
Ildikanzoloto, Ltd.
Kazakovo GGP, LLC
Kaltagay, Ltd.

Kamensky quarry, Ltd.
Quartz, PC Ltd.
Keys rudnikOAO
Royal, LLC
Ksenevskaya mine, Inc.
Mineral, LLC
Mokla, Ltd.

Nergeoprom, Ltd.
Enrichment Plant, LLC
The prize, Ltd.
Mine Aprelkovo, Inc.
Sirius, c / a, LLC
Sludyanka, Inc.
Taiga a / c, LLC
Uryum FCA, Ltd.
Uryumkan, Ltd.
Ust-Kara mine, Inc.
Chitageologorazvedka, FGUGP
Shilka a / c, Inc.
Shirinsky, Ltd.
South, LLC

IRKUTSK REGION

Bilibino Hydropower, LLC
Borodino a / c, LLC
Top Bodaibo, Ltd.
Vitim, a / s Company
The highest, Inc.
Garichev, Ltd.
Hydraulics, LLC
Grain-Star SAM, LLC
Daksib, Ltd.
Far Forest, Inc.
Druse, Ltd.
Gold Bodaibo, Ltd.
Gold Rus, LLC
Irkutsk, a / c, LLC
Kadan, a / c, LLC
Caravan, Ltd.
Lena a / c, LLC
Lenzoloto FCA, Inc.
Lensib, Inc.
Mama GRK Ltd.
Marakan, Inc.
Hope, LLC
Nadezhdinskoye, Inc.
New Ugakhan, Ltd.
Firstborn, Inc.
Priiskovaya, Inc.
Progress-M, OOO
Retcon, GPP Company
Bright, Inc.
Sevzoto, Inc.
Siberia, a / c, LLC
Sukhoi Log, the GSC Company
Uganaha, Ltd.
Gloom River 2, LLC
Khomolkho, Inc.
Shapovalovsky, Ltd.

KEMEROVO REGION

Altai mine, Inc.
Golden pole, a / s Company
Koryak Autonomous
Kamgold, Inc.
Kamchatka, a / s Company
Koryakgeoldobycha, Inc.
North GGP, LLC
Krasnoyarsk Territory
Angara-North a / c, LLC
Artemovskaya, SAMs of
Turquoise, Ltd.
Vasilevsky Rudnik, Inc.
WSI, LLC
Gerfed, Inc.
Gold Field Ltd.
The dredge mine, a / c, LLC
Krasnoyarskgeologiya, Inc.
Polyus CJSC ZDK
Mine the Caspian Sea, Ltd.
RemServis CRP, LLC
Mine Udereysky, Inc.
Ruthenium, Ltd.
Sayan FCA, Ltd.
North, ZAO ZDK
Siberia FCA, Ltd.
Sibzolotorazvedka, Inc.
Sisim, Ltd.
Sovrudnik, Ltd.
Udereysky mine, Inc.

MAGADAN REGION

Avec Plus, LLC
Agate, Ltd.
Alif, Ltd.
Alkene, Ltd.
Anasco, Ltd.
Argentum, LLC
Ardagh, Ltd.
AUM, Ltd.
Aurum Plus, LLC
Bacharach, Ltd.
Barium, Ltd.
GDK Berelekh "JSC
Berelekh 2, LLC
Bolonoyskaya dike, Ltd.
Berm, c / a
Vector Research Department, Inc.
Veotrak, Ltd.
Whist, Ltd.
East Co., Ltd.
Knight, LLC
Time, PC
Geo, Inc.
Coat of Arms, LLC

Company GCI, LLC
Globe, Ltd.
Gloria Gold, Inc.
Gold-X, LLC
Horizon Kolyma, Ltd.
Goldkom, Ltd.
Mining, LLC
Mining, LLC
GP, LLC
Delta, MUP
Pomegranate, Inc.
Denezhkin Stone, LLC
Detrinskoe Hydropower JSC
Diana, Ltd.
Dynamo, Ltd.
Dnepr, Ltd.
Dnepr-Gold, LLC
Domant, Ltd.
Double, Ltd.
DEYA, Ltd.
Zolotinka, Ltd.
The Golden Calf, Ltd.
ZolotoProfi, Ltd.
Ilica, Ltd.
Indra, Ltd.
Kaabi, Ltd.
Cascade, LLC
Kwan, Ltd.
Kolyma gold, LLC
Kolyma Lada-Service Ltd.
Kolyma-Electrum, Ltd.
Kolyma placer, Inc.
Congo, LLC
Conglomerate FCA, Ltd.
Corvette, Ltd.
Emery, LLC
Corundum-M, OOO
Corundum Plus, LLC
Krivbass, Ltd.
Krohn-D Co., Ltd.
Kuranah, Ltd.
Kurchatov, a / c, LLC
Magadan Mining Company, Ltd.
Magas, Ltd.
May Day, LLC

Max DCP, LLC
Matrosov Mine, Inc.
Marion, LLC
M.A.YA., Ltd.
Gorge, Ltd.
Mineral, LLC
Mulkan National Handicraft, Ltd.
Natran, Ltd.

Nedra, Ltd.
Nedra FCA, Ltd.
Nelkobazoloto, Inc.
Nera, Ltd.
New path, Ltd.
Olbot a / c, LLC
Omolonskaya SAM, Inc.
Omsukchanskaya Hydropower JSC
Onyx, LLC
Parangon GBF, Ltd.
Paris, OOO
The party, Ltd.
Placer, Inc.
Search for a / c
Finder, LLC
Field, LLC
Landfill, LLC
Progress a / c, LLC
Prospector, LLC
Rise, LLC
Remstroymash, Inc.
River, LLC
Northeast, LLC
Magadan Silver, Inc.
Silver Company, Inc.
Silver Territory, Inc.
Synthesis, Ltd.
Scala, Inc.
Slavonic origin, Ltd.
Snow DCP, LLC
Promote, LLC
Commonwealth Hydropower, LLC
Calm, LLC
Srednekan a / c, LLC
Stalker, Ltd.
Title, LLC
Sysymanzoloto SUGOK, Inc.
Seter, Ltd.
Taiga Plus, LLC
Topolovka, Ltd.
Thor, Ltd.
Work-2, OOO
T Cement Ltd.
Ugakhan, Ltd.
Umar, Ltd.
Utinka, Ltd.
Fatum-Plus, LLC
Company GCI, LLC
KHATYN, Ltd.
Horse, LLC
Tea Uryan Gold, Inc.
Spur, LLC
Evengold, Ltd.
El Dorado, LLC

Elf, LLC
Energia, a / c, LLC
Yarolga, Ltd.

MOSCOW

Sibproekt, Ltd.

NOVOSIBIRSK REGION

Helion, Ltd.
Pole TCC, LLC
Salair, Ltd.
Suenga a / c, LLC

ORENBURG REGION

Letos, Ltd.
Mednogorsky GMT, LLC
Ormet, Inc.
South Ural FCA, Inc.

PERM REGION

Miner, LLC
Primorsky Krai
GRK & R, Inc.
East PGRK, Inc.
The eastern shore, Ltd.

Mining Company, Ltd.
Green City, LLC
Azure, DCP, LLC
Priiskovaya a / c, Inc.
Seaside GRK, Inc.
Pacific A / C, Inc.
Unicom, Ltd.
YAKKOM, Ltd.
The Republic of Sakha (Yakutia)
Aldanzoloto, Inc.
Aldgold, Inc. GDK
Diamond, Ltd.
Alchanets, Ltd.
Amburdak, Ltd.
Brindak a / c, LLC
Dzhugdzhur-A c / a, LLC
Drazhnik a / c, LLC
Western GRK, Inc.
Star, LLC
Gold Seligdara, Inc.
Gold Verkhoyanie Plant, JSC
Gold Ynykchana, c / a of
Indgold, Ltd.
Indigirka gang, PC
Inyali, Ltd.
Spark, LLC

Spark Plus, LLC
Cedar, LLC
Continent, LLC
Komdragmetall SUE
Litos, Ltd.
World c / a, LLC
Multan, National A / C, LLC
Mars, Ltd.
Nera Gold, LLC
Nedra Nerungri
Neryungri Metallic, Ltd.
Nimgerkan, a / c, LLC
Nirungan, Ltd.
New and / sec PC
Nord, LLC
Nyulka, Ltd.
Oymyakonsky Plant, LLC
Oymyakon, Ltd.
Omega, LLC
Omoloy KRO, SEC
+ Orion Group, LLC
Flame a / c, pc
Flame-2, a / c, LLC
Search, LLC
Search, PC c / a
Progress, LLC
Romis, Ltd.
Mine Duet, Ltd.
Rederga, Ltd.
Sarylakh-Antimony, Inc.
Saha-East, LLC
Saha Gold, LLC
North, Ltd. (Verkhoyansk district)
Seligdar, Inc.
Soyuz-02, LLC
The satellite, a / c
Sunnagin, Ltd.
Timpton Gold, LLC
Tal, a / c, LLC
Topaz, LLC
Tyrkanda, Ltd.
Tours, LLC
Uduma, Ltd.
Faust, Ltd.
The company Romis, Ltd.
Hoth a / c, LLC
Yakutskgeologiya GUGGP of Sakha (Yakutia)
Amber, LLC

SAKHALIN REGION

East-2, a / c

SVERDLOVSK REGION

Berezovsky RU, LLC
Valentorsky copper mine, Ltd.
Vector, LLC
Secondary precious metals, LLC
GeoPoisk, Ltd.
Geoprid, Ltd.
Hephaestus PKF, Ltd.
Degtyarskoye RU, Inc.
Gold of Northern Urals, JSC
Ekaterinburg Industry Group Co., Ltd.
Iridium LLC
Magistral, Ltd.
Maminskoe GRK, Inc.
Mehta, Ltd.
Nev'yansky mine and / PC
Neiva, a / c
Palladium, Ltd.
Polevskaya, Hydropower JSC
Promeks TK, Ltd.
Pulsar, Ltd.
Russian Copper Company, Inc.
Rhodium, Ltd.
Sukhoi Log, LLC
Ural-Quartz, Ltd.
Ural-Gold, LLC
Urals-Nord, a / c
Ural fracturing, Ltd.
Uralelectromed of
Fartagh a / c, LLC
South Zaozersky mine, a / c

REPUBLIC OF TUVA

East, LLC
Ojna, a / c
Tardan Gold, LLC
Geological Expedition of Tuva
Khanty-Mansiysk
Berezovsky REP, Inc.
Nedra PC, LLC
Ural, Ltd.

KHABAROVSK KRAI

Alpha BHP a / c, LLC
Amgun-1 a / c, Inc.
Amour a / c, Inc.
Love of Gold, LLC
White Mountain, LLC
East a / c, pc
Welcome Co., Ltd.
Far Eastern Resources, Inc.
Dalnevostochnik FCA, Ltd.
Dawn of a / c, LLC
Compass geo-service NPF, Ltd.

Marekan GGP, LLC
MNV, Inc.
Niemann a / c, LLC
Okhotsk Hydropower JSC
Plast Hydropower, LLC
Coastal, PC a / c
Primorye, a / c, PC
Ros-DV, LLC
Enthusiast, Ltd.

REPUBLIC OF KHAKASSIA

Aurum, Ltd.
Dawan, a / c, LLC
Jess, LLC (JES)
Golden Valley a / c, LLC
Gold Star of the FCA, Inc.
Irgiredmet & Noyon NGOs, Inc.
Kommunarovskiy mine, Inc.
Sayan field, Ltd.
Siberia FCA, Ltd.
Sora Mining, LLC

CHELYABINSK REGION

Alexandrinsk GRK, Ltd.
Verhneuralsk ore, Inc.
East, Inc.
GEOTEK NPP, LLC
Hydraulics, Inc.
Etkulzoloto, Inc.
Golden Fleece a / c, Inc.
Inhul, Ltd.
Karabashmed, Inc.
Karabashsky Steel Works, Ltd.
Mauksky mine, Inc.
Miasszoloto, Inc.
Terra Gold, LLC
Chelyabinsk Zinc Plant OJSC
Efa, Ltd.
Yuzhuralzoloto SC, Inc.

CHUKOTKA

Anyui, Ltd.
Arctic, Ltd.
Valkaray, of the Civil Code
Karalveem mine, Inc.
Quasar-LTD, LLC
Dome, FCA, LLC
League, LLC
Beam, a / c, LLC
Oil and gas, Ltd.
Polaris, a / c, LLC
Polar Star a / c, Inc.
Progress, LLC

Northern Gold, Inc.
North c / a, LLC
Shining a / c, LLC
Chukotka, a / c, LLC
Chukotka Hydropower JSC
Chukotka Trade Co., Ltd.
Shakhtar a / c, LLC

TRADE REGULATIONS IMPORTANT FOR BUSINESS ACTIVITY

TRADE BARRIERS

In 1994, import duties were increasing to a trade-weighted average of 11 percent. In March 1997 these rates were revised to raise the floor (except for a small list of zero-duty goods) to five percent and lower the ceiling (except for a few luxury goods) to 30 percent. In , the Government raised tariffs on alcoholic drinks and chicken, resulting in an average weighted tariff of 14 percent, as calculated by the IMF. A three-percentage point tariff increase on all imports was enacted in July 1998 as a revenue-enhancing measure. Although this import surcharge has been presented as a temporary measure, it is unclear when it might be revoked.

Besides tariffs, there are two other types of charges applied to imports: excise tax and value-added-tax (VAT). Excise tax applies to a number of luxury goods, alcohol, cigarettes and autos, and varies from 20 percent to 570 percent on a price- exclusive basis. The VAT rate is now 20 percent, with the exception of foodstuffs (for which VAT is 12 percent), and is applied to the import price plus tariff plus excise tax.

CUSTOMS VALUATION

Customs duties are payable on the customs value of goods in hard currency or rubles at the current exchange rate. The customs value is generally considered to be the CIF price of the goods imported. A customs processing fee of 0.15 percent of the goods□ actual cost is also levied. According to customs regulations, customs processing should take no longer than one month. If goods are refused by Russian Customs, regulations call for their return to the country of origin.

IMPORT LICENSES

Import licenses are required for importation of various goods, including ethyl alcohol and vodka, combat and sporting weapons, self-defense articles, explosives, military and ciphering equipment, radioactive materials and waste including uranium, strong poisons and narcotics, and precious metals, alloys and stones. Most import licenses are issued by the Russian Ministry of Foreign Economic Relations and Trade (MinFERT) or its regional branches, and controlled by the State Customs Committee. Licenses for sporting weapons and self-defense articles are issued by the Interior Ministry.

RUSSIAN EXPORT CONTROLS

Presidential Decree 245 of March 1997 lifted the need for MinFERT permission to export "strategically important raw materials," such as oil and gas, non-ferrous metals, fertilizers, cellulose, grain, fish products, and electric power. The decree also abolished the list of "special exporters." However, export of oil and gas is controlled in a practical sense by the Ministry of Fuel and Energy's granting of access to the export pipeline. Also, weapons, military equipment and dual-use materials and technology continue to require export licenses. Exports of "strategically important raw materials" still require registration with MinFERT.

UNITED STATES EXPORT CONTROLS

Certain high-technology or dual-use (civilian and military) products are be subject to United States Government export restrictions, possibly including requirements for pre-license chacks and/or post-shipment verifications. In addition, in July 1998, President Clinton banned U.S. exports to seven Russian enterprises suspected of collaboration with Iran in the development of ballistic missile and/or nuclear weapons capabilities. Prospective exporters with questions are advised to contact the Export Counseling Division of the U.S. Department of Commerce Bureau of Export Administration (contact information is found in Appendix E of this report).

IMPORT/EXPORT DOCUMENTATION

Importers are required to complete a Russian customs freight declaration for every item imported. The declaration form consists of 54 paragraphs and should be completed in the Russian language for presentation to Customs authorities. Certificates of origin and conformity (see "Product Standards" below) should also be presented at customs. Exporters are required to complete an export declaration and, if necessary, present the appropriate export license at customs. In addition, currency control authorities require the issuance of a "passport" for both exports and imports to ensure that hard currency earnings are repatriated to Russia and transfers of hard currency payments for imports is for goods actually received and properly valued.

TEMPORARY ENTRY

Temporary imports by foreign companies which are accredited with Russian government authorities are exempt from customs duties. This applies to goods imported only for company use and for one year only. Companies not accredited with Russian government authorities are charged 3 percent of the total cost of the product on a monthly basis. In this case, total cost equals original product price plus all import taxes.

PRODUCT STANDARDS

Many products imported for sale into the Russian Federation are required to have a certificate of conformity issued by the Russian State Standards Committee (GOSSTANDART). GOSSTANDART tests and certifies products according to Russian Government standards, rather than other widely-accepted international standards (e.g., the ISO-9000 system). GOSSTANDART and its authorized agents are the chief sources for certification in Russia. However, other agencies are involved in certification of certain products, including the Ministry of Agriculture (food products), the Ministry of Health (medical devices and pharmaceuticals), the State Communications Committee (telecommunications equipment and services), the State Mining and Industrial Inspectorate GOSGORTECHNADZOR (equipment for the mining, oil and gas industries) and others.

Testing protocols from the IECEE (electrical equipment) and the IECQ (electrical components), both of which fall under the International Electrotechnical Commission, from Underwriters Laboratories, and other bodies are accepted by GOSSTANDART and help to expedite certification by the Russian agency. The certificate of conformity is valid for 3 years and must accompany every shipment. Copies of the certificate are acceptable if original seals of the U.S. company holding the original certificate accompany the copy. Russian retailers are obliged to have on hand certificates for all imported products sold in their stores; violation of this requirement can bring penalties of up to the equivalent of $10,000.

PRODUCT LABELING

New regulations on labeling for non-food products came into force on July 1, 1998, augmenting food labelling requirements which took effect previously. Companies are advised to check their compliance with these requirements before shipping products. Regulations can be obtained from Russia□s State Committee on Standardization and Metrology, also known as Gosstandart (see contact information in Appendix E).

FREE TRADE ZONES/WAREHOUSES

There are no actual free trade zones in Russia. There are some free economic zones designed to encourage investments in specific areas, as well as free customs zones and free warehouses. Customs duties do not apply in free customs zones and free warehouses. Some production and wholesale transactions can take place within these zones, but not retail sales. The storage period is not limited. Free customs zones and free warehouses are located in customs areas (airports, seaports, railway and truck terminals).

MEMBERSHIP IN FREE TRADE ARRANGEMENTS

Russia does not participate currently in any free trade arrangements, although it is attempting to finalize a customs union with members of the CIS. Russia has an association agreement with the European Union (effective December 1997), proposes to join the World Trade Organization, and currently receives MFN treatment and GSP status from the United States.

TRADE AND PROJECT FINANCING

BANKING SYSTEM

After private banks were allowed beginning in the late 1980s, their number in Russia reached a peak of over 2,500 in 1997. Although there are over 1,600 licensed banks, the sector has been in a period of consolidation since mid-1997. Bank lending has been limited, due to weak credit analysis, lack of international accounting practices and ineffective bankruptcy laws. Almost 23 percent of the financial institutions are rated in critical condition, and while these banks account for only 2.9 percent of total banking assets, there is growing concern that a devaluation could undermine many smaller, weaker banks in Russia, along with a few of the larger ones.

Russian banks remain small by world standards (Sberbank, the largest, had a capital base of $1.3 billion in January , ranking it below the world's top 500 banks). Most Russian banks are much smaller; about 80 percent have capital of only $1 million or less, and only 4 percent have capital greater than $5 million. The large majority of small banks are reliant on highly specialized transactions or perform treasury functions for small enterprises. The largest banks offer a full range of modern banking services. However, commercial lending remains a small share of business, and long-term lending (over 1 year) accounts for less than 10 percent of credits. Most business is focused on trading of various types of securities, foreign exchange dealing, and to a lesser degree in project and trade finance. Almost 800 banks have a license to deal in foreign exchange, including 270 banks which possess a general license.

The relative stability of the ruble, lower inflation and falling yields in government securities market have limited commercial banks' profit-making opportunities during the past few years. At the same time, capital inadequacy, a continuing enterprise payment arrears problem, real estate problems, and a pervasive lack of banking experience have put strains on the banking system and prompted predictions of a major shakeout in the industry. Based on past experience, few creditors of failed banks recover much, if any of their deposits.

In 1993, Citibank and Chase Manhattan Bank became the first U.S. banks to receive general licenses to open subsidiaries in Russia. The new commercial banking bill, which took effect in January , explicitly permits foreign banks to establish full-service subsidiaries in Russia, though it gives the Central Bank of Russia (CBR) the ability to use reciprocity as a criteria for granting approval. Republic National Bank of New York has taken advantage of the new law to obtain a license and recently began full-service operations. More recently, American Express has received permission to open a representative office in Russia.

CURRENCY CONTROL AND REGULATION ISSUES

Regulations that took effect in January 1994 ban the use of foreign currency in cash transactions. Under these regulations, businesses in Russia are no longer permitted to accept cash payments in dollars or other hard currency. Non-cash transactions (e.g. credit/debit cards and checks) are not affected by the new regulations, so establishments that previously accepted payment via credit cards continue to do so. Stores that sell imported goods are still allowed to mark prices in dollars. At the time of purchase clerks convert the dollar price into rubles. Through the exchange rate they employ, merchants pass on the additional costs they will incur when they convert the rubles back into hard currency to restock inventories. Russian resident entities are still required to convert 50 percent of their foreign-currency revenues from exports into rubles. The foreign currency must be sold through MICEX or authorized foreign exchange dealers.

In an effort to limit outflow of capital, the CBR introduced a computerized export control system to monitor the flow of goods out of the country and the flow of hard currency back in. The system, which unites for the first time banking and export controls, requires exporters to obtain a special "passport" from a commercial bank, which enters the trade in a computer database. Customs agents register the actual export of the goods in the database and the commercial bank completes the cycle by entering receipt of the payment. Strategic exports, including energy and several types of metals, were subject to the new regime as of January 1, 1994. The system took effect for all other types of goods on March 1, 1994.

Effective January 1, , the CBR, in an effort to disrupt the use of illegitimate contracts for imports into Russia (and resulting capital flight from Russia), instituted an "import passport" system in addition to the already existing export control system. The system requires issuance of a "passport" by the importer's bank for payment against a specific import contract. The importer will have 180 days either to document the entry of the goods with the Russian Customs Service or return the hard currency issued in payment. Failure to comply with this regulation may make the importer liable for a hard currency penalty in the amount of the payment.

GENERAL FINANCING AVAILABILITY

The financing environment in Russia continues to improve with the growing Westernization of the economy; however, high domestic interest rates continue to limit Russian enterprises□ access to working capital. While the Russian banking system as a whole is inexperienced in project financing, a number of Western investment banks and venture funds are operating locally. In addition, a number of bilateral and multilateral financing programs provide more opportunities for traders and investors. The use of limited recourse project financing remains hampered by the immaturity of commercial legislation, including contract enforcement, asset title, the rights of debt and equity holders, performance responsibility of contractors and dispute settlement, among others.

HOW TO FINANCE EXPORTS; METHODS OF PAYMENT

Companies new to exporting to Russia should insist on payment in advance for goods and services. This is, in fact, the normal procedure in Russia for most transactions. Letters of credit are issued by Russian banks only in those cases where the Russian customer can deposit the requisite funds in its account ahead of time, and Western banks generally will only confirm letters of credit on that basis as well. Once a firm has established a strong relationship with a Russian trading partner, the U.S. firm may consider extending short-term credit as a way to bolster sales volume. This should be done with caution, and after careful evaluation.

For some large transactions, where up-front payment from Russian buyers may be impractical, financing may be provided by a bank, export credit agency or venture fund. In cases where lease transactions are appropriate, exporters should insist on three to four months' lease payment upon delivery.

Perhaps as many as twenty private Russian banks now offer forfaiting and factoring services. However, the volume and value of transactions using these techniques have yet to attain levels at which they are either profitable or self-sustaining. Given the endemic non-liquidity in the Russian economy, cross-border leasing may become an important alternative to export sales. At present, less than five percent of imported equipment is leased, including equipment for the aerospace, energy, transportation, pharmaceutical, forestry and fishing industries.

COUNTERTRADE AND PROMISSORY NOTES

Because of low liquidity throughout the Russian economy, many U.S. and other foreign companies which pursue business here are surprised to learn that, in some industries and regions, upwards of seventy or eighty percent of economic activity is conducted on a non-cash basis. In many transactions, goods or services are sold for other goods which can be used directly -- or more typically, sold -- by the original seller, who may have better access to cash-paying third-party customers than the original customer which made the payment-in-goods. While such barter deals can be more complex than cash transactions, U.S. firms should not dismiss them out-of-hand, for they can be just as profitable, and can help a company win a market foothold which it might not otherwise obtain. As in cash transactions, however, companies are advised to stay closely engaged in all aspects of the deal, to ensure that the payer meets commitments on schedule.

Promissory notes (in Russian, veksels), denominated in rubles, are often offerred by Russian companies or government entities in lieu of cash. While many veksels are issued by reliable companies, others are issued by firms with no credit records, or worse. U.S. companies are advised not to accept promissory notes as direct payment, but may find it worthwhile to rely on Russian banks or □veksel brokers□ as intermediaries who will accept the final risk of the promissory notes and ensure that the U.S. exporter is paid in cash.

THE U.S. EXPORT-IMPORT BANK

The U.S. Eximbank initially began lending to support U.S. exports to Russia in 1992, offering loans based on sovereign guarantees from the Russian Government. With Russia's tightening budget constraints increasingly limiting the Russian Government's willingness and ability to offer sovereign guarantees over the past several years, Eximbank has sought more creative ways to finance transactions. Eximbank's Oil and Gas Framework Agreement relied on pledges of exported oil to guarantee loans, and Exim has supported eight transactions for the oil sector, worth more than $1 billion. Russia's Gazprom withdrew from a similar arrangemnet in 1997, citing concerns over possible U.S. sanctions. Eximbank has also explored cooperatitve financing with major Russian banks on a small scale, and is also considering work with local governments in Moscow and St.Petersburg. Companies which wish to investigate whether Eximbank financing may be available for particular transactions should contact Eximbank directly (contact information is found in Appendix E of this report).

PARTIAL LIST OF PRIVATE COMMERCIAL BANKS

The Russian banking system is undergoing a period of change, during which significant disruptions may occur. The Financial Institutions Development Project (FIDP), financed by loans from the World Bank and the EBRD and grants from the European Union and the Japanese Government, aims to promote a stable and efficient banking system. The FIDP is administered by representatives of the Russian Ministry of Finance, the CBR, the Ministry of Economy, and the Council of Ministers. Banks are "accredited" to the FIDP based on recommendations of the World Bank and EBRD, and an analysis of bank financial statements prepared according to International Accounting Standards (IAS) by one of the major international accounting firms resident in Russia. While the information accumulated in the accreditation process is confidential, any foreign firm wishing to establish a banking relationship with an FIDP bank is free to request copies of their IAS financial statements. The following banks are currently accredited by the FIDP, and should be able to provide IAS financial statements prepared by Western auditors upon request:

Moscow Banks: Alpha Bank, Bank Vozrozhdenie, Inkombank, Konversebank, Kredit Moskva, Moscow Industrial Bank, Avtobank, Bank Imperial, Mezhkombank, Bank Menatep, Mosbusinessbank,

Uneximbank, Stolichniy Savings Bank, Bank Moskovskiy Delovoi Mir, Most Bank, Neftekhimbank, Probusinessbank, Rossiskiy Kredit and Toribank.

Regional Banks: Bank Petrovskiy (St. Petersburg), Promstroibank (St. Petersburg), Bank St. Petersburg (St. Petersburg), Dalrybbank (Vladivostok), Dalnevostochniy Bank (Vladivostok), Nizhnegorodskiy Bankisrskiy Dom (Nizhny Novgorod), Uralpromstroibank (Yekaterinburg), Omskpromstroibank (Omsk), Investbank (Kaliningrad), Bashprombank (Ufa) and Kuzbassotzbank (Kemerovo).

BUSINESS TRAVEL

BUSINESS CULTURE AND CUSTOMS

One challenging aspect of doing business here is bridging the substantial cultural gulf between Russians and Americans. Russian business culture is different, and visitors should not assume that Russians with who they are dealing have adopted or understood American business practice. For example:

-Russian decision-making is still highly centralized in most organizations.

-While Americans prefer to base their business relationships on legally-binding contracts, many Russians still doubt the value of their business laws and courts. In contrast, many Russian business dealings are based on strong personal relationships, with contracts considered merely a formality.

-Many Russians want to keep wealth and business deals secret.

-Westerners may think "win-win," while Russians may think "win-lose."

TRAVEL ADVISORY AND VISAS

The State Department issues travel advisories when political unrest warrants. Travel to Chechnya and surrounding regions is extremely dangerous due to continued political tension in the area. Two U.S. citizens have disappeared in Chechnya and remain missing; and local separatists have taken hostages on several occasions. Public gatherings and demonstrations occur frequently in Russia, particularly in Moscow. Although such demonstrations are usually peaceful, travelers are urged to exercise caution in areas where large groups are gathered.

Travelers may need to cross great distances, especially in Siberia and the Far East, to obtain services from Russian Government organizations, the U.S. Embassy in Moscow or U.S. consulates in St. Petersburg, Yekaterinburg or Vladivostok.

All Americans traveling to or transiting through Russia by any means of transportation must have a passport and visa. Travelers who arrive without a passport or entry visa may be subject to large fines, days of processing requirements imposed by Russian officials, and/or immediate departure by route of entry (at the traveler's expense).

Visas, other than for transit purposes, are issued based on support from a Russian individual or organization - the sponsor. It is very important to know who your sponsor is and how he or she can be contacted, as Russian law requires the sponsor to apply for replacement, extension or changes to your visa. The U.S. Embassy and Consulates cannot act as a sponsor. Tourists should contact their tour company or hotel in advance for information on visa sponsorship.

All foreigners must have an exit visa to depart. For short stays, the exit visa is issued along with the entry visa. For longer stays, the exit visa must be obtained by the sponsor after the traveler's arrival. All travelers who spend more than three days in Russia must register their visa through their hotel or sponsor. Visitors who overstay their visa's validity, even for one day, or neglect to register their visa, may be prevented from leaving. Errors in dates or other information on the visa can occur, and it is helpful to have someone who reads Russian check the visa before departing the United States. Travelers should have all points of entry and all itinerary points in the Russian Federation printed on their visa, in order to avoid potential difficulties in registering their visas and lengthy delays in travel. Due to the possibility of random document checks by police, U.S. citizens should carry their original or photocopies of the passports and registered visas. Failure to provide proper documentation can result in detention and/or heavy fines.

Americans can receive assistance from the Russian Embassy□s Consular Division. The Consulate moved in early 1998, and is now located at 2641 Tunlaw Road, NW, Washington, DC, 20007. The Russian Consulate can be reached at (202) 939-8907 or fax 202-483-7579. Travelers can also receive assistance from the Russian Consulates in New York, San Francisco or Seattle.

Russian Holidays

January 1	**--New Year's Day**
January 7	**--Christmas (Orthodox)**
March 8	**--International Women's Day**
May 1	**--International Labor Day**
May 2	**--Spring Day**
May 9	**--World War II Victory Day**
June 12	**--Independence Day**
November 7	**--Revolution Day**
December 12	**--Constitution Day**

When holidays fall on weekends, Russian authorities announce during the week prior to the holiday whether the holiday will be celebrated on the preceding Friday or following Monday.

TRANSPORTATION

Air travel within Russia is occasionally erratic, but is increasingly on-schedule, and the overall quality of service continues to improve. Russian-based airlines (such as Transaero) certified to operate internationally usually meet higher standards than domestic-only carriers. Moscow has four major airports which ring the city. Most international flights enter Moscow through Sheremetyevo II, although Transaero has a direct flight to Sheremetyevo I from Los Angeles. Travelers may continue to other Russian cities from any of the other three airports. Travel time to the departure airport can be as much as an hour and a half from Sheremetyevo II, and ample time must be allowed for passport control, customs clearance and baggage retrieval. St. Petersburg's airport (Pulkovo) has two terminals: Pulkovo I (domestic flights) and Pulkovo II (international flights).

A good way to get around Russia is by train. Between cities as close as St. Petersburg and Moscow, travelers can generally ride overnight trains, although occasional incidents of theft and other crimes on trains have made this mode less safe, especially for unaccompanied passengers. Inclement weather, erratic maintenance and a culture of aggressive driving make road conditions throughout Russia highly variable. Drivers and pedestrians should exercise extreme caution to avoid accidents, which are common. Traffic police sometimes stop motorists to extract cash "fines," and bandits occasionally prey on travelers, especially in isolated areas.

In Moscow and St. Petersburg, the metro (subway) is an efficient and inexpensive, if crowded, means of transport. Signs are in Russian, so it is helpful to learn the Cyrillic alphabet before you come. Marked taxis are increasingly present in Moscow, but not in other cities. US&FCS recommends that short-term business travelers consider renting a car and driver for extensive excursions, or hire taxis through their hotels for shorter jaunts.

CRIME AGAINST PERSONS

Recent police statistics for Moscow report an overall decline in crime, though drug-related crimes, murders, and kidnappings have increased, and street crime, sometimes violent, remains a continuing problem. The crime rate in Moscow is still below that of many major U.S. cities, and the rate is generally much lower in regions of Russia outside major cities (however, terrorist activity is a threat in and around Chechnya, including the adjacent republics of Dagestan and Ingushetia).

In Moscow, the most prevalent crime is theft, primarily from hotel rooms and train compartments, and by pickpockets and bands of street criminals. While there is little overt anti-American sentiment in Russia, Westerners are often targeted because of their perceived wealth, and street criminals operate in areas frequented by tourists and business travelers. Most foreigners are easily identifiable on Russian streets. In April 1998, a series of violent attacks in Moscow by gangs of skinheads against persons of African and Asian origin led to issuance of a travel warning to American citizens cautioning them of the possibility of such attacks.

To reduce the risk of personal crime, U.S. businesspeople should be alert to their surroundings and guard belongings in hotels, restaurants and other high-density tourist areas. Do not assume that you can blend in on the street. Do not leave valuables in hotel rooms -- keep your passport and visa with you at all times, and retain copies in separate locations in case of loss or theft of the originals. Be alert to theft and assault in metro stations, on metro trains, and on inter-city trains (when traveling on overnight trains, secure the door to your compartment with some sort of jamming device). While many Muscovites flag private hacker vehicles for rides, this is a risky form of transport that should be avoided, and travelers are advised to use only marked taxis. Finally, American business people who utilize local services for banking, security and medical treatment should limit the information provided to the minimum required, as reports have been received indicating that some individuals working in these sectors have passed confidential credit/financial, banking and medical information to organized crime gangs who use it to make extortion threats against foreigners.

US AND COUNTRY CONTACTS

RUSSIAN GOVERNMENT AGENCIES

Following is a listing of selected Russian government offices with responsibilities affecting business. This is not an exhaustive list, and companies seeking contact information for particular federal or regional government offices not appearing here are encouraged to contact the U.S. Commercial Service in Russia. (A listing of Russian Consulates - for obtaining visas for Russia - in the United States is found in Chapter IX of this report.) The country code for telephone and fax numbers in Russia is 7. City codes appear in parentheses.

Ministry of Economic Development and Trade
1/3, 1st Tverskaya Yamskaya., Moscow
Tel: (095) 200-5298, fax (095) 251-6995

Ministry of Finance
Ulitsa Ilyinka 9, Entrance 1, Moscow
Tel: (095) 298-9130; Fax: (095) 925-0889

Ministry of Energy
7, Kitaigorodskiy Proyezd, Moscow 103074
Tel: (095) 220-5200; Fax: (095) 975-2045 (International Dept.)

Ministry of Agriculture and Food
Orlikov Pereulok, 1/11, Moscow
Tel: (095) 207-4243 Fax: (095) 207-6437

Ministry of Communications & Information Technology
7, Tverskaya Ul., Moscow 103375
Tel: (095) 292-7100; Fax:(095) 230-2097

Ministry of Anti-Monopoly and Entrepreneurship
11, Sadovaya-Kudrinskaya Ul., Moscow, 123231
Tel: (095) 252-7445; fax: (095) 254-8300

Ministry of Taxes and Levies
23, Neglinnaya Ul., Moscow, 103381
Tel: (095) 925-4847; fax: (095) 913-6112

Ministry of Finance of the Russian Federation
9, Ilyinka Street, Moscow
(Accreditation of banking, auditing firms)
Tel: (095) 298-9959; Fax: (095) 913-4311

Central Bank of Russia
Sergey Vladimirovich Tatarinov, Head of External and Public Relations
12 Neglinnaya Street, Moscow, 103016
Tel: (095) 923-1081; Fax: (095) 921-5476

State Customs Committee
1a, Komsomolskaya Ploshchad, Moscow 107842
Tel: (095) 975-1918; Fax: (095) 975-4823
Internet site: custom-house.ru

State Committee for Standardization, Metrology and Certification (GOSSTANDART)
9, Leninskiy Prospekt, Moscow 117049
Tel: (095) 236-6208, -4044; Fax: (095) 236-6231, 237-6032
Internet site: www.gost.ru

State Committee for Construction and Housing Policy (Gosstroy)
8, Stroiteley Ul., Bldg. 2, Moscow, 117987
Tel: (095) 930-1755; Fax: (095) 938-2202

State Statistics Committee (Russian official economic data)
39 Myasnitskaya Ul.
Moscow 103450, Russia
Tel: (095) 207-4676; Fax: (095) 207-4891

Russian Agency for Patents and Trademarks (Rospatent)
30-1 Berezhkovskaya Nab., Moscow 121858, Russia
Tel. (095) 243-5509, 240-3295; Fax: (095)-956-4374
Internet site: www.rupto.ru

Russian Copyright Agency
6a, Bolshaya Bronnaya Ul., Moscow 103670
Tel: (095) 203-2996, -4599; Fax: (095) 200-1263

SELECTED REGIONAL GOVERNMENTS

Moscow City Administration
13 Tverskaya Ulitsa, 103032, Moscow
Tel: (095) 229-6360; Fax: (095) 883-6208

St. Petersburg City Administration
1, Smolny, St. Petersburg
Tel: (812) 271-0767; Fax: (812) 276-1633

Leningrad Oblast
Suvorovskiy Prospekt, 67, St. Petersburg, 193311
Tel: (812) 278-5587; Fax: (812) 274-5986

Sverdlovsk Oblast Administration
1, Oktyabrskaya Ploshchad, Yekaterinburg 620031
Tel: (3432) 51-54-97, 58-96-56; Fax: (3432) 51-98-70

Yekaterinburg City Administration
1, Oktyabrskaya Ploshchad, Yekaterinburg 620031
Tel: (3432) 51-13-07, 51-43-83; Fax: (3432) 51-90-05

Primorskiy Territorial Administration
Committee for Foreign Economic Relations and Regional Trade
22 Svetlanskaya ulitsa, 690110, Vladivostok
Tel: (4232) 22-08-52; Fax: (4232) 22-10-19
E-mail: chernous@primorsky.ru

Khabarovsk Territorial Administration
Foreign Economic Relations Dept.
56 ul.K.Marksa, Khabarovsk
Tel/fax: (4212) 32-41-21

Sakhalin Regional Administration
Department of Foreign Economic Relations
32 Kommunisticheskiy prospect, "Sakhincenter", office 242
693000, Yuzhno-Sakhalinsk
Tel: (42422) 3-25-69 Fax: (42422) 3-49-08
E-mail: up_forecon@adm.sakhalin.ru

CONTACTS FOR COMPANY REGISTRATION

State Registration Chamber of the Russian Federation
3/5, Smolenskiy Bulvar
Moscow 119835, Russian Federation
Tel: (095) 246-8649, 246-3486; E-mail: srcinfo@corbina.ru
Tel/Fax: (095) 245-2090
Internet site: www.palata.ru

Chamber of Commerce and Industry of the Russian Federation
Department of Accreditation
6, Ilyinka Street, Office 104
Moscow 103684
Tel: (095) 929-0260 Fax: (095) 929-0170

Registration Chamber of the Moscow City Administration
Branch, Registration of Foreign Companies
22, Pilyugina Street
Moscow 117393
Head of Branch Office
Tel: (095) 132-0500; Fax: (095) 202-2787

Moscow Chamber of Commerce and Industry
(Registration of Foreign Companies)
22 Pilyugina Street
Moscow 117393, Russian Federation

Tel: (095) 132-7396,132-7255; tel/fax: (095) 132-0047
E-mail: mtpp@glasnet.ru

BASIC TITLES ON RUSSIA

IMPORTANT!
All publications are updated annually!
Please contact IBP, Inc. at ibpusa3@gmail.com for the latest ISBNs and additional information

TITLE
Russia 1000 Largest Industrial Companies Directory
Russia 1000 Largest Industrial Companies Directory
Russia 500 Largest Industrial Companies Directory
Russia 500 Largest Industrial Companies Directory
Russia A "Spy" Guide - Strategic Information and Developments
Russia A Spy" Guide"
Russia Advertising Directory
Russia Advertising Directory
Russia Air Force Handbook
Russia Air Force Handbook
Russia and CIS Countries Chambers of Commerce Directory
Russia and CIS Countries Chambers of Commerce Directory
Russia and NIS Mineral Industry Handbook - Strategic Information and Regulations Vol. 1
Russia and NIS Mineral Industry Handbook - Strategic Information and Regulations Vol. 1
Russia and NIS Mineral Industry Handbook - Strategic Information and Regulations Vol. 2
Russia and NIS Mineral Industry Handbook - Strategic Information and Regulations Vol. 2
Russia Army Weapon Systems Handbook
Russia Army Weapon Systems Handbook
Russia Army Weapon Systems Handbook
Russia Army, National Security and Defense Policy Handbook
Russia Army, National Security and Defense Policy Handbook
Russia Automobile Industry Directory
Russia Automobile Industry Directory
Russia Aviation and Aerospace Industry Handbook Vol. 1
Russia Aviation and Aerospace Industry Handbook Vol. 1
Russia Aviation and Aerospace Industry Handbook Vol. 1
Russia Aviation and Aerospace Industry Handbook Vol. 2
Russia Aviation and Aerospace Industry Handbook Vol. 2
Russia Banking & Financial Market Handbook
Russia Banking & Financial Market Handbook
Russia Banks and Financial Institutions Handbook
Russia Banks and Financial Institutions Handbook
Russia Beer and Non Alcoholic Beverages Producers Directory
Russia Beer and Non Alcoholic Beverages Producers Directory
Russia Building Materials Industry Directory
Russia Building Materials Industry Directory
Russia Business and Investment Opportunities Yearbook

TITLE
Russia Business and Investment Opportunities Yearbook
Russia Business and Investment Opportunities Yearbook Volume 1 Strategic Information and Opportunities
Russia Business and Investment Opportunities Yearbook Volume 2 Leading Export-Import, Business, Investment Opportunities and Projects
Russia Business and Investment Services Handbook
Russia Business and Investment Services Handbook
Russia Business Intelligence Report - Practical Information, Opportunities, Contacts
Russia Business Intelligence Report - Practical Information, Opportunities, Contacts
Russia Business Law Handbook - Strategic Information and Basic Laws
Russia Business Law Handbook - Strategic Information and Basic Laws
Russia Business Law Handbook - Strategic Information and Basic Laws
Russia Business Law Handbook - Strategic Information and Basic Laws
Russia Business Law Handbook Volume 2 Investment and Trade Laws Volume 2 Investment and Trade Laws
Russia Business Success Guide - Basic Practical Information and Contacts
Russia Business Survival Guide
Russia Business Survival Guide
Russia Charity, Religious and Non Profit organizations Directory
Russia Charity, Religious and Non Profit organizations Directory
Russia Clothing & Textile Industry Handbook
Russia Clothing & Textile Industry Handbook
Russia Coal Mining Industry Business Intelligence Report - Practical Information, Opportunities, Contacts
Russia Coal Mining Industry Business Intelligence Report - Practical Information, Opportunities, Contacts
Russia Coal Mining Industry Directory
Russia Coal Mining Industry Directory
Russia Company Laws and Regulations Handbook
Russia Company Laws and Regulations Handbook - Strategic Information and Basic Laws
Russia Computers Video TV Electronics Producers Directory
Russia Computers Video TV Electronics Producers Directory
Russia Constitution and Citizenship Laws Handbook - Strategic Information and Basic Laws
Russia Country Study Guide - Strategic Information and Developments Vol.1 History, National Identity, Politics
Russia Country Study Guide - Strategic Information and Developments Volt 2. Economy, Industry, Regional Development
Russia Country Study Guide - Strategic Information and Developments Volt 3. Army and National Security
Russia Country Study Guide - Strategic Information and Developments Volume 1 Strategic Information and Developments
Russia Country Study Guide - Strategic Information and Developments Volume 2. Economy, Industry, Regional Development
Russia Country Study Guide - Strategic Information and Developments Volume 3. Army and National Security
Russia Criminal Laws, Regulations and Procedures Handbook - Strategic Information, Regulations, Procedures
Russia Customs, Trade Regulations and Procedures Handbook

TITLE
Russia Customs, Trade Regulations and Procedures Handbook
Russia Defense Industry Directory
Russia Diplomatic and International Contacts Directory
Russia Diplomatic and International Contacts Directory
Russia Diplomatic Handbook - Strategic Information and Developments
Russia Diplomatic Handbook - Strategic Information and Developments
Russia Ecology & Nature Protection Handbook
Russia Ecology & Nature Protection Handbook
Russia Ecology & Nature Protection Laws and Regulation Handbook
Russia Economic & Development Strategy Handbook
Russia Economic & Development Strategy Handbook
Russia Economic, Business and Investment Statistics Yearbook
Russia Economic, Business and Investment Statistics Yearbook
Russia Education System and Policy Handbook
Russia Electoral, Political Parties Laws and Regulations Handbook - Strategic Information, Regulations, Procedures
Russia Electrical Engineering Industry Directory
Russia Electrical Engineering Industry Directory
Russia Electronic and Telecommunications Equipment Producers Directory
Russia Electronic and Telecommunications Equipment Producers Directory
Russia Energy Policy, Laws and Regulation Handbook
Russia Energy Policy, Laws and Regulations Handbook
Russia Energy Policy, Laws and Regulations Handbook
Russia Energy Sector Handbook
Russia Energy Sector Handbook
Russia Executive Government Encyclopedic Directory
Russia Executive Government Encyclopedic Directory
Russia Executive Government Encyclopedic Directory 2011 VOL 2
Russia Executive Government Encyclopedic Directory 2011 VOL 2
Russia Executive Government Encyclopedic Directory 2012 VOL 2
Russia Executive Government Encyclopedic Directory VOL 1
Russia Executive Government Encyclopedic Directory VOL 1
Russia Executive Government Encyclopedic Directory VOL 1 2012
Russia Executive Government Encyclopedic Directory VOL 2
Russia Executive Government Encyclopedic Directory VOL 2 2011
Russia Exporters and Importers Directory
Russia Exporters and Importers Directory
Russia Export-Import and Business Directory volt 1
Russia Export-Import and Business Directory volt 2
Russia Export-Import and Business Directory Volume 1
Russia Export-Import and Business Directory Volume 2
Russia Ferrous and Non Ferrous Metallurgy Business Intelligence Report - Practical Information, Opportunities, Contacts
Russia Ferrous and Non Ferrous Metallurgy Business Intelligence Report - Practical Information, Opportunities, Contacts

TITLE
Russia Fishing and Fish Processing Industry
Russia Fishing and Fish Processing Industry
Russia Foreign Policy and Government Guide
Russia Foreign Policy and Government Guide
Russia Foreign Policy and National Security Yearbook Volume 1 Strategic Information and Regulations
Russia Forestry and Timber Industry Directory
Russia Forestry and Timber Industry Directory
Russia Gaming Industry Investment and Business Guide - Strategic and Practical Information
Russia Gaming Industry Investment and Business Guide - Strategic and Practical Information
Russia Gold Mining Industry Business Intelligence Report - Practical Information, Opportunities, Contacts
Russia Gold Mining Industry Business Intelligence Report - Practical Information, Opportunities, Contacts
Russia Gold Mining Industry Directory
Russia Gold Mining Industry Directory
Russia Government and Business Contacts Handbook
Russia Government and Business Contacts Handbook
Russia Government Guide: 1000+ Top Government Officials
Russia Government Guide: 1000+ Top Government Officials
Russia Healthcare Sector Organization, Management and Payment Systems Handbook - Strategic Information, Programs and Regulations
Russia Hotels Directory
Russia Hotels Directory
Russia Immigration Laws and Regulations Handbook - Strategic Information and Basic Laws
Russia Industrial and Business Directory
Russia Industrial and Business Directory
Russia Insolvency (Bankruptcy) Laws and Regulations Handbook - Strategic Information and Basic Laws
Russia Intelligence & Security Activities & Operations Handbook
Russia Intelligence & Security Activities & Operations Handbook
Russia Internet and E-Commerce Investment and Business Guide - Strategic and Practical Information: Regulations and Opportunities
Russia Internet and E-Commerce Investment and Business Guide - Strategic and Practical Information: Regulations and Opportunities
Russia Investment and Business Guide - Strategic and Practical Information
Russia Investment and Business Guide - Strategic and Practical Information
Russia Investment and Business Guide - Strategic and Practical Information
Russia Investment and Business Guide - Strategic and Practical Information
Russia Investment and Business Guide Volume 2 Business, Investment Opportunities and Incentives
Russia Investment and Business Profile - Basic Information and Contacts for Succesful investment and Business Activity
Russia Investment and Trade Laws and Regulations Handbook
Russia Justice System and National Police Handbook
Russia Justice System and National Police Handbook
Russia KGB Handbook: Past, Present, Future
Russia KGB Handbook: Past, Present, Future
Russia Labor Laws and Regulations Handbook - Strategic Information and Basic Laws
Russia Land Ownership and Agriculture Laws Handbook

TITLE
Russia Leather Fur and Tanning Industry Directory
Russia Leather Fur and Tanning Industry Directory
Russia Mass Media Directory
Russia Mass Media Directory
Russia Medical & Pharmaceutical Industry Handbook
Russia Medical & Pharmaceutical Industry Handbook
Russia Metal Working Industry Directory
Russia Metal Working Industry Directory
Russia Metallurgy Industry Directory
Russia Metallurgy Industry Directory
Russia Mineral & Mining Sector Investment and Business Guide - Strategic and Practical Information
Russia Mineral & Mining Sector Investment and Business Guide - Strategic and Practical Information
Russia Mining & Gold Mining Industry Directory
Russia Mining & Gold Mining Industry Directory
Russia Mining Industry Business Opportunities Handbook
Russia Mining Industry Business Opportunities Handbook
Russia Mining Industry Directory (Building Materials)
Russia Mining Industry Directory (Building Materials)
Russia Mining Laws and Regulations Handbook
Russia National Development Strategy Handbook: Important Programs and Developments
Russia National Security and Defense Policy Handbook
Russia National Security and Defense Policy Handbook
Russia Navy Handbook: History and Modern Situation
Russia Navy Handbook: History and Modern Situation
Russia Northern Regions Regional Investment & Business Guide
Russia NUCLEAR INDUSTRY Business Opportunities Handbook
Russia NUCLEAR INDUSTRY Business Opportunities Handbook
Russia Oil & Gas Industry Business Opportunities Handbook
Russia Oil & Gas Industry Business Opportunities Handbook
Russia Oil & Gas Sector Business & Investment Opportunities Yearbook
Russia Oil & Gas Sector Business & Investment Opportunities Yearbook
Russia Oil and Gas Exploration Laws and Regulation Handbook
Russia Oil and Gas Industry Encyclopedic Directory
Russia Oil and Gas Industry Encyclopedic Directory
Russia Oil and Gas Industry Producers Directory
Russia Oil and Gas Industry Producers Directory
Russia Oil Refining and Gas Processing Companies Handbook
Russia Oil Refining and Gas Processing Companies Handbook
Russia Orthodox Church Guide
Russia Orthodox Church Guide
Russia Parliament Encyclopedic Directory
Russia Parliament Encyclopedic Directory
Russia Parliament Guide
Russia Parliament Guide

TITLE
Russia Political Atlas
Russia Political Atlas
Russia Political Parties Directory
Russia Political Parties Directory
Russia Power Industry Directory
Russia Power Industry Directory
Russia Precious Metals Mining Industry Business Intelligence Report - Practical Information, Opportunities, Contacts
Russia Precious Metals Mining Industry Business Intelligence Report - Practical Information, Opportunities, Contacts
Russia President Vladimir Putin Handbook - Foreign and Domestic Policy
Russia President Vladimir Putin Rule: Achievements, Problems and Future Strategies
Russia Privatization Programs and Regulations Handbook
Russia Privatization Programs and Regulations Handbook
Russia Publishing Printing and Copying Industry Directory
Russia Publishing Printing and Copying Industry Directory
Russia Pulp & Paper Products Industry Directory
Russia Pulp & Paper Products Industry Directory
Russia Pulp and Paper Industry Directory
Russia Pulp and Paper Industry Directory
Russia Radio, TV and Electronic Equipment Producers Directory
Russia Radio, TV and Electronic Equipment Producers Directory
Russia Recent Economic and Political Developments Yearbook
Russia Recent Economic and Political Developments Yearbook
Russia Recent Economic and Political Developments Yearbook
Russia Regional Economic and Business Atlas
Russia Regional Economic and Business Atlas
Russia Regional Economic and Business Atlas Volume 2
Russia Regional Government Encyclopedic Directory
Russia Regional Government Encyclopedic Directory
Russia Regional Investment & Business Guide
Russia Regional Investment & Business Guide
Russia Regional Investment & Business Guide Volume 5 Siberia
Russia Research & Development Policy Handbook
Russia Research & Development Policy Handbook
Russia Research & Development Policy Handbook
Russia Research Institutions and Scientists Directory
Russia Research Institutions and Scientists Directory
Russia Sanitary and Bathroom Equipment Industry Directory
Russia Sanitary and Bathroom Equipment Industry Directory
Russia Scrap and Waste Processing Industry Directory
Russia Scrap and Waste Processing Industry Directory
Russia Space Agency and Programs Handbook
Russia Space Agency and Programs Handbook
Russia Space Programs and Exploration Handbook

TITLE
Russia Space Programs and Exploration Handbook
Russia Special and Working Clothing Industry Directory
Russia Special and Working Clothing Industry Directory
Russia Starting Business (Incorporating) in Russia Guide
Russia Starting Business (Incorporating) in....Guide
Russia Tax Guide
Russia Tax Guide
Russia Tax Guide Volume 1 Strategic Information and Basic Regulations
Russia Taxation Laws and Regulations Handbook
Russia Telecom & Broadcasting Equipment Producers Directory
Russia Telecom & Broadcasting Equipment Producers Directory
Russia Telecom Laws and Regulations Handbook
Russia Telecommunication Industry Business Opportunities Handbook
Russia Telecommunication Industry Business Opportunities Handbook
Russia Telecommunication Industry Directory
Russia Telecommunication Industry Directory
Russia Textile Industry Directory
Russia Textile Industry Directory
Russia Tires Rubber and Related Products Industry Directory
Russia Tires Rubber and Related Products Industry Directory
Russia Today Atlas: For Business and Political Decision Makers
Russia Today Atlas: For Business and Political Decision Makers
Russia Top Scientists and Researchers Handbook: Members of the Russian Academy of Sciences
Russia Top Scientists and Researchers Handbook: Members of the Russian Academy of Sciences
Russia Trade Directory: Wholesale Trading Companies
Russia Trade Directory: Wholesale Trading Companies
Russia Transportation Companies Directory
Russia Transportation Companies Directory
Russia Transportation Policy and Regulations Handbook
Russia Universities and Colleges Directory
Russia Universities and Colleges Directory
Russia Vodka and Hard Liquors Industry Directory
Russia Vodka and Hard Liquors Industry Directory
Russia ZIP Codes Directory
Russia ZIP Codes Directory
Russia: Adygey Republic Regional Investment & Business Guide
Russia: Adygey Republic Regional Investment & Business Guide
Russia: Astrakhan Province Regional Investment & Business Guide
Russia: Astrakhan Province Regional Investment & Business Guide
Russia: Bashkortostan Republic Regional Investment & Business Guide
Russia: Bashkortostan Republic Regional Investment & Business Guide
Russia: Belgorod Province Regional Investment & Business Guide
Russia: Belgorod Province Regional Investment & Business Guide
Russia: Bryansk Province Regional Investment & Business Guide

TITLE
Russia: Bryansk Province Regional Investment & Business Guide
Russia: Buryat Republic Regional Investment & Business Guide
Russia: Buryat Republic Regional Investment & Business Guide
Russia: Chelyabinsk Province Regional Investment & Business Guide
Russia: Chelyabinsk Province Regional Investment & Business Guide
Russia: Chita Province Regional Investment & Business Guide
Russia: Chita Province Regional Investment & Business Guide
Russia: Chuvash Republic Regional Investment & Business Guide
Russia: Chuvash Republic Regional Investment & Business Guide
Russia: Dagestan Republic Regional Investment & Business Guide
Russia: Dagestan Republic Regional Investment & Business Guide
Russia: How to Invest, Start and Run Profitable Business in Russia Guide - Practical Information, Opportunities, Contacts
Russia: Ingush Republic Regional Investment & Business Guide
Russia: Ingush Republic Regional Investment & Business Guide
Russia: Irkutsk Province Regional Investment & Business Guide
Russia: Irkutsk Province Regional Investment & Business Guide
Russia: Ivanovo Province Regional Investment & Business Guide
Russia: Ivanovo Province Regional Investment & Business Guide
Russia: Karachay-Cherkess Republic Regional Investment & Business Guide
Russia: Karachay-Cherkess Republic Regional Investment & Business Guide
Russia: Karelian Republic Regional Investment & Business Guide
Russia: Karelian Republic Regional Investment & Business Guide
Russia: Kemerovo Province Regional Investment & Business Guide
Russia: Kemerovo Province Regional Investment & Business Guide
Russia: Khabarovsk Province Regional Investment & Business Guide
Russia: Khabarovsk Territory Regional Investment & Business Guide
Russia: Khakass Republic Regional Investment & Business Guide
Russia: Khakass Republic Regional Investment & Business Guide
Russia: Kirov Province Regional Investment & Business Guide
Russia: Kirov Province Regional Investment & Business Guide
Russia: Komi Republic Regional Investment & Business Guide
Russia: Komi Republic Regional Investment & Business Guide
Russia: Kurgan Province Regional Investment & Business Guide
Russia: Kurgan Province Regional Investment & Business Guide
Russia: Kursk Province Regional Investment & Business Guide
Russia: Kursk Province Regional Investment & Business Guide
Russia: Leningrad Province Regional Investment & Business Guide
Russia: Leningrad Province Regional Investment & Business Guide
Russia: Magadan Province Regional Investment & Business Guide
Russia: Magadan Province Regional Investment & Business Guide
Russia: Mariy El Republic Regional Investment & Business Guide
Russia: Mariy El Republic Regional Investment & Business Guide
Russia: Mordovian Republic Regional Investment & Business Guide
Russia: Mordovian Republic Regional Investment & Business Guide

TITLE
Russia: Moscow City Investment & Business Guide
Russia: Moscow City Investment & Business Guide
Russia: Moscow Province Regional Investment & Business Guide
Russia: Moscow Province Regional Investment & Business Guide
Russia: Murmansk Province Regional Investment & Business Guide
Russia: Murmansk Province Regional Investment & Business Guide
Russia: Nizhniy Novgorod Province Regional Investment & Business Guide
Russia: Nizhniy Novgorod Province Regional Investment & Business Guide
Russia: North Osetian Republic Regional Investment & Business Guide
Russia: North Osetian Republic Regional Investment & Business Guide
Russia: Novgorod Province Regional Investment & Business Guide
Russia: Novgorod Province Regional Investment & Business Guide
Russia: Novosibirsk Province Regional Investment & Business Guide
Russia: Novosibirsk Province Regional Investment & Business Guide
Russia: Omsk Province Regional Investment & Business Guide
Russia: Omsk Province Regional Investment & Business Guide
Russia: Orenburg Province Regional Investment & Business Guide
Russia: Orenburg Province Regional Investment & Business Guide
Russia: Oryol Province Regional Investment & Business Guide
Russia: Oryol Province Regional Investment & Business Guide
Russia: Rostov Province Regional Investment & Business Guide
Russia: Rostov Province Regional Investment & Business Guide
Russia: Ryazan Province Regional Investment & Business Guide
Russia: Ryazan Province Regional Investment & Business Guide
Russia: Sakha (Yakut) Republic Regional Investment & Business Guide
Russia: Sakhalin Regional Investment & Business Guide
Russia: Sakhalin Regional Investment & Business Guide
Russia: Samara Province Regional Investment & Business Guide
Russia: Samara Province Regional Investment & Business Guide
Russia: Saratov Regional Investment & Business Guide
Russia: Saratov Regional Investment & Business Guide
Russia: Smolensk Province Regional Investment & Business Guide
Russia: Smolensk Province Regional Investment & Business Guide
Russia: St. Petersburg (Russia) Investment & Business Guide
Russia: St. Petersburg Business and Investment Opportunities Yearbook
Russia: St. Petersburg Business Law Handbook - Strategic Information and Basic Laws
Russia: St. Petersburg City Business and Investment Opportunities Yearbook
Russia: St. Petersburg City Investment & Business Guide
Russia: St. Petersburg, Russia: A Spy" Guide"
Russia: Stavropol Province Regional Investment & Business Guide
Russia: Stavropol Territory Regional Investment & Business Guide
Russia: Sverdlovsk Province Regional Investment & Business Guide
Russia: Sverdlovsk Province Regional Investment & Business Guide
Russia: Tambov Province Regional Investment & Business Guide

TITLE
Russia: Tambov Province Regional Investment & Business Guide
Russia: Tatarstan Republic Regional Investment & Business Guide
Russia: Tatarstan Republic Regional Investment & Business Guide
Russia: Tomsk Province Regional Investment & Business Guide
Russia: Tomsk Province Regional Investment & Business Guide
Russia: Tula Province Regional Investment & Business Guide
Russia: Tula Province Regional Investment & Business Guide
Russia: Tver Province Regional Investment & Business Guide
Russia: Tver Province Regional Investment & Business Guide
Russia: Tyumen Province Regional Investment & Business Guide
Russia: Tyumen Province Regional Investment & Business Guide
Russia: Tyva Republic Regional Investment & Business Guide
Russia: Tyva Republic Regional Investment & Business Guide
Russia: Udmurt Republic Regional Investment & Business Guide
Russia: Udmurt Republic Regional Investment & Business Guide
Russia: Vladimir Province Regional Investment & Business Guide
Russia: Vladimir Province Regional Investment & Business Guide
Russia: Volgograd Province Regional Investment & Business Guide
Russia: Volgograd Province Regional Investment & Business Guide
Russia: Vologda Province Regional Investment & Business Guide
Russia: Vologda Province Regional Investment & Business Guide
Russia: Voronezh Province Regional Investment & Business Guide
Russia: Voronezh Province Regional Investment & Business Guide
Russian Federation Fishing and Aquaculture Industry Handbook - Strategic Information, Regulations, Opportunities
Russian Federation Investment, Trade Strategy and Agreements Handbook - Strategic Information and Basic Agreements
Russian KGB Handbook: Past, Present, Future
Russian KGB Handbook: Past, Present, Future
Russian Law Firms and Legal Services Companies Directory
Russian Law Firms and Legal Services Companies Directory
Russian Navy Handbook: History and Modern Situation
Russian Navy Handbook: History and Modern Situation
Russian Regional Economic and Business Atlas Volume 2 2011
Russian Regional Economic and Business Atlas Volume 2 2012
Russian Regional Investment Guide: Strategic and Practical Information (World Investment and Business Guide - Strategic and Practical Information Library)
Russia-NATO Cooperation Handbook
Russia-NATO Cooperation Handbook

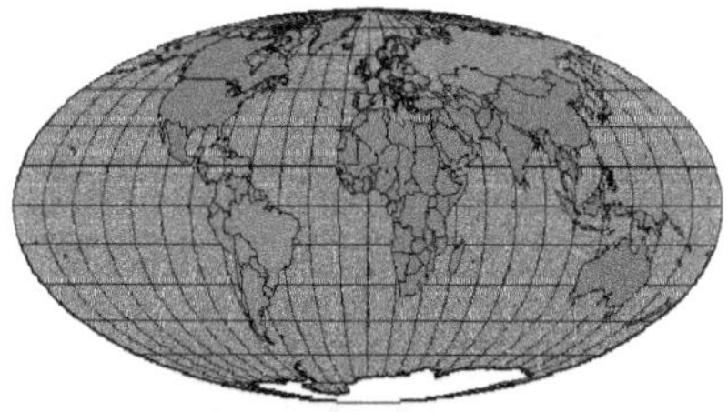

WORLD MINERAL AND MINING SECTOR INVESTMENT AND BUSINESS GUIDES LIBRARY

Price: $149.95 Each

1. Afghanistan Mineral and Mining Sector Investment and Business Guide - Strategic Information and Regulations
2. Albania Mineral and Mining Sector Investment and Business Guide - Strategic Information and Regulations
3. Algeria Mineral and Mining Sector Investment and Business Guide - Strategic Information and Regulations
4. Angola Mineral and Mining Sector Investment and Business Guide - Strategic Information and Regulations
5. Argentina Mineral and Mining Sector Investment and Business Guide - Strategic Information and Regulations
6. Armenia Mineral and Mining Sector Investment and Business Guide - Strategic Information and Regulations
7. Australia Mineral and Mining Sector Investment and Business Guide - Strategic Information and Regulations
8. Austria Mineral and Mining Sector Investment and Business Guide - Strategic Information and Regulations
9. Azerbaijan Mineral and Mining Sector Investment and Business Guide - Strategic Information and Regulations
10. Bahrain Mineral and Mining Sector Investment and Business Guide - Strategic Information and Regulations
11. Bangladesh Mineral and Mining Sector Investment and Business Guide - Strategic Information and Regulations
12. Belarus Mineral and Mining Sector Investment and Business Guide - Strategic Information and Regulations
13. Belgium Mineral and Mining Sector Investment and Business Guide - Strategic Information and Regulations
14. Benin Mineral and Mining Sector Investment and Business Guide - Strategic Information and Regulations
15. Bolivia Mineral and Mining Sector Investment and Business Guide - Strategic Information and Regulations
16. Bosnia and Herzegovina Mineral and Mining Sector Investment and Business Guide - Strategic Information and Regulations
17. Botswana Mineral and Mining Sector Investment and Business Guide - Strategic Information and Regulations
18. Brazil Mineral and Mining Sector Investment and Business Guide - Strategic Information and Regulations
19. Brunei Mineral and Mining Sector Investment and Business Guide - Strategic Information and Regulations
20. Bulgaria Mineral and Mining Sector Investment and Business Guide - Strategic Information and Regulations
21. Burkina Faso Mineral and Mining Sector Investment and Business Guide - Strategic Information and Regulations
22. Burundi Mineral and Mining Sector Investment and Business Guide - Strategic Information and Regulations
23. Cambodia Mineral and Mining Sector Investment and Business Guide - Strategic Information and Regulations
24. Cameroon Mineral and Mining Sector Investment and Business Guide - Strategic Information and Regulations
25. Canada Mineral and Mining Sector Investment and Business Guide - Strategic Information and Regulations
26. Cape Verde Mineral and Mining Sector Investment and Business Guide - Strategic Information and

---

For additional analytical, business and investment opportunities information, please contact Global Investment & Business Center, USA at (202) 546-2103. Fax: (202) 546-3275. E-mail: ibpusa@comcast.net

Regulations
27. Cayman Islands Mineral and Mining Sector Investment and Business Guide - Strategic Information and Regulations
28. Central African Republic Mineral and Mining Sector Investment and Business Guide - Strategic Information and Regulations
29. Chad Mineral and Mining Sector Investment and Business Guide - Strategic Information and Regulations
30. Chile Mineral and Mining Sector Investment and Business Guide - Strategic Information and Regulations
31. China Mineral and Mining Sector Investment and Business Guide - Strategic Information and Regulations
32. Colombia Mineral and Mining Sector Investment and Business Guide - Strategic Information and Regulations
33. Comoros Mineral and Mining Sector Investment and Business Guide - Strategic Information and Regulations
34. Congo Mineral and Mining Sector Investment and Business Guide - Strategic Information and Regulations
35. Congo, Dem. Republic Mineral and Mining Sector Investment and Business Guide - Strategic Information and Regulations
36. Cook Islands Mineral and Mining Sector Investment and Business Guide - Strategic Information and Regulations
37. Costa Rica Mineral and Mining Sector Investment and Business Guide - Strategic Information and Regulations
38. Cote d'Ivoire Mineral and Mining Sector Investment and Business Guide - Strategic Information and Regulations
39. Croatia Mineral and Mining Sector Investment and Business Guide - Strategic Information and Regulations
40. Cuba Mineral and Mining Sector Investment and Business Guide - Strategic Information and Regulations
41. Czech Republic Mineral and Mining Sector Investment and Business Guide - Strategic Information and Regulations
42. Denmark Mineral and Mining Sector Investment and Business Guide - Strategic Information and Regulations
43. Djibouti Mineral and Mining Sector Investment and Business Guide - Strategic Information and Regulations
44. Dominican Republic Mineral and Mining Sector Investment and Business Guide - Strategic Information and Regulations
45. Dubai Mineral and Mining Sector Investment and Business Guide - Strategic Information and Regulations
46. Ecuador Mineral and Mining Sector Investment and Business Guide - Strategic Information and Regulations
47. Egypt Mineral and Mining Sector Investment and Business Guide - Strategic Information and Regulations
48. El Salvador Mineral and Mining Sector Investment and Business Guide - Strategic Information and Regulations
49. Equatorial Guinea Mineral and Mining Sector Investment and Business Guide - Strategic Information and Regulations
50. Eritrea Mineral and Mining Sector Investment and Business Guide - Strategic Information and Regulations
51. Estonia Mineral and Mining Sector Investment and Business Guide - Strategic Information and Regulations
52. Ethiopia Mineral and Mining Sector Investment and Business Guide - Strategic Information and Regulations
53. Fiji Mineral and Mining Sector Investment and Business Guide - Strategic Information and Regulations
54. Finland Mineral and Mining Sector Investment and Business Guide - Strategic Information and Regulations
55. France Mineral and Mining Sector Investment and Business Guide - Strategic Information and Regulations
56. Gabon Mineral and Mining Sector Investment and Business Guide - Strategic Information and Regulations
57. Gambia Mineral and Mining Sector Investment and Business Guide - Strategic Information and Regulations
58. Georgia Mineral and Mining Sector Investment and Business Guide - Strategic Information and Regulations
59. Germany Mineral and Mining Sector Investment and Business Guide - Strategic Information and Regulations
60. Ghana Mineral and Mining Sector Investment and Business Guide - Strategic Information and Regulations
61. Greece Mineral and Mining Sector Investment and Business Guide - Strategic Information and Regulations
62. Greenland Mineral and Mining Sector Investment and Business Guide - Strategic Information and Regulations

63. Guatemala Mineral and Mining Sector Investment and Business Guide - Strategic Information and Regulations
64. Guinea Mineral and Mining Sector Investment and Business Guide - Strategic Information and Regulations
65. Guinea-Bissau Mineral and Mining Sector Investment and Business Guide - Strategic Information and Regulations
66. Guyana Mineral and Mining Sector Investment and Business Guide - Strategic Information and Regulations
67. Haiti Mineral and Mining Sector Investment and Business Guide - Strategic Information and Regulations
68. Honduras Mineral and Mining Sector Investment and Business Guide - Strategic Information and Regulations
69. Hungary Mineral and Mining Sector Investment and Business Guide - Strategic Information and Regulations
70. Iceland Mineral and Mining Sector Investment and Business Guide - Strategic Information and Regulations
71. India Mineral and Mining Sector Investment and Business Guide - Strategic Information and Regulations
72. Indonesia Mineral and Mining Sector Investment and Business Guide - Strategic Information and Regulations
73. Iran Mineral and Mining Sector Investment and Business Guide - Strategic Information and Regulations
74. Iraq Mineral and Mining Sector Investment and Business Guide - Strategic Information and Regulations
75. Ireland Mineral and Mining Sector Investment and Business Guide - Strategic Information and Regulations
76. Israel Mineral and Mining Sector Investment and Business Guide - Strategic Information and Regulations
77. Italy Mineral and Mining Sector Investment and Business Guide - Strategic Information and Regulations
78. Jamaica Mineral and Mining Sector Investment and Business Guide - Strategic Information and Regulations
79. Japan Mineral and Mining Sector Investment and Business Guide - Strategic Information and Regulations
80. Jordan Mineral and Mining Sector Investment and Business Guide - Strategic Information and Regulations
81. Kazakhstan Mineral and Mining Sector Investment and Business Guide - Strategic Information and Regulations
82. Kenya Mineral and Mining Sector Investment and Business Guide - Strategic Information and Regulations
83. Korea, South Mineral and Mining Sector Investment and Business Guide - Strategic Information and Regulations
84. Kuwait Mineral and Mining Sector Investment and Business Guide - Strategic Information and Regulations
85. Kyrgyzstan Mineral and Mining Sector Investment and Business Guide - Strategic Information and Regulations
86. Laos Mineral and Mining Sector Investment and Business Guide - Strategic Information and Regulations
87. Latvia Mineral and Mining Sector Investment and Business Guide - Strategic Information and Regulations
88. Lesotho Mineral and Mining Sector Investment and Business Guide - Strategic Information and Regulations
89. Liberia Mineral and Mining Sector Investment and Business Guide - Strategic Information and Regulations
90. Libya Mineral and Mining Sector Investment and Business Guide - Strategic Information and Regulations
91. Lithuania Mineral and Mining Sector Investment and Business Guide - Strategic Information and Regulations
92. Macedonia Republic Mineral and Mining Sector Investment and Business Guide - Strategic Information and Regulations
93. Madagascar Mineral and Mining Sector Investment and Business Guide - Strategic Information and Regulations
94. Malawi Mineral and Mining Sector Investment and Business Guide - Strategic Information and Regulations
95. Malaysia Mineral and Mining Sector Investment and Business Guide - Strategic Information and Regulations
96. Mali Mineral and Mining Sector Investment and Business Guide - Strategic Information and Regulations
97. Mauritania Mineral and Mining Sector Investment and Business Guide - Strategic Information and Regulations
98. Mauritius Mineral and Mining Sector Investment and Business Guide - Strategic Information and Regulations
99. Mexico Mineral and Mining Sector Investment and Business Guide - Strategic Information and Regulations

100. Moldova Mineral and Mining Sector Investment and Business Guide - Strategic Information and Regulations
101. Mongolia Mineral and Mining Sector Investment and Business Guide - Strategic Information and Regulations
102. Morocco Mineral and Mining Sector Investment and Business Guide - Strategic Information and Regulations
103. Mozambique Mineral and Mining Sector Investment and Business Guide - Strategic Information and Regulations
104. Myanmar Mineral and Mining Sector Investment and Business Guide - Strategic Information and Regulations
105. Namibia Mineral and Mining Sector Investment and Business Guide - Strategic Information and Regulations
106. Nepal Mineral and Mining Sector Investment and Business Guide - Strategic Information and Regulations
107. Netherlands Mineral and Mining Sector Investment and Business Guide - Strategic Information and Regulations
108. New Zealand Mineral and Mining Sector Investment and Business Guide - Strategic Information and Regulations
109. Nicaragua Mineral and Mining Sector Investment and Business Guide - Strategic Information and Regulations
110. Niger Mineral and Mining Sector Investment and Business Guide - Strategic Information and Regulations
111. Nigeria Mineral and Mining Sector Investment and Business Guide - Strategic Information and Regulations
112. Norway Mineral and Mining Sector Investment and Business Guide - Strategic Information and Regulations
113. Oman Mineral and Mining Sector Investment and Business Guide - Strategic Information and Regulations
114. Pakistan Mineral and Mining Sector Investment and Business Guide - Strategic Information and Regulations
115. Papua New Guinea Mineral and Mining Sector Investment and Business Guide - Strategic Information and Regulations
116. Paraguay Mineral and Mining Sector Investment and Business Guide - Strategic Information and Regulations
117. Peru Mineral and Mining Sector Investment and Business Guide - Strategic Information and Regulations
118. Philippines Mineral and Mining Sector Investment and Business Guide - Strategic Information and Regulations
119. Poland Mineral and Mining Sector Investment and Business Guide - Strategic Information and Regulations
120. Portugal Mineral and Mining Sector Investment and Business Guide - Strategic Information and Regulations
121. Qatar Mineral and Mining Sector Investment and Business Guide - Strategic Information and Regulations
122. Romania Mineral and Mining Sector Investment and Business Guide - Strategic Information and Regulations
123. Russia Mineral and Mining Sector Investment and Business Guide - Strategic Information and Regulations
124. Rwanda Mineral and Mining Sector Investment and Business Guide - Strategic Information and Regulations
125. Sao Tome and Principe Mineral and Mining Sector Investment and Business Guide - Strategic Information and Regulations
126. Saudi Arabia Mineral and Mining Sector Investment and Business Guide - Strategic Information and Regulations
127. Senegal Mineral and Mining Sector Investment and Business Guide - Strategic Information and Regulations
128. Serbia Mineral and Mining Sector Investment and Business Guide - Strategic Information and Regulations
129. Sierra Leone Mineral and Mining Sector Investment and Business Guide - Strategic Information and Regulations
130. Slovakia Mineral and Mining Sector Investment and Business Guide - Strategic Information and Regulations
131. Slovenia Mineral and Mining Sector Investment and Business Guide - Strategic Information and Regulations
132. Somalia Mineral and Mining Sector Investment and Business Guide - Strategic Information and Regulations
133. South Africa Mineral and Mining Sector Investment and Business Guide - Strategic Information and Regulations
134. Spain Mineral and Mining Sector Investment and Business Guide - Strategic Information and Regulations
135. Sri Lanka Mineral and Mining Sector Investment and Business Guide - Strategic Information and Regulations
136. Sudan Mineral and Mining Sector Investment and Business Guide - Strategic Information and Regulations

137. Suriname Mineral and Mining Sector Investment and Business Guide - Strategic Information and Regulations
138. Swaziland Mineral and Mining Sector Investment and Business Guide - Strategic Information and Regulations
139. Sweden Mineral and Mining Sector Investment and Business Guide - Strategic Information and Regulations
140. Syria Mineral and Mining Sector Investment and Business Guide - Strategic Information and Regulations
141. Taiwan Mineral and Mining Sector Investment and Business Guide - Strategic Information and Regulations
142. Tajikistan Mineral and Mining Sector Investment and Business Guide - Strategic Information and Regulations
143. Tanzania Mineral and Mining Sector Investment and Business Guide - Strategic Information and Regulations
144. Thailand Mineral and Mining Sector Investment and Business Guide - Strategic Information and Regulations
145. Togo Mineral and Mining Sector Investment and Business Guide - Strategic Information and Regulations
146. Trinidad and Tobago Mineral and Mining Sector Investment and Business Guide - Strategic Information and Regulations
147. Tunisia Mineral and Mining Sector Investment and Business Guide - Strategic Information and Regulations
148. Turkey Mineral and Mining Sector Investment and Business Guide - Strategic Information and Regulations
149. Turkmenistan Mineral and Mining Sector Investment and Business Guide - Strategic Information and Regulations
150. Uganda Mineral and Mining Sector Investment and Business Guide - Strategic Information and Regulations
151. Ukraine Mineral and Mining Sector Investment and Business Guide - Strategic Information and Regulations
152. United Arab Emirates Mineral and Mining Sector Investment and Business Guide - Strategic Information and Regulations
153. United Kingdom Mineral and Mining Sector Investment and Business Guide - Strategic Information and Regulations
154. United States Mineral and Mining Sector Investment and Business Guide - Strategic Information and Regulations
155. Uruguay Mineral and Mining Sector Investment and Business Guide - Strategic Information and Regulations
156. Uzbekistan Mineral and Mining Sector Investment and Business Guide - Strategic Information and Regulations
157. Venezuela Mineral and Mining Sector Investment and Business Guide - Strategic Information and Regulations
158. Vietnam Mineral and Mining Sector Investment and Business Guide - Strategic Information and Regulations
159. Yemen Mineral and Mining Sector Investment and Business Guide - Strategic Information and Regulations
160. Zambia Mineral and Mining Sector Investment and Business Guide - Strategic Information and Regulations
161. Zimbabwe Mineral and Mining Sector Investment and Business Guide - Strategic Information and Regulations

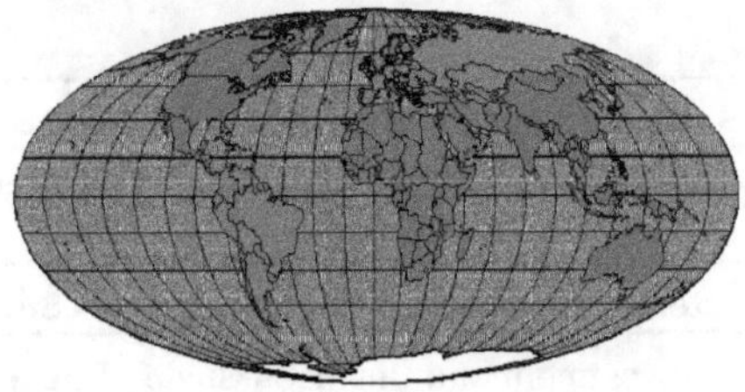

WORLD BUSINESS AND INVESTMENT OPPORTUNITIES YEARBOOK LIBRARY

World Business Information Catalog, USA: http://www.ibpus.com
Email: ibpusa3@gmail.com

Price: $99.95 Each

TITLE
Abkhazia (Republic of Abkhazia) Business and Investment Opportunities Yearbook Volume 1 Strategic, Practical Information and Opportunities
Afghanistan Business and Investment Opportunities Yearbook Volume 1 Strategic, Practical Information and Opportunities
Aland Business and Investment Opportunities Yearbook Volume 1 Strategic, Practical Information and Opportunities
Albania Business and Investment Opportunities Yearbook Volume 1 Strategic, Practical Information and Opportunities
Algeria Business and Investment Opportunities Yearbook Volume 1 Strategic, Practical Information and Opportunities
Andorra Business and Investment Opportunities Yearbook Volume 1 Strategic, Practical Information and Opportunities
Angola Business and Investment Opportunities Yearbook Volume 1 Strategic, Practical Information and Opportunities
Anguilla Business and Investment Opportunities Yearbook Volume 1 Strategic, Practical Information and Opportunities
Antigua and Barbuda Business and Investment Opportunities Yearbook Volume 1 Strategic, Practical Information and Opportunities
Antilles (Netherlands) Business and Investment Opportunities Yearbook Volume 1 Strategic, Practical Information and Opportunities
Argentina Business and Investment Opportunities Yearbook Volume 1 Strategic, Practical Information and Opportunities
Armenia Business and Investment Opportunities Yearbook Volume 1 Strategic, Practical Information and Opportunities
Aruba Business and Investment Opportunities Yearbook Volume 1 Strategic, Practical Information and Opportunities
Australia Business and Investment Opportunities Yearbook Volume 1 Strategic, Practical Information and Opportunities
Austria Business and Investment Opportunities Yearbook Volume 1 Strategic, Practical Information and Opportunities
Azerbaijan Business and Investment Opportunities Yearbook Volume 1 Strategic, Practical Information and Opportunities
Bahamas Business and Investment Opportunities Yearbook Volume 1 Strategic, Practical Information and Opportunities
Bahrain Business and Investment Opportunities Yearbook Volume 1 Strategic, Practical Information and Opportunities
Bangladesh Business and Investment Opportunities Yearbook Volume 1 Strategic, Practical Information and Opportunities
Barbados Business and Investment Opportunities Yearbook Volume 1 Strategic, Practical Information and Opportunities
Belarus Business and Investment Opportunities Yearbook Volume 1 Strategic, Practical Information and Opportunities

For additional analytical, business and investment opportunities information,
Please contact Global Investment & Business Center, USA
at (202) 546-2103. Fax: (202) 546-3275. E-mail: ibpusa3@gmail.com

TITLE
Belgium Business and Investment Opportunities Yearbook Volume 1 Strategic, Practical Information and Opportunities
Belize Business and Investment Opportunities Yearbook Volume 1 Strategic, Practical Information and Opportunities
Benin Business and Investment Opportunities Yearbook Volume 1 Strategic, Practical Information and Opportunities
Bermuda Business and Investment Opportunities Yearbook Volume 1 Strategic, Practical Information and Opportunities
Bhutan Business and Investment Opportunities Yearbook Volume 1 Strategic, Practical Information and Opportunities
Bolivia Business and Investment Opportunities Yearbook Volume 1 Strategic, Practical Information and Opportunities
Bosnia and Herzegovina Business and Investment Opportunities Yearbook Volume 1 Strategic, Practical Information and Opportunities
Botswana Business and Investment Opportunities Yearbook Volume 1 Strategic, Practical Information and Opportunities
Brazil Business and Investment Opportunities Yearbook Volume 1 Strategic, Practical Information and Opportunities
Brunei Business and Investment Opportunities Yearbook Volume 1 Strategic, Practical Information and Opportunities
Bulgaria Business and Investment Opportunities Yearbook Volume 1 Strategic, Practical Information and Opportunities
Burkina Faso Business and Investment Opportunities Yearbook Volume 1 Strategic, Practical Information and Opportunities
Burundi Business and Investment Opportunities Yearbook Volume 1 Strategic, Practical Information and Opportunities
Cambodia Business and Investment Opportunities Yearbook Volume 1 Strategic, Practical Information and Opportunities
Cameroon Business and Investment Opportunities Yearbook Volume 1 Strategic, Practical Information and Opportunities
Canada Business and Investment Opportunities Yearbook Volume 1 Strategic, Practical Information and Opportunities
Cape Verde Business and Investment Opportunities Yearbook Volume 1 Strategic, Practical Information and Opportunities
Cayman Islands Business and Investment Opportunities Yearbook Volume 1 Strategic, Practical Information and Opportunities
Central African Republic Business and Investment Opportunities Yearbook Volume 1 Strategic, Practical Information and Opportunities
Chad Business and Investment Opportunities Yearbook Volume 1 Strategic, Practical Information and Opportunities
Chile Business and Investment Opportunities Yearbook Volume 1 Strategic, Practical Information and Opportunities
China Business and Investment Opportunities Yearbook Volume 1 Strategic, Practical Information and Opportunities
Colombia Business and Investment Opportunities Yearbook Volume 1 Strategic, Practical Information and Opportunities
Comoros Business and Investment Opportunities Yearbook Volume 1 Strategic, Practical Information and Opportunities
Congo Business and Investment Opportunities Yearbook Volume 1 Strategic, Practical Information and Opportunities
Congo, Democratic Republic Business and Investment Opportunities Yearbook Volume 1 Strategic, Practical Information and Opportunities
Cook Islands Business and Investment Opportunities Yearbook Volume 1 Strategic, Practical Information and Opportunities
Costa Rica Business and Investment Opportunities Yearbook Volume 1 Strategic, Practical Information and Opportunities

TITLE
Cote d'Ivoire Business and Investment Opportunities Yearbook Volume 1 Strategic, Practical Information and Opportunities
Croatia Business and Investment Opportunities Yearbook Volume 1 Strategic, Practical Information and Opportunities
Cuba Business and Investment Opportunities Yearbook Volume 1 Strategic, Practical Information and Opportunities
Cyprus Business and Investment Opportunities Yearbook Volume 1 Strategic, Practical Information and Opportunities
Czech Republic Business and Investment Opportunities Yearbook Volume 1 Strategic, Practical Information and Opportunities
Denmark Business and Investment Opportunities Yearbook Volume 1 Strategic, Practical Information and Opportunities
Djibouti Business and Investment Opportunities Yearbook Volume 1 Strategic, Practical Information and Opportunities
Dominica Business and Investment Opportunities Yearbook Volume 1 Strategic, Practical Information and Opportunities
Dominican Republic Business and Investment Opportunities Yearbook Volume 1 Strategic, Practical Information and Opportunities
Ecuador Business and Investment Opportunities Yearbook Volume 1 Strategic, Practical Information and Opportunities
Egypt Business and Investment Opportunities Yearbook Volume 1 Strategic, Practical Information and Opportunities
El Salvador Business and Investment Opportunities Yearbook Volume 1 Strategic, Practical Information and Opportunities
Equatorial Guinea Business and Investment Opportunities Yearbook Volume 1 Strategic, Practical Information and Opportunities
Eritrea Business and Investment Opportunities Yearbook Volume 1 Strategic, Practical Information and Opportunities
Estonia Business and Investment Opportunities Yearbook Volume 1 Strategic, Practical Information and Opportunities
Ethiopia Business and Investment Opportunities Yearbook Volume 1 Strategic, Practical Information and Opportunities
Falkland Islands Business and Investment Opportunities Yearbook Volume 1 Strategic, Practical Information and Opportunities
Faroes Islands Business and Investment Opportunities Yearbook Volume 1 Strategic, Practical Information and Opportunities
Fiji Business and Investment Opportunities Yearbook Volume 1 Strategic, Practical Information and Opportunities
Finland Business and Investment Opportunities Yearbook Volume 1 Strategic, Practical Information and Opportunities
France Business and Investment Opportunities Yearbook Volume 1 Strategic, Practical Information and Opportunities
Gabon Business and Investment Opportunities Yearbook Volume 1 Strategic, Practical Information and Opportunities
Gambia Business and Investment Opportunities Yearbook Volume 1 Strategic, Practical Information and Opportunities
Georgia Business and Investment Opportunities Yearbook Volume 1 Strategic, Practical Information and Opportunities
Germany Business and Investment Opportunities Yearbook Volume 1 Strategic, Practical Information and Opportunities
Ghana Business and Investment Opportunities Yearbook Volume 1 Strategic, Practical Information and Opportunities
Gibraltar Business and Investment Opportunities Yearbook Volume 1 Strategic, Practical Information and Opportunities
Greece Business and Investment Opportunities Yearbook Volume 1 Strategic, Practical Information and Opportunities

TITLE
Greenland Business and Investment Opportunities Yearbook Volume 1 Strategic, Practical Information and Opportunities
Grenada Business and Investment Opportunities Yearbook Volume 1 Strategic, Practical Information and Opportunities
Guam Business and Investment Opportunities Yearbook Volume 1 Strategic, Practical Information and Opportunities
Guatemala Business and Investment Opportunities Yearbook Volume 1 Strategic, Practical Information and Opportunities
Guernsey Business and Investment Opportunities Yearbook Volume 1 Strategic, Practical Information and Opportunities
Guinea Business and Investment Opportunities Yearbook Volume 1 Strategic, Practical Information and Opportunities
Guinea-Bissau Business and Investment Opportunities Yearbook Volume 1 Strategic, Practical Information and Opportunities
Guyana Business and Investment Opportunities Yearbook Volume 1 Strategic, Practical Information and Opportunities
Haiti Business and Investment Opportunities Yearbook Volume 1 Strategic, Practical Information and Opportunities
Honduras Business and Investment Opportunities Yearbook Volume 1 Strategic, Practical Information and Opportunities
Hungary Business and Investment Opportunities Yearbook Volume 1 Strategic, Practical Information and Opportunities
Iceland Business and Investment Opportunities Yearbook Volume 1 Strategic, Practical Information and Opportunities
India Business and Investment Opportunities Yearbook Volume 1 Strategic, Practical Information and Opportunities
Indonesia Business and Investment Opportunities Yearbook Volume 1 Strategic, Practical Information and Opportunities
Iran Business and Investment Opportunities Yearbook Volume 1 Strategic, Practical Information and Opportunities
Iraq Business and Investment Opportunities Yearbook Volume 1 Strategic, Practical Information and Opportunities
Ireland Business and Investment Opportunities Yearbook Volume 1 Strategic, Practical Information and Opportunities
Israel Business and Investment Opportunities Yearbook Volume 1 Strategic, Practical Information and Opportunities
Italy Business and Investment Opportunities Yearbook Volume 1 Strategic, Practical Information and Opportunities
Jamaica Business and Investment Opportunities Yearbook Volume 1 Strategic, Practical Information and Opportunities
Japan Business and Investment Opportunities Yearbook Volume 1 Strategic, Practical Information and Opportunities
Jersey Business and Investment Opportunities Yearbook Volume 1 Strategic, Practical Information and Opportunities
Jordan Business and Investment Opportunities Yearbook Volume 1 Strategic, Practical Information and Opportunities
Kazakhstan Business and Investment Opportunities Yearbook Volume 1 Strategic, Practical Information and Opportunities
Kenya Business and Investment Opportunities Yearbook Volume 1 Strategic, Practical Information and Opportunities
Kiribati Business and Investment Opportunities Yearbook Volume 1 Strategic, Practical Information and Opportunities
Korea, North Business and Investment Opportunities Yearbook Volume 1 Strategic, Practical Information and Opportunities
Korea, South Business and Investment Opportunities Yearbook Volume 1 Strategic, Practical Information and Opportunities

TITLE
Kosovo Business and Investment Opportunities Yearbook Volume 1 Strategic, Practical Information and Opportunities
Kurdistan Business and Investment Opportunities Yearbook Volume 1 Strategic, Practical Information and Opportunities
Kuwait Business and Investment Opportunities Yearbook Volume 1 Strategic, Practical Information and Opportunities
Kyrgyzstan Business and Investment Opportunities Yearbook Volume 1 Strategic, Practical Information and Opportunities
Laos Business and Investment Opportunities Yearbook Volume 1 Strategic, Practical Information and Opportunities
Latvia Business and Investment Opportunities Yearbook Volume 1 Strategic, Practical Information and Opportunities
Lebanon Business and Investment Opportunities Yearbook Volume 1 Strategic, Practical Information and Opportunities
Lesotho Business and Investment Opportunities Yearbook Volume 1 Strategic, Practical Information and Opportunities
Liberia Business and Investment Opportunities Yearbook Volume 1 Strategic, Practical Information and Opportunities
Libya Business and Investment Opportunities Yearbook Volume 1 Strategic, Practical Information and Opportunities
Liechtenstein Business and Investment Opportunities Yearbook Volume 1 Strategic, Practical Information and Opportunities
Lithuania Business and Investment Opportunities Yearbook Volume 1 Strategic, Practical Information and Opportunities
Luxembourg Business and Investment Opportunities Yearbook Volume 1 Strategic, Practical Information and Opportunities
Macao Business and Investment Opportunities Yearbook Volume 1 Strategic, Practical Information and Opportunities
Macedonia Business and Investment Opportunities Yearbook Volume 1 Strategic, Practical Information and Opportunities
Madagascar Business and Investment Opportunities Yearbook Volume 1 Strategic, Practical Information and Opportunities
Madeira Business and Investment Opportunities Yearbook Volume 1 Strategic, Practical Information and Opportunities
Malawi Business and Investment Opportunities Yearbook Volume 1 Strategic, Practical Information and Opportunities
Malaysia Business and Investment Opportunities Yearbook Volume 1 Strategic, Practical Information and Opportunities
Maldives Business and Investment Opportunities Yearbook Volume 1 Strategic, Practical Information and Opportunities
Mali Business and Investment Opportunities Yearbook Volume 1 Strategic, Practical Information and Opportunities
Malta Business and Investment Opportunities Yearbook Volume 1 Strategic, Practical Information and Opportunities
Man Business and Investment Opportunities Yearbook Volume 1 Strategic, Practical Information and Opportunities
Marshall Islands Business and Investment Opportunities Yearbook Volume 1 Strategic, Practical Information and Opportunities
Mauritania Business and Investment Opportunities Yearbook Volume 1 Strategic, Practical Information and Opportunities
Mauritius Business and Investment Opportunities Yearbook Volume 1 Strategic, Practical Information and Opportunities
Mayotte Business and Investment Opportunities Yearbook Volume 1 Strategic, Practical Information and Opportunities
Mexico Business and Investment Opportunities Yearbook Volume 1 Strategic, Practical Information and Opportunities

TITLE
Micronesia Business and Investment Opportunities Yearbook Volume 1 Strategic, Practical Information and Opportunities
Moldova Business and Investment Opportunities Yearbook Volume 1 Strategic, Practical Information and Opportunities
Monaco Business and Investment Opportunities Yearbook Volume 1 Strategic, Practical Information and Opportunities
Mongolia Business and Investment Opportunities Yearbook Volume 1 Strategic, Practical Information and Opportunities
Montserrat Business and Investment Opportunities Yearbook Volume 1 Strategic, Practical Information and Opportunities
Montenegro Business and Investment Opportunities Yearbook Volume 1 Strategic, Practical Information and Opportunities
Morocco Business and Investment Opportunities Yearbook Volume 1 Strategic, Practical Information and Opportunities
Mozambique Business and Investment Opportunities Yearbook Volume 1 Strategic, Practical Information and Opportunities
Myanmar Business and Investment Opportunities Yearbook Volume 1 Strategic, Practical Information and Opportunities
Nagorno-Karabakh Republic Business and Investment Opportunities Yearbook Volume 1 Strategic, Practical Information and Opportunities
Namibia Business and Investment Opportunities Yearbook Volume 1 Strategic, Practical Information and Opportunities
Nauru Business and Investment Opportunities Yearbook Volume 1 Strategic, Practical Information and Opportunities
Nepal Business and Investment Opportunities Yearbook Volume 1 Strategic, Practical Information and Opportunities
Netherlands Business and Investment Opportunities Yearbook Volume 1 Strategic, Practical Information and Opportunities
New Caledonia Business and Investment Opportunities Yearbook Volume 1 Strategic, Practical Information and Opportunities
New Zealand Business and Investment Opportunities Yearbook Volume 1 Strategic, Practical Information and Opportunities
Nicaragua Business and Investment Opportunities Yearbook Volume 1 Strategic, Practical Information and Opportunities
Niger Business and Investment Opportunities Yearbook Volume 1 Strategic, Practical Information and Opportunities
Nigeria Business and Investment Opportunities Yearbook Volume 1 Strategic, Practical Information and Opportunities
Niue Business and Investment Opportunities Yearbook Volume 1 Strategic, Practical Information and Opportunities
Northern Cyprus (Turkish Republic of Northern Cyprus) Business and Investment Opportunities Yearbook Volume 1 Strategic, Practical Information and Opportunities
Northern Mariana Islands Business and Investment Opportunities Yearbook Volume 1 Strategic, Practical Information and Opportunities
Norway Business and Investment Opportunities Yearbook Volume 1 Strategic, Practical Information and Opportunities
Oman Business and Investment Opportunities Yearbook Volume 1 Strategic, Practical Information and Opportunities
Pakistan Business and Investment Opportunities Yearbook Volume 1 Strategic, Practical Information and Opportunities
Palau Business and Investment Opportunities Yearbook Volume 1 Strategic, Practical Information and Opportunities
Palestine (West Bank & Gaza) Business and Investment Opportunities Yearbook Volume 1 Strategic, Practical Information and Opportunities
Panama Business and Investment Opportunities Yearbook Volume 1 Strategic, Practical Information and Opportunities

TITLE
Papua New Guinea Business and Investment Opportunities Yearbook Volume 1 Strategic, Practical Information and Opportunities
Paraguay Business and Investment Opportunities Yearbook Volume 1 Strategic, Practical Information and Opportunities
Peru Business and Investment Opportunities Yearbook Volume 1 Strategic, Practical Information and Opportunities
Philippines Business and Investment Opportunities Yearbook Volume 1 Strategic, Practical Information and Opportunities
Pitcairn Islands Business and Investment Opportunities Yearbook Volume 1 Strategic, Practical Information and Opportunities
Poland Business and Investment Opportunities Yearbook Volume 1 Strategic, Practical Information and Opportunities
Polynesia French Business and Investment Opportunities Yearbook Volume 1 Strategic, Practical Information and Opportunities
Portugal Business and Investment Opportunities Yearbook Volume 1 Strategic, Practical Information and Opportunities
Qatar Business and Investment Opportunities Yearbook Volume 1 Strategic, Practical Information and Opportunities
Romania Business and Investment Opportunities Yearbook Volume 1 Strategic, Practical Information and Opportunities
Russia Business and Investment Opportunities Yearbook Volume 1 Strategic, Practical Information and Opportunities
Rwanda Business and Investment Opportunities Yearbook Volume 1 Strategic, Practical Information and Opportunities
Sahrawi Arab Democratic Republic Volume 1 Strategic Information and Developments
Saint Kitts and Nevis Business and Investment Opportunities Yearbook Volume 1 Strategic, Practical Information and Opportunities
Saint Lucia Business and Investment Opportunities Yearbook Volume 1 Strategic, Practical Information and Opportunities
Saint Vincent and The Grenadines Business and Investment Opportunities Yearbook Volume 1 Strategic, Practical Information and Opportunities
Samoa (American) A Business and Investment Opportunities Yearbook Volume 1 Strategic, Practical Information and Opportunities
Samoa (Western) Business and Investment Opportunities Yearbook Volume 1 Strategic, Practical Information and Opportunities
San Marino Business and Investment Opportunities Yearbook Volume 1 Strategic, Practical Information and Opportunities
Sao Tome and Principe Business and Investment Opportunities Yearbook Volume 1 Strategic, Practical Information and Opportunities
Saudi Arabia Business and Investment Opportunities Yearbook Volume 1 Strategic, Practical Information and Opportunities
Scotland Business and Investment Opportunities Yearbook Volume 1 Strategic, Practical Information and Opportunities
Senegal Business and Investment Opportunities Yearbook Volume 1 Strategic, Practical Information and Opportunities
Serbia Business and Investment Opportunities Yearbook Volume 1 Strategic, Practical Information and Opportunities
Seychelles Business and Investment Opportunities Yearbook Volume 1 Strategic, Practical Information and Opportunities
Sierra Leone Business and Investment Opportunities Yearbook Volume 1 Strategic, Practical Information and Opportunities
Singapore Business and Investment Opportunities Yearbook Volume 1 Strategic, Practical Information and Opportunities
Slovakia Business and Investment Opportunities Yearbook Volume 1 Strategic, Practical Information and Opportunities

TITLE
Slovenia Business and Investment Opportunities Yearbook Volume 1 Strategic, Practical Information and Opportunities
Solomon Islands Business and Investment Opportunities Yearbook Volume 1 Strategic, Practical Information and Opportunities
Somalia Business and Investment Opportunities Yearbook Volume 1 Strategic, Practical Information and Opportunities
South Africa Business and Investment Opportunities Yearbook Volume 1 Strategic, Practical Information and Opportunities
Spain Business and Investment Opportunities Yearbook Volume 1 Strategic, Practical Information and Opportunities
Sri Lanka Business and Investment Opportunities Yearbook Volume 1 Strategic, Practical Information and Opportunities
St. Helena Business and Investment Opportunities Yearbook Volume 1 Strategic, Practical Information and Opportunities
St. Pierre & Miquelon Business and Investment Opportunities Yearbook Volume 1 Strategic, Practical Information and Opportunities
Sudan (Republic of the Sudan) Business and Investment Opportunities Yearbook Volume 1 Strategic, Practical Information and Opportunities
Sudan South Business and Investment Opportunities Yearbook Volume 1 Strategic, Practical Information and Opportunities
Suriname Business and Investment Opportunities Yearbook Volume 1 Strategic, Practical Information and Opportunities
Swaziland Business and Investment Opportunities Yearbook Volume 1 Strategic, Practical Information and Opportunities
Sweden Business and Investment Opportunities Yearbook Volume 1 Strategic, Practical Information and Opportunities
Switzerland Business and Investment Opportunities Yearbook Volume 1 Strategic, Practical Information and Opportunities
Syria Business and Investment Opportunities Yearbook Volume 1 Strategic, Practical Information and Opportunities
Taiwan Business and Investment Opportunities Yearbook Volume 1 Strategic, Practical Information and Opportunities
Tajikistan Business and Investment Opportunities Yearbook Volume 1 Strategic, Practical Information and Opportunities
Tanzania Business and Investment Opportunities Yearbook Volume 1 Strategic, Practical Information and Opportunities
Thailand Business and Investment Opportunities Yearbook Volume 1 Strategic, Practical Information and Opportunities
Timor Leste (Democratic Republic of Timor-Leste) Business and Investment Opportunities Yearbook Volume 1 Strategic, Practical Information and Opportunities
Togo Business and Investment Opportunities Yearbook Volume 1 Strategic, Practical Information and Opportunities
Tonga Business and Investment Opportunities Yearbook Volume 1 Strategic, Practical Information and Opportunities
Trinidad and Tobago Business and Investment Opportunities Yearbook Volume 1 Strategic, Practical Information and Opportunities
Tunisia Business and Investment Opportunities Yearbook Volume 1 Strategic, Practical Information and Opportunities
Turkey Business and Investment Opportunities Yearbook Volume 1 Strategic, Practical Information and Opportunities
Turkmenistan Business and Investment Opportunities Yearbook Volume 1 Strategic, Practical Information and Opportunities
Turks & Caicos Business and Investment Opportunities Yearbook Volume 1 Strategic, Practical Information and Opportunities
Tuvalu Business and Investment Opportunities Yearbook Volume 1 Strategic, Practical Information and Opportunities

TITLE
Uganda Business and Investment Opportunities Yearbook Volume 1 Strategic, Practical Information and Opportunities
Ukraine Business and Investment Opportunities Yearbook Volume 1 Strategic, Practical Information and Opportunities
United Arab Emirates Business and Investment Opportunities Yearbook Volume 1 Strategic, Practical Information and Opportunities
United Kingdom Business and Investment Opportunities Yearbook Volume 1 Strategic, Practical Information and Opportunities
United States Business and Investment Opportunities Yearbook Volume 1 Strategic, Practical Information and Opportunities
Uruguay Business and Investment Opportunities Yearbook Volume 1 Strategic, Practical Information and Opportunities
Uzbekistan Business and Investment Opportunities Yearbook Volume 1 Strategic, Practical Information and Opportunities
Vanuatu Business and Investment Opportunities Yearbook Volume 1 Strategic, Practical Information and Opportunities
Vatican City (Holy See) Business and Investment Opportunities Yearbook Volume 1 Strategic, Practical Information and Opportunities
Venezuela Business and Investment Opportunities Yearbook Volume 1 Strategic, Practical Information and Opportunities
Vietnam Business and Investment Opportunities Yearbook Volume 1 Strategic, Practical Information and Opportunities
Virgin Islands, British Business and Investment Opportunities Yearbook Volume 1 Strategic, Practical Information and Opportunities
Wake Atoll Business and Investment Opportunities Yearbook Volume 1 Strategic, Practical Information and Opportunities
Wallis & Futuna Business and Investment Opportunities Yearbook Volume 1 Strategic, Practical Information and Opportunities
Western Sahara Business and Investment Opportunities Yearbook Volume 1 Strategic, Practical Information and Opportunities
Yemen Business and Investment Opportunities Yearbook Volume 1 Strategic, Practical Information and Opportunities
Zambia Business and Investment Opportunities Yearbook Volume 1 Strategic, Practical Information and Opportunities
Zimbabwe Business and Investment Opportunities Yearbook Volume 1 Strategic, Practical Information and Opportunities

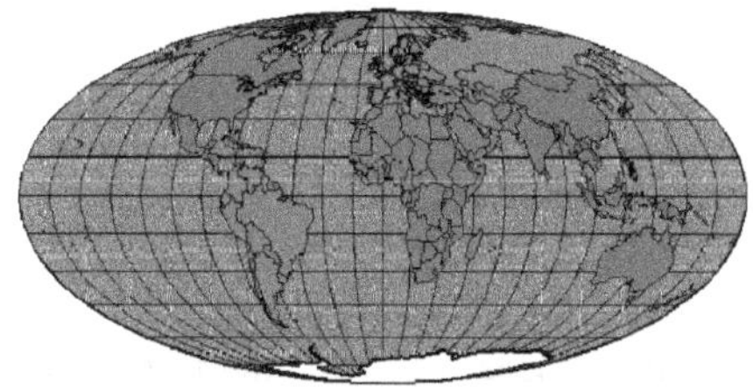

TITLE
Cape Verde Investment and Business Guide Volume 1 Strategic and Practical Information
Cayman Islands Investment and Business Guide Volume 1 Strategic and Practical Information
Central African Republic Investment and Business Guide Volume 1 Strategic and Practical Information
Chad Investment and Business Guide Volume 1 Strategic and Practical Information
Chile Investment and Business Guide Volume 1 Strategic and Practical Information
China Investment and Business Guide Volume 1 Strategic and Practical Information
Colombia Investment and Business Guide Volume 1 Strategic and Practical Information
Comoros Investment and Business Guide Volume 1 Strategic and Practical Information
Congo Investment and Business Guide Volume 1 Strategic and Practical Information
Congo, Democratic Republic Investment and Business Guide Volume 1 Strategic and Practical Information
Cook Islands Investment and Business Guide Volume 1 Strategic and Practical Information
Costa Rica Investment and Business Guide Volume 1 Strategic and Practical Information
Cote d'Ivoire Investment and Business Guide Volume 1 Strategic and Practical Information
Croatia Investment and Business Guide Volume 1 Strategic and Practical Information
Cuba Investment and Business Guide Volume 1 Strategic and Practical Information
Cyprus Investment and Business Guide Volume 1 Strategic and Practical Information
Czech Republic Investment and Business Guide Volume 1 Strategic and Practical Information
Denmark Investment and Business Guide Volume 1 Strategic and Practical Information
Djibouti Investment and Business Guide Volume 1 Strategic and Practical Information
Dominica Investment and Business Guide Volume 1 Strategic and Practical Information
Dominican Republic Investment and Business Guide Volume 1 Strategic and Practical Information
Ecuador Investment and Business Guide Volume 1 Strategic and Practical Information
Egypt Investment and Business Guide Volume 1 Strategic and Practical Information
El Salvador Investment and Business Guide Volume 1 Strategic and Practical Information
Equatorial Guinea Investment and Business Guide Volume 1 Strategic and Practical Information
Eritrea Investment and Business Guide Volume 1 Strategic and Practical Information
Estonia Investment and Business Guide Volume 1 Strategic and Practical Information
Ethiopia Investment and Business Guide Volume 1 Strategic and Practical Information
Falkland Islands Investment and Business Guide Volume 1 Strategic and Practical Information
Faroes Islands Investment and Business Guide Volume 1 Strategic and Practical Information
Fiji Investment and Business Guide Volume 1 Strategic and Practical Information
Finland Investment and Business Guide Volume 1 Strategic and Practical Information
France Investment and Business Guide Volume 1 Strategic and Practical Information
Gabon Investment and Business Guide Volume 1 Strategic and Practical Information
Gambia Investment and Business Guide Volume 1 Strategic and Practical Information
Georgia Investment and Business Guide Volume 1 Strategic and Practical Information
Germany Investment and Business Guide Volume 1 Strategic and Practical Information
Ghana Investment and Business Guide Volume 1 Strategic and Practical Information
Gibraltar Investment and Business Guide Volume 1 Strategic and Practical Information
Greece Investment and Business Guide Volume 1 Strategic and Practical Information
Greenland Investment and Business Guide Volume 1 Strategic and Practical Information
Grenada Investment and Business Guide Volume 1 Strategic and Practical Information
Guam Investment and Business Guide Volume 1 Strategic and Practical Information
Guatemala Investment and Business Guide Volume 1 Strategic and Practical Information
Guernsey Investment and Business Guide Volume 1 Strategic and Practical Information
Guinea Investment and Business Guide Volume 1 Strategic and Practical Information

TITLE
Guinea-Bissau Investment and Business Guide Volume 1 Strategic and Practical Information
Guyana Investment and Business Guide Volume 1 Strategic and Practical Information
Haiti Investment and Business Guide Volume 1 Strategic and Practical Information
Honduras Investment and Business Guide Volume 1 Strategic and Practical Information
Hungary Investment and Business Guide Volume 1 Strategic and Practical Information
Iceland Investment and Business Guide Volume 1 Strategic and Practical Information
India Investment and Business Guide Volume 1 Strategic and Practical Information
Indonesia Investment and Business Guide Volume 1 Strategic and Practical Information
Iran Investment and Business Guide Volume 1 Strategic and Practical Information
Iraq Investment and Business Guide Volume 1 Strategic and Practical Information
Ireland Investment and Business Guide Volume 1 Strategic and Practical Information
Israel Investment and Business Guide Volume 1 Strategic and Practical Information
Italy Investment and Business Guide Volume 1 Strategic and Practical Information
Jamaica Investment and Business Guide Volume 1 Strategic and Practical Information
Japan Investment and Business Guide Volume 1 Strategic and Practical Information
Jersey Investment and Business Guide Volume 1 Strategic and Practical Information
Jordan Investment and Business Guide Volume 1 Strategic and Practical Information
Kazakhstan Investment and Business Guide Volume 1 Strategic and Practical Information
Kenya Investment and Business Guide Volume 1 Strategic and Practical Information
Kiribati Investment and Business Guide Volume 1 Strategic and Practical Information
Korea, North Investment and Business Guide Volume 1 Strategic and Practical Information
Korea, South Investment and Business Guide Volume 1 Strategic and Practical Information
Kosovo Investment and Business Guide Volume 1 Strategic and Practical Information
Kurdistan Investment and Business Guide Volume 1 Strategic and Practical Information
Kuwait Investment and Business Guide Volume 1 Strategic and Practical Information
Kyrgyzstan Investment and Business Guide Volume 1 Strategic and Practical Information
Laos Investment and Business Guide Volume 1 Strategic and Practical Information
Latvia Investment and Business Guide Volume 1 Strategic and Practical Information
Lebanon Investment and Business Guide Volume 1 Strategic and Practical Information
Lesotho Investment and Business Guide Volume 1 Strategic and Practical Information
Liberia Investment and Business Guide Volume 1 Strategic and Practical Information
Libya Investment and Business Guide Volume 1 Strategic and Practical Information
Liechtenstein Investment and Business Guide Volume 1 Strategic and Practical Information
Lithuania Investment and Business Guide Volume 1 Strategic and Practical Information
Luxembourg Investment and Business Guide Volume 1 Strategic and Practical Information
Macao Investment and Business Guide Volume 1 Strategic and Practical Information
Macedonia Investment and Business Guide Volume 1 Strategic and Practical Information
Madagascar Investment and Business Guide Volume 1 Strategic and Practical Information
Madeira Investment and Business Guide Volume 1 Strategic and Practical Information
Malawi Investment and Business Guide Volume 1 Strategic and Practical Information
Malaysia Investment and Business Guide Volume 1 Strategic and Practical Information
Maldives Investment and Business Guide Volume 1 Strategic and Practical Information
Mali Investment and Business Guide Volume 1 Strategic and Practical Information
Malta Investment and Business Guide Volume 1 Strategic and Practical Information
Man Investment and Business Guide Volume 1 Strategic and Practical Information
Marshall Islands Investment and Business Guide Volume 1 Strategic and Practical Information

TITLE
Mauritania Investment and Business Guide Volume 1 Strategic and Practical Information
Mauritius Investment and Business Guide Volume 1 Strategic and Practical Information
Mayotte Investment and Business Guide Volume 1 Strategic and Practical Information
Mexico Investment and Business Guide Volume 1 Strategic and Practical Information
Micronesia Investment and Business Guide Volume 1 Strategic and Practical Information
Moldova Investment and Business Guide Volume 1 Strategic and Practical Information
Monaco Investment and Business Guide Volume 1 Strategic and Practical Information
Mongolia Investment and Business Guide Volume 1 Strategic and Practical Information
Montserrat Investment and Business Guide Volume 1 Strategic and Practical Information
Montenegro Investment and Business Guide Volume 1 Strategic and Practical Information
Morocco Investment and Business Guide Volume 1 Strategic and Practical Information
Mozambique Investment and Business Guide Volume 1 Strategic and Practical Information
Myanmar Investment and Business Guide Volume 1 Strategic and Practical Information
Nagorno-Karabakh Republic Investment and Business Guide Volume 1 Strategic and Practical Information
Namibia Investment and Business Guide Volume 1 Strategic and Practical Information
Nauru Investment and Business Guide Volume 1 Strategic and Practical Information
Nepal Investment and Business Guide Volume 1 Strategic and Practical Information
Netherlands Investment and Business Guide Volume 1 Strategic and Practical Information
New Caledonia Investment and Business Guide Volume 1 Strategic and Practical Information
New Zealand Investment and Business Guide Volume 1 Strategic and Practical Information
Nicaragua Investment and Business Guide Volume 1 Strategic and Practical Information
Niger Investment and Business Guide Volume 1 Strategic and Practical Information
Nigeria Investment and Business Guide Volume 1 Strategic and Practical Information
Niue Investment and Business Guide Volume 1 Strategic and Practical Information
Northern Cyprus (Turkish Republic of Northern Cyprus) Volume 1 Strategic Information and Developments
Northern Mariana Islands Investment and Business Guide Volume 1 Strategic and Practical Information
Norway Investment and Business Guide Volume 1 Strategic and Practical Information
Oman Investment and Business Guide Volume 1 Strategic and Practical Information
Pakistan Investment and Business Guide Volume 1 Strategic and Practical Information
Palau Investment and Business Guide Volume 1 Strategic and Practical Information
Palestine (West Bank & Gaza) Investment and Business Guide Volume 1 Strategic and Practical Information
Panama Investment and Business Guide Volume 1 Strategic and Practical Information
Papua New Guinea Investment and Business Guide Volume 1 Strategic and Practical Information
Paraguay Investment and Business Guide Volume 1 Strategic and Practical Information
Peru Investment and Business Guide Volume 1 Strategic and Practical Information
Philippines Investment and Business Guide Volume 1 Strategic and Practical Information
Pitcairn Islands Investment and Business Guide Volume 1 Strategic and Practical Information
Poland Investment and Business Guide Volume 1 Strategic and Practical Information
Polynesia French Investment and Business Guide Volume 1 Strategic and Practical Information
Portugal Investment and Business Guide Volume 1 Strategic and Practical Information
Qatar Investment and Business Guide Volume 1 Strategic and Practical Information
Romania Investment and Business Guide Volume 1 Strategic and Practical Information
Russia Investment and Business Guide Volume 1 Strategic and Practical Information
Rwanda Investment and Business Guide Volume 1 Strategic and Practical Information
Sahrawi Arab Democratic Republic Volume 1 Strategic Information and Developments
Saint Kitts and Nevis Investment and Business Guide Volume 1 Strategic and Practical Information

TITLE
Saint Lucia Investment and Business Guide Volume 1 Strategic and Practical Information
Saint Vincent and The Grenadines Investment and Business Guide Volume 1 Strategic and Practical Information
Samoa (American) A Investment and Business Guide Volume 1 Strategic and Practical Information
Samoa (Western) Investment and Business Guide Volume 1 Strategic and Practical Information
San Marino Investment and Business Guide Volume 1 Strategic and Practical Information
Sao Tome and Principe Investment and Business Guide Volume 1 Strategic and Practical Information
Saudi Arabia Investment and Business Guide Volume 1 Strategic and Practical Information
Scotland Investment and Business Guide Volume 1 Strategic and Practical Information
Senegal Investment and Business Guide Volume 1 Strategic and Practical Information
Serbia Investment and Business Guide Volume 1 Strategic and Practical Information
Seychelles Investment and Business Guide Volume 1 Strategic and Practical Information
Sierra Leone Investment and Business Guide Volume 1 Strategic and Practical Information
Singapore Investment and Business Guide Volume 1 Strategic and Practical Information
Slovakia Investment and Business Guide Volume 1 Strategic and Practical Information
Slovenia Investment and Business Guide Volume 1 Strategic and Practical Information
Solomon Islands Investment and Business Guide Volume 1 Strategic and Practical Information
Somalia Investment and Business Guide Volume 1 Strategic and Practical Information
South Africa Investment and Business Guide Volume 1 Strategic and Practical Information
Spain Investment and Business Guide Volume 1 Strategic and Practical Information
Sri Lanka Investment and Business Guide Volume 1 Strategic and Practical Information
St. Helena Investment and Business Guide Volume 1 Strategic and Practical Information
St. Pierre & Miquelon Investment and Business Guide Volume 1 Strategic and Practical Information
Sudan (Republic of the Sudan) Investment and Business Guide Volume 1 Strategic and Practical Information
Sudan South Investment and Business Guide Volume 1 Strategic and Practical Information
Suriname Investment and Business Guide Volume 1 Strategic and Practical Information
Swaziland Investment and Business Guide Volume 1 Strategic and Practical Information
Sweden Investment and Business Guide Volume 1 Strategic and Practical Information
Switzerland Investment and Business Guide Volume 1 Strategic and Practical Information
Syria Investment and Business Guide Volume 1 Strategic and Practical Information
Taiwan Investment and Business Guide Volume 1 Strategic and Practical Information
Tajikistan Investment and Business Guide Volume 1 Strategic and Practical Information
Tanzania Investment and Business Guide Volume 1 Strategic and Practical Information
Thailand Investment and Business Guide Volume 1 Strategic and Practical Information
Timor Leste (Democratic Republic of Timor-Leste) Investment and Business Guide Volume 1 Strategic and Practical Information
Togo Investment and Business Guide Volume 1 Strategic and Practical Information
Tonga Investment and Business Guide Volume 1 Strategic and Practical Information
Trinidad and Tobago Investment and Business Guide Volume 1 Strategic and Practical Information
Tunisia Investment and Business Guide Volume 1 Strategic and Practical Information
Turkey Investment and Business Guide Volume 1 Strategic and Practical Information
Turkmenistan Investment and Business Guide Volume 1 Strategic and Practical Information
Turks & Caicos Investment and Business Guide Volume 1 Strategic and Practical Information
Tuvalu Investment and Business Guide Volume 1 Strategic and Practical Information
Uganda Investment and Business Guide Volume 1 Strategic and Practical Information
Ukraine Investment and Business Guide Volume 1 Strategic and Practical Information
United Arab Emirates Investment and Business Guide Volume 1 Strategic and Practical Information

TITLE
United Kingdom Investment and Business Guide Volume 1 Strategic and Practical Information
United States Investment and Business Guide Volume 1 Strategic and Practical Information
Uruguay Investment and Business Guide Volume 1 Strategic and Practical Information
Uzbekistan Investment and Business Guide Volume 1 Strategic and Practical Information
Vanuatu Investment and Business Guide Volume 1 Strategic and Practical Information
Vatican City (Holy See) Investment and Business Guide Volume 1 Strategic and Practical Information
Venezuela Investment and Business Guide Volume 1 Strategic and Practical Information
Vietnam Investment and Business Guide Volume 1 Strategic and Practical Information
Virgin Islands, British Investment and Business Guide Volume 1 Strategic and Practical Information
Wake Atoll Investment and Business Guide Volume 1 Strategic and Practical Information
Wallis & Futuna Investment and Business Guide Volume 1 Strategic and Practical Information
Western Sahara Investment and Business Guide Volume 1 Strategic and Practical Information
Yemen Investment and Business Guide Volume 1 Strategic and Practical Information
Zambia Investment and Business Guide Volume 1 Strategic and Practical Information
Zimbabwe Investment and Business Guide Volume 1 Strategic and Practical Information

www.ingramcontent.com/pod-product-compliance
Lightning Source LLC
LaVergne TN
LVHW080038210926
848481LV00011B/3226